Shugo Chara!

8

PEACH-PIT

Translated by
Satsuki Yamashita

Adapted by
Nunzio DeFilippis and Christina Weir

Lettered by
North Market Street Graphics

BALLANTINE BOOKS • NEW YORK

Shugo Chara! volume 8 is a work of fiction. Names, characters, places, and incidents are the products of the author's imagination or are used fictitiously. Any resemblance to actual events, locales, or persons, living or dead, is entirely coincidental.

A Del Rey Manga/Kodansha Trade Paperback Original

Published in the United States by Del Rey, an imprint of The Random House Publishing Group, a division of Random House, Inc., New York.

Publication rights arranged through Kodansha Ltd.

First published in Japan in 2008 by Kodansha Ltd., Tokyo

ISBN 978-0-345-51431-8

Original cover design by Akiko Omo

Printed in the United States of America

www.delreymanga.com

9 8 7 6 5 4 3 2 1

Translator: Satsuki Yamashita
Adapters: Nunzio DeFilippis and Christina Weir
Lettering: North Market Street Graphics

Contents

Honorifics Explained

Throughout the Del Rey Manga books, you will find Japanese honorifics left intact in the translations. For those not familiar with how the Japanese use honorifics and, more important, how they differ from American honorifics, we present this brief overview.

Politeness has always been a critical facet of Japanese culture. Ever since the feudal era, when Japan was a highly stratified society, use of honorifics—which can be defined as polite speech that indicates relationship or status—has played an essential role in the Japanese language. When addressing someone in Japanese, an honorific usually takes the form of a suffix attached to one's name (example: "Asuna-san"), is used as a title at the end of one's name, or appears in place of the name itself (example: "Negi-sensei," or simply "Sensei").

Honorifics can be expressions of respect or endearment. In the context of manga and anime, honorifics give insight into the nature of the relationship between characters. Many English translations leave out these important honorifics and therefore distort the feel of the original Japanese. Because Japanese honorifics contain nuances that English honorifics lack, it is our policy at Del Rey not to translate them. Here, instead, is a guide to some of the honorifics you may encounter in Del Rey Manga.

-san: This is the most common honorific and is equivalent to Mr., Miss, Ms., or Mrs. It is the all-purpose honorific and can be used in any situation where politeness is required.

-sama: This is one level higher than "-san" and is used to confer great respect.

-dono: This comes from the word "tono," which means "lord." It is an even higher level than "-sama" and confers utmost respect.

-kun: This suffix is used at the end of boys' names to express familiarity or endearment. It is also sometimes used by men among friends, or when addressing someone younger or of a lower station.

-chan: This is used to express endearment, mostly toward girls. It is also used for little boys, pets, and even among lovers. It gives a sense of childish cuteness.

Bozu: This is an informal way to refer to a boy, similar to the English terms "kid" and "squirt."

Sempai/
Senpai: This title suggests that the addressee is one's senior in a group or organization. It is most often used in a school setting, where underclassmen refer to their upperclassmen as "sempai." It can also be used in the workplace, such as when a newer employee addresses an employee who has seniority in the company.

Kohai: This is the opposite of "sempai" and is used toward underclassmen in school or newcomers in the workplace. It connotes that the addressee is of a lower station.

Sensei: Literally meaning "one who has come before," this title is used for teachers, doctors, or masters of any profession or art.

-[blank]: This is usually forgotten in these lists, but it is perhaps the most significant difference between Japanese and English. The lack of honorific means that the speaker has permission to address the person in a very intimate way. Usually, only family, spouses, or very close friends have this kind of permission. Known as *yobisute*, it can be gratifying when someone who has earned the intimacy starts to call one by one's name without an honorific. But when that intimacy hasn't been earned, it can be very insulting.

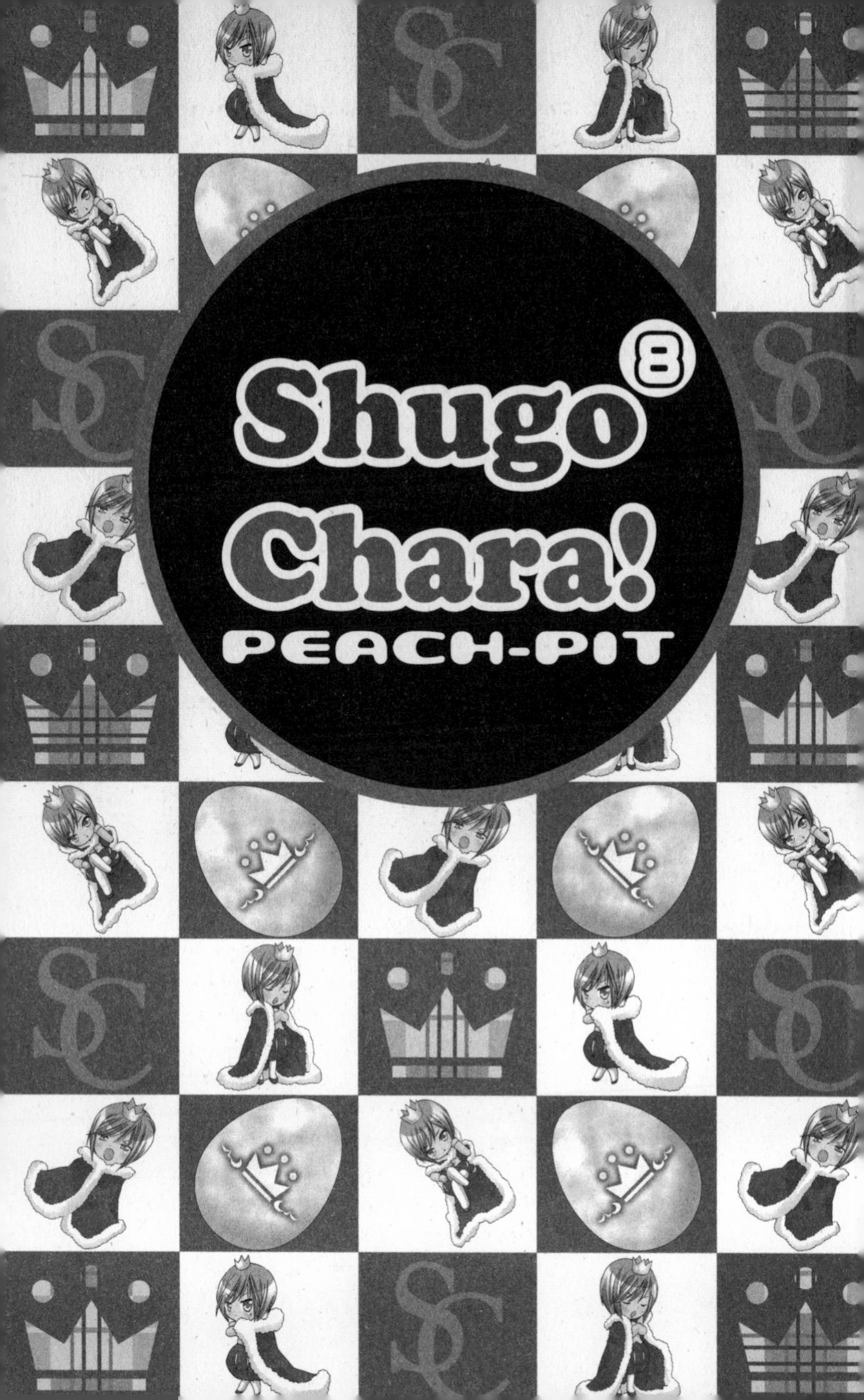
8
Shugo Chara!
PEACH-PIT

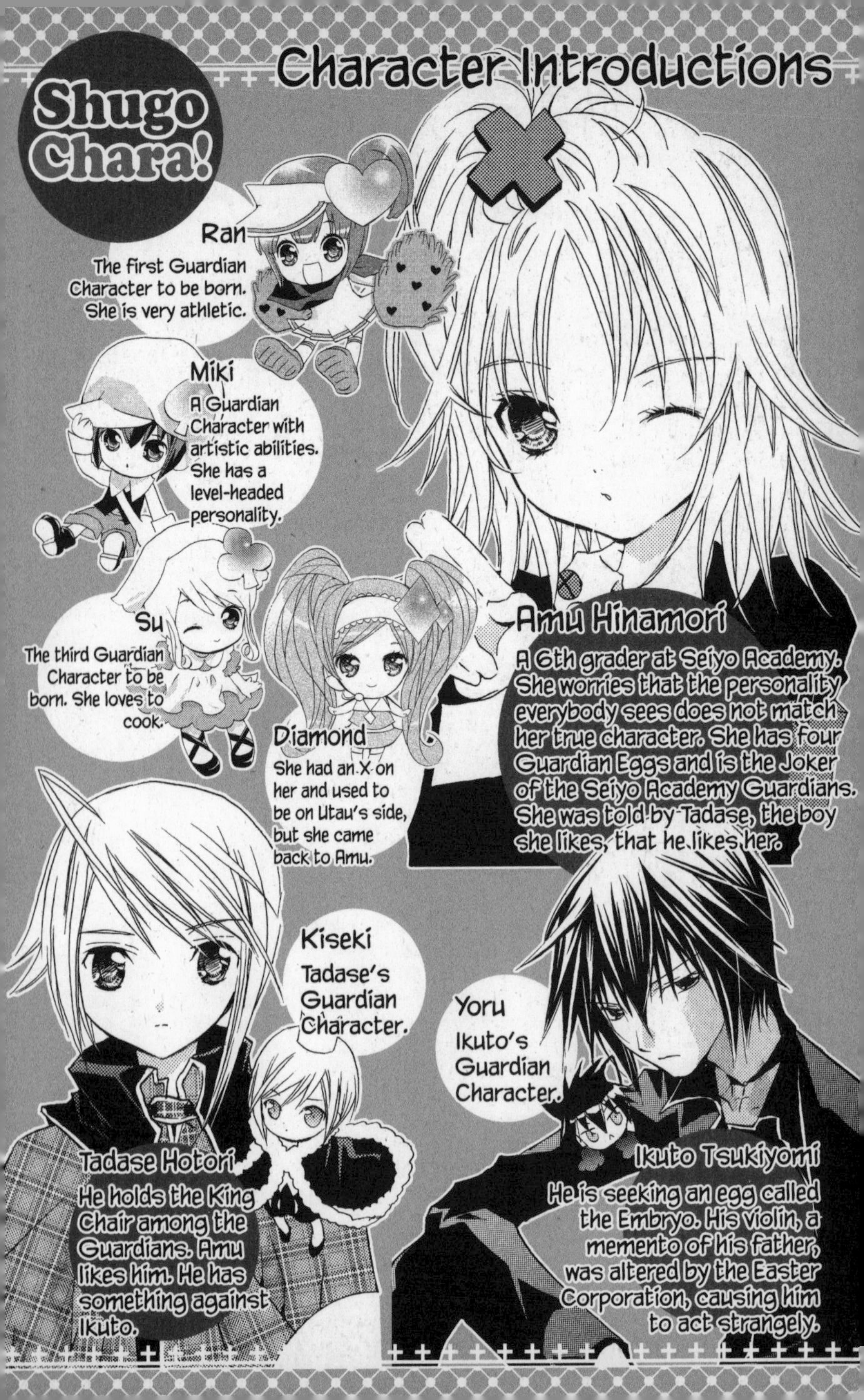
Character Introductions
Shugo Chara!
Ran
The first Guardian Character to be born. She is very athletic.
Miki
A Guardian Character with artistic abilities. She has a level-headed personality.
Su
The third Guardian Character to be born. She loves to cook.
Diamond
She had an X on her and used to be on Utau's side, but she came back to Amu.
Amu Hinamori
A 6th grader at Seiyo Academy. She worries that the personality everybody sees does not match her true character. She has four Guardian Eggs and is the Joker of the Seiyo Academy Guardians. She was told by Tadase, the boy she likes, that he likes her.
Kiseki
Tadase's Guardian Character.
Yoru
Ikuto's Guardian Character.
Tadase Hotori
He holds the King Chair among the Guardians. Amu likes him. He has something against Ikuto.
Ikuto Tsukiyomi
He is seeking an egg called the Embryo. His violin, a memento of his father, was altered by the Easter Corporation, causing him to act strangely.

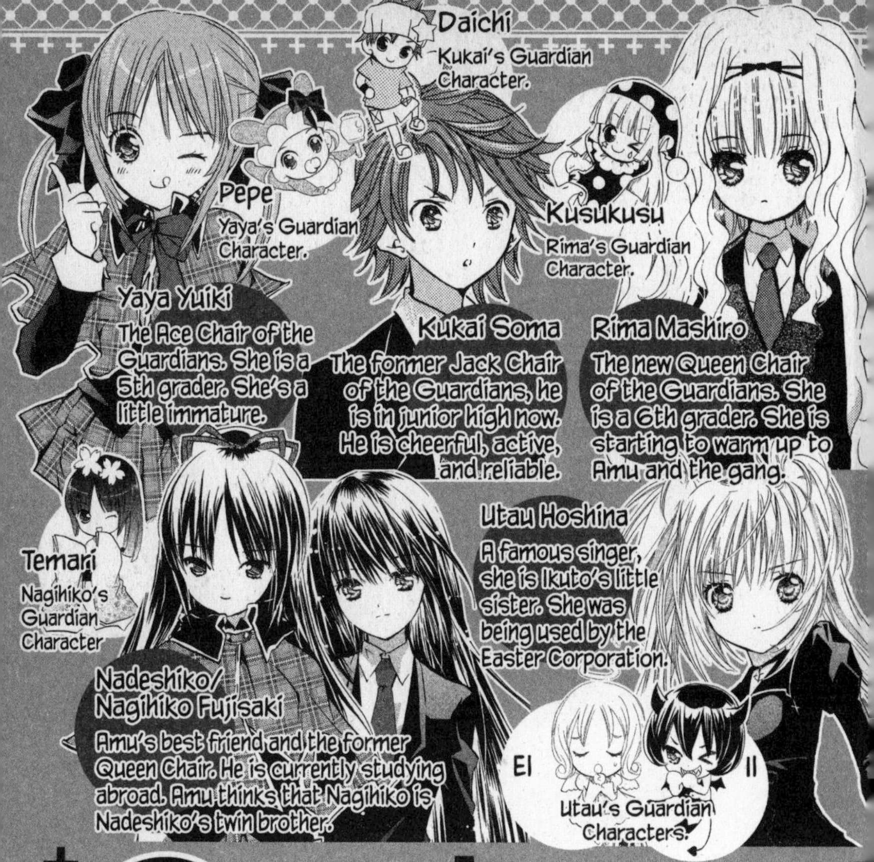
Daichi
Kukai's Guardian Character.
Kusukusu
Rima's Guardian Character.
Rima Mashiro
The new Queen Chair of the Guardians. She is a 6th grader. She is starting to warm up to Amu and the gang.
Kukai Soma
The former Jack Chair of the Guardians, he is in junior high now. He is cheerful, active, and reliable.
Pepe
Yaya's Guardian Character.
Yaya Yuiki
The Ace Chair of the Guardians. She is a 5th grader. She's a little immature.
Utau Hoshina
A famous singer, she is Ikuto's little sister. She was being used by the Easter Corporation.
Temari
Nagihiko's Guardian Character
Nadeshiko/ Nagihiko Fujisaki
Amu's best friend and the former Queen Chair. He is currently studying abroad. Amu thinks that Nagihiko is Nadeshiko's twin brother.
Il
El
Utau's Guardian Characters.

The Story So Far

● Amu comes across as cool. But that isn't who she really is. Deep inside, she is shy and a little cynical. One day, she wished she could be more true to herself, and the next day she found three eggs in her bed! Ran, Miki, and Su hatched from the eggs. They are Amu's "Guardian Characters." Amu was recruited to become one of the Guardians at Seiyo Academy, and ever since, she's become good friends with other kids who have Guardian Characters.

● As the Joker of the Guardians, Amu's job is to find Heart's Eggs with X's on them and save them. But it seems that the Easter Corporation is looking for an egg known as the Embryo, and collecting countless X Eggs. The Easter Corporation's next target is Ikuto. They altered his violin and are using it to control Ikuto and make him collect X Eggs!

● During winter break, Amu let Ikuto stay in her room secretly. But Tadase came over and told her that he was in love with her and Ikuto heard everything. Tadase was hurt, and now, Ikuto has fallen into the Easter Corporation's hands!!

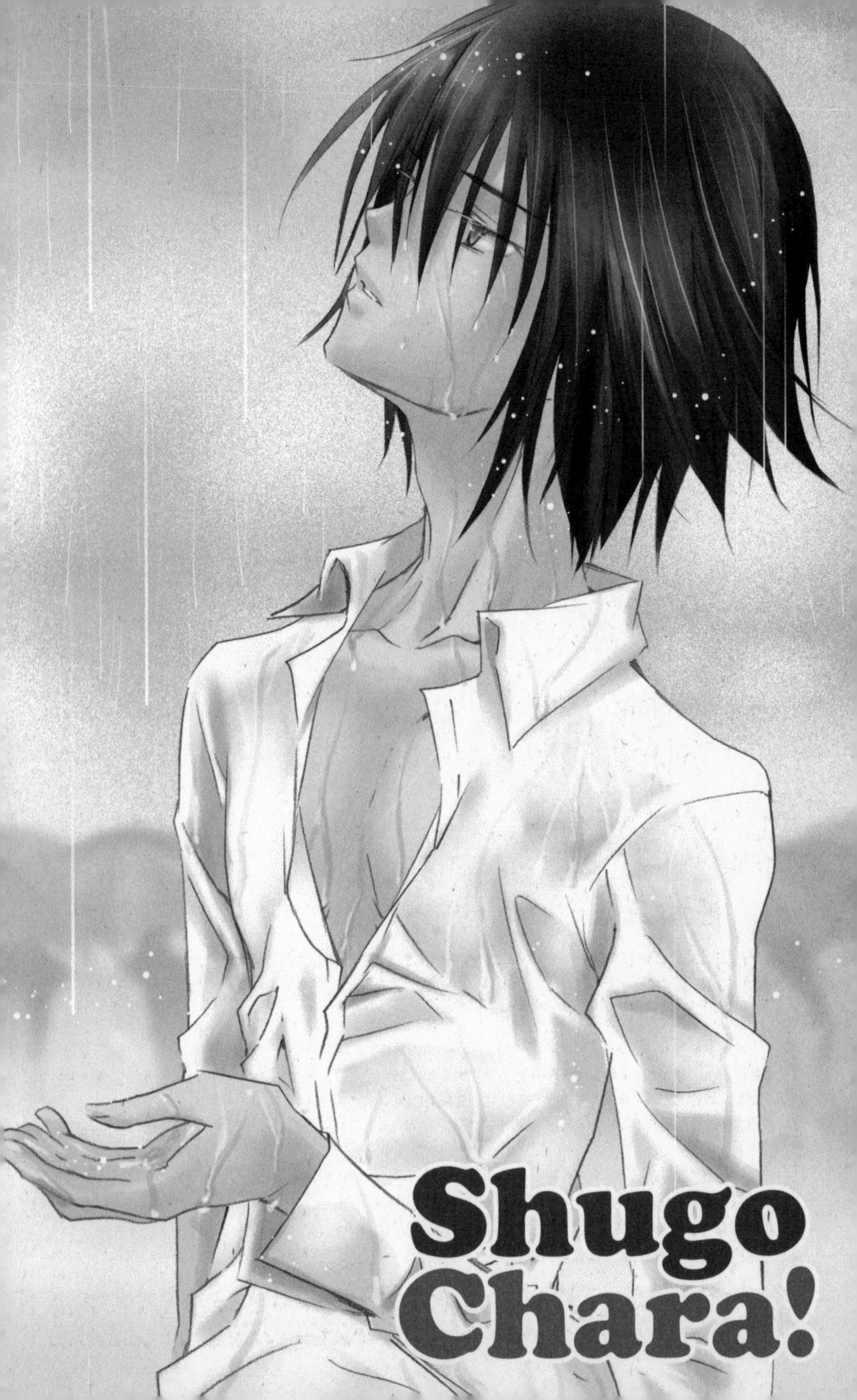
Shugo
Chara!

If we don't do something Ikuto's going to die!

All because of that purple violin!!

What happened, Yoru?

I don't know what to do!

Start at the beginning.

MEOWWW

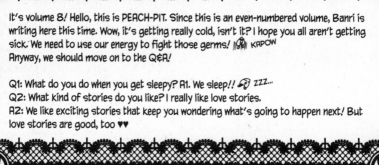

It's volume 8! Hello, this is PEACH-PIT. Since this is an even-numbered volume, Banri is writing here this time. Wow, it's getting really cold, isn't it? I hope you all aren't getting sick. We need to use our energy to fight those germs! KAPOW
Anyway, we should move on to the Q&A!

Q1: What do you do when you get sleepy? A1. We sleep!! ZZZ...
Q2: What kind of stories do you like? I really like love stories.
A2: We like exciting stories that keep you wondering what's going to happen next! But love stories are good, too ♥♥

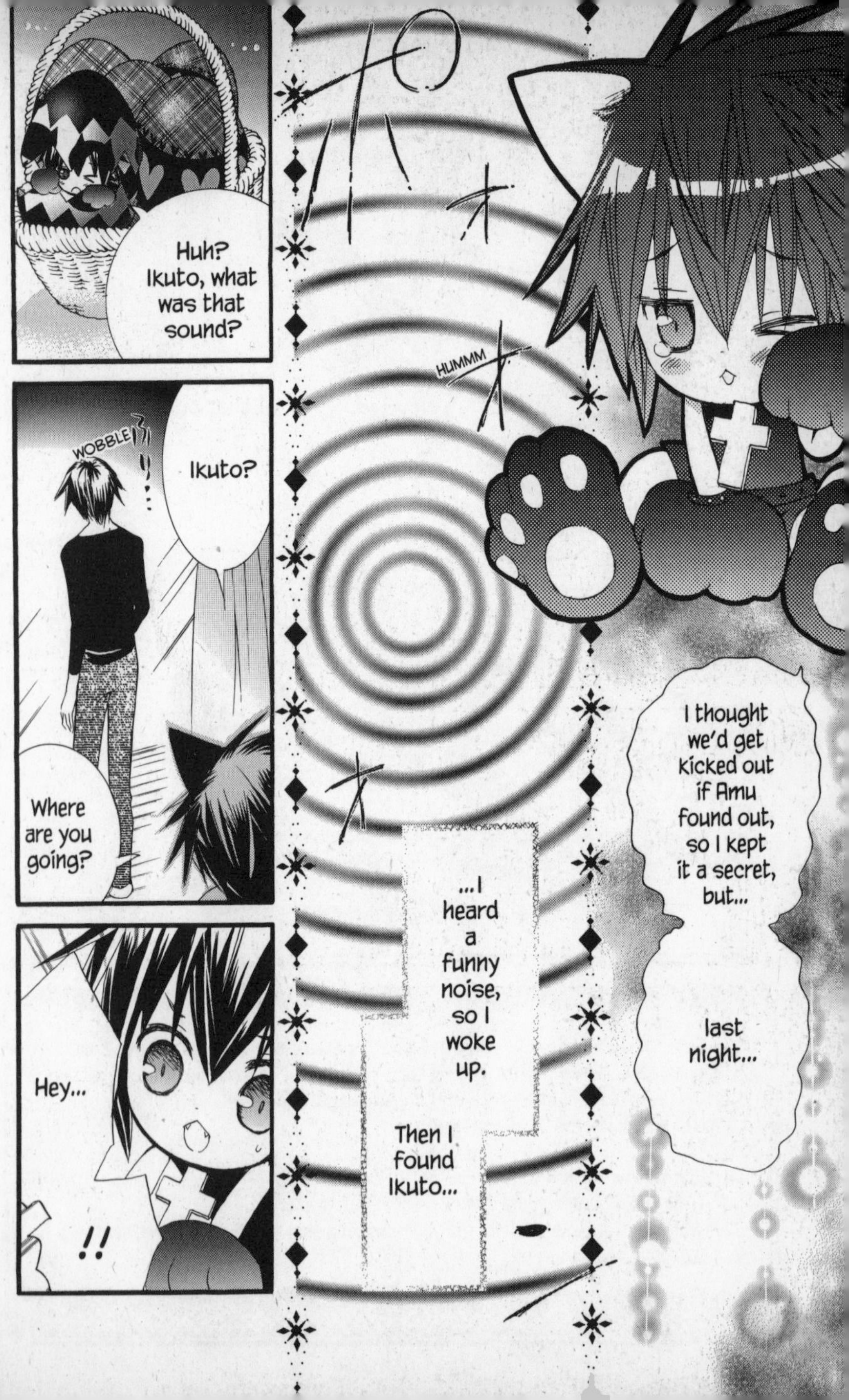
HUMMM
I thought we'd get kicked out if Amu found out, so I kept it a secret, but...
last night...
...I heard a funny noise, so I woke up.
Then I found Ikuto...
Huh? Ikuto, what was that sound?
Ikuto?
WOBBLE
Where are you going?
Hey...
!!

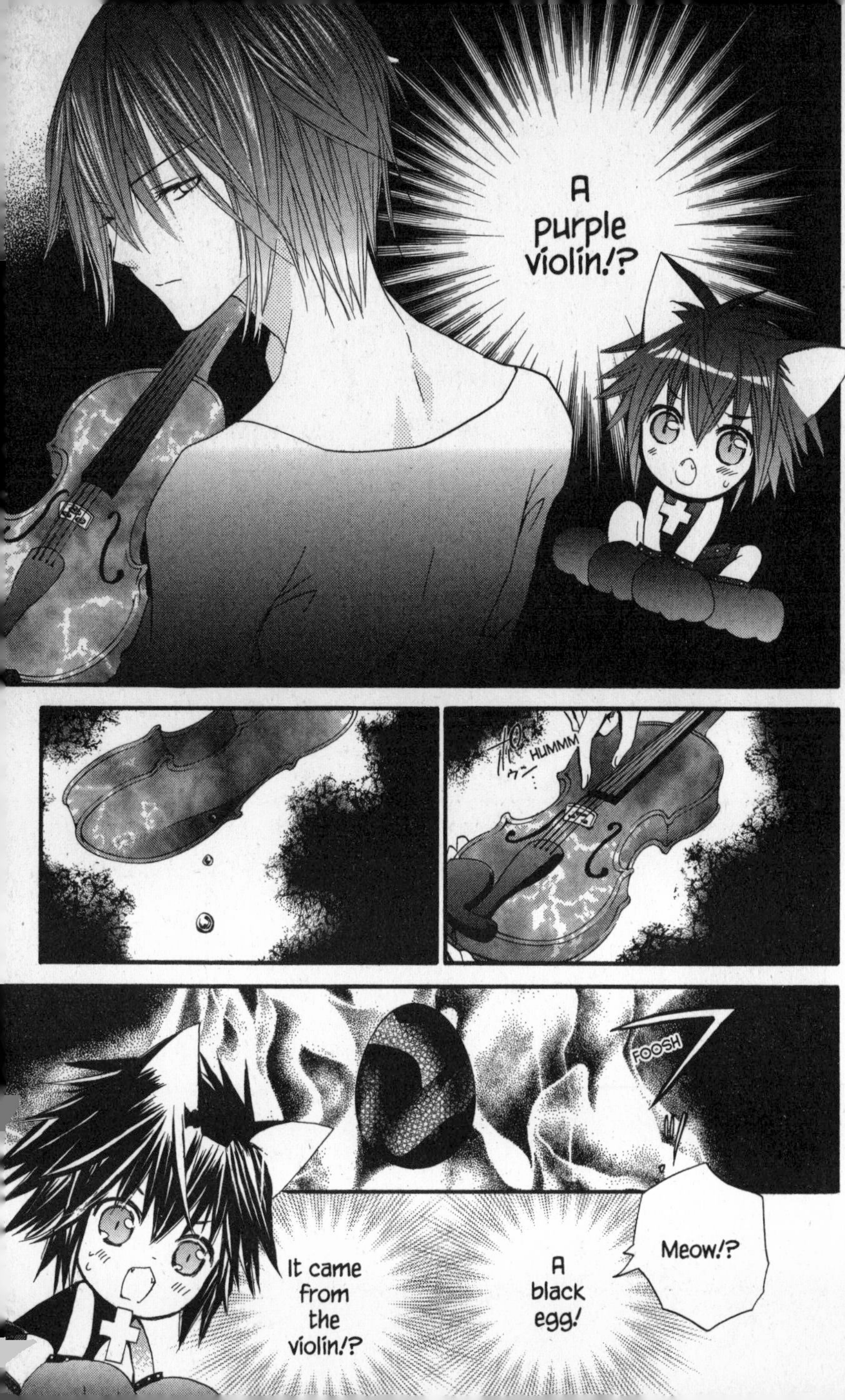
A purple violin!?
HUMMM
FOOSH
Meow!?
A black egg!
It came from the violin!?

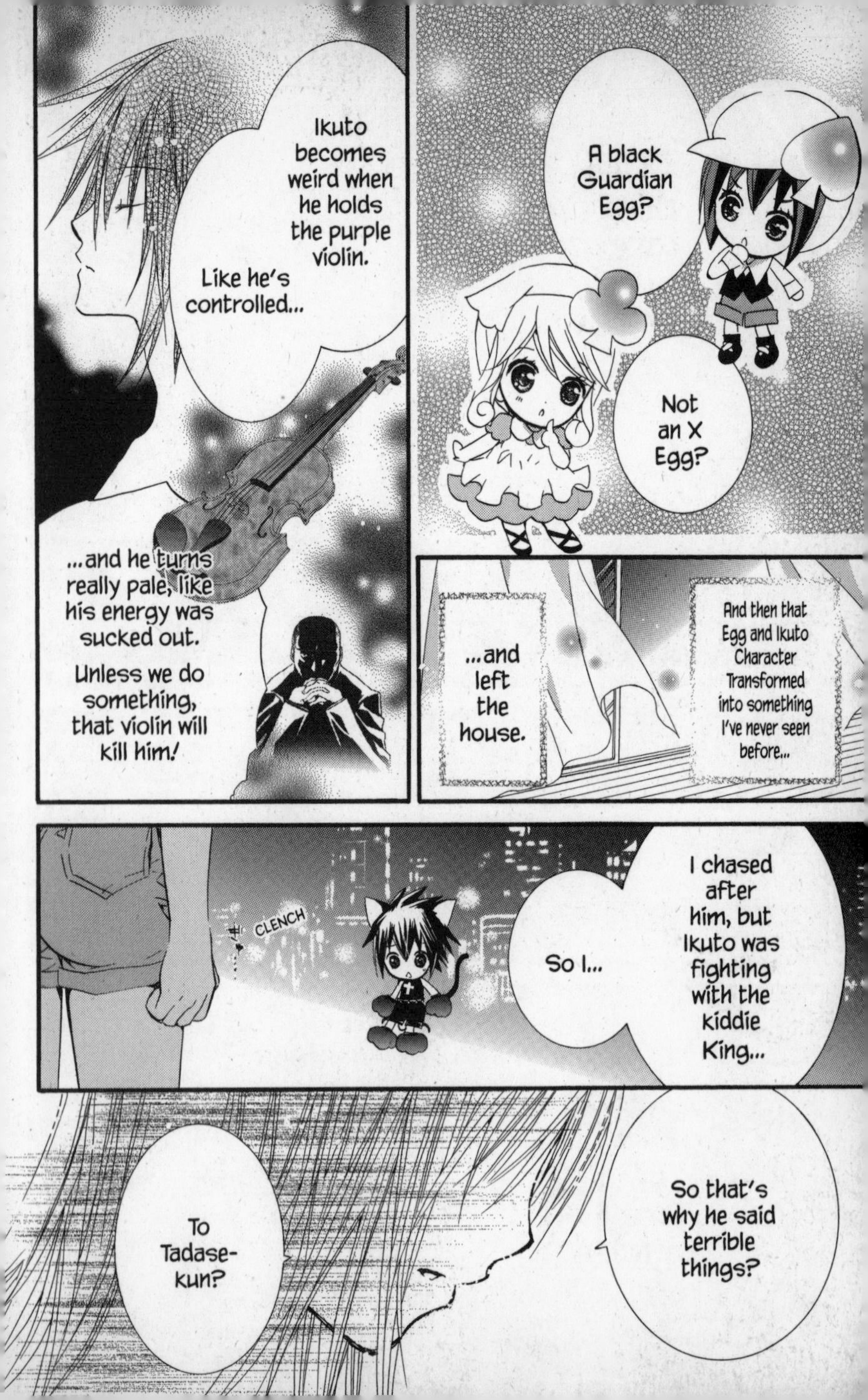
A black Guardian Egg?
Not an X Egg?
And then that Egg and Ikuto Character Transformed into something I've never seen before...
...and left the house.
Ikuto becomes weird when he holds the purple violin.
Like he's controlled...
...and he turns really pale, like his energy was sucked out.
Unless we do something, that violin will kill him!
I chased after him, but Ikuto was fighting with the kiddie King...
So I...
CLENCH
So that's why he said terrible things?
To Tadase-kun?

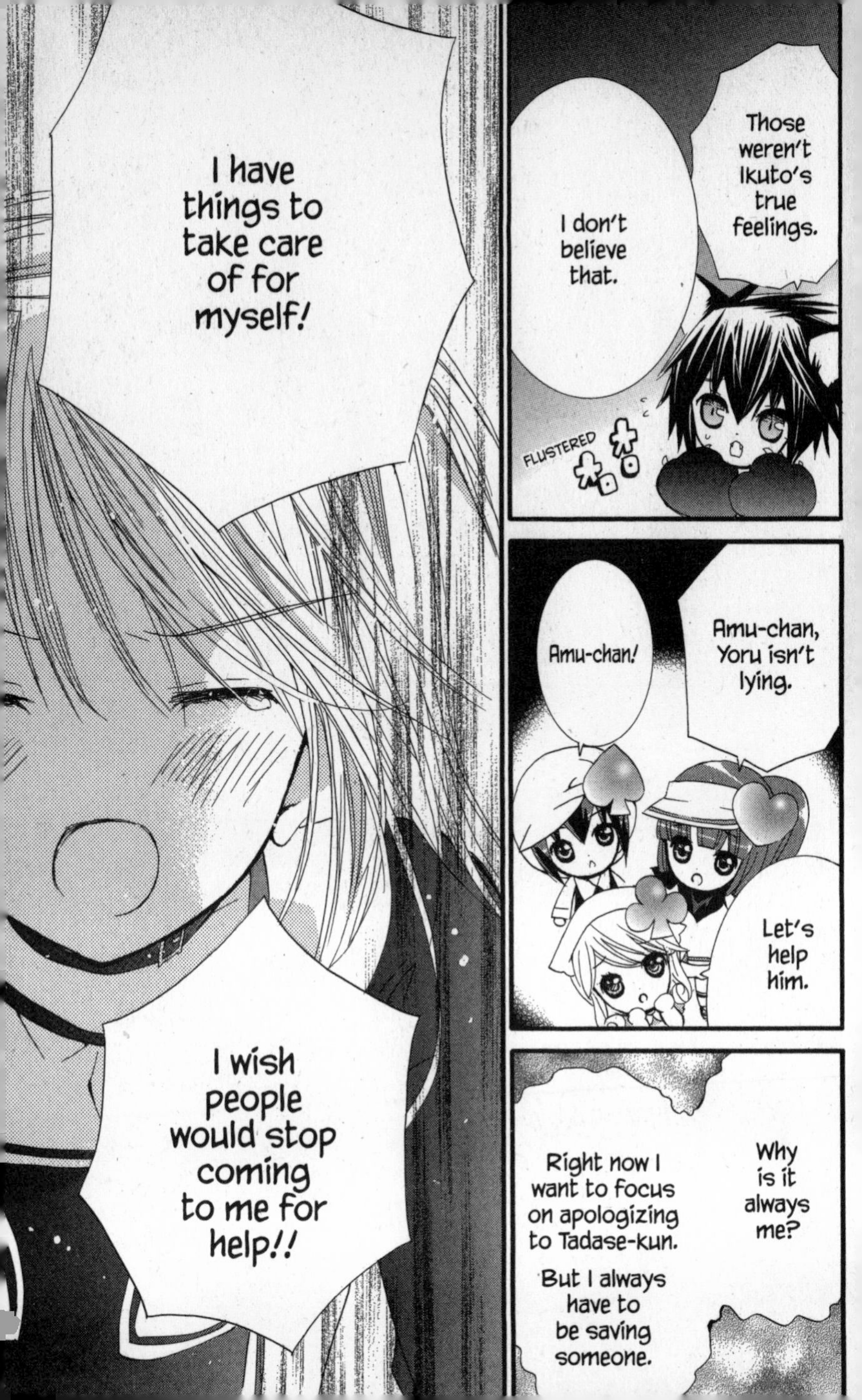
Those weren't Ikuto's true feelings.
I don't believe that.
FLUSTERED
Amu-chan, Yoru isn't lying.
Amu-chan!
Let's help him.
Why is it always me?
Right now I want to focus on apologizing to Tadase-kun.
But I always have to be saving someone.
I have things to take care of for myself!
I wish people would stop coming to me for help!!

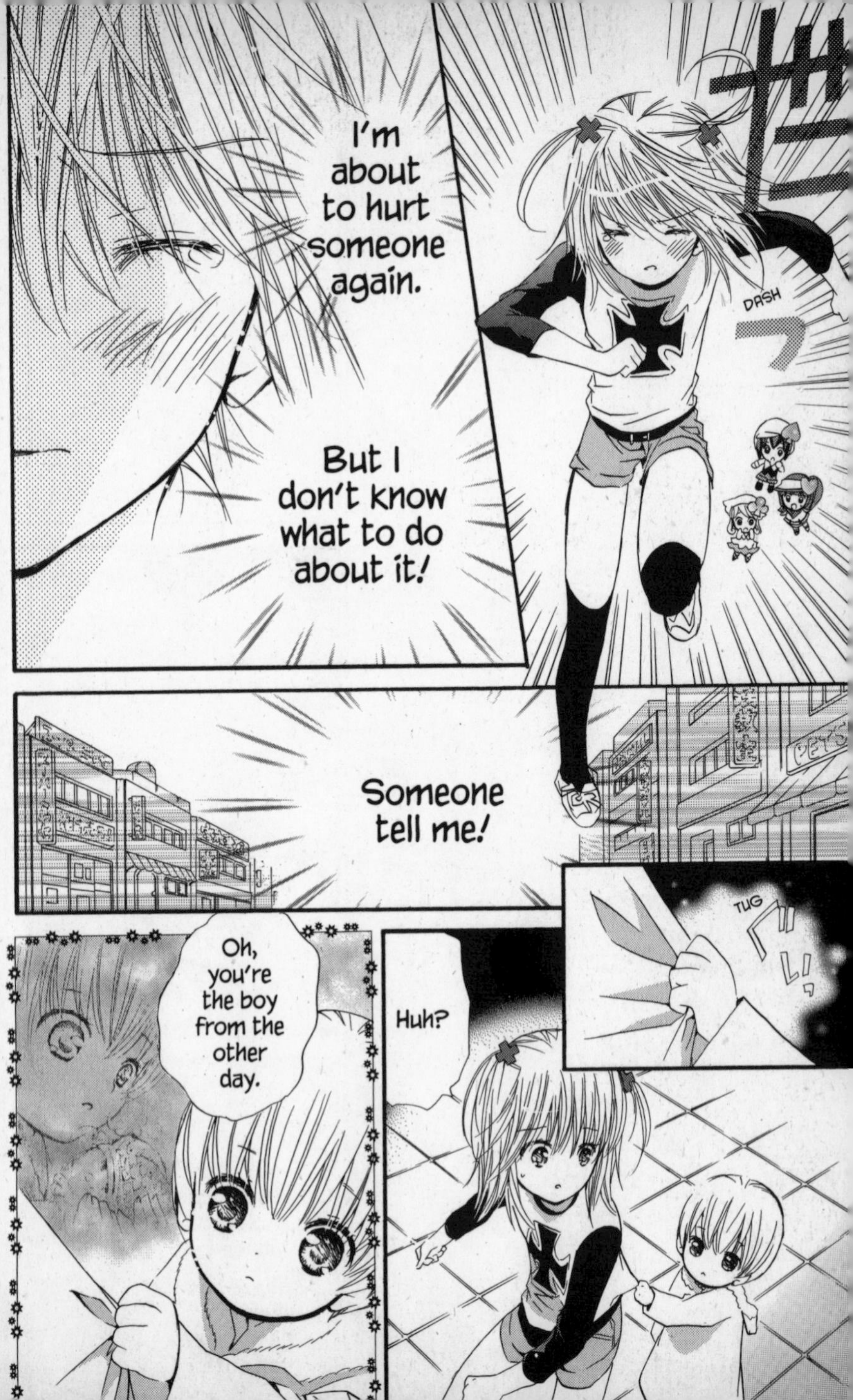
DASH
I'm about to hurt someone again.
But I don't know what to do about it!
Someone tell me!
TUG
Huh?
Oh, you're the boy from the other day.

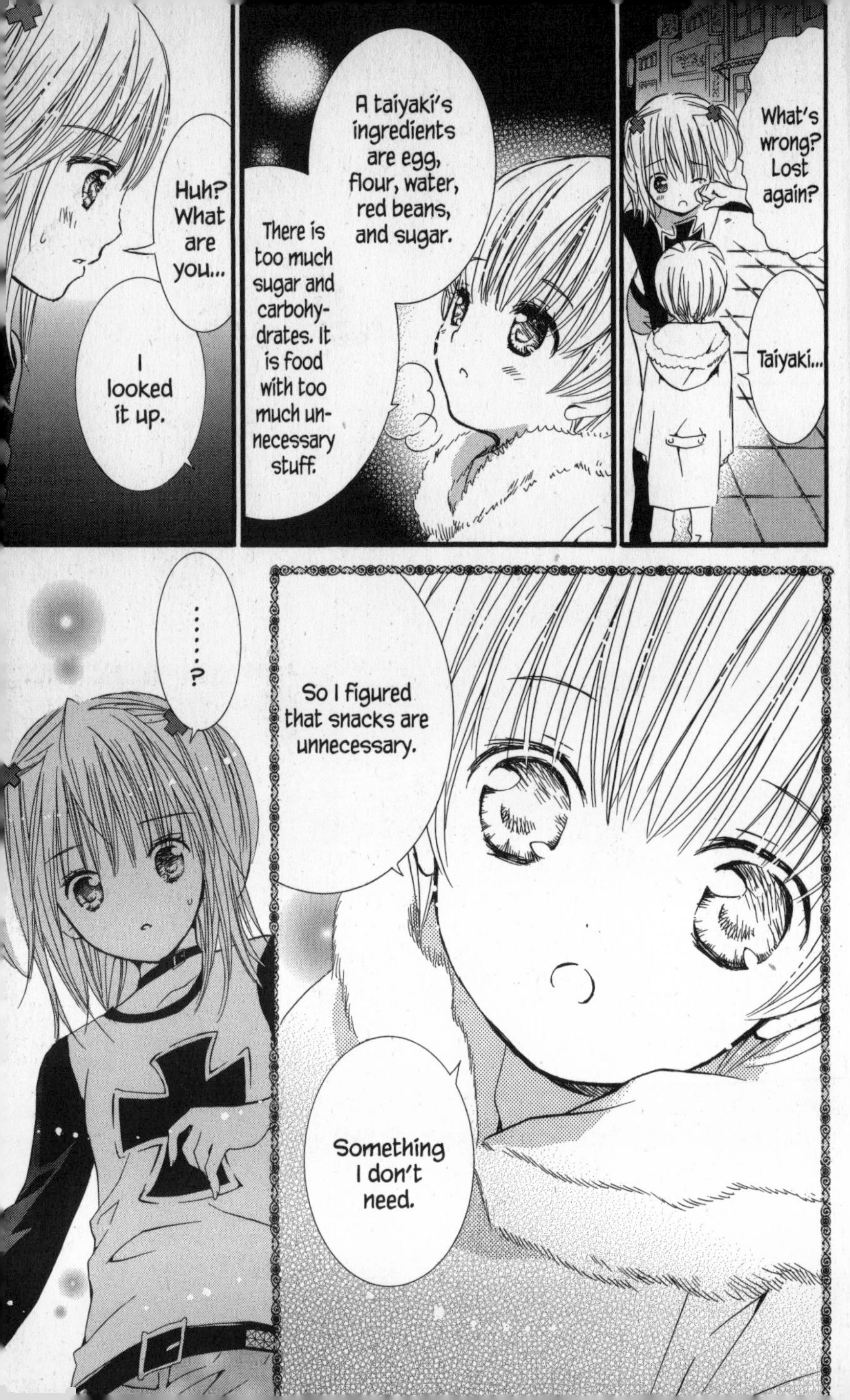
What's wrong? Lost again?
Taiyaki...
A taiyaki's ingredients are egg, flour, water, red beans, and sugar.
There is too much sugar and carbohydrates. It is food with too much unnecessary stuff.
Huh? What are you...
I looked it up.
So I figured that snacks are unnecessary.
Something I don't need.
......?

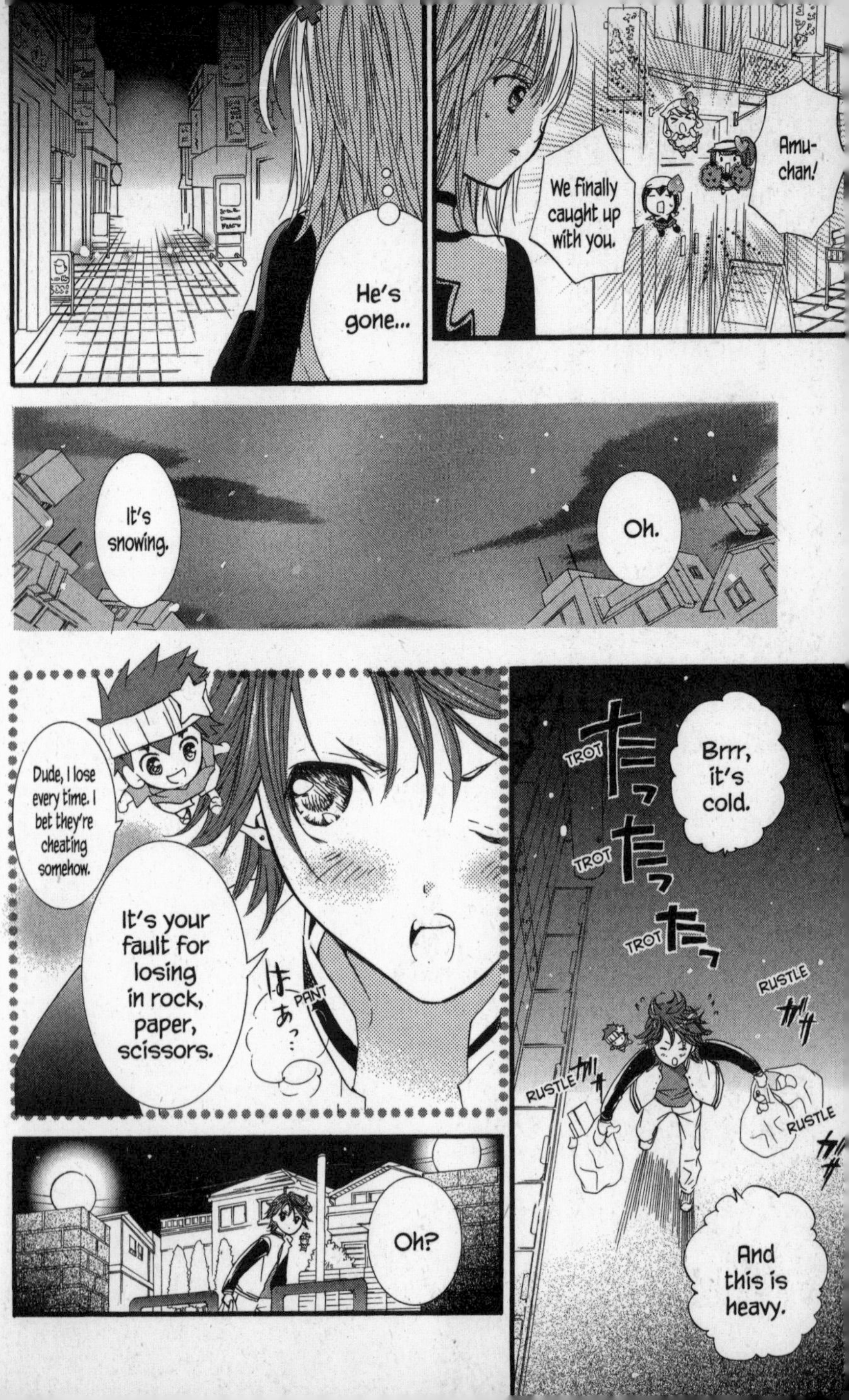
Amu-chan!
We finally caught up with you.
He's gone...
Oh.
It's your snowing.
TROT たっ
TROT たっ
TROT たっ
Brrr, it's cold.
RUSTLE ガサ
RUSTLE ガサ
RUSTLE ガサ
And this is heavy.
It's your fault for losing in rock, paper, scissors.
Dude, I lose every time. I bet they're cheating somehow.
PANT はあっ
Oh?

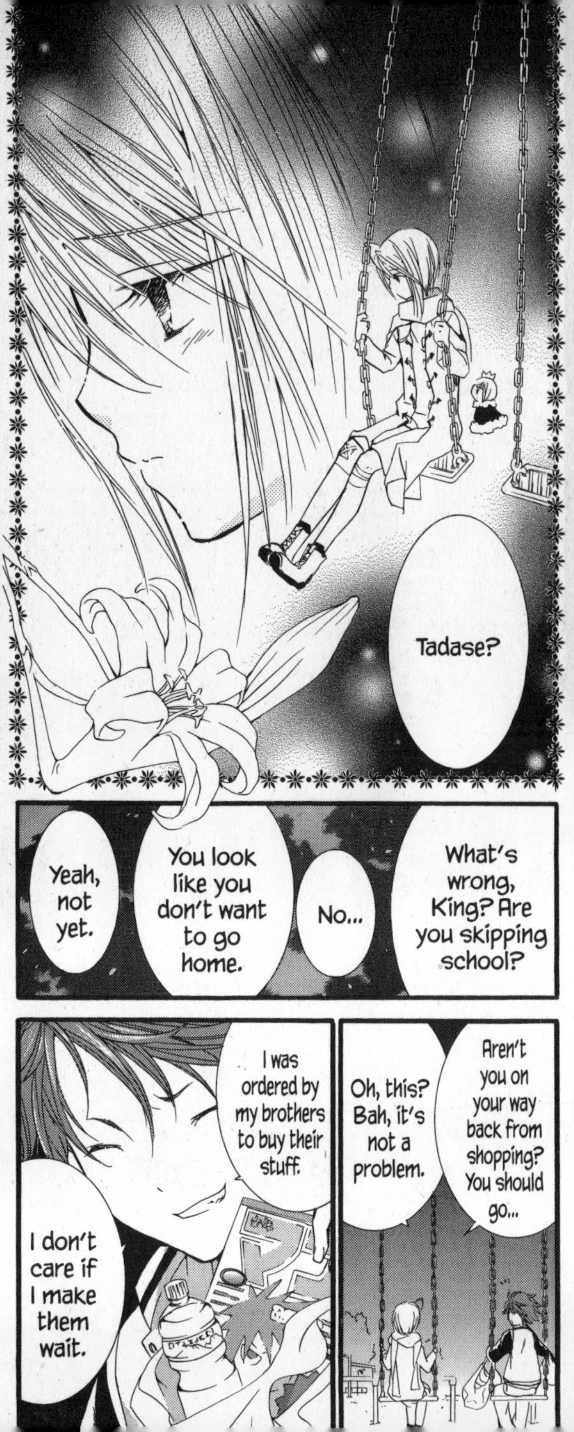
Tadase?
What's wrong, King? Are you skipping school?
No...
You look like you don't want to go home.
Yeah, not yet.
Aren't you on your way back from shopping? You should go...
Oh, this? Bah, it's not a problem.
I was ordered by my brothers to buy their stuff.
I don't care if I make them wait.

character profile

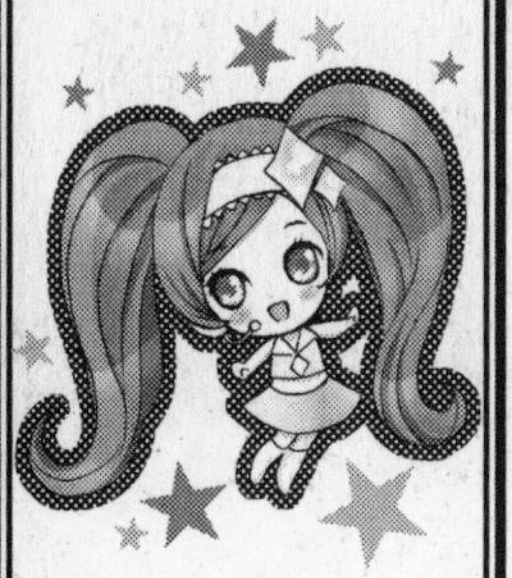

Diamond
(real name unknown)
Guardian Character of: Amu
Special Skill: ?
Hates: ?

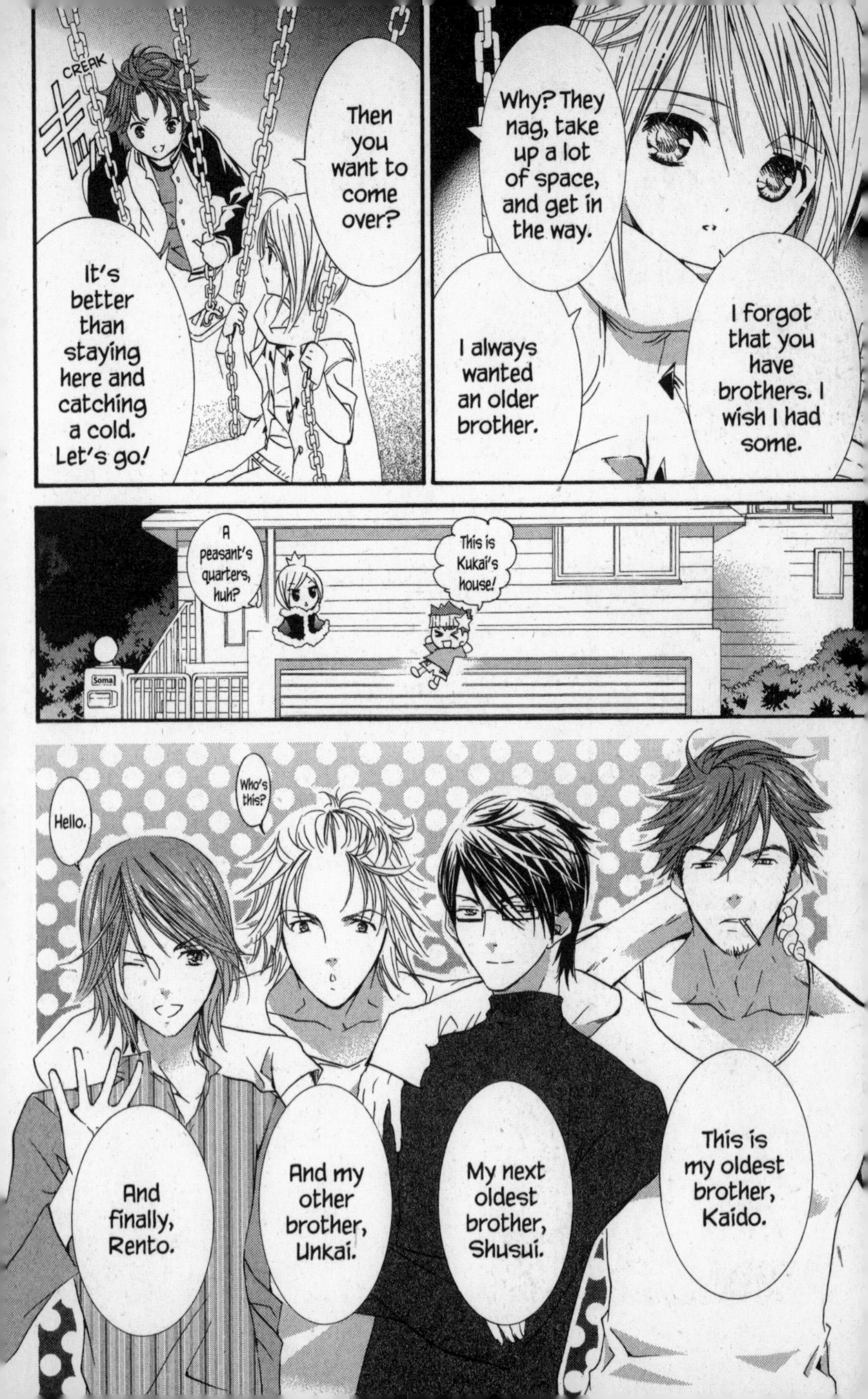
I forgot that you have brothers. I wish I had some.
Why? They nag, take up a lot of space, and get in the way.
I always wanted an older brother.
Then you want to come over?
CREAK
It's better than staying here and catching a cold. Let's go!
This is Kukai's house!
A peasant's quarters, huh?
Soma
Who's this?
Hello.
This is my oldest brother, Kaido.
My next oldest brother, Shusui.
And my other brother, Unkai.
And finally, Rento.

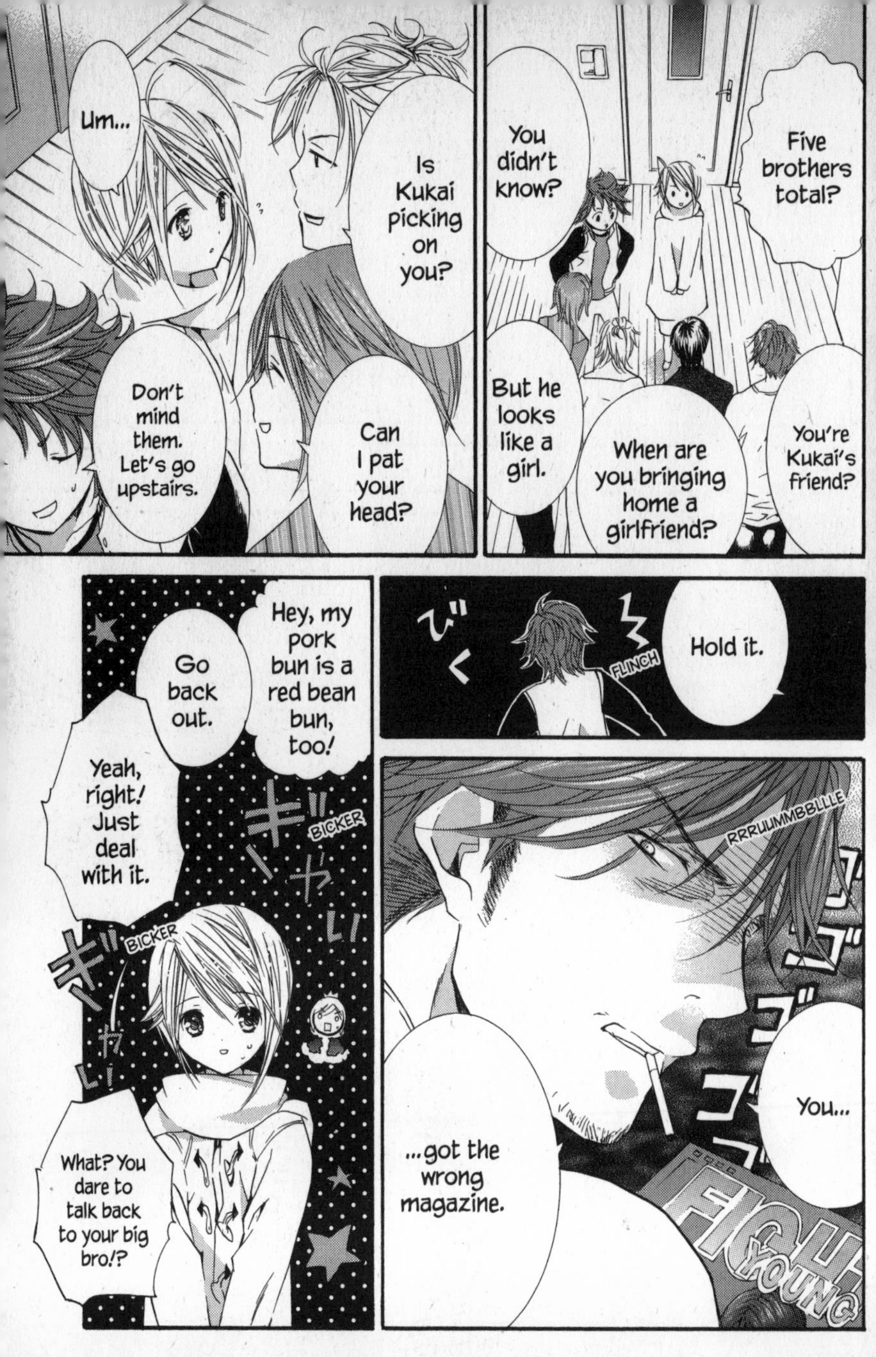
Five brothers total?
You didn't know?
You're Kukai's friend?
When are you bringing home a girlfriend?
But he looks like a girl.
Is Kukai picking on you?
Um...
Can I pat your head?
Don't mind them. Let's go upstairs.
Hold it.
FLINCH
You...
...got the wrong magazine.
RRRUUMMBBLLLE
YOUNG
Hey, my pork bun is a red bean bun, too!
Go back out.
Yeah, right! Just deal with it.
BICKER
BICKER
What? You dare to talk back to your big bro!?

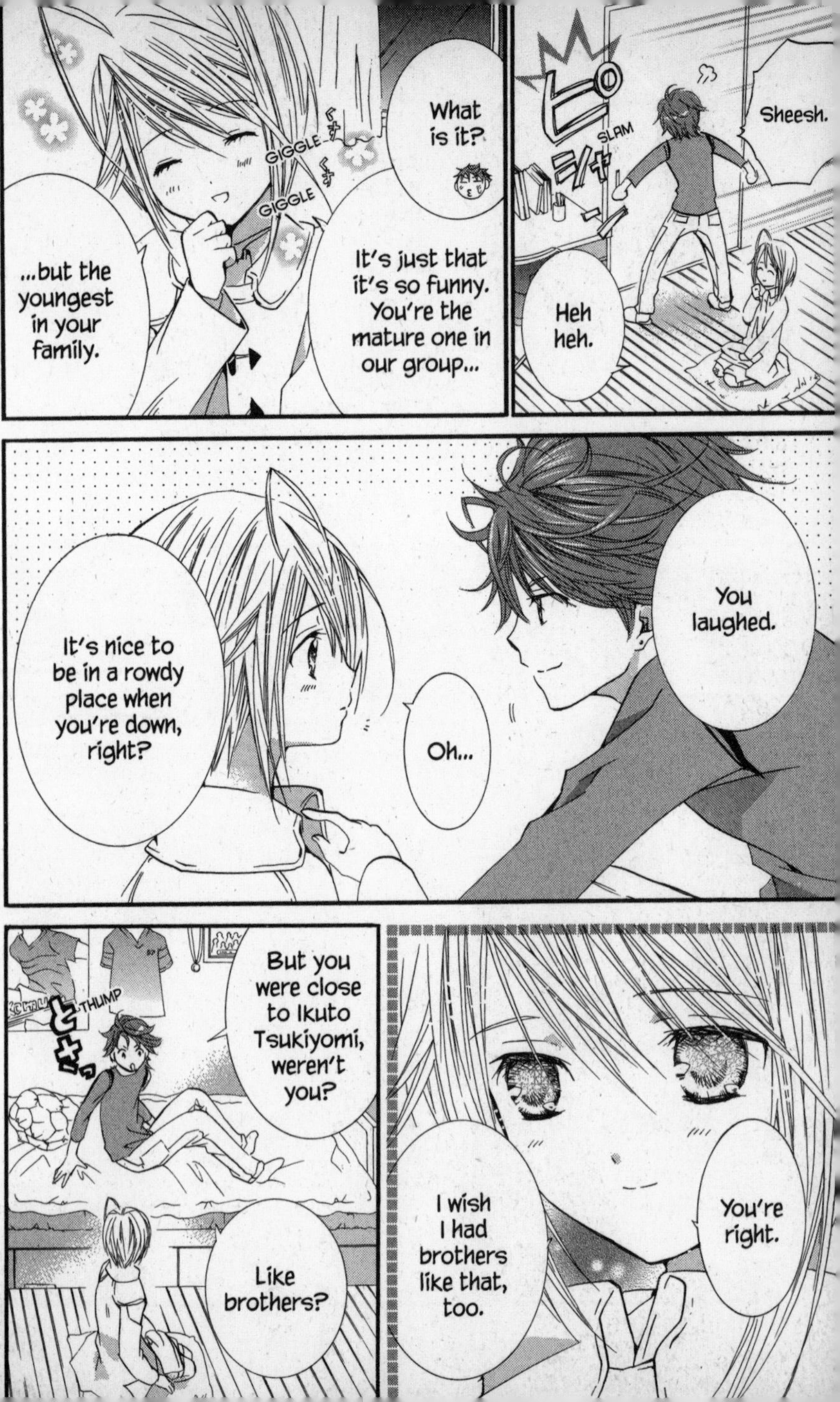
Sheesh.
SLAM
Heh heh.
What is it?
GIGGLE
GIGGLE
It's just that it's so funny. You're the mature one in our group...
...but the youngest in your family.
You laughed.
Oh...
It's nice to be in a rowdy place when you're down, right?
You're right.
I wish I had brothers like that, too.
THUMP
But you were close to Ikuto Tsukiyomi, weren't you?
Like brothers?

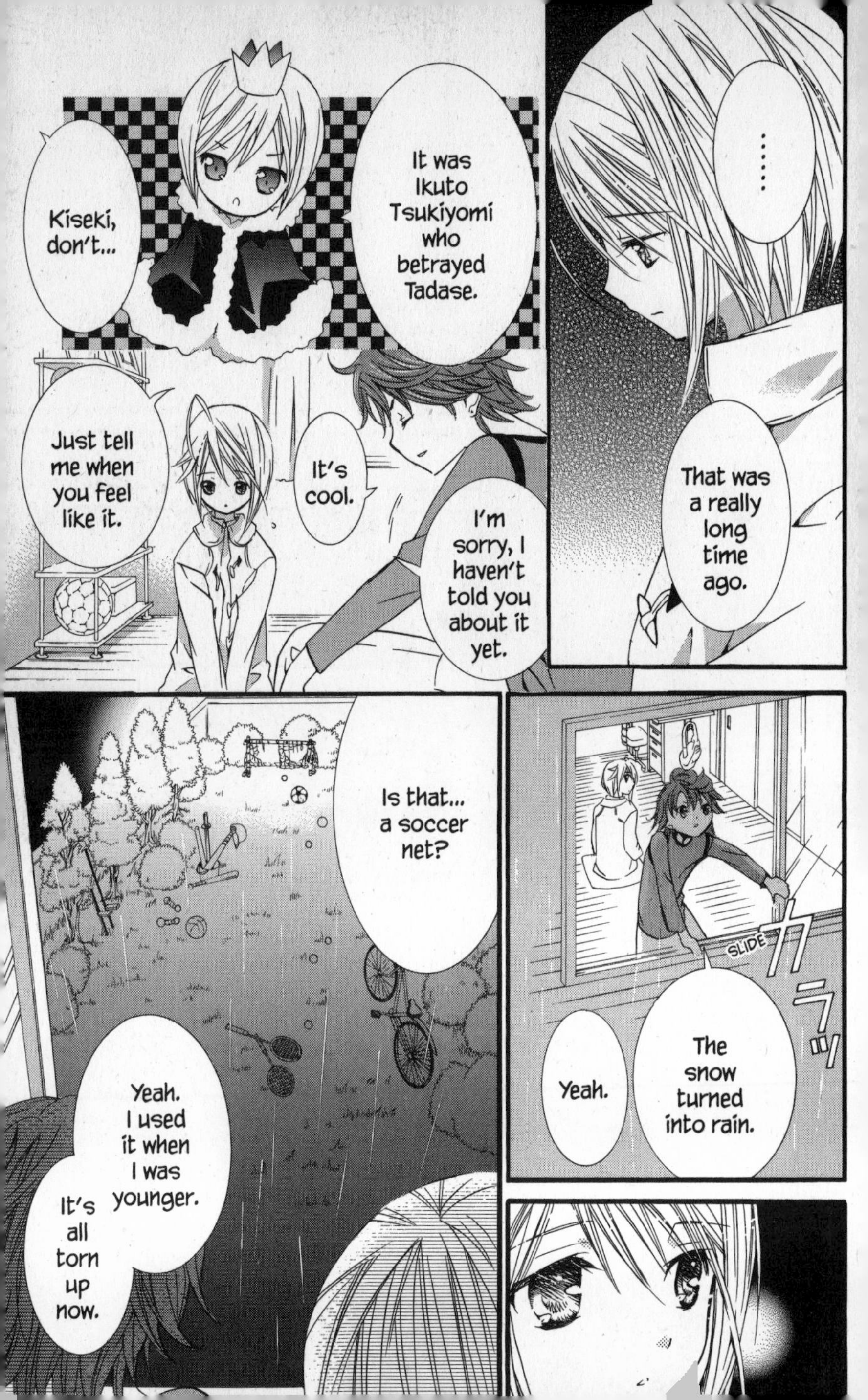
......
That was a really long time ago.
It was Ikuto Tsukiyomi who betrayed Tadase.
Kiseki, don't...
I'm sorry, I haven't told you about it yet.
It's cool.
Just tell me when you feel like it.
SLIDE
カラッ
The snow turned into rain.
Yeah.
Is that... a soccer net?
Yeah. I used it when I was younger.
It's all torn up now.

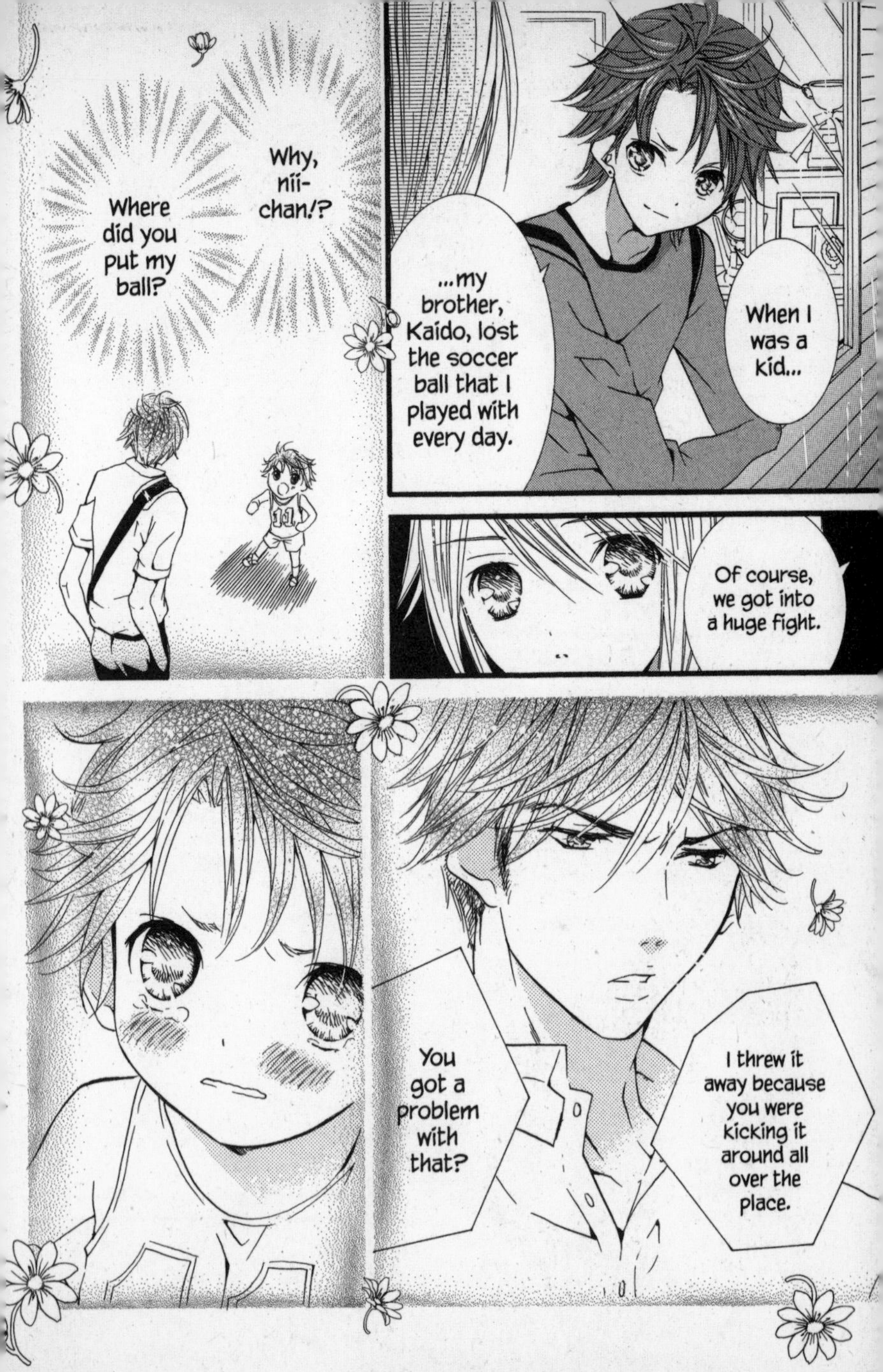
When I was a kid...
...my brother, Kaido, lost the soccer ball that I played with every day.
Of course, we got into a huge fight.
Why, nii-chan!?
Where did you put my ball?
I threw it away because you were kicking it around all over the place.
You got a problem with that?

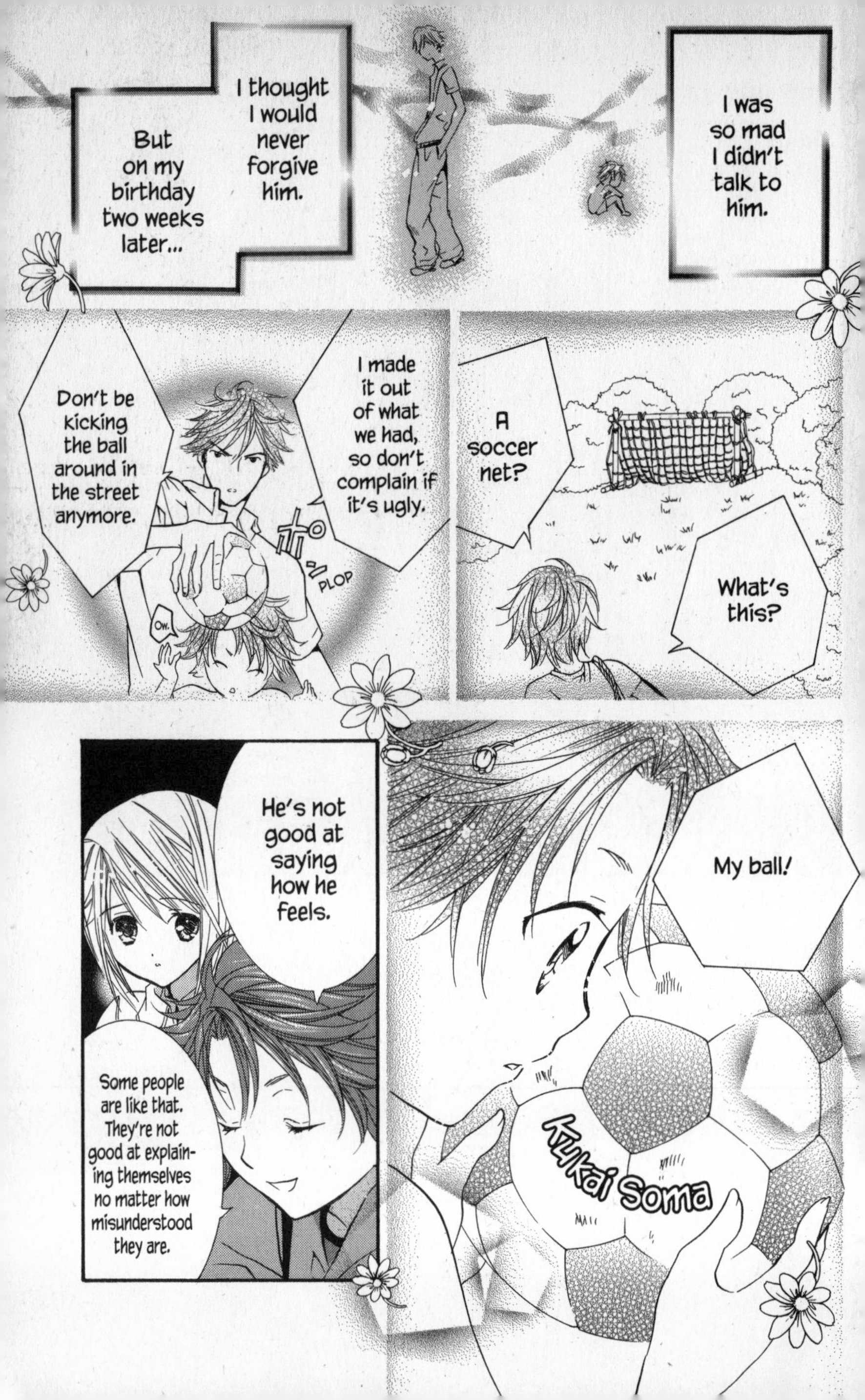
I was so mad I didn't talk to him.
I thought I would never forgive him.
But on my birthday two weeks later...
What's this?
A soccer net?
I made it out of what we had, so don't complain if it's ugly.
PLOP
Don't be kicking the ball around in the street anymore.
Ow.
My ball!
Kukai Soma
He's not good at saying how he feels.
Some people are like that. They're not good at explaining themselves no matter how misunderstood they are.

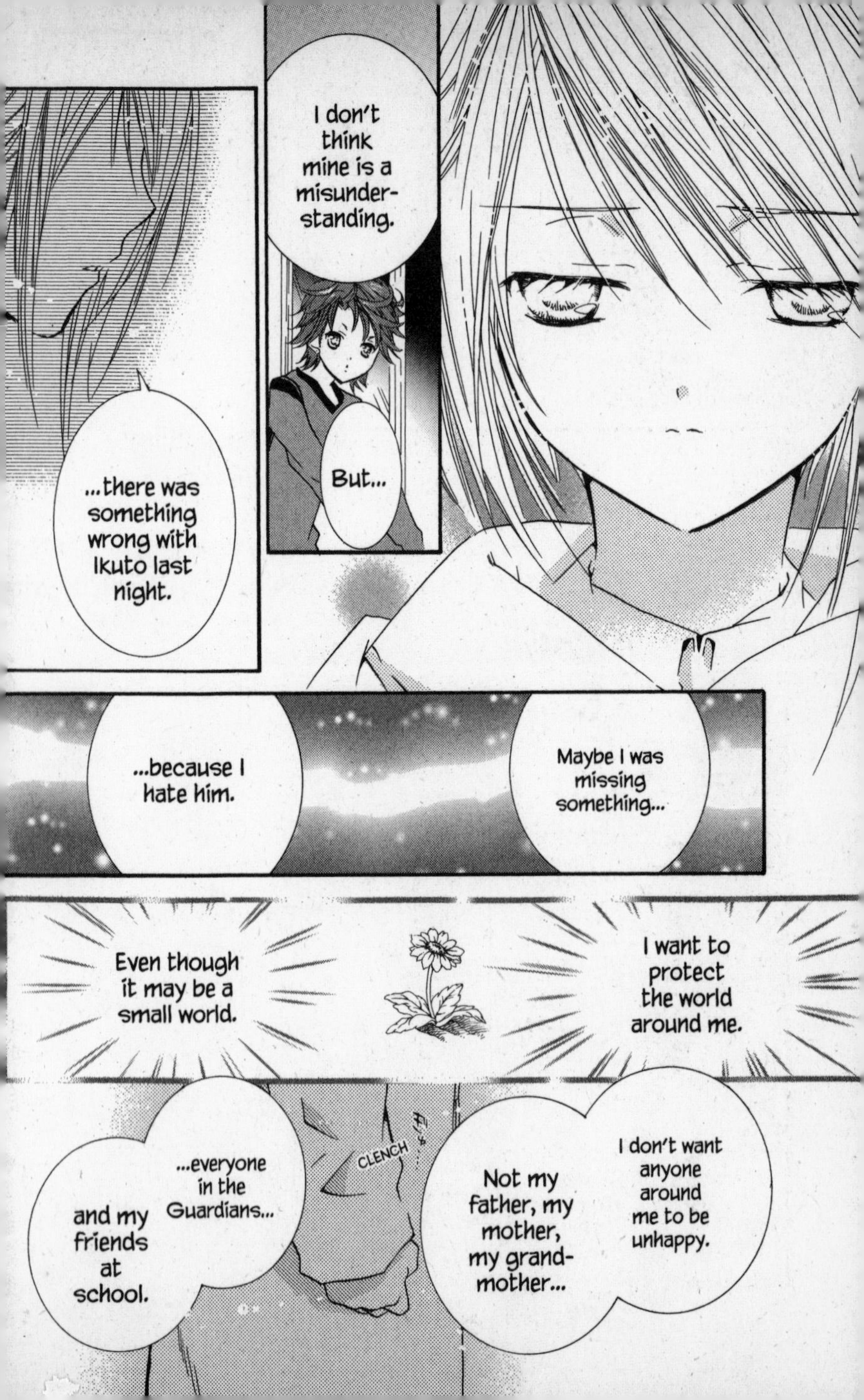
I don't think mine is a misunderstanding.
But...
...there was something wrong with Ikuto last night.
Maybe I was missing something...
...because I hate him.
I want to protect the world around me.
Even though it may be a small world.
I don't want anyone around me to be unhappy.
Not my father, my mother, my grand-mother...
CLENCH
...everyone in the Guardians...
and my friends at school.

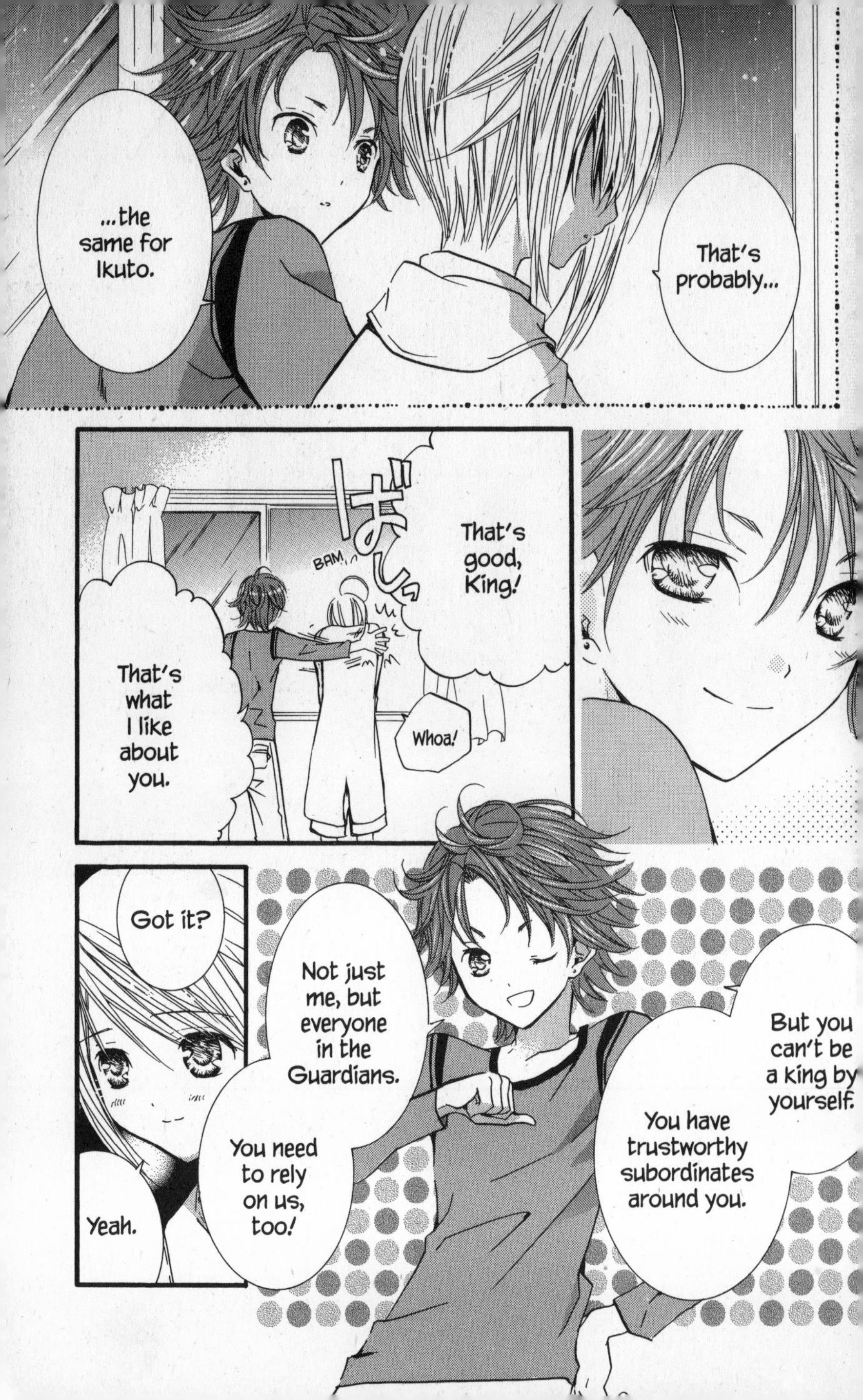
That's probably...
...the same for Ikuto.
That's good, King!
BAM
Whoa!
That's what I like about you.
But you can't be a king by yourself.
You have trustworthy subordinates around you.
Not just me, but everyone in the Guardians.
You need to rely on us, too!
Got it?
Yeah.

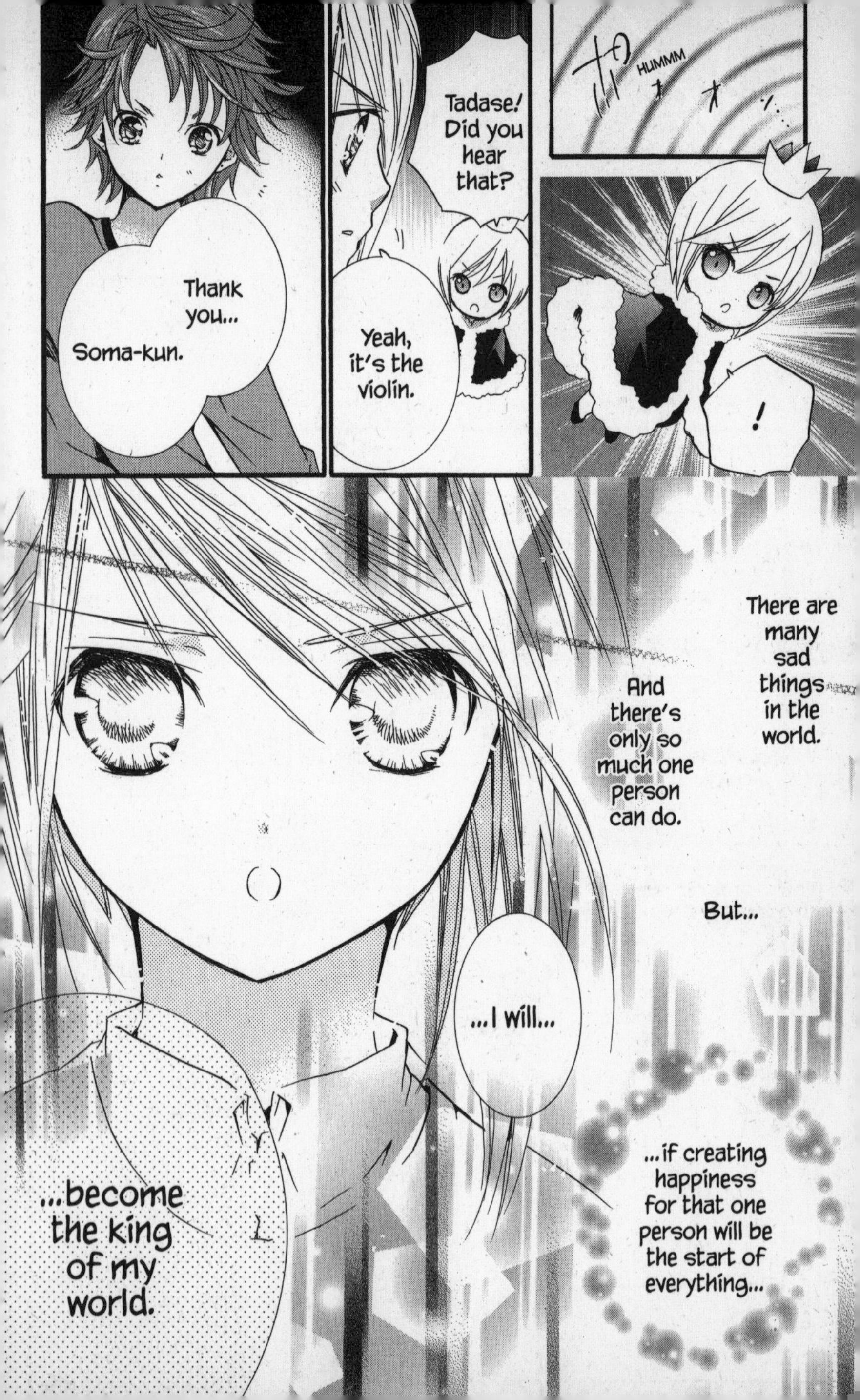
HUMMM
!
Tadase! Did you hear that?
Yeah, it's the violin.
Thank you... Soma-kun.
There are many sad things in the world.
And there's only so much one person can do.
But...
...if creating happiness for that one person will be the start of everything...
...I will...
...become the king of my world.

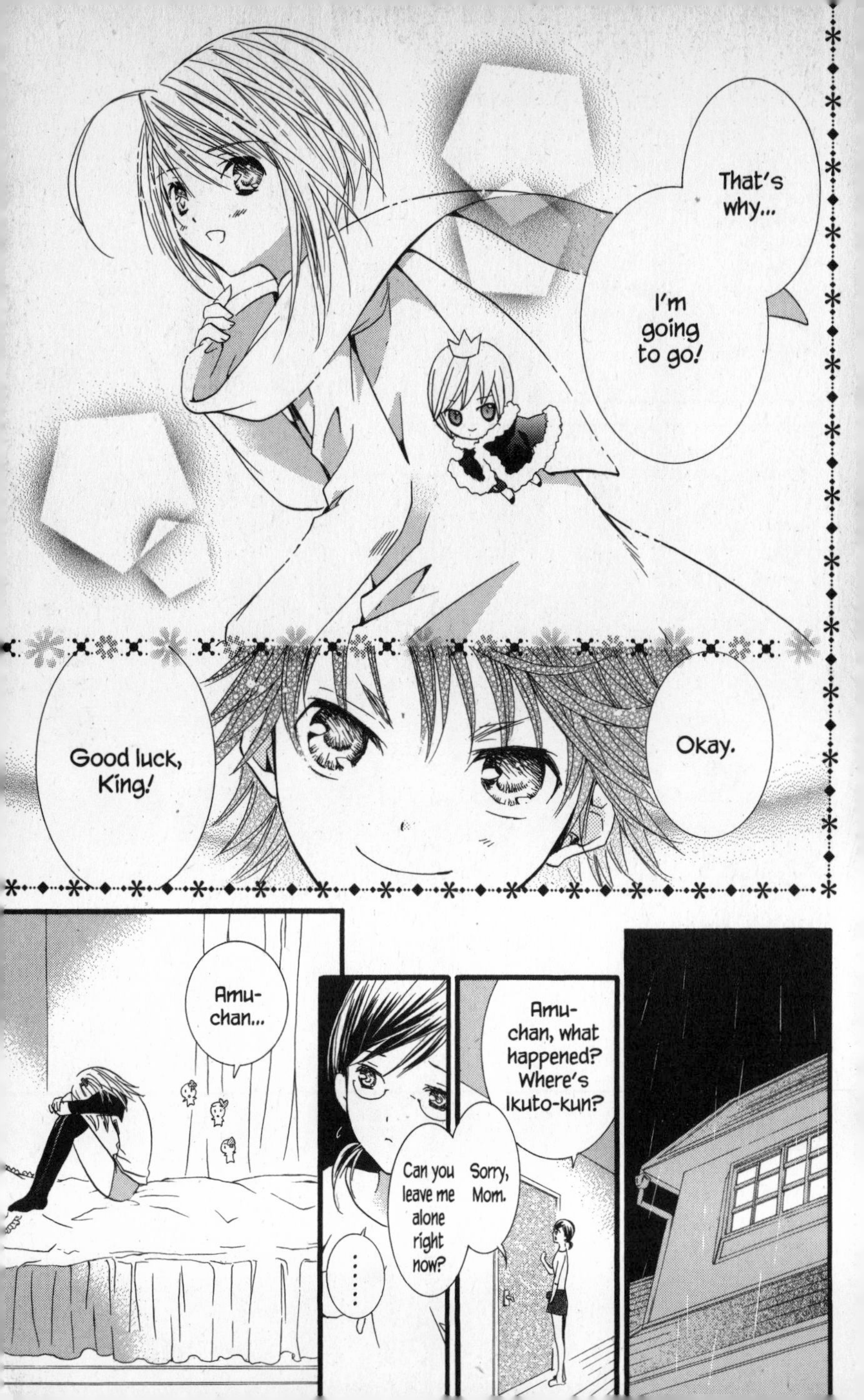
That's why...
I'm going to go!
Okay.
Good luck, King!
Amu-chan, what happened? Where's Ikuto-kun?
Sorry, Mom.
Can you leave me alone right now?
......
Amu-chan...

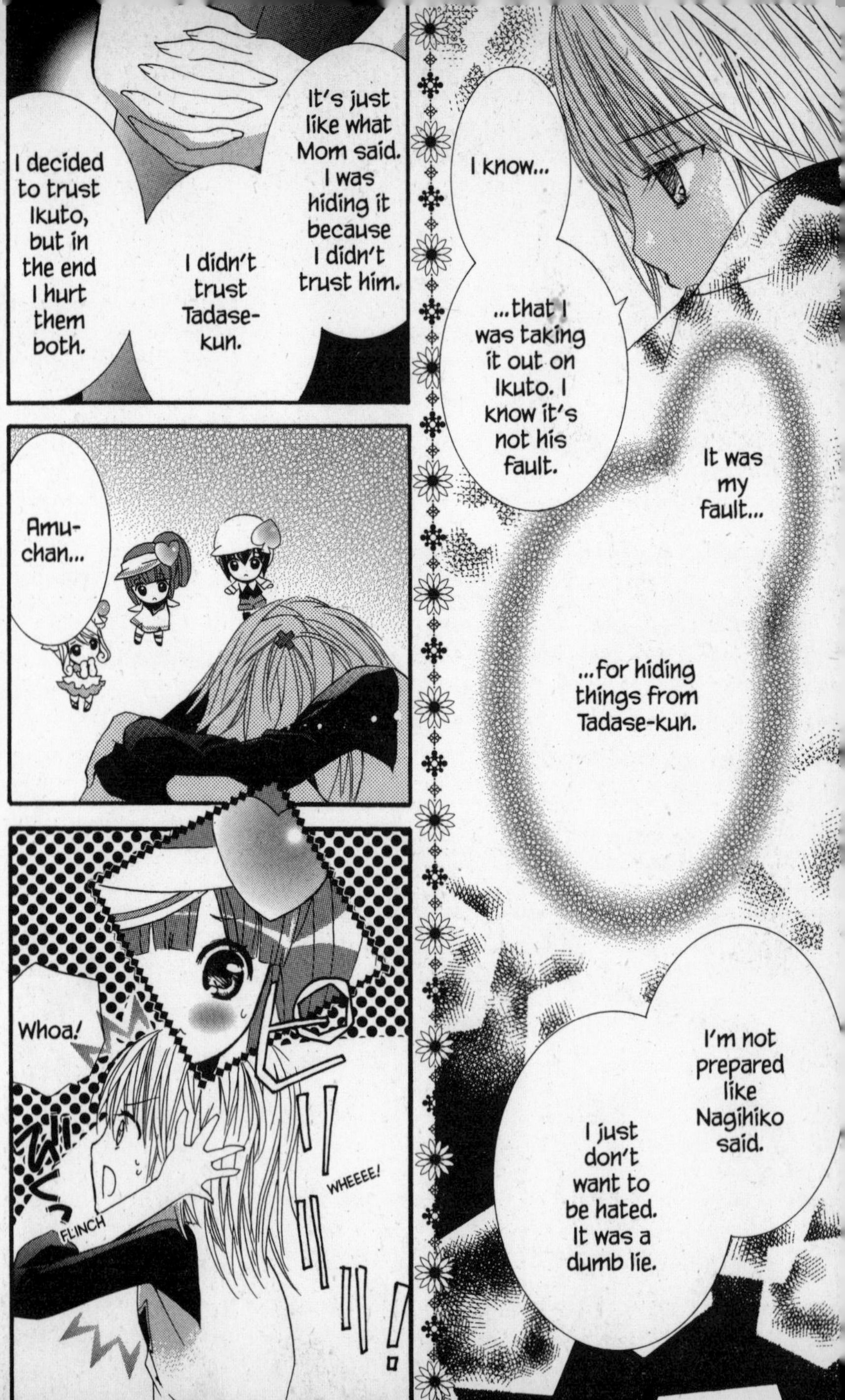
I know...
...that I was taking it out on Ikuto. I know it's not his fault.
It was my fault...
...for hiding things from Tadase-kun.
I'm not prepared like Nagihiko said.
I just don't want to be hated. It was a dumb lie.
It's just like what Mom said. I was hiding it because I didn't trust him.
I didn't trust Tadase-kun.
I decided to trust Ikuto, but in the end I hurt them both.
Amu-chan...
Whoa!
WHEEEE!
FLINCH

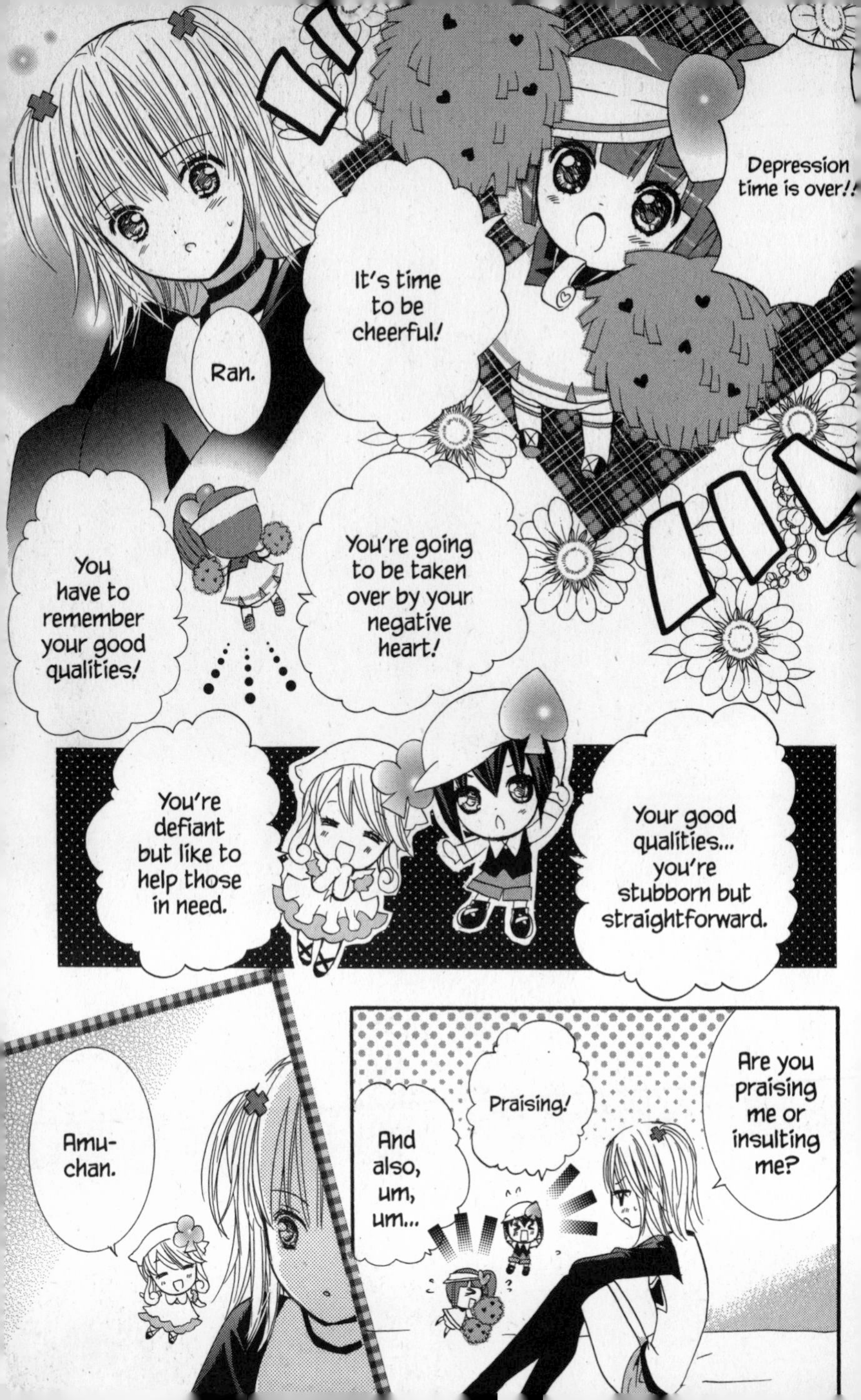

Depression time is over!!
It's time to be cheerful!
Ran.
You're going to be taken over by your negative heart!
You have to remember your good qualities!
Your good qualities... you're stubborn but straightforward.
You're defiant but like to help those in need.
Are you praising me or insulting me?
Praising!
And also, um, um...
Amu-chan.

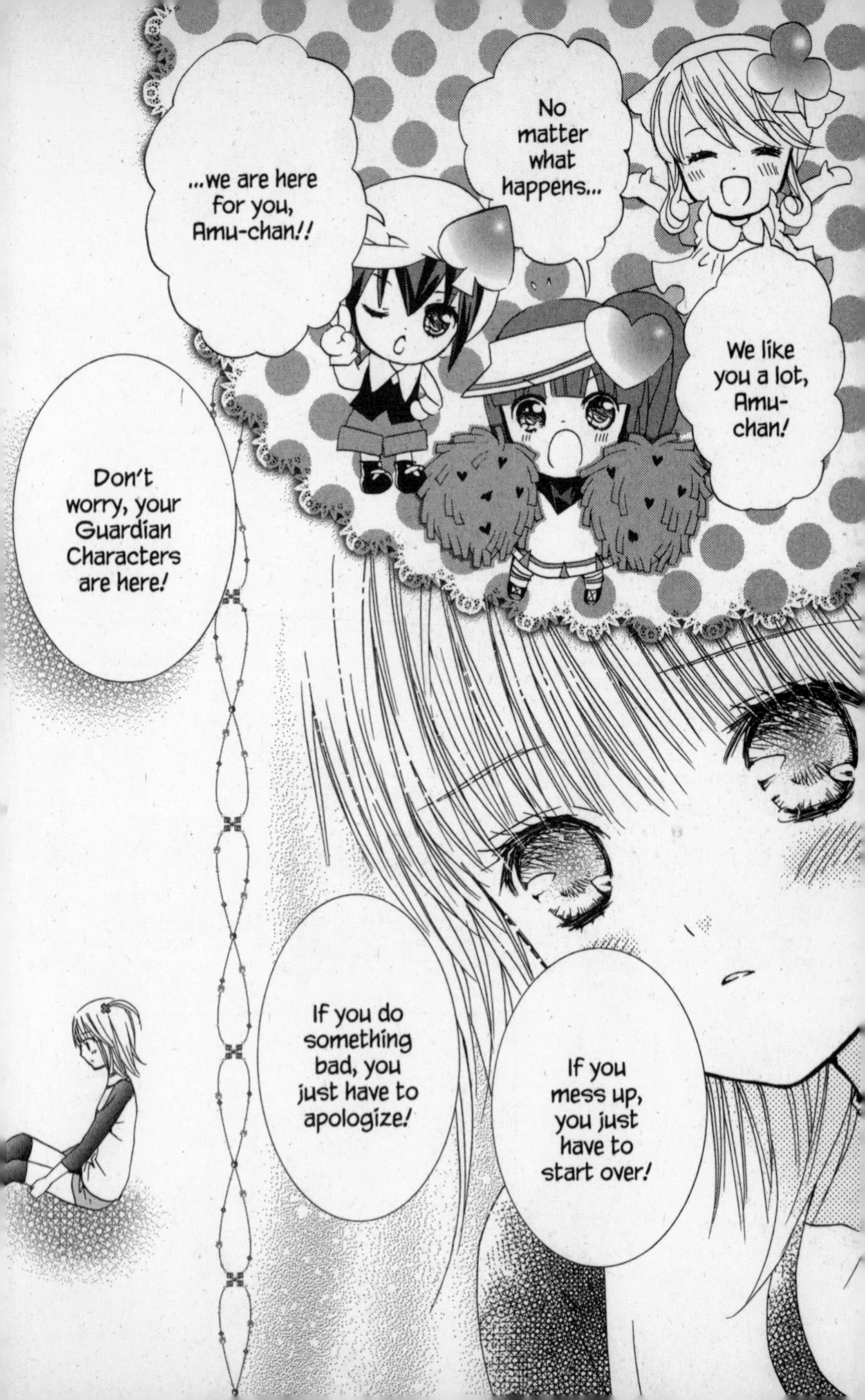
We like you a lot, Amu-chan!
No matter what happens...
...we are here for you, Amu-chan!!
Don't worry, your Guardian Characters are here!
If you mess up, you just have to start over!
If you do something bad, you just have to apologize!

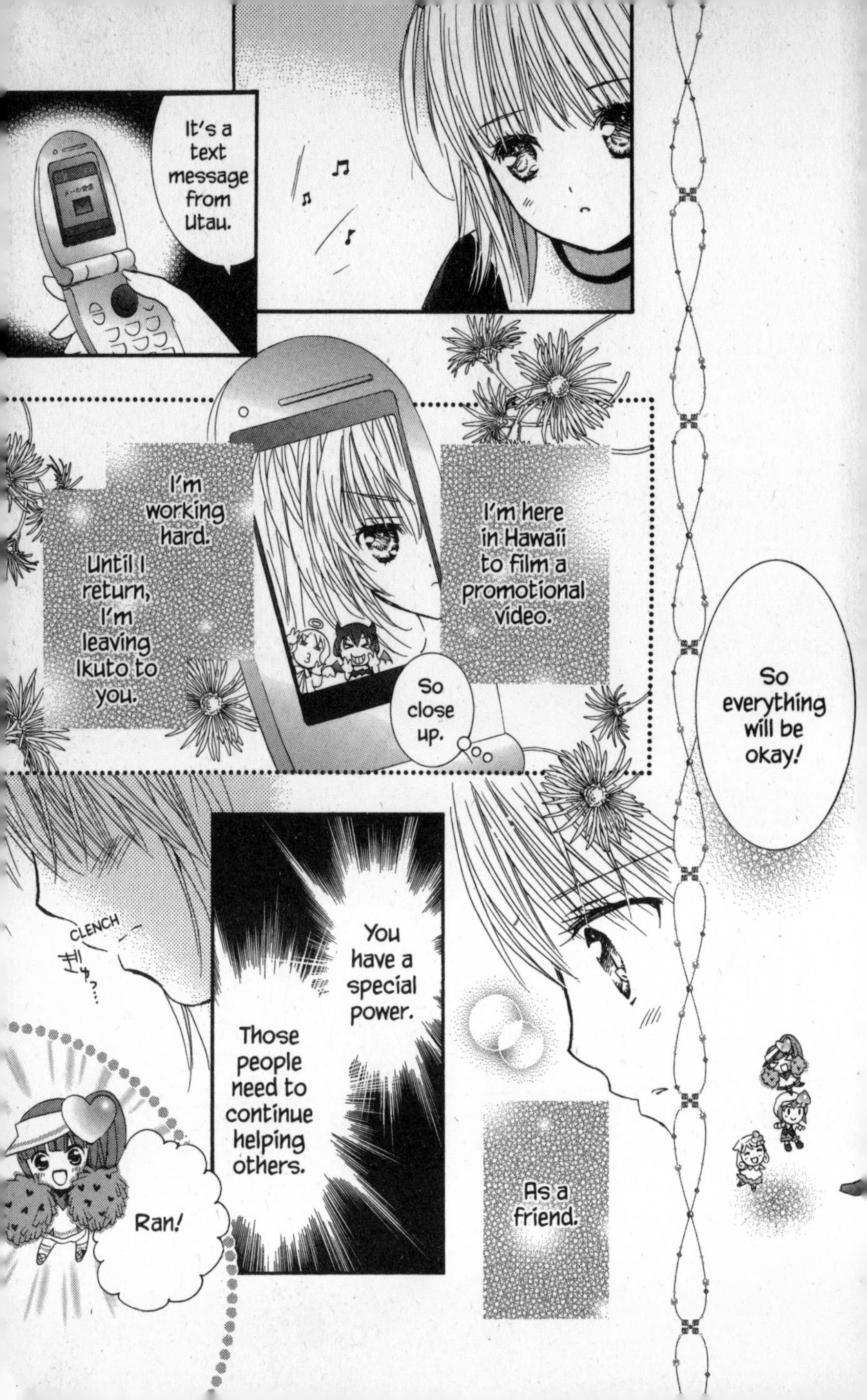

It's a text message from Utau.
I'm here in Hawaii to film a promotional video.
I'm working hard.
Until I return, I'm leaving Ikuto to you.
So close up.
So everything will be okay!
As a friend.
You have a special power.
Those people need to continue helping others.
CLENCH
ぎゅっ…
Ran!

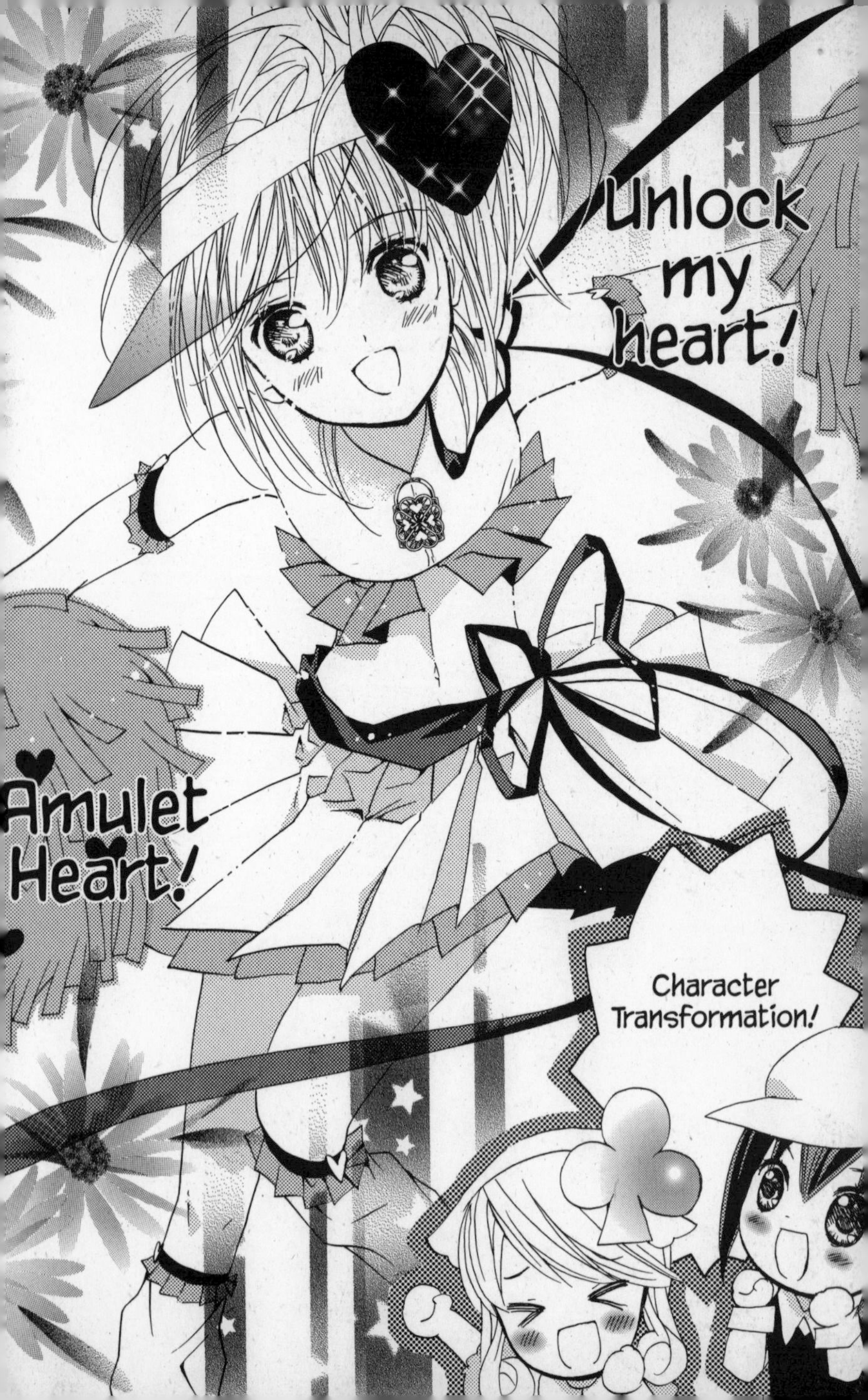
Unlock my heart!
Character Transformation!
Amulet Heart!

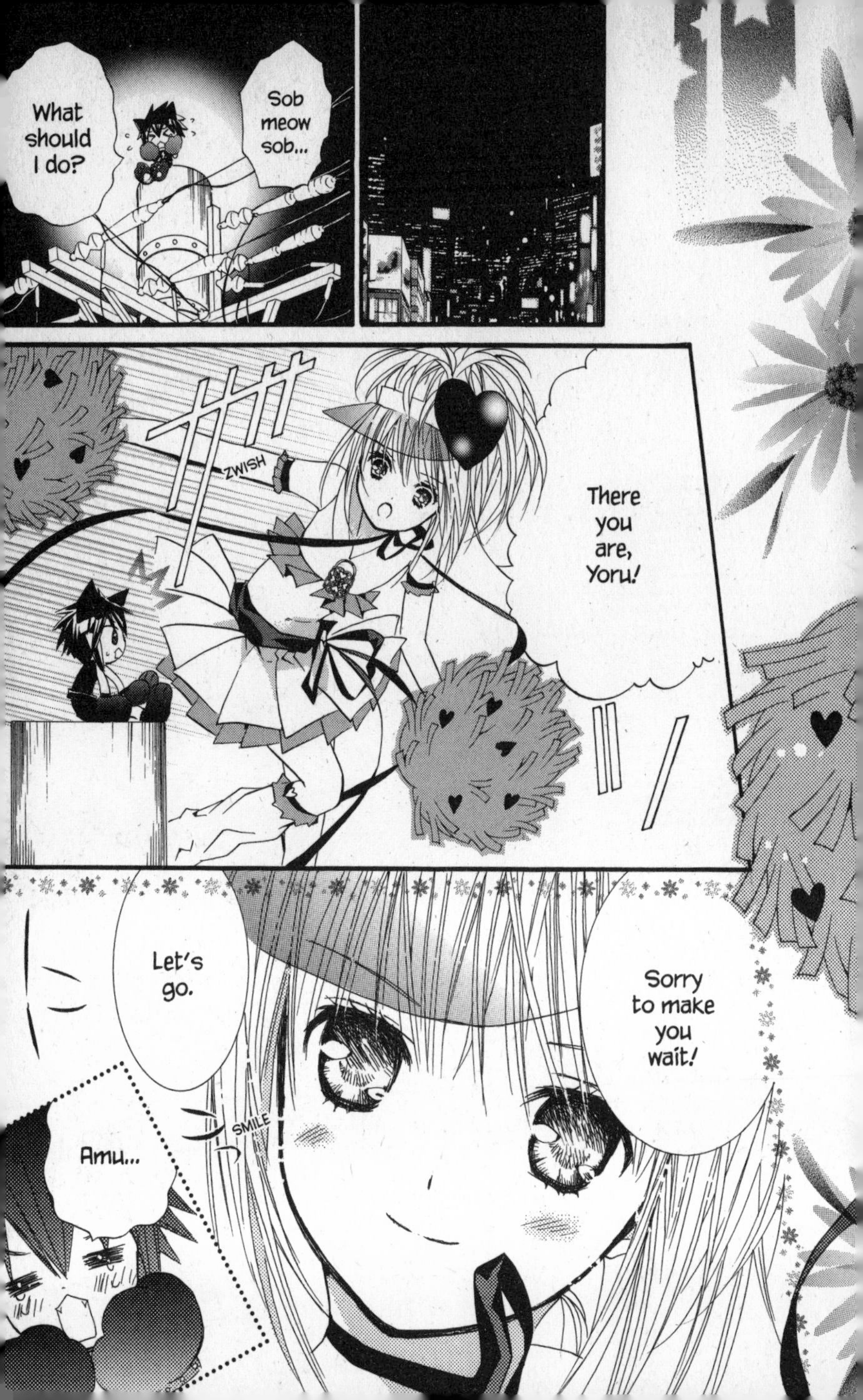
Sob meow sob...
What should I do?
There you are, Yoru!
ZWISH
Sorry to make you wait!
Let's go.
SMILE
Amu...

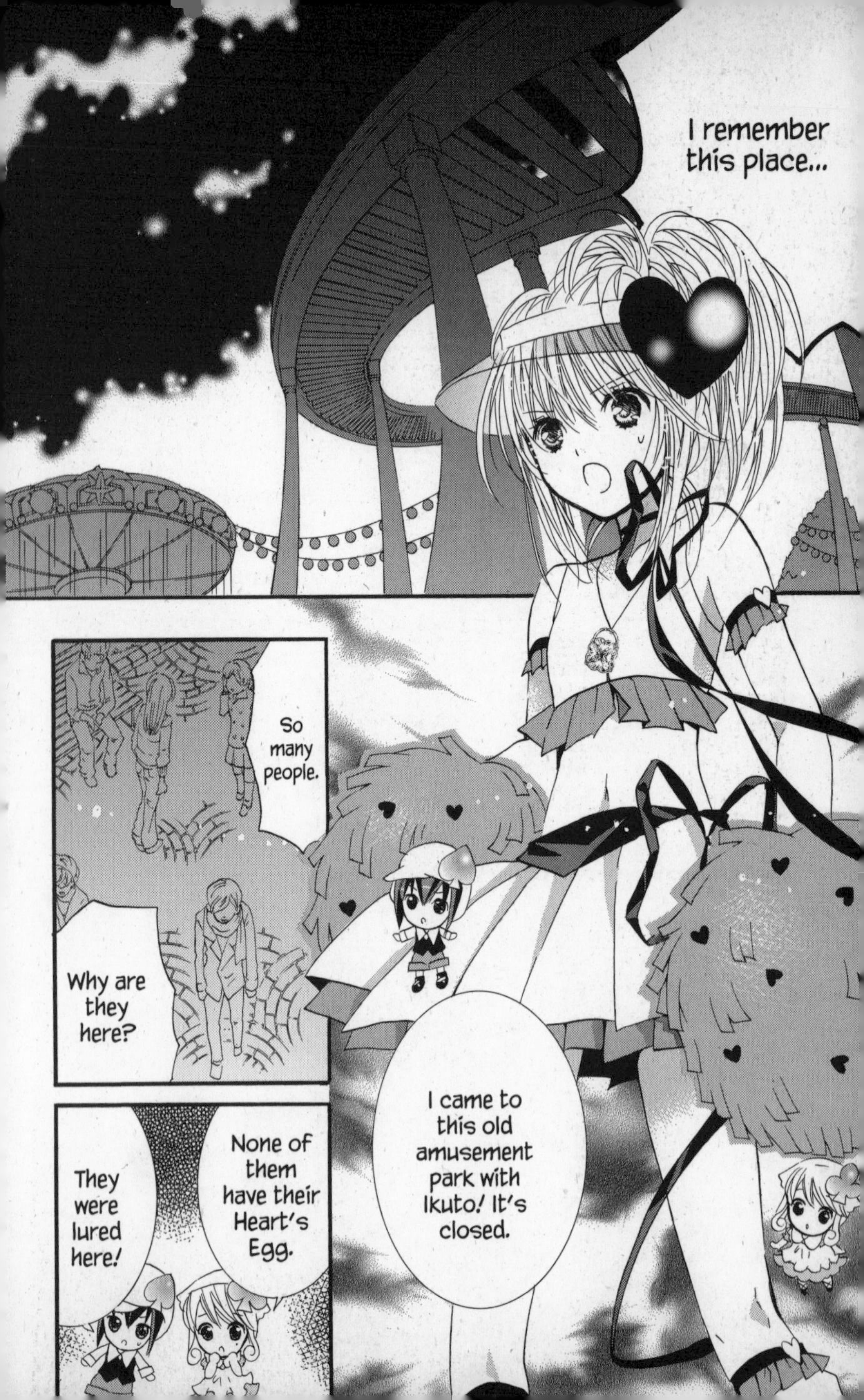
I remember this place...
I came to this old amusement park with Ikuto! It's closed.
So many people.
Why are they here?
None of them have their Heart's Egg.
They were lured here!

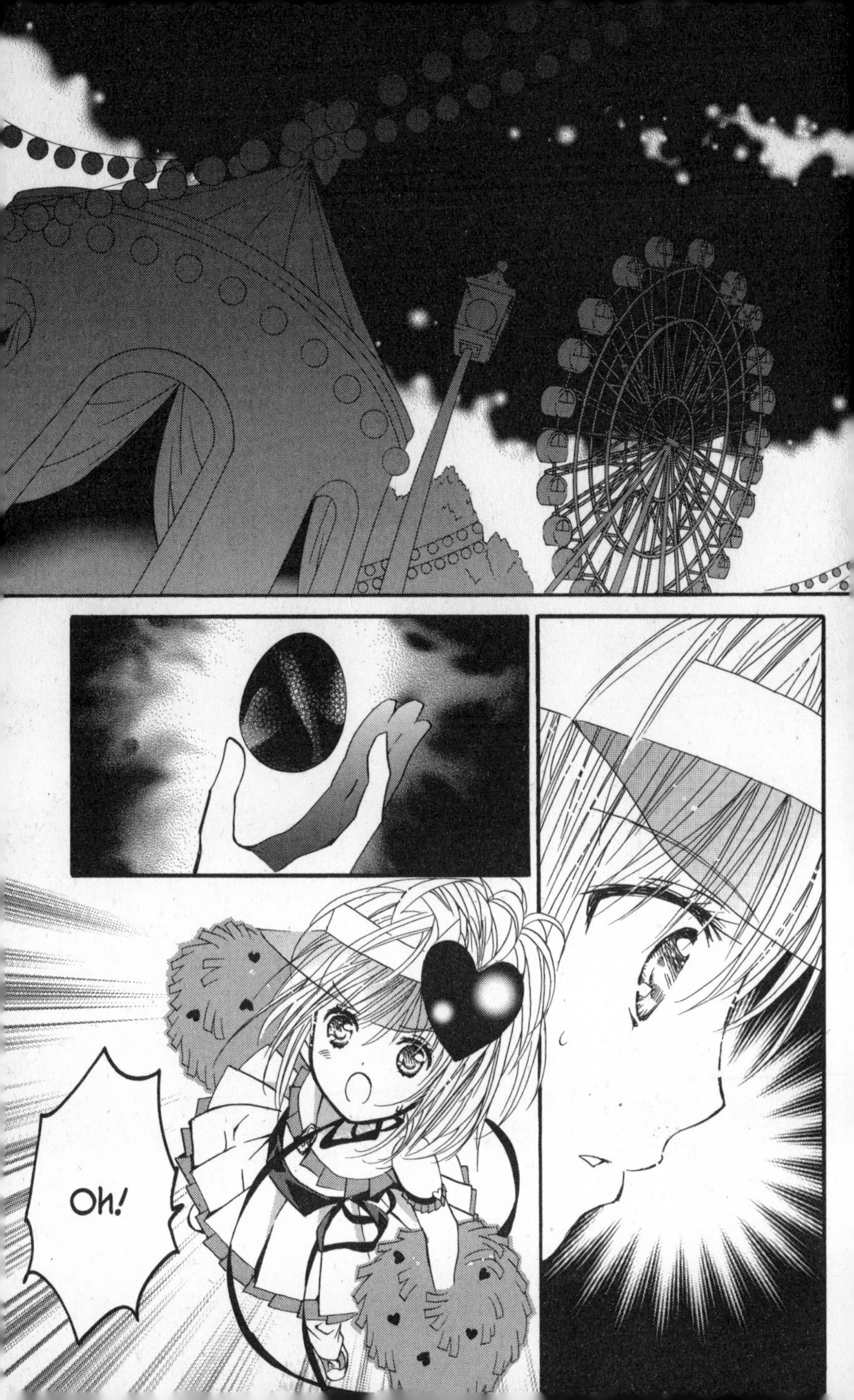
Oh!

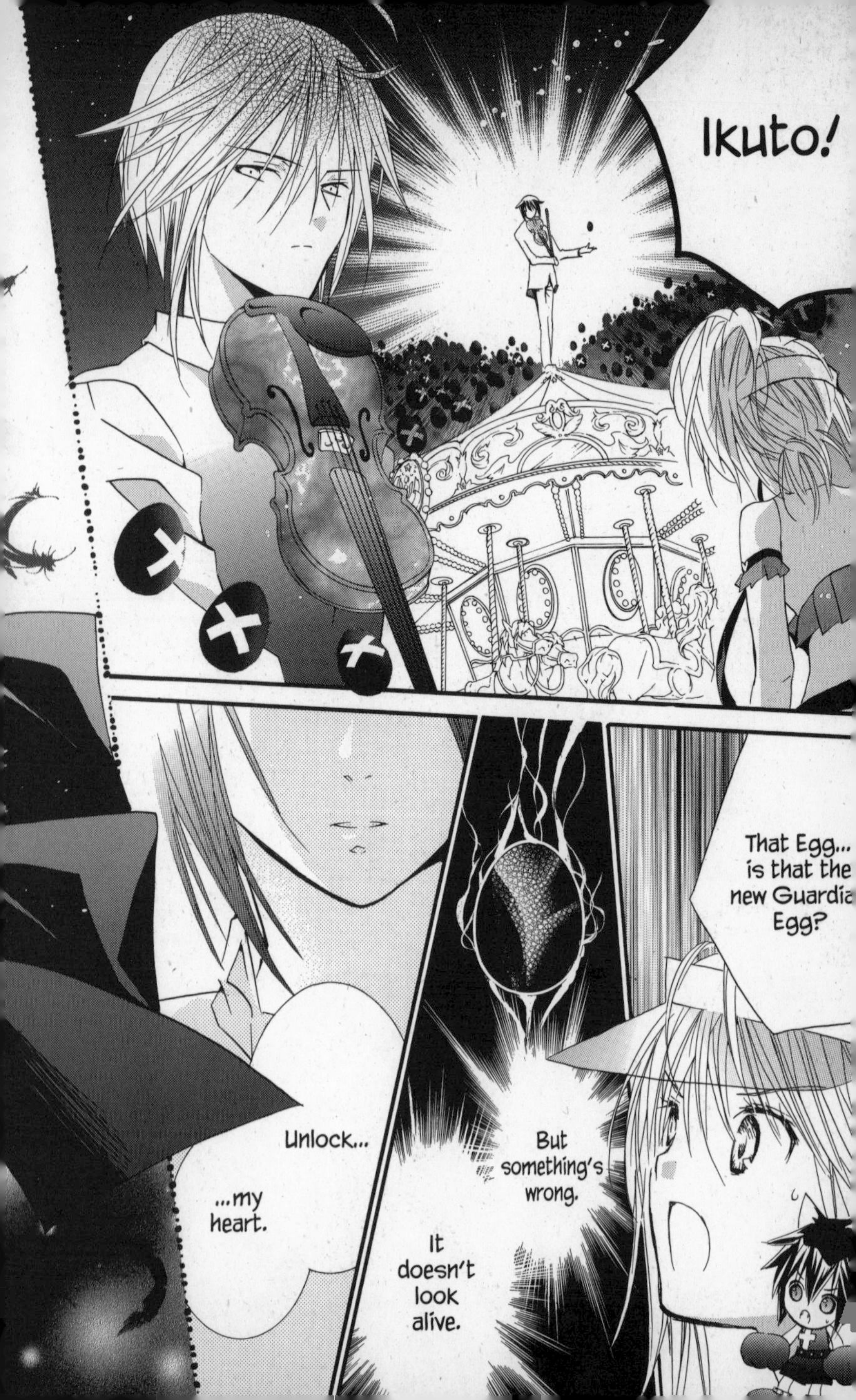
Ikuto!
That Egg... is that the new Guardia Egg?
But something's wrong.
It doesn't look alive.
Unlock...
...my heart.

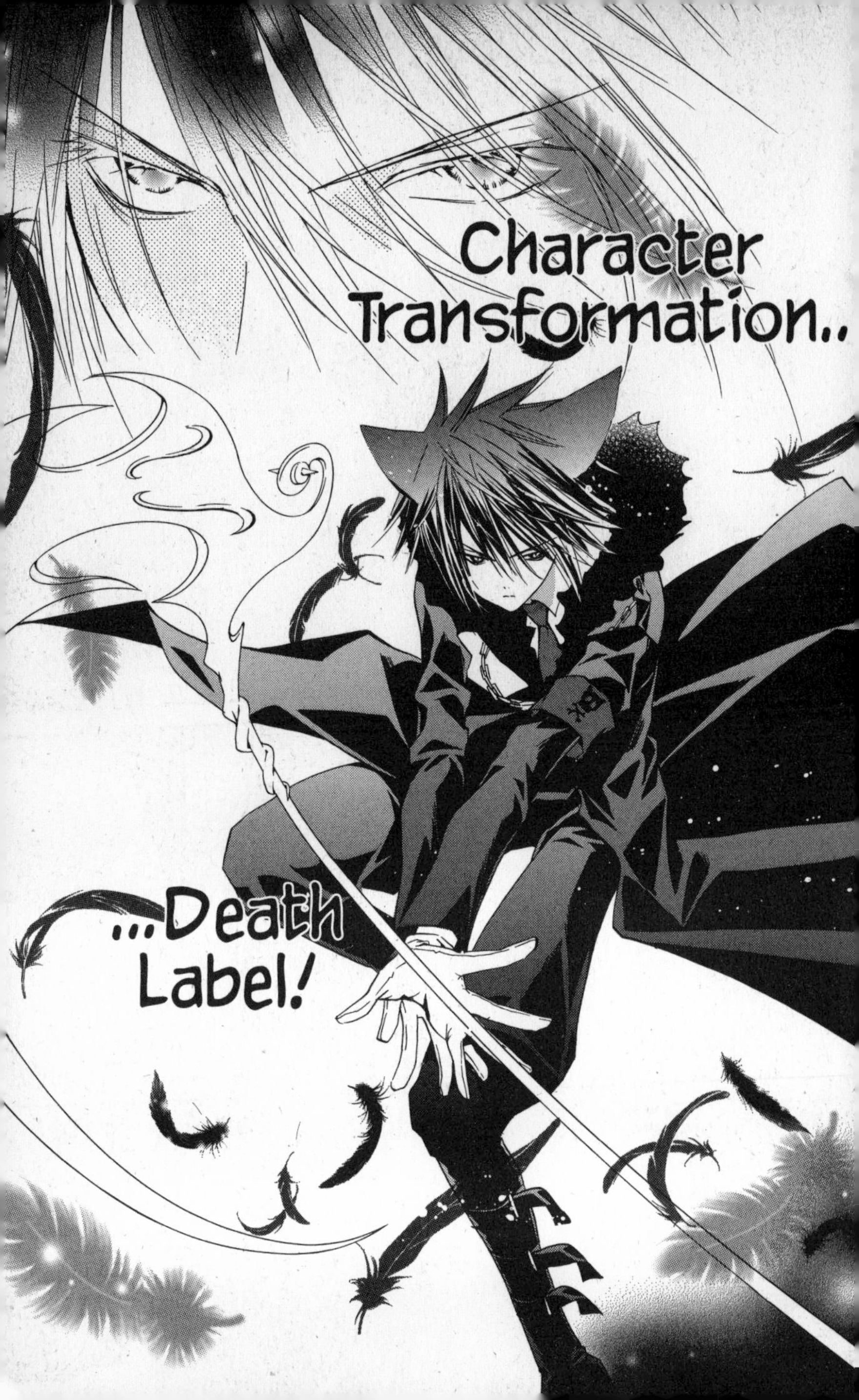
Character Transformation..
...Death Label!

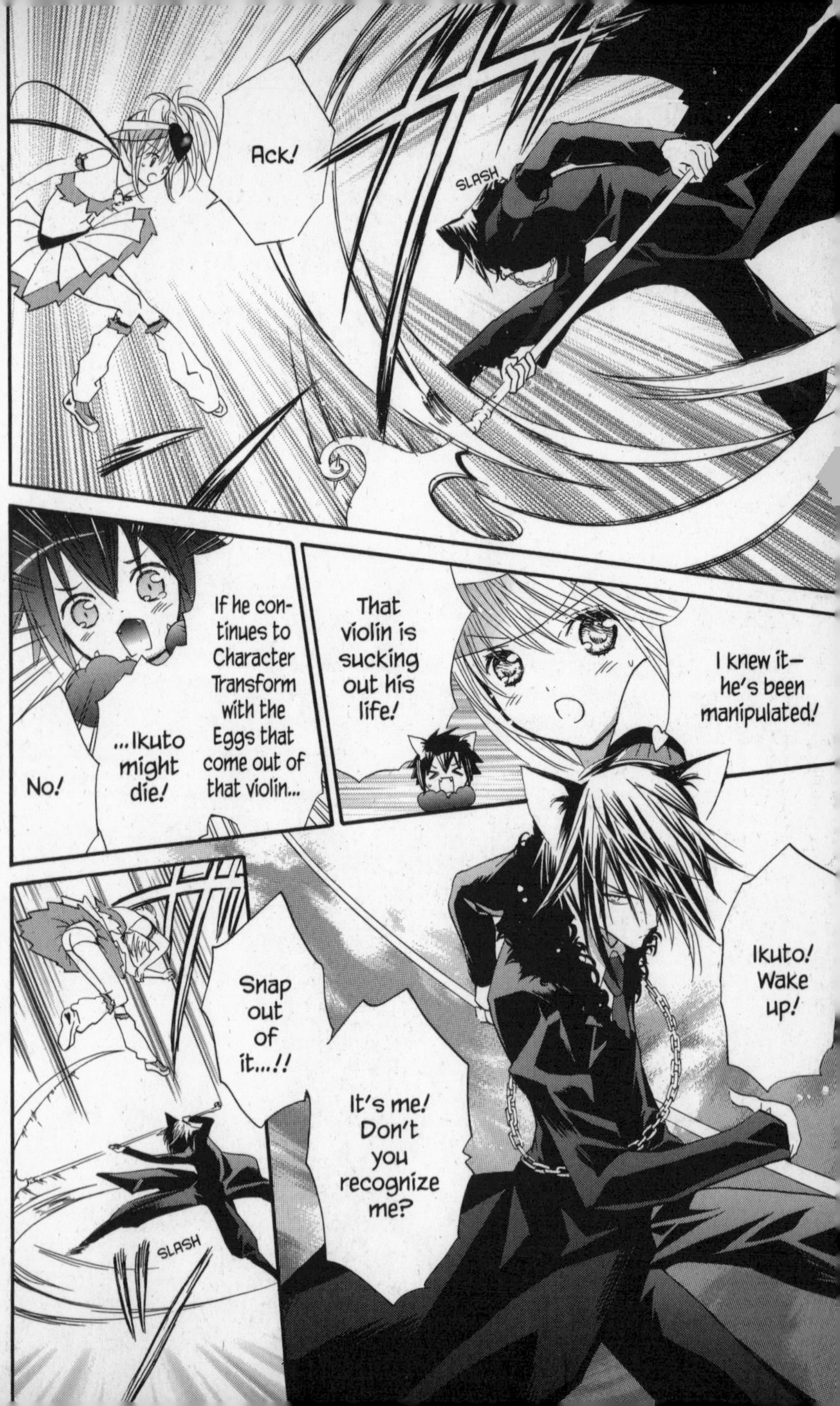
SLASH
Ack!
I knew it—he's been manipulated!
That violin is sucking out his life!
If he continues to Character Transform with the Eggs that come out of that violin...
...Ikuto might die!
No!
Ikuto! Wake up!
Snap out of it...!!
It's me! Don't you recognize me?
SLASH

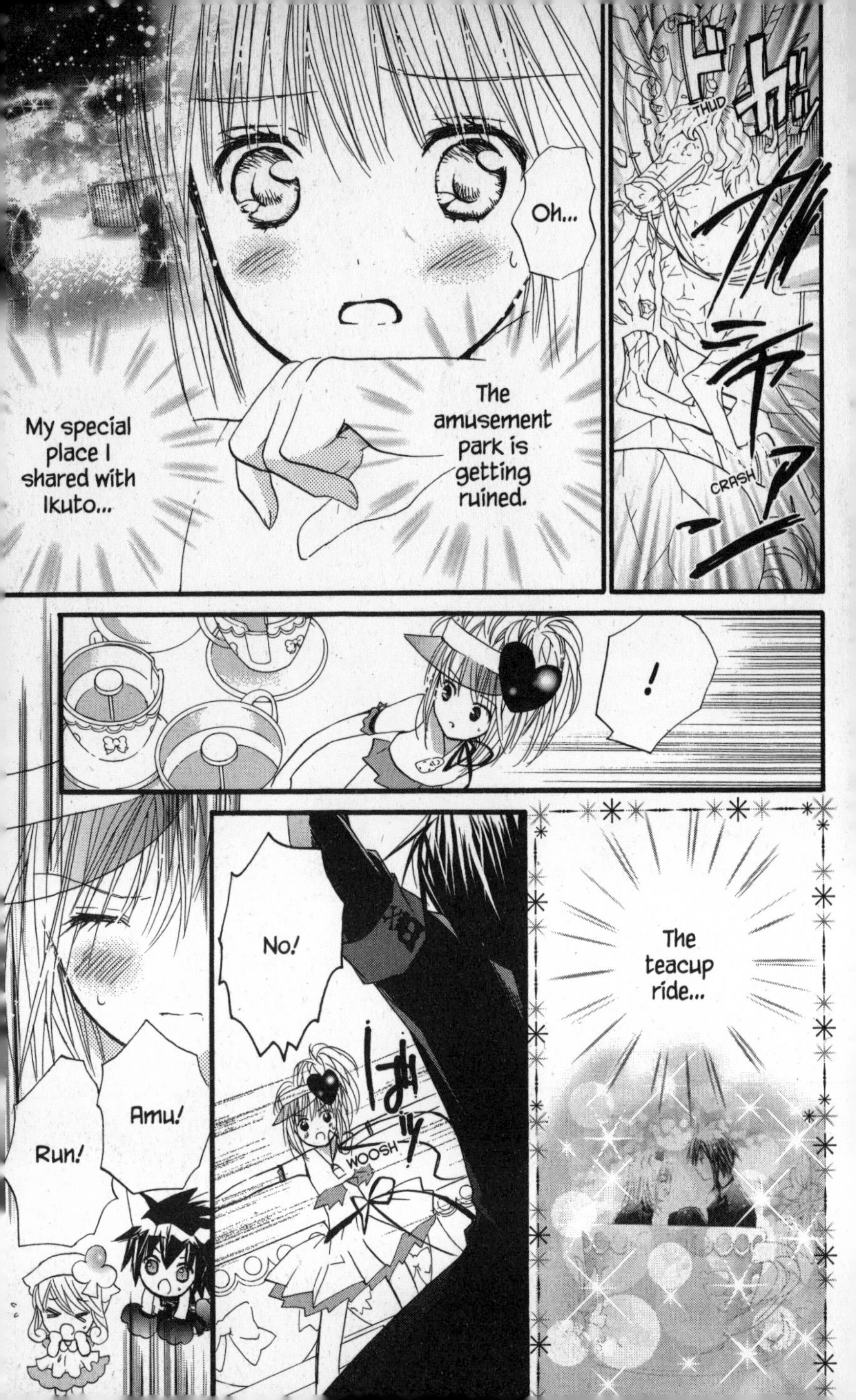
THUD
CRASH
Oh...
The amusement park is getting ruined.
My special place I shared with Ikuto...
!
The teacup ride...
No!
WOOSH
Amu!
Run!

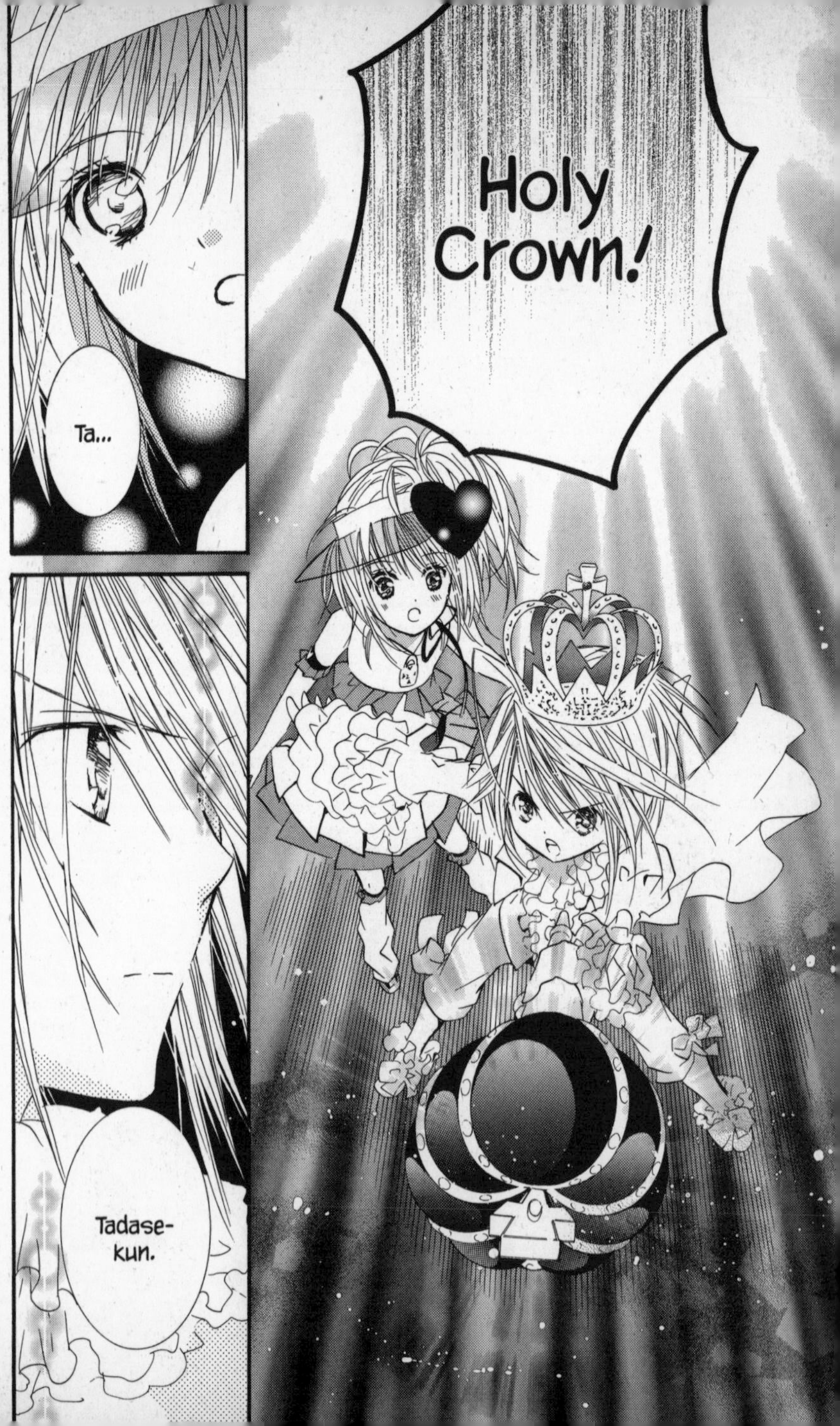
Holy Crown!
Ta...
Tadase-kun.

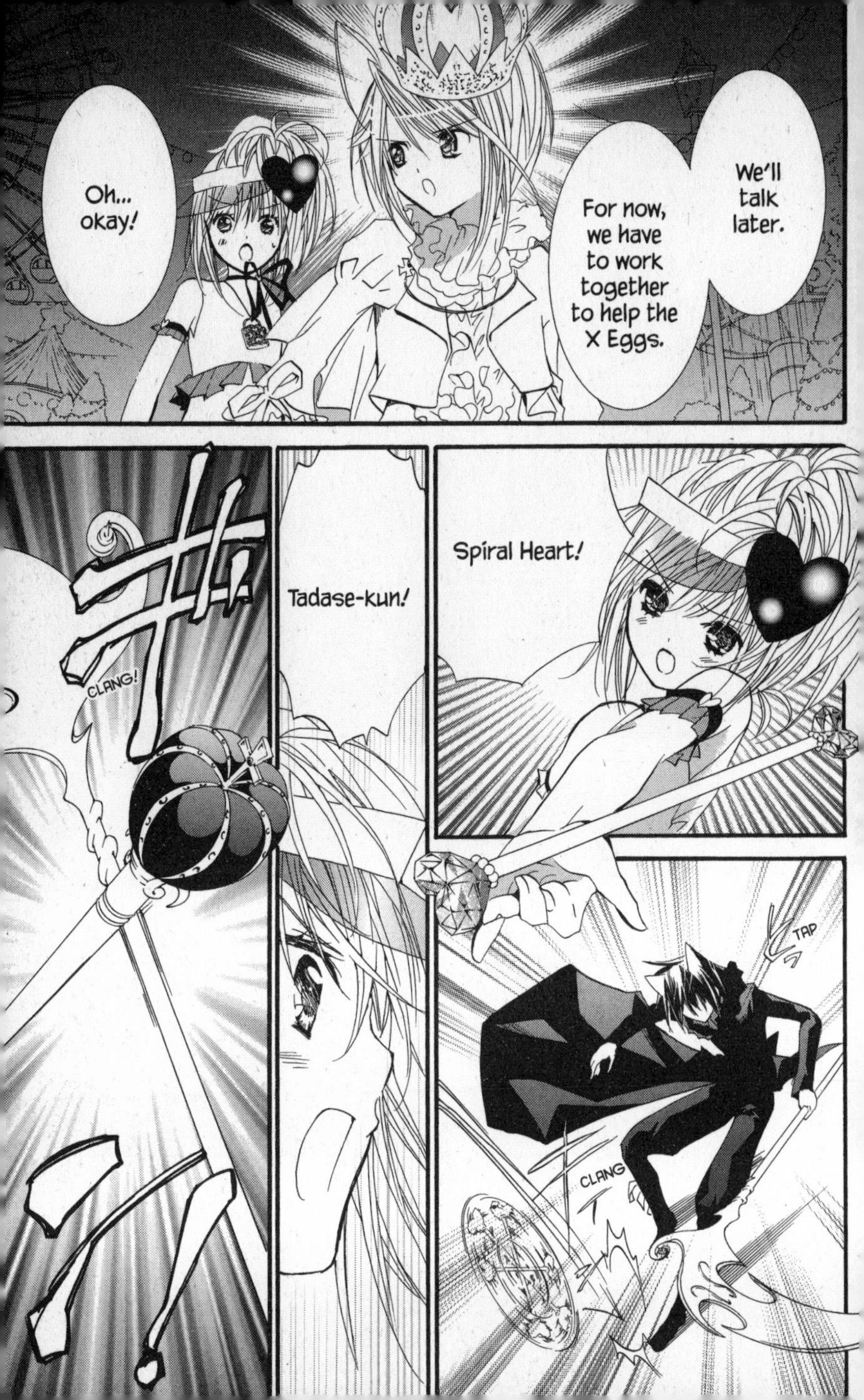
We'll talk later.
For now, we have to work together to help the X Eggs.
Oh... okay!
Spiral Heart!
TAP
CLANG
Tadase-kun!
CLANG!

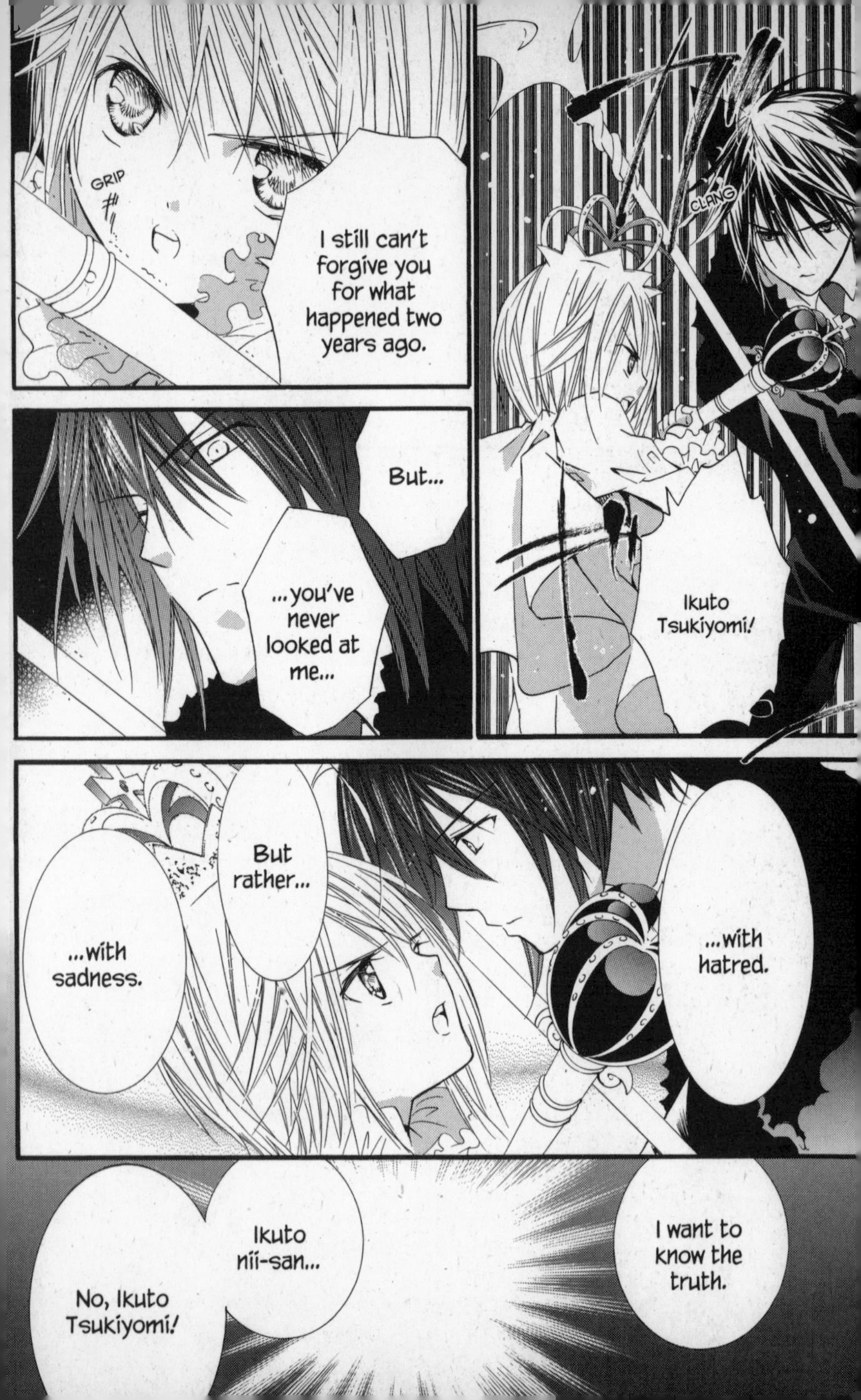
CLANG
Ikuto Tsukiyomi!
I still can't forgive you for what happened two years ago.
GRIP
But...
...you've never looked at me...
...with hatred.
But rather...
...with sadness.
I want to know the truth.
Ikuto nii-san...
No, Ikuto Tsukiyomi!

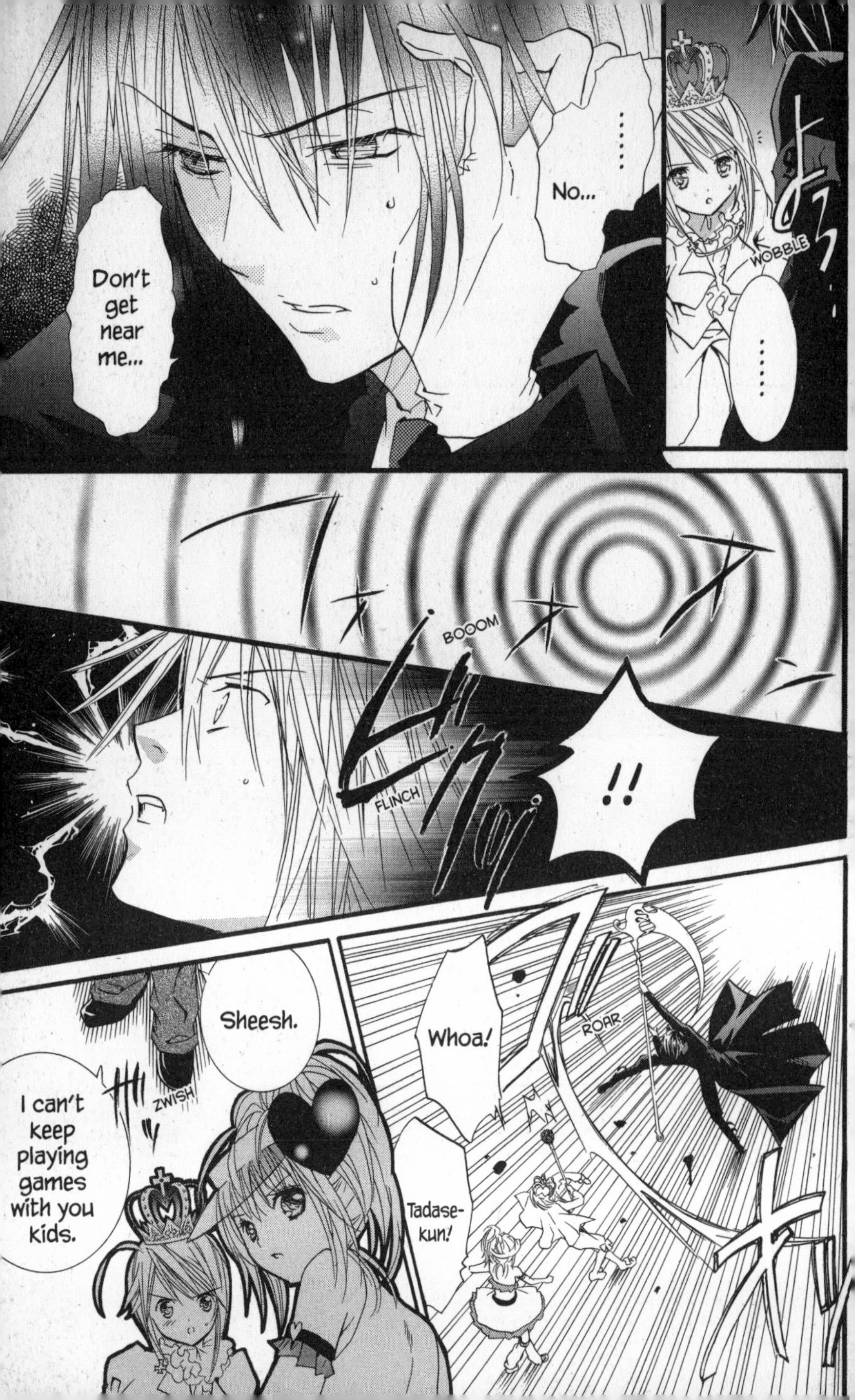
WOBBLE
......
......
No...
Don't get near me...
BOOOM
FLINCH
!!
Whoa!
ROAR
Tadase-kun!
Sheesh.
ZWISH
I can't keep playing games with you kids.

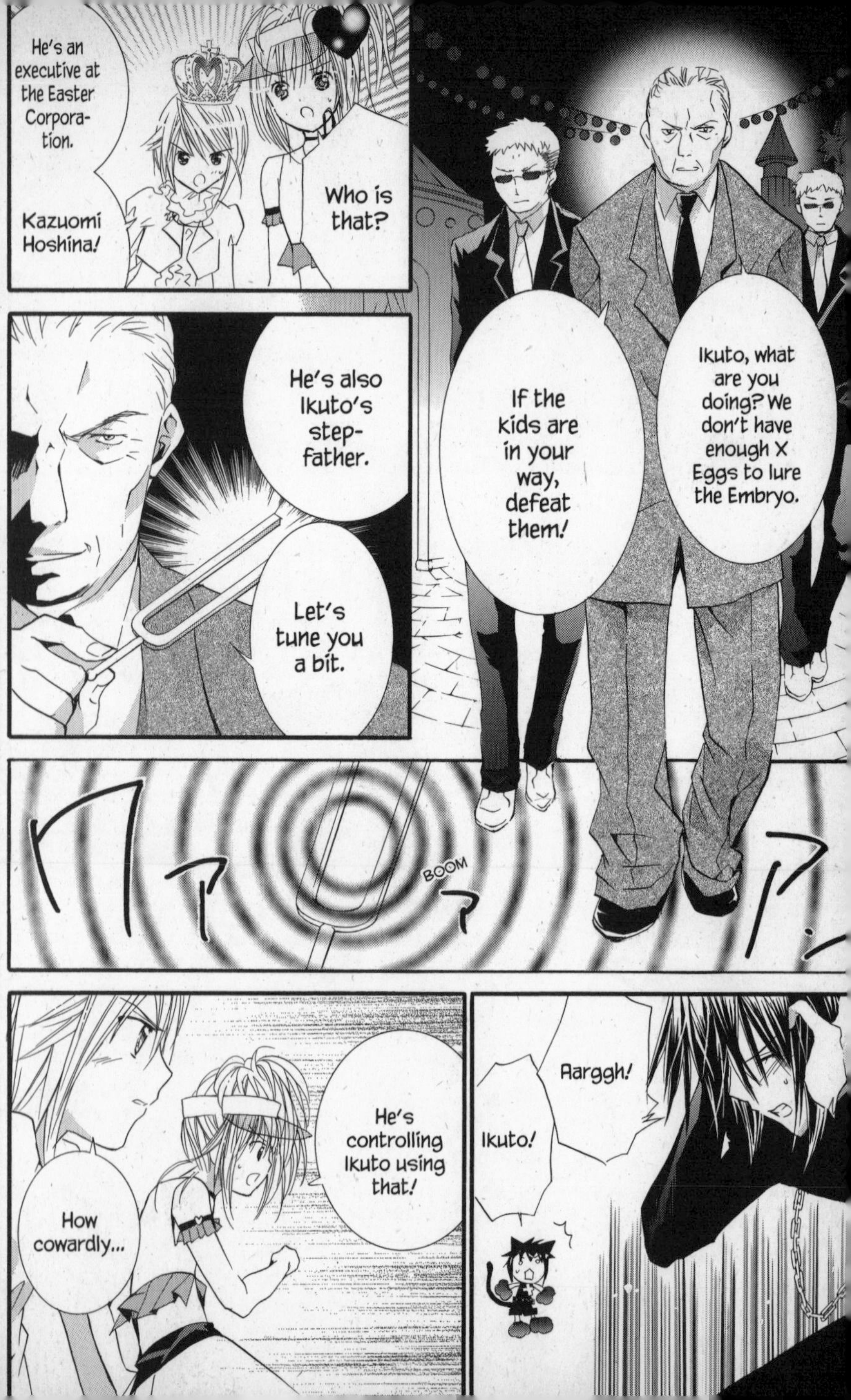
Ikuto, what are you doing? We don't have enough X Eggs to lure the Embryo.
If the kids are in your way, defeat them!
Who is that?
He's an executive at the Easter Corporation.
Kazuomi Hoshina!
He's also Ikuto's step-father.
Let's tune you a bit.
BOOM
Aarggh!
Ikuto!
He's controlling Ikuto using that!
How cowardly...

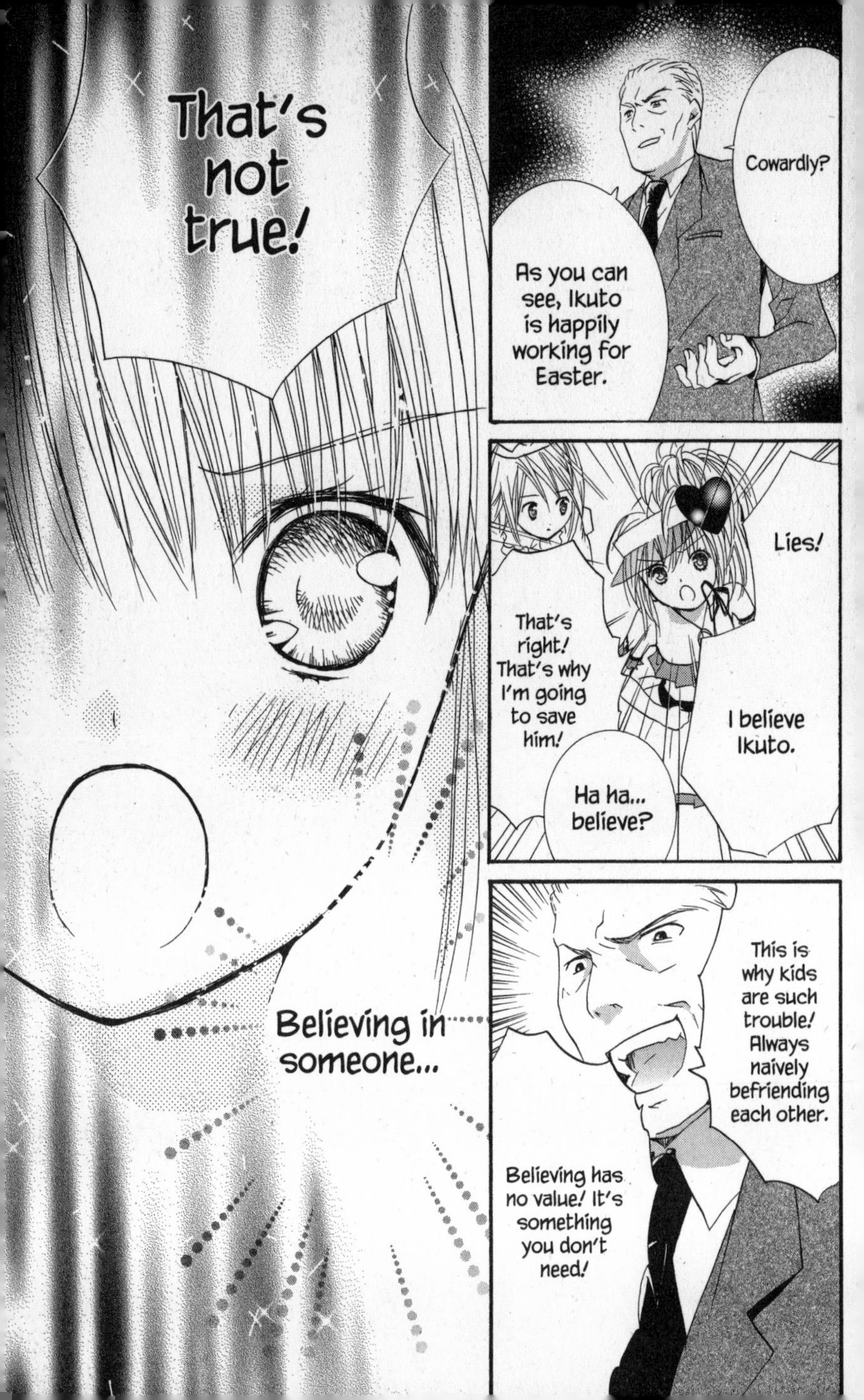
Cowardly?
As you can see, Ikuto is happily working for Easter.
Lies!
That's right! That's why I'm going to save him!
I believe Ikuto.
Ha ha... believe?
This is why kids are such trouble! Always naively befriending each other.
Believing has no value! It's something you don't need!
That's not true!
Believing in someone...

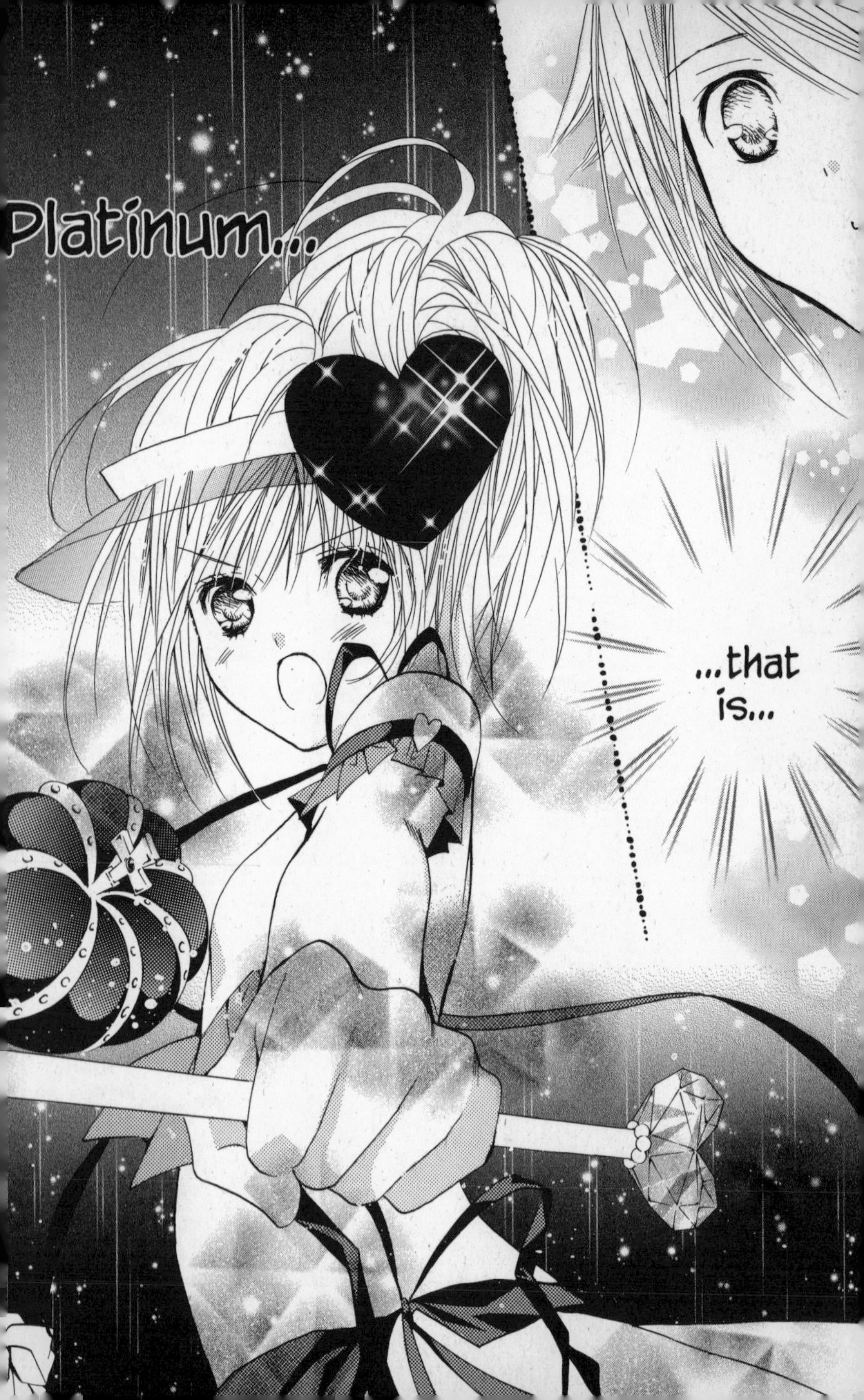
...that is...
Platinum...

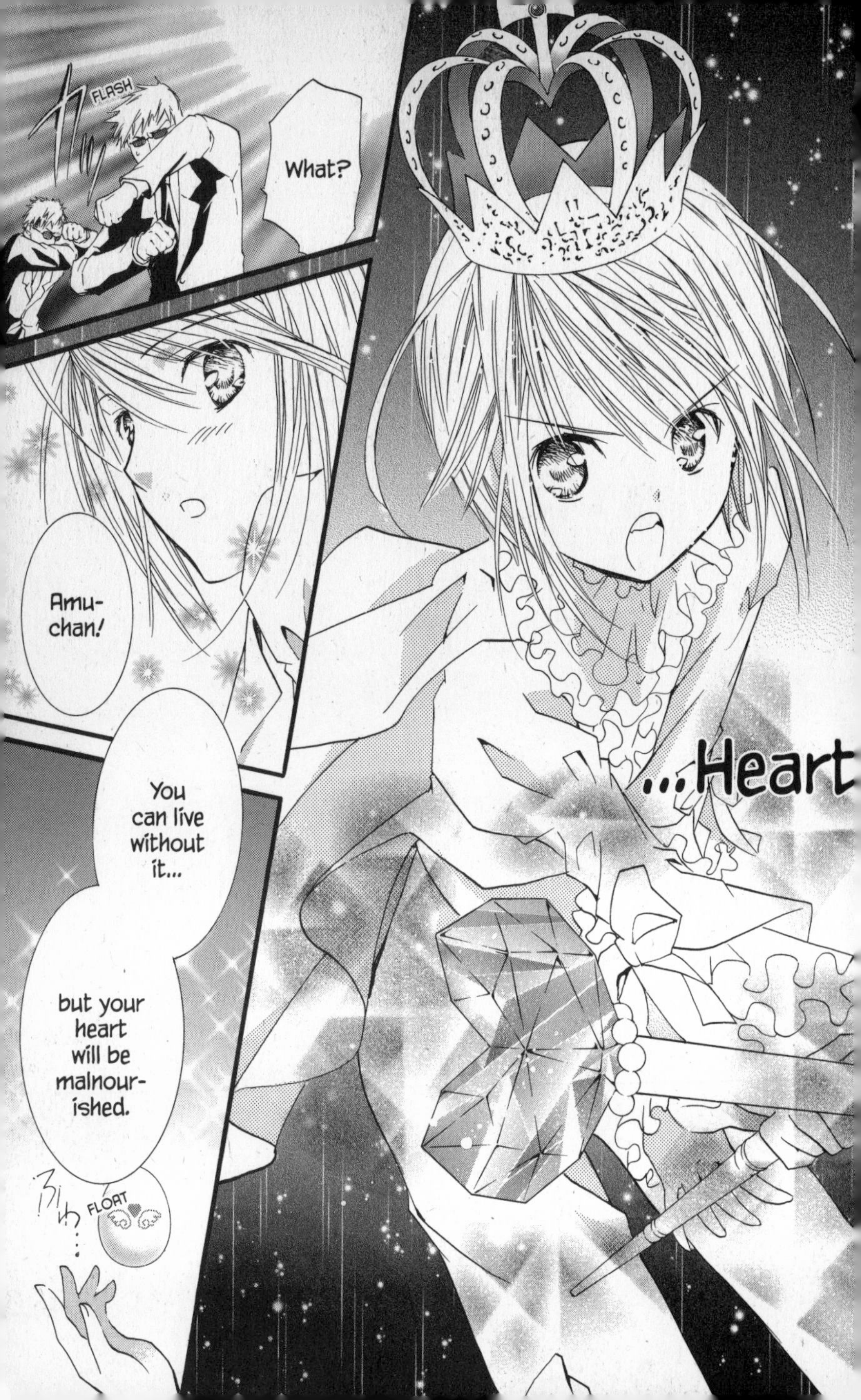
...Heart
FLASH
What?
Amu-chan!
You can live without it...
but your heart will be malnourished.
FLOAT

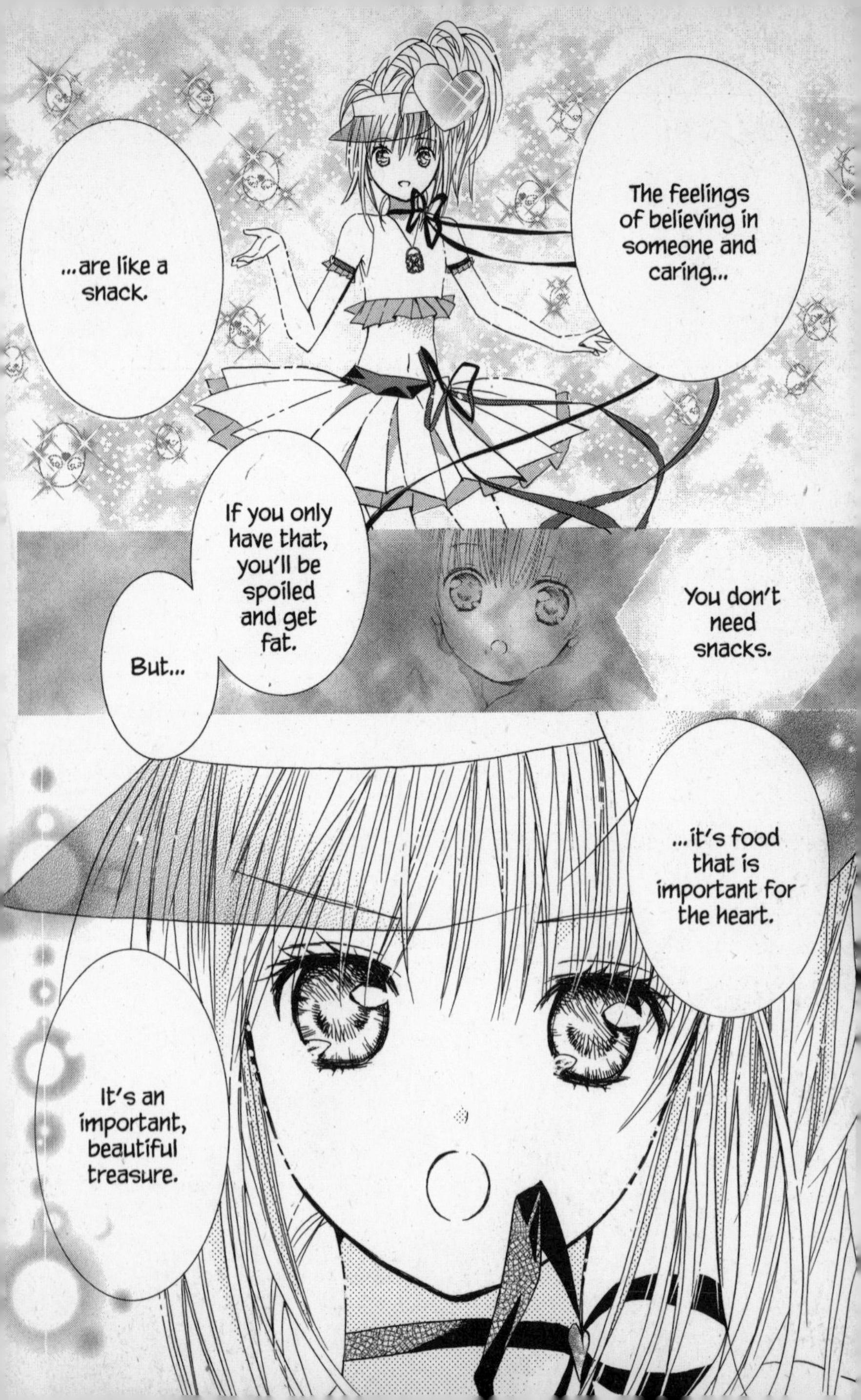
The feelings of believing in someone and caring...
...are like a snack.
You don't need snacks.
If you only have that, you'll be spoiled and get fat.
But...
...it's food that is important for the heart.
It's an important, beautiful treasure.

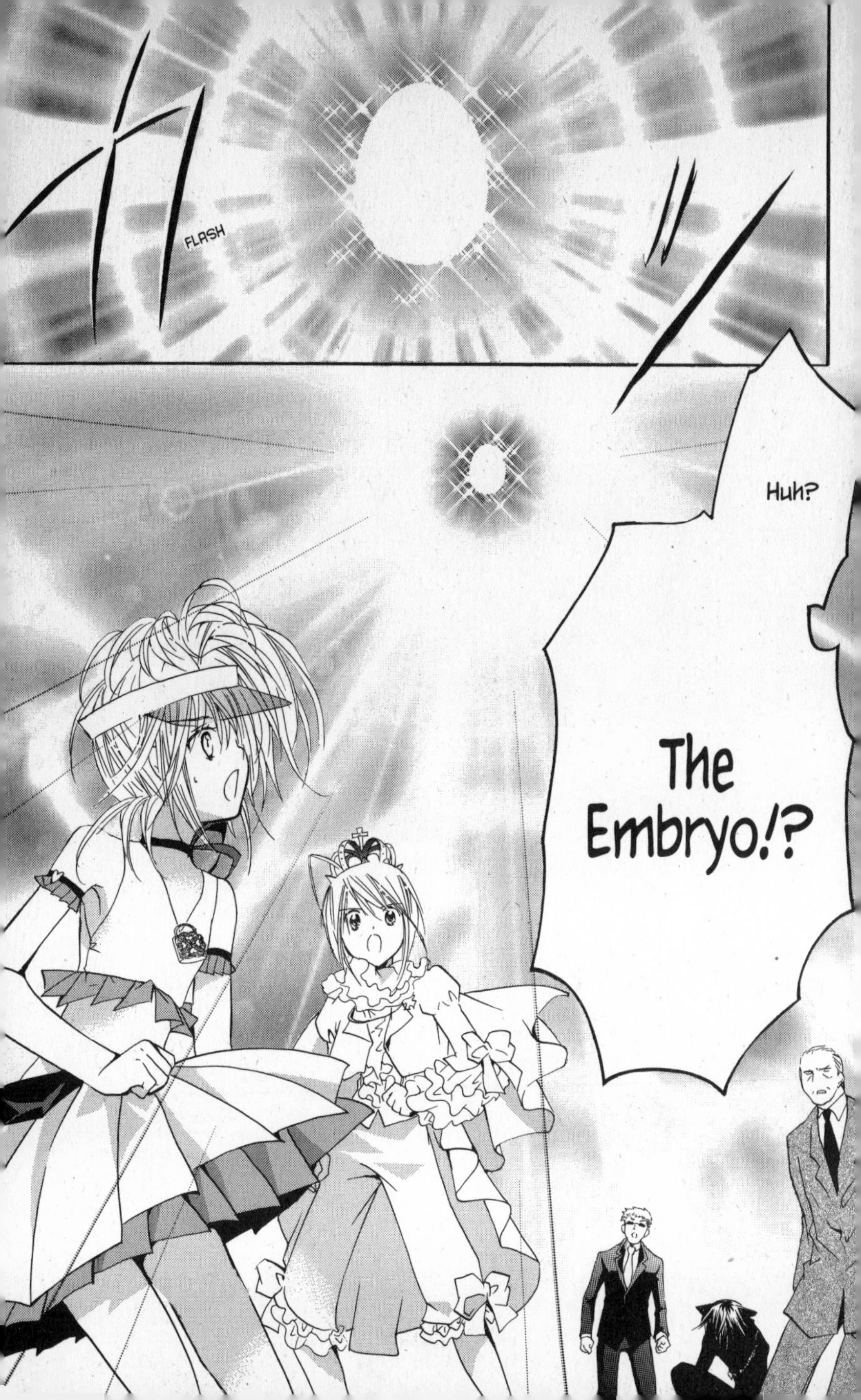
FLASH
Huh?
The Embryo!?

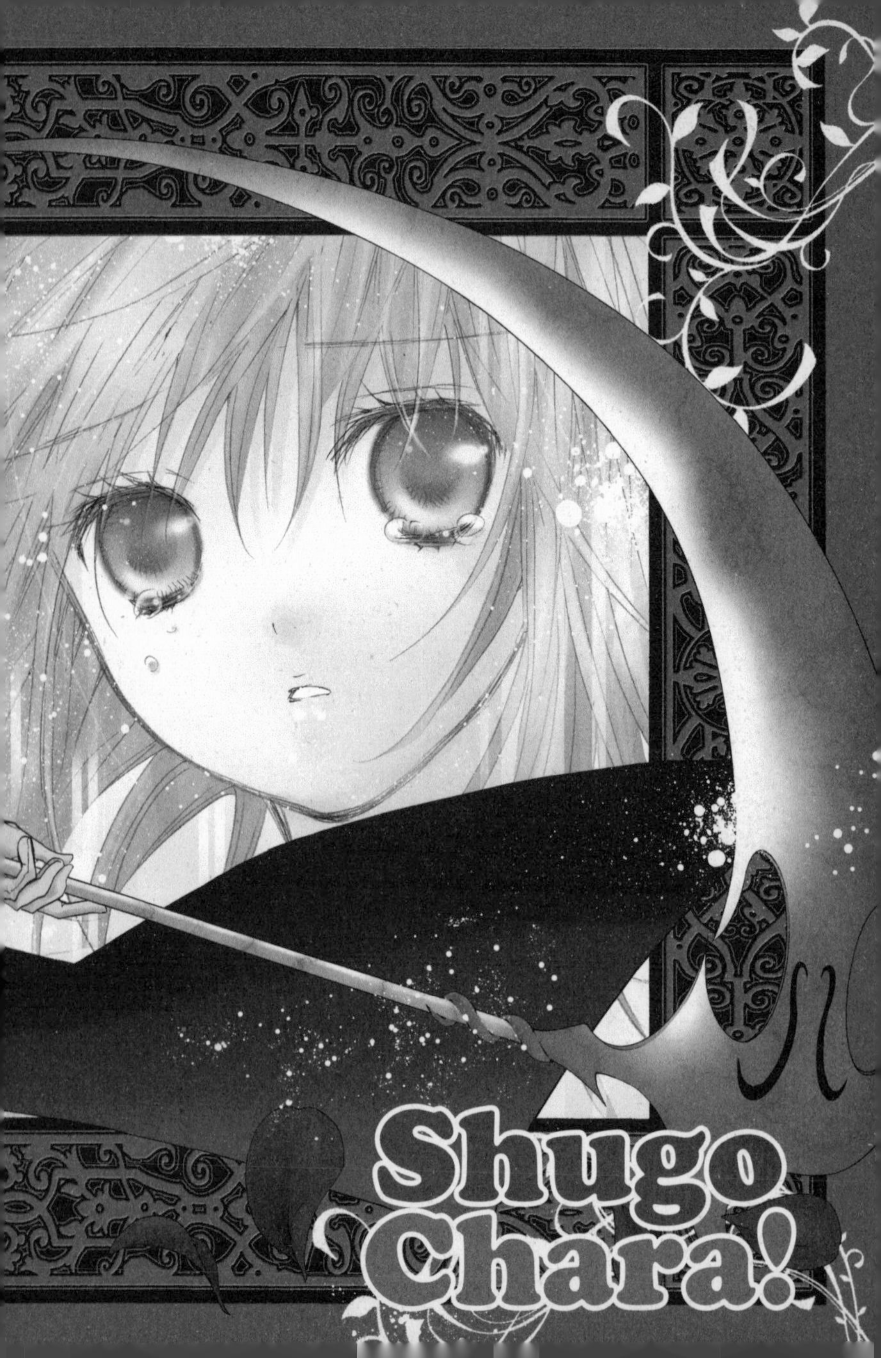
Shugo Chara!

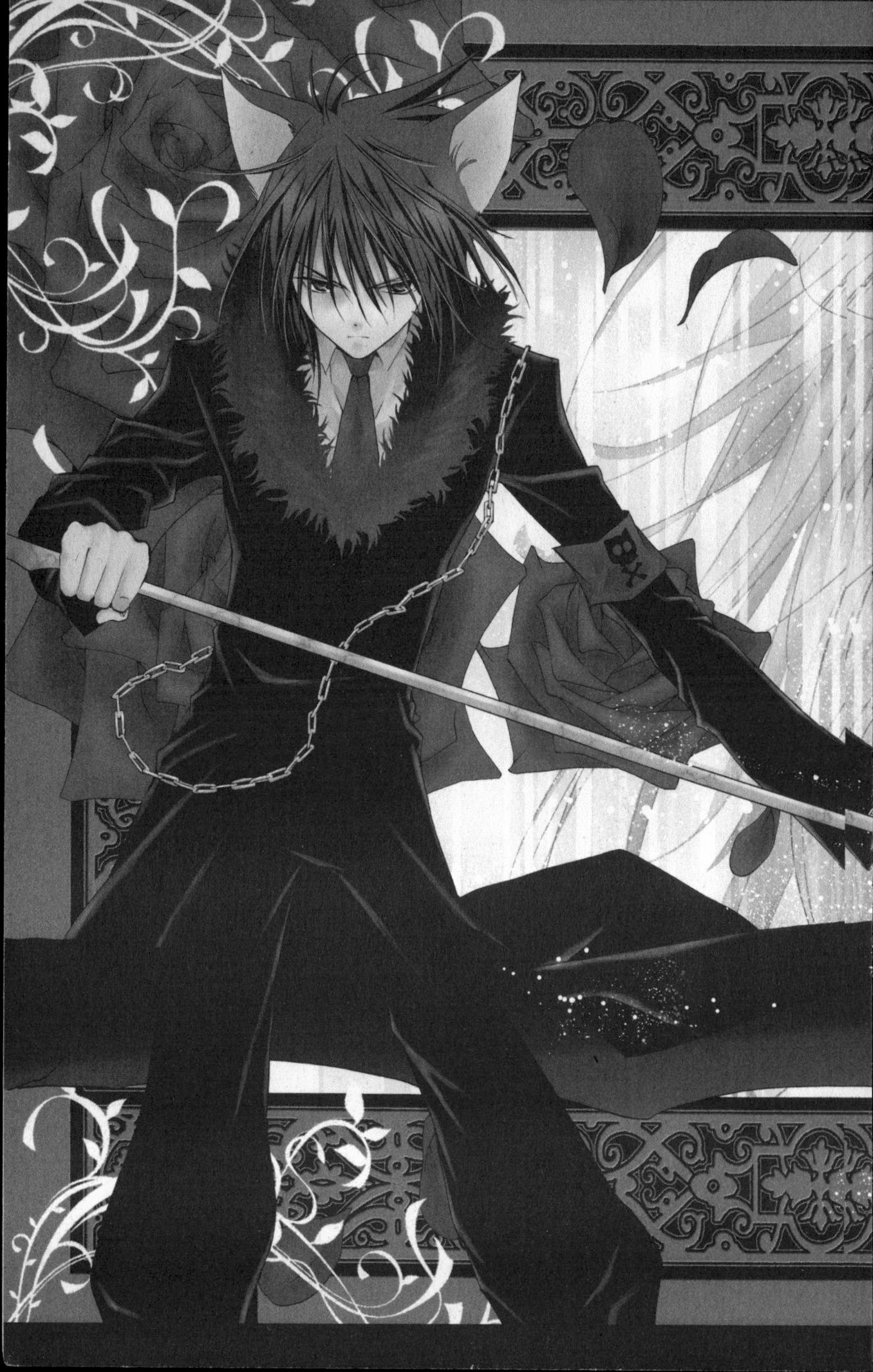

Shugo Chara!

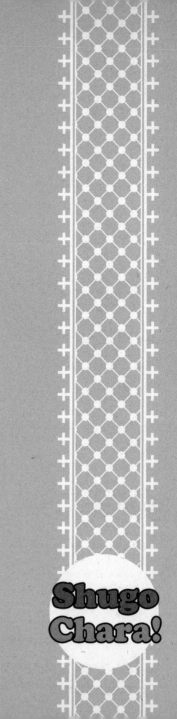

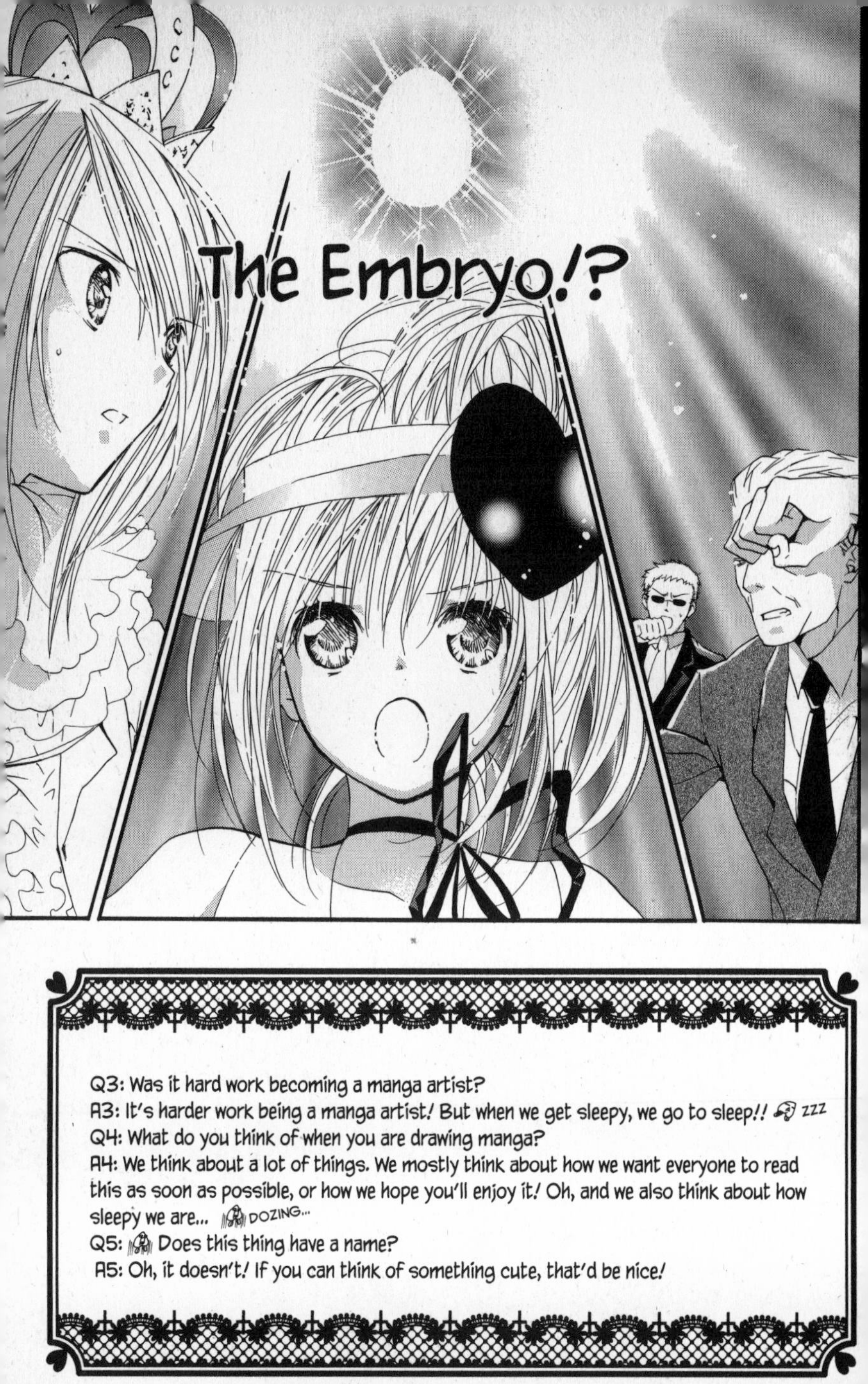
The Embryo!?

Q3: Was it hard work becoming a manga artist?
A3: It's harder work being a manga artist! But when we get sleepy, we go to sleep!! ZZZ
Q4: What do you think of when you are drawing manga?
A4: We think about a lot of things. We mostly think about how we want everyone to read this as soon as possible, or how we hope you'll enjoy it! Oh, and we also think about how sleepy we are... DOZING...
Q5: Does this thing have a name?
A5: Oh, it doesn't! If you can think of something cute, that'd be nice!

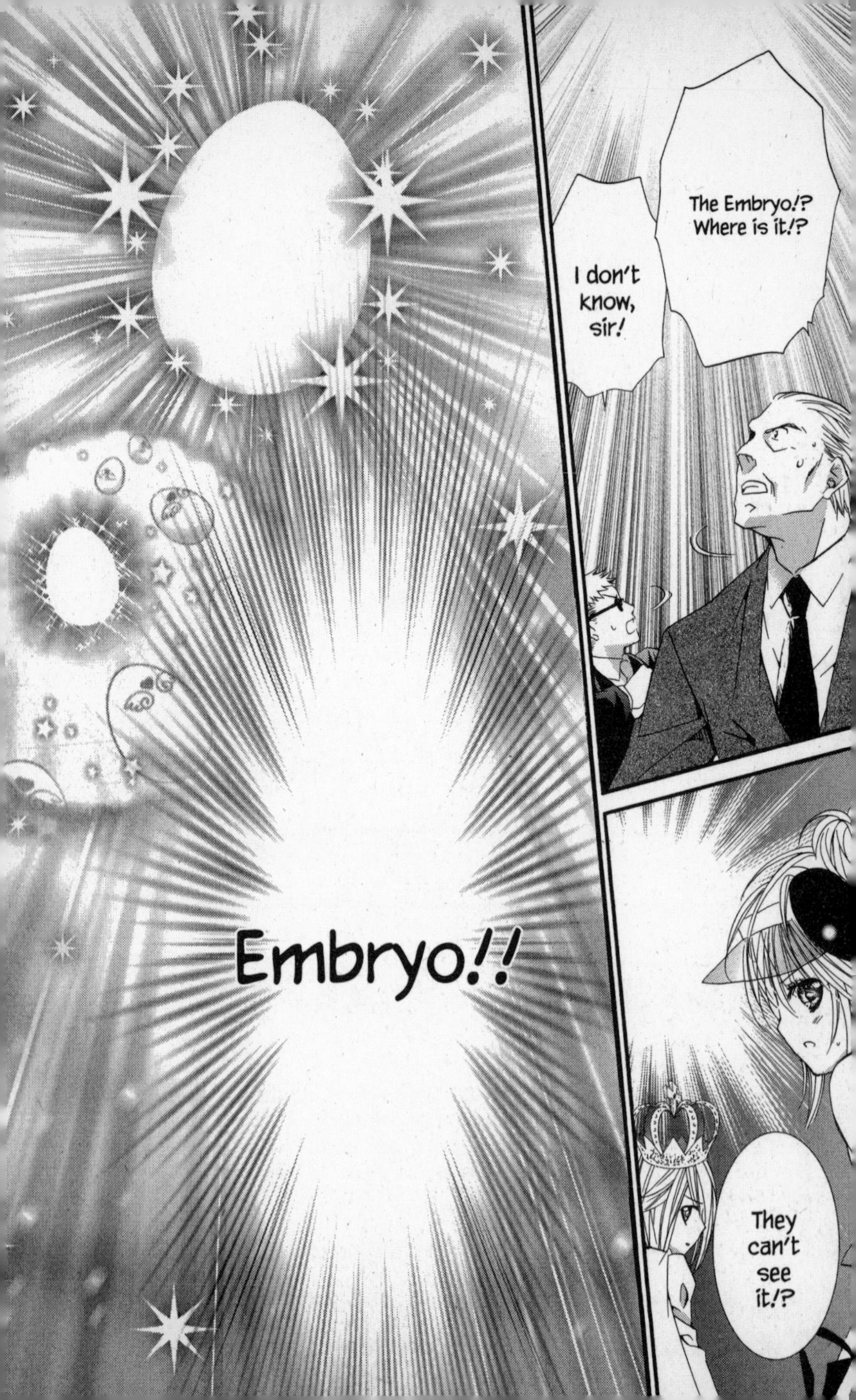
The Embryo!? Where is it!?
I don't know, sir!
They can't see it!?
Embryo!!

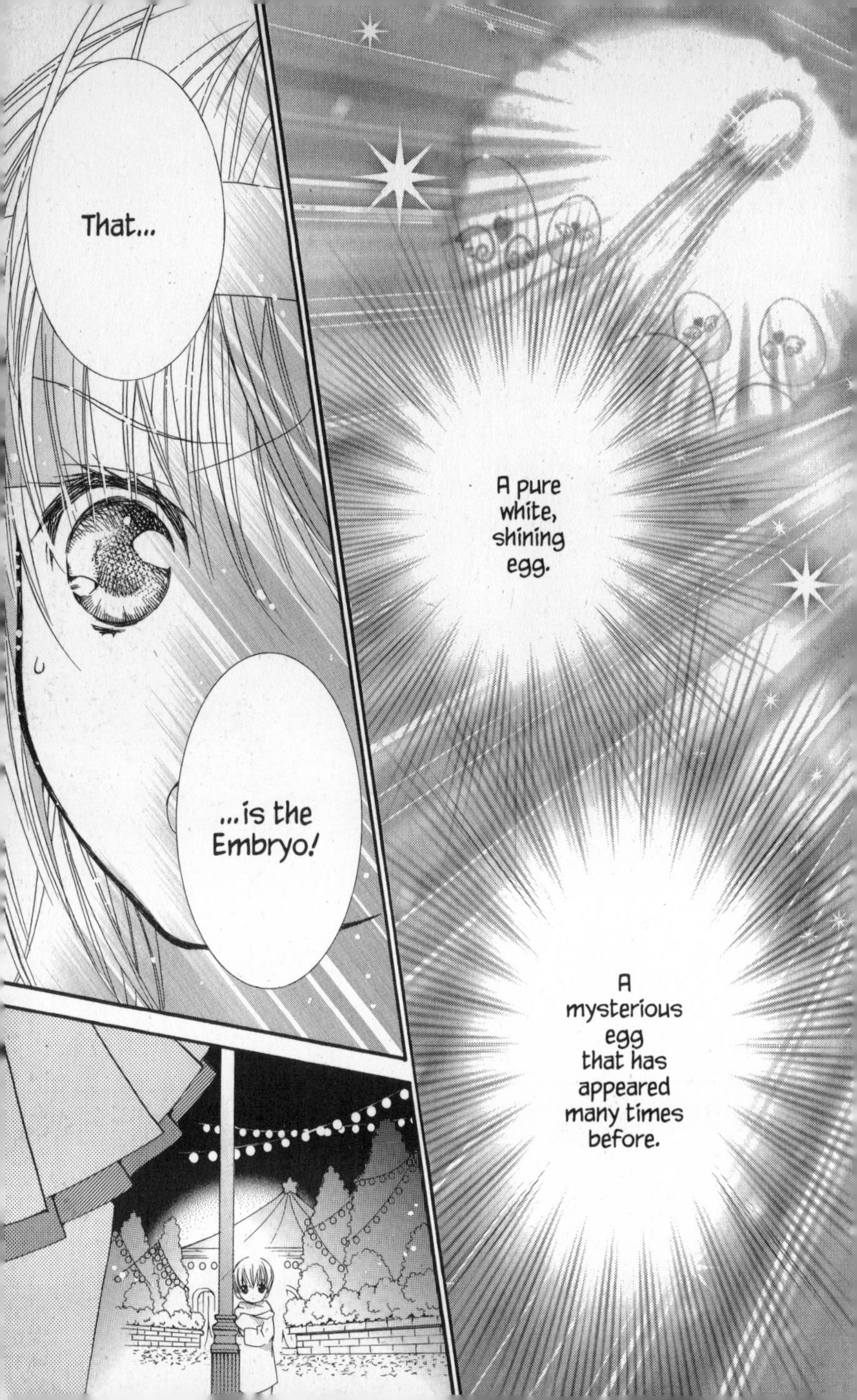
A pure white, shining egg.
A mysterious egg that has appeared many times before.
That...
...is the Embryo!

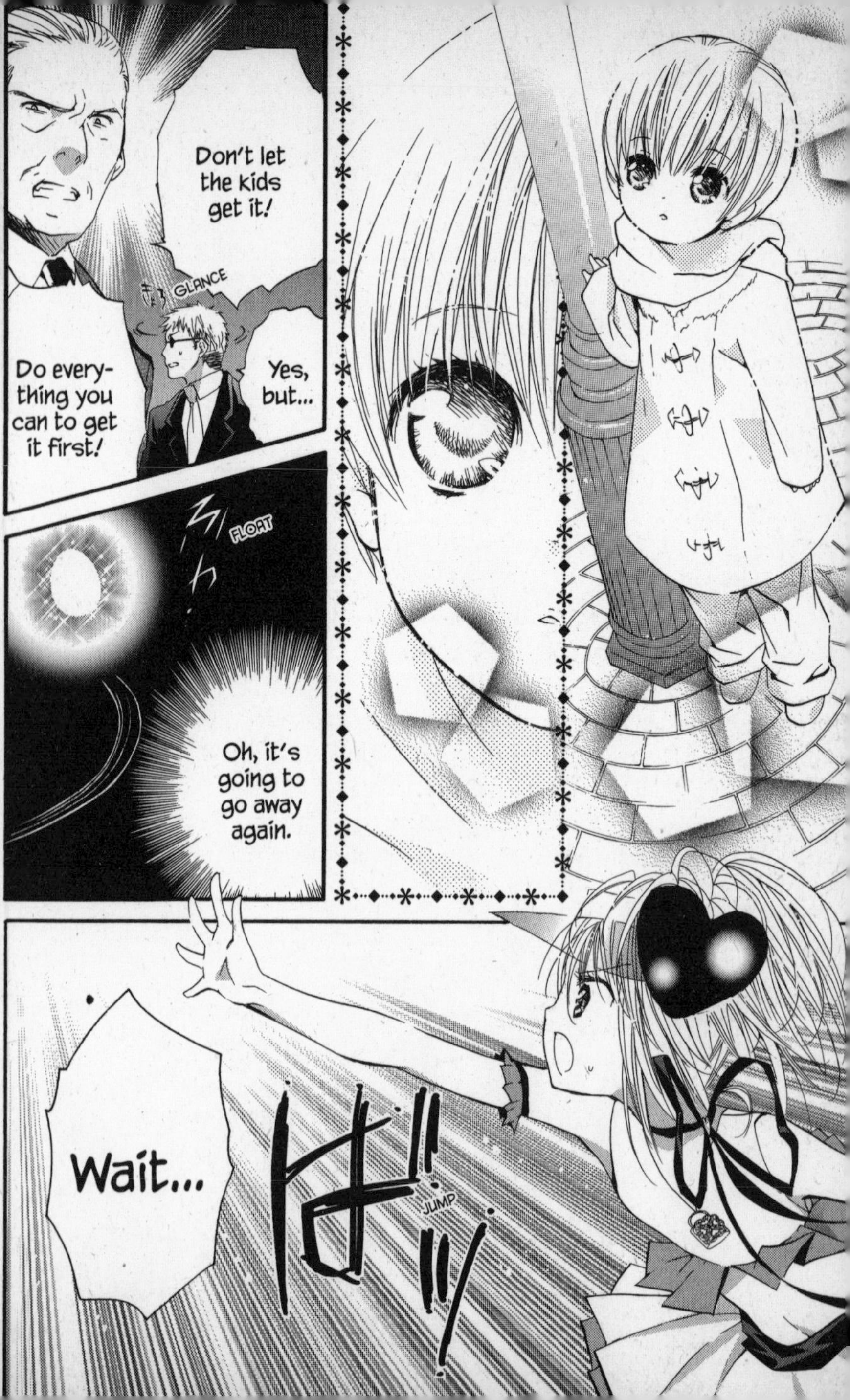
Don't let the kids get it!
GLANCE
Yes, but...
Do every-thing you can to get it first!
FLOAT
Oh, it's going to go away again.
Wait...
JUMP

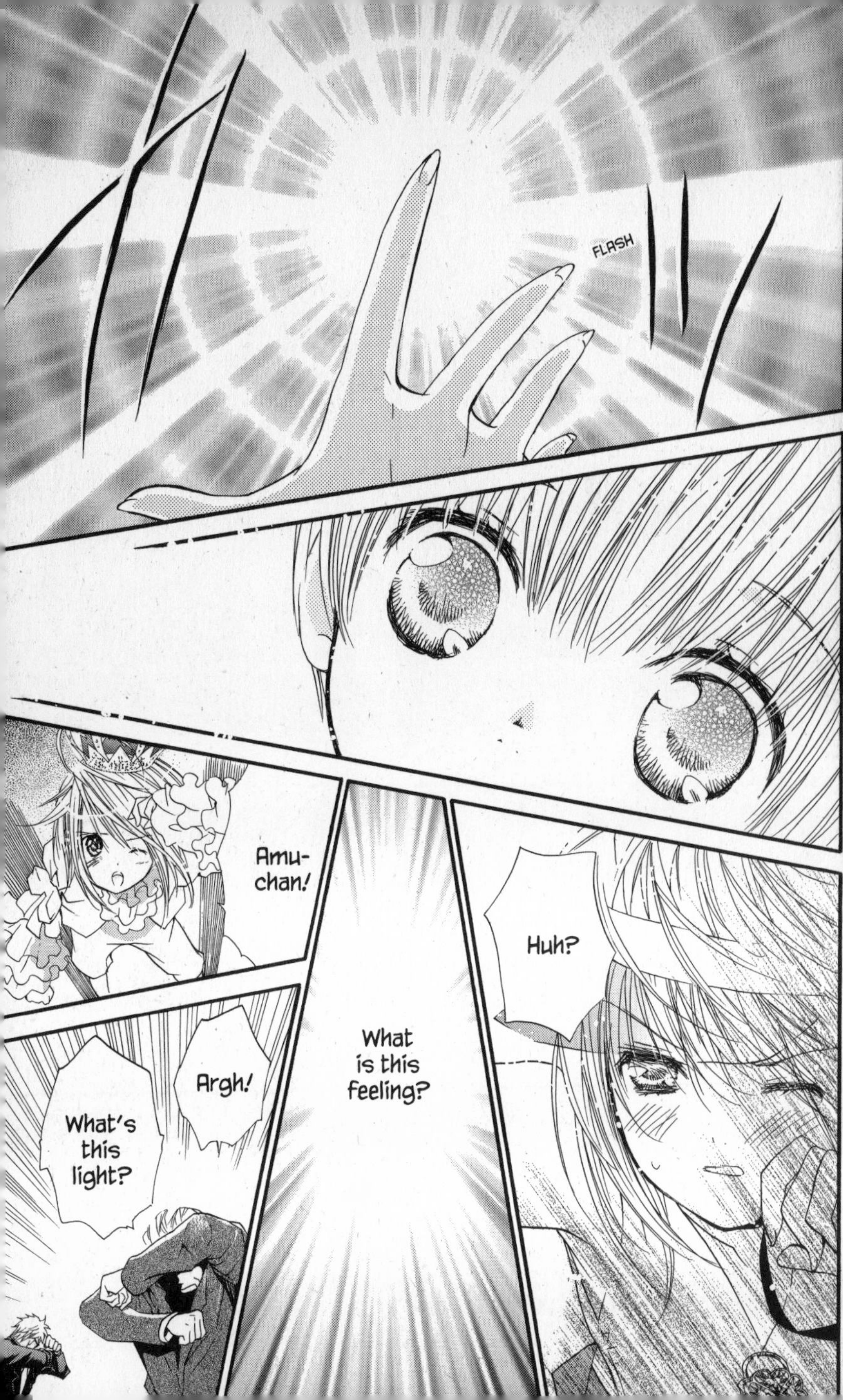
FLASH
Huh?
What is this feeling?
Amu-chan!
Argh!
What's this light?

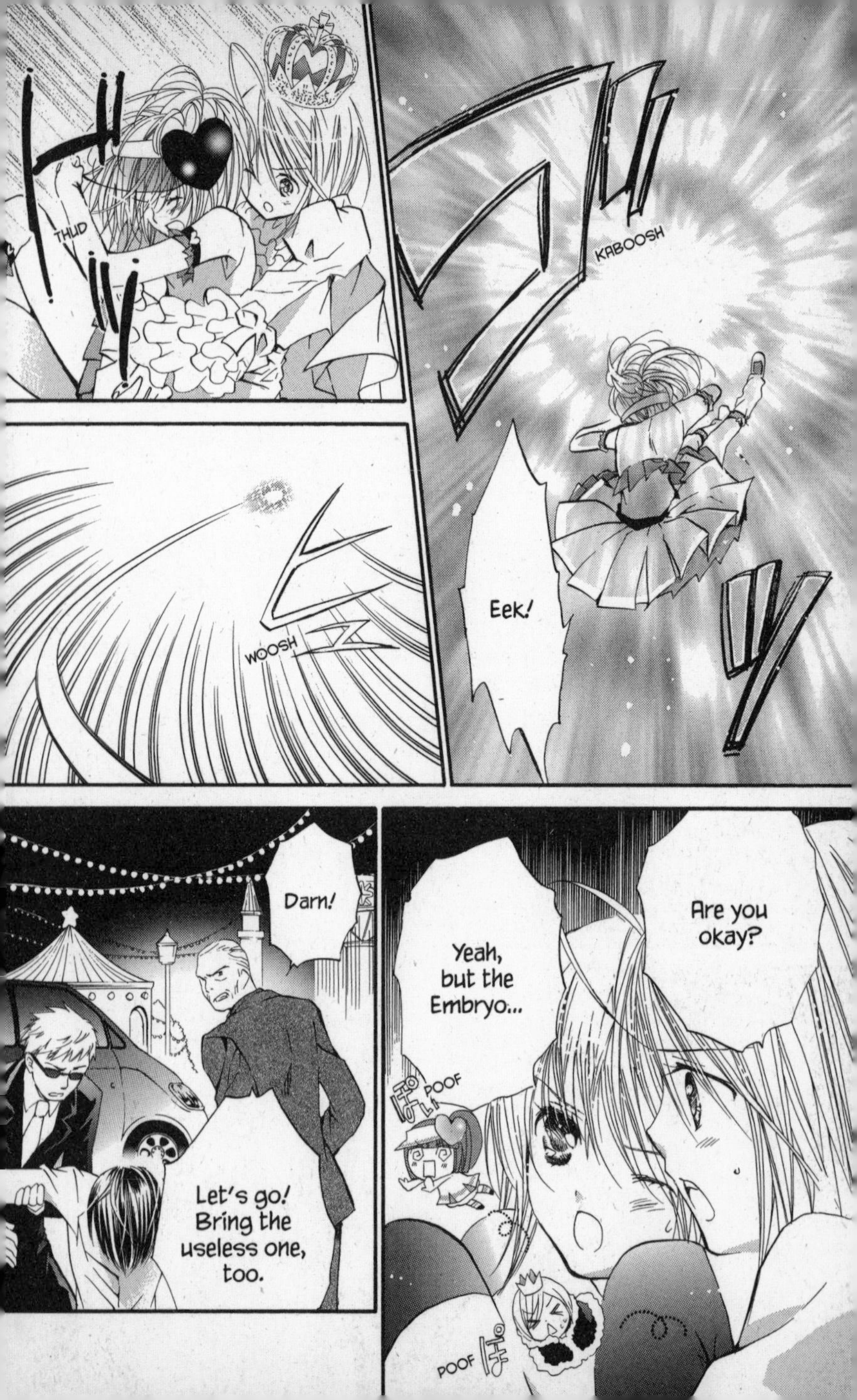
KABOOSH
Eek!
THUD
WOOSH
Are you okay?
Yeah, but the Embryo...
POOF
POOF
Darn!
Let's go! Bring the useless one, too.

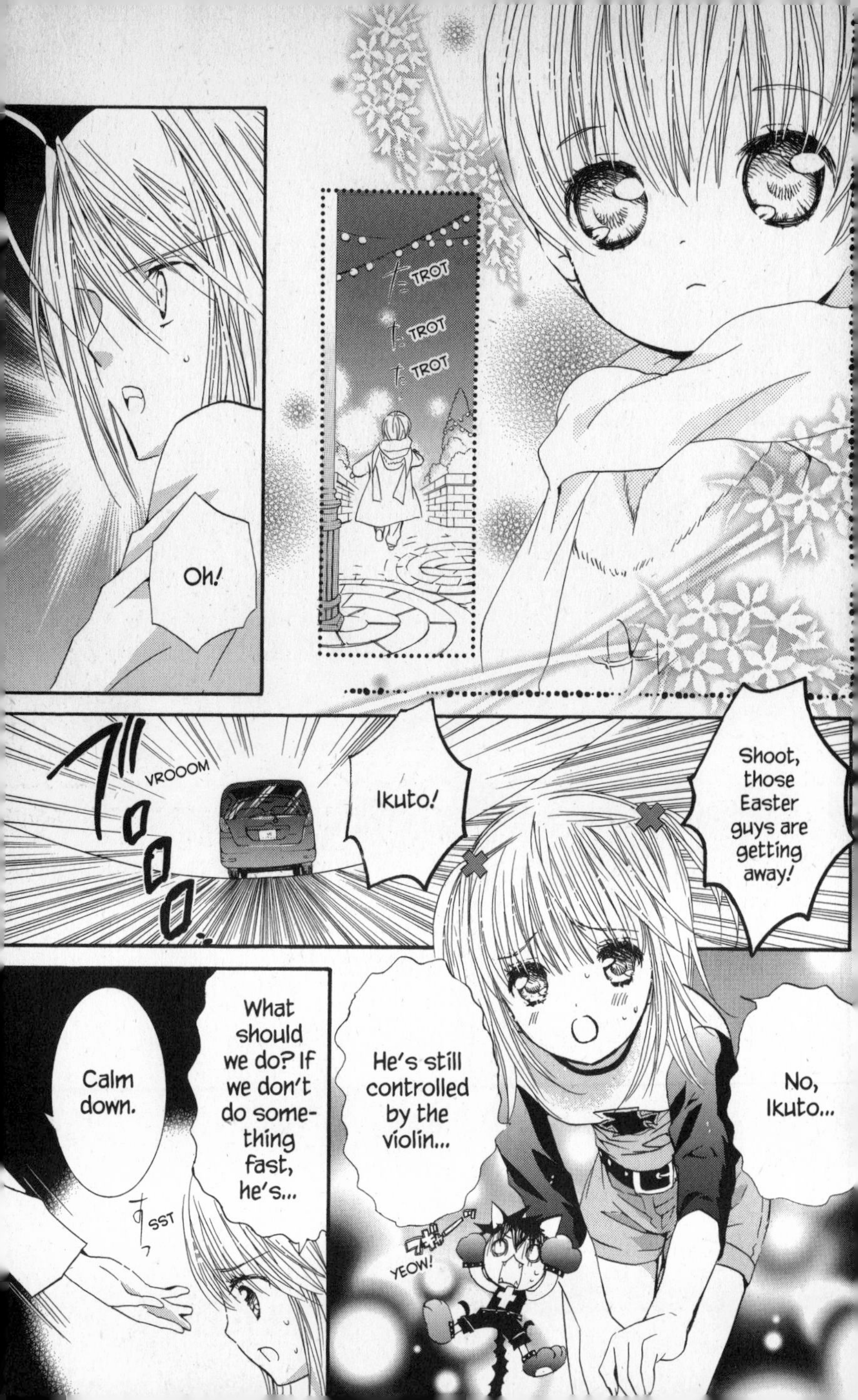
TROT
TROT
TROT
Oh!
Shoot, those Easter guys are getting away!
Ikuto!
VROOOM
No, Ikuto...
He's still controlled by the violin...
YEOW!
What should we do? If we don't do something fast, he's...
SST
Calm down.

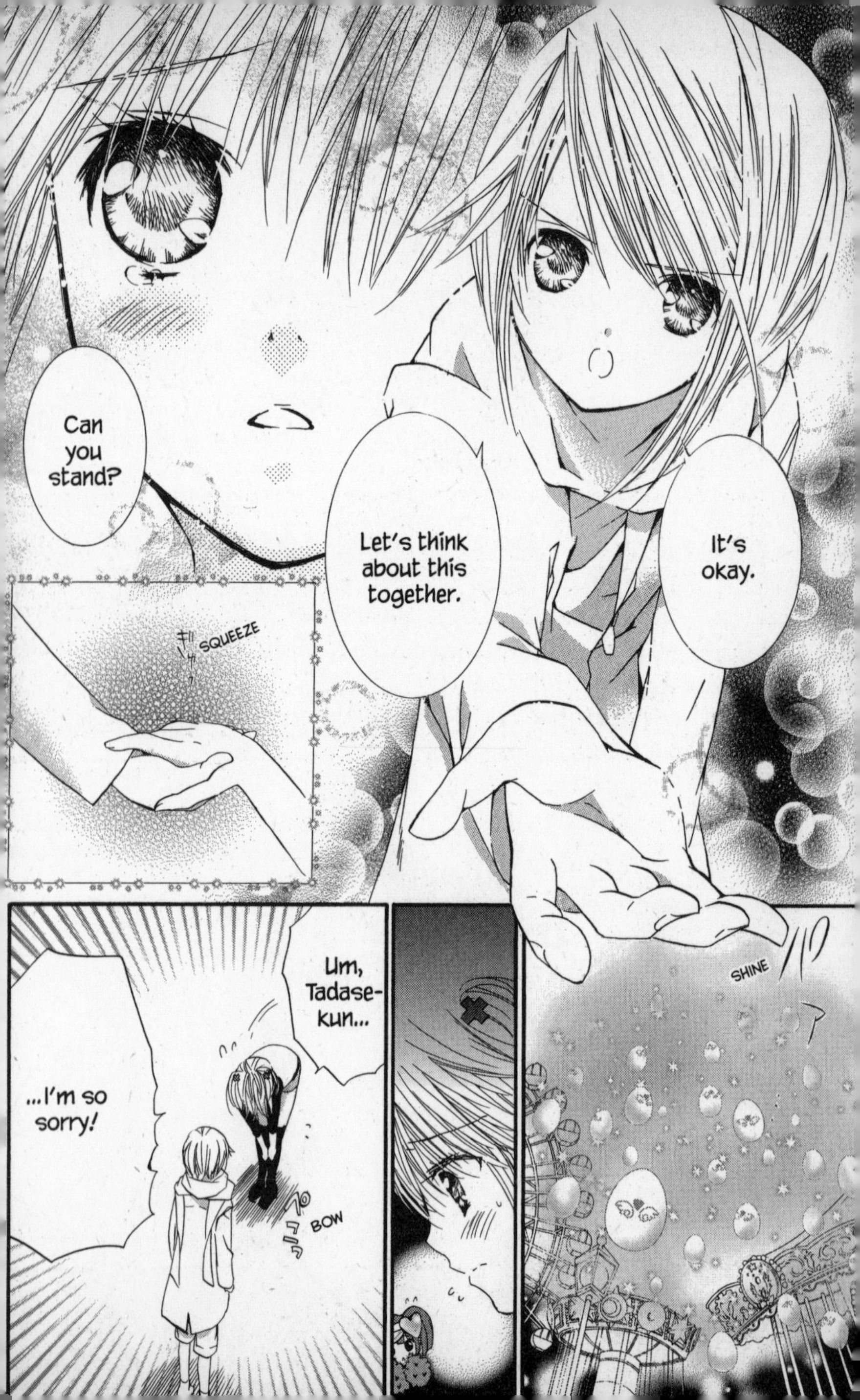
It's okay.
Let's think about this together.
Can you stand?
SQUEEZE
SHINE
Um, Tadase-kun...
...I'm so sorry!
BOW

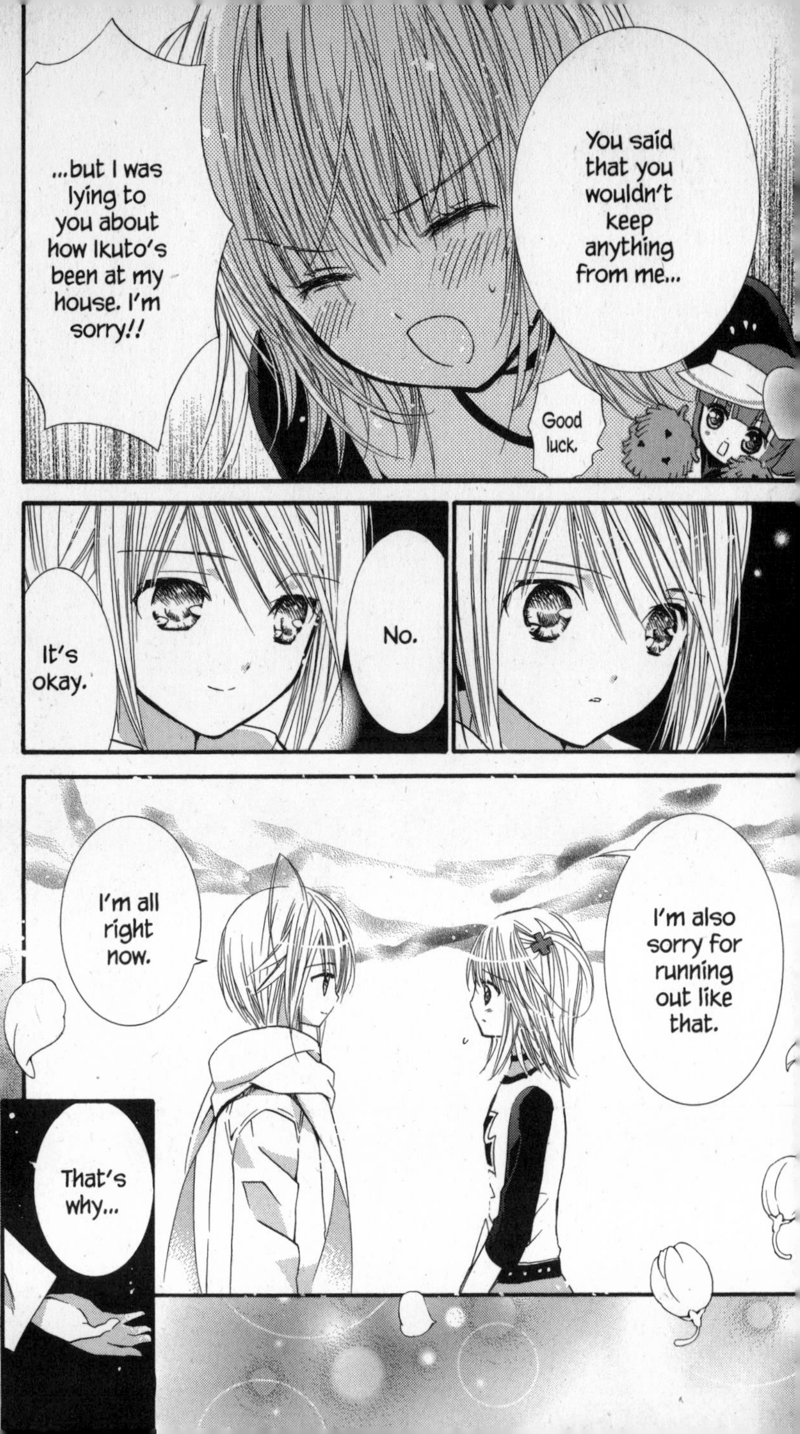
You said that you wouldn't keep anything from me...
...but I was lying to you about how Ikuto's been at my house. I'm sorry!!
Good luck.
No.
It's okay.
I'm also sorry for running out like that.
I'm all right now.
That's why...

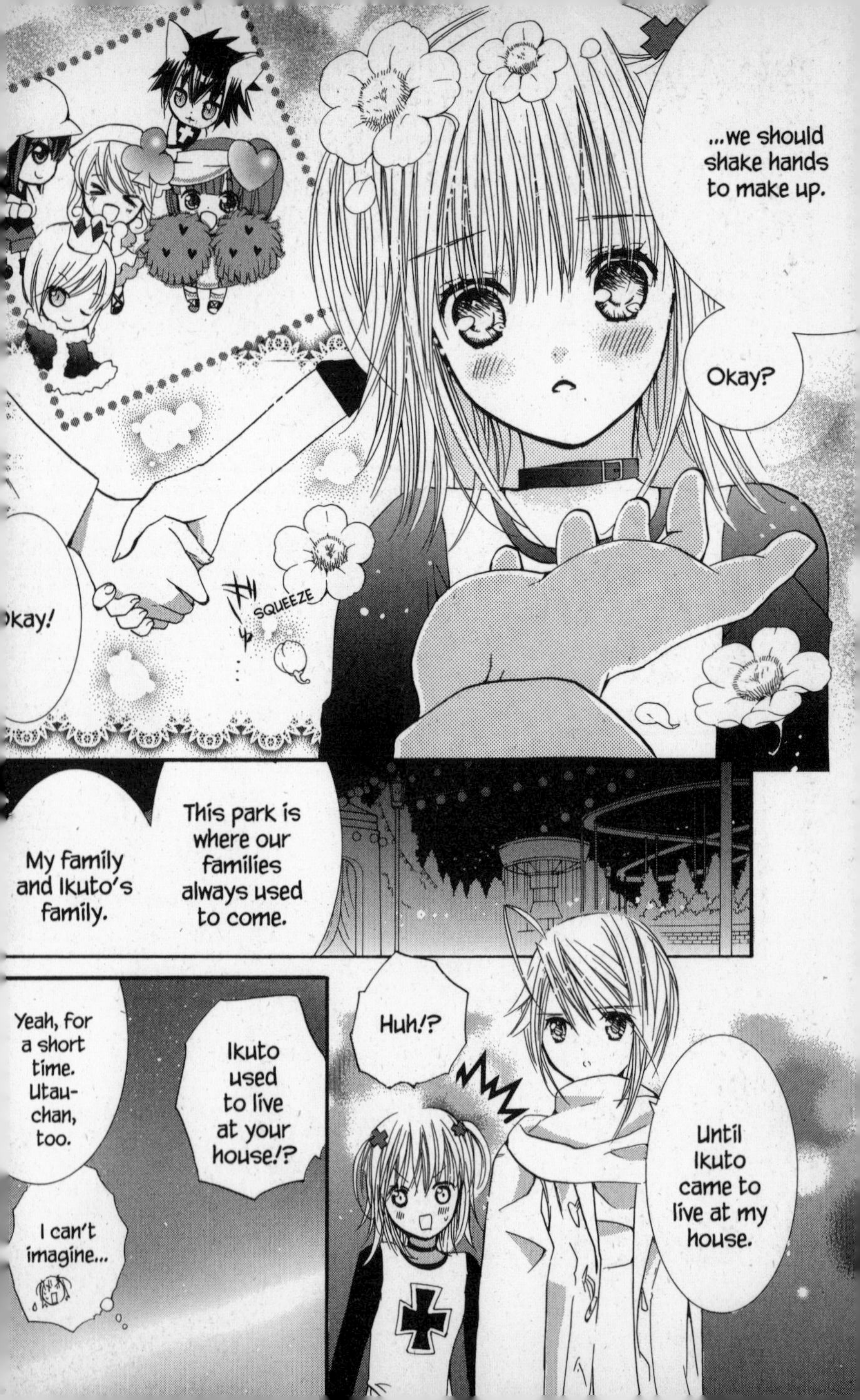
...we should shake hands to make up.
Okay?
Okay!
SQUEEZE
This park is where our families always used to come.
My family and Ikuto's family.
Until Ikuto came to live at my house.
Huh!?
Ikuto used to live at your house!?
Yeah, for a short time. Utau-chan, too.
I can't imagine...

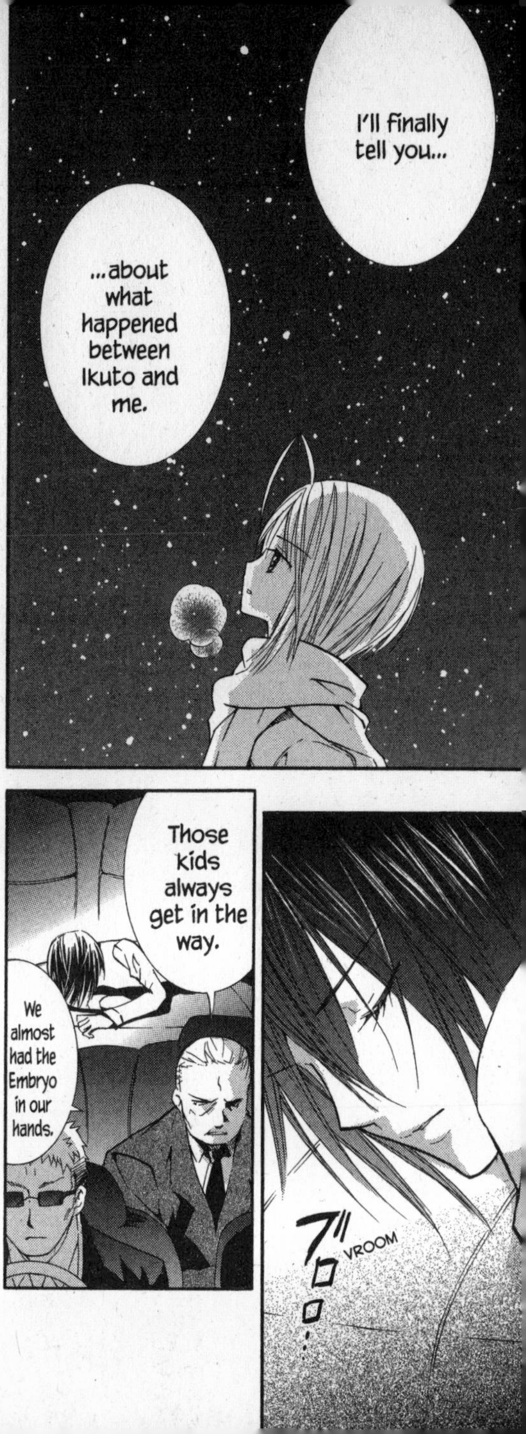
I'll finally tell you...
...about what happened between Ikuto and me.
VROOM
Those kids always get in the way.
We almost had the Embryo in our hands.

character profile

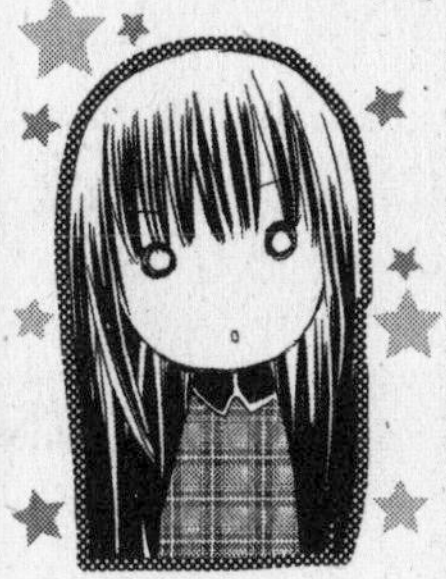

Nagihiko Fujisaki

Birthday: 7/4
Blood Type: AB
Sign: Cancer
Guardian Characters: Rhythm
Temari

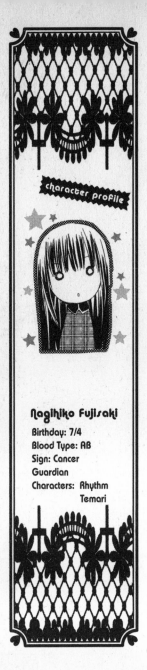

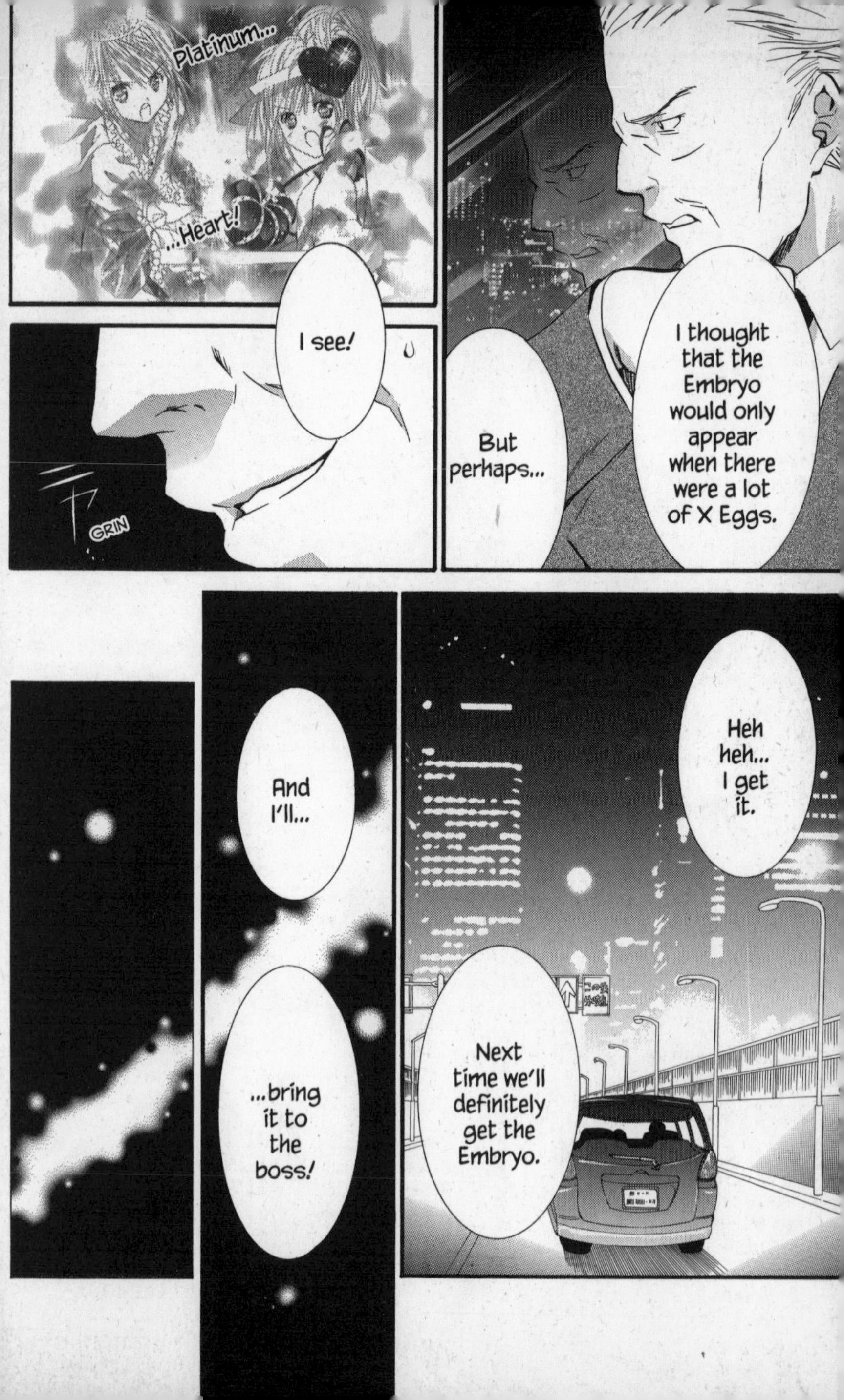
I thought that the Embryo would only appear when there were a lot of X Eggs.
But perhaps...
Platinum...
...Heart!
I see!
ニヤ
GRIN
Heh heh... I get it.
Next time we'll definitely get the Embryo.
And I'll...
...bring it to the boss!

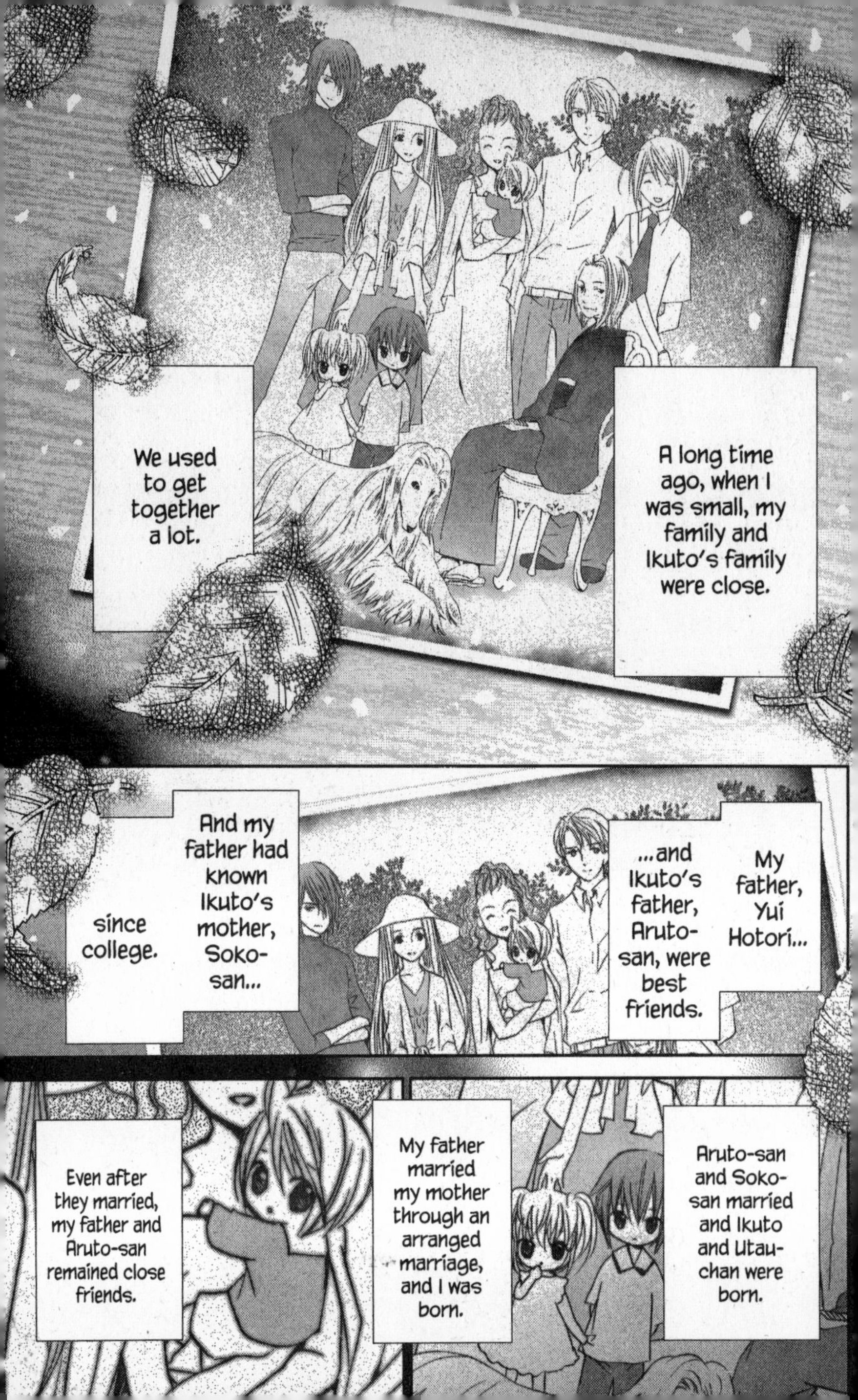
A long time ago, when I was small, my family and Ikuto's family were close.
We used to get together a lot.
My father, Yui Hotori...
...and Ikuto's father, Aruto-san, were best friends.
And my father had known Ikuto's mother, Soko-san...
since college.
Aruto-san and Soko-san married and Ikuto and Utau-chan were born.
My father married my mother through an arranged marriage, and I was born.
Even after they married, my father and Aruto-san remained close friends.

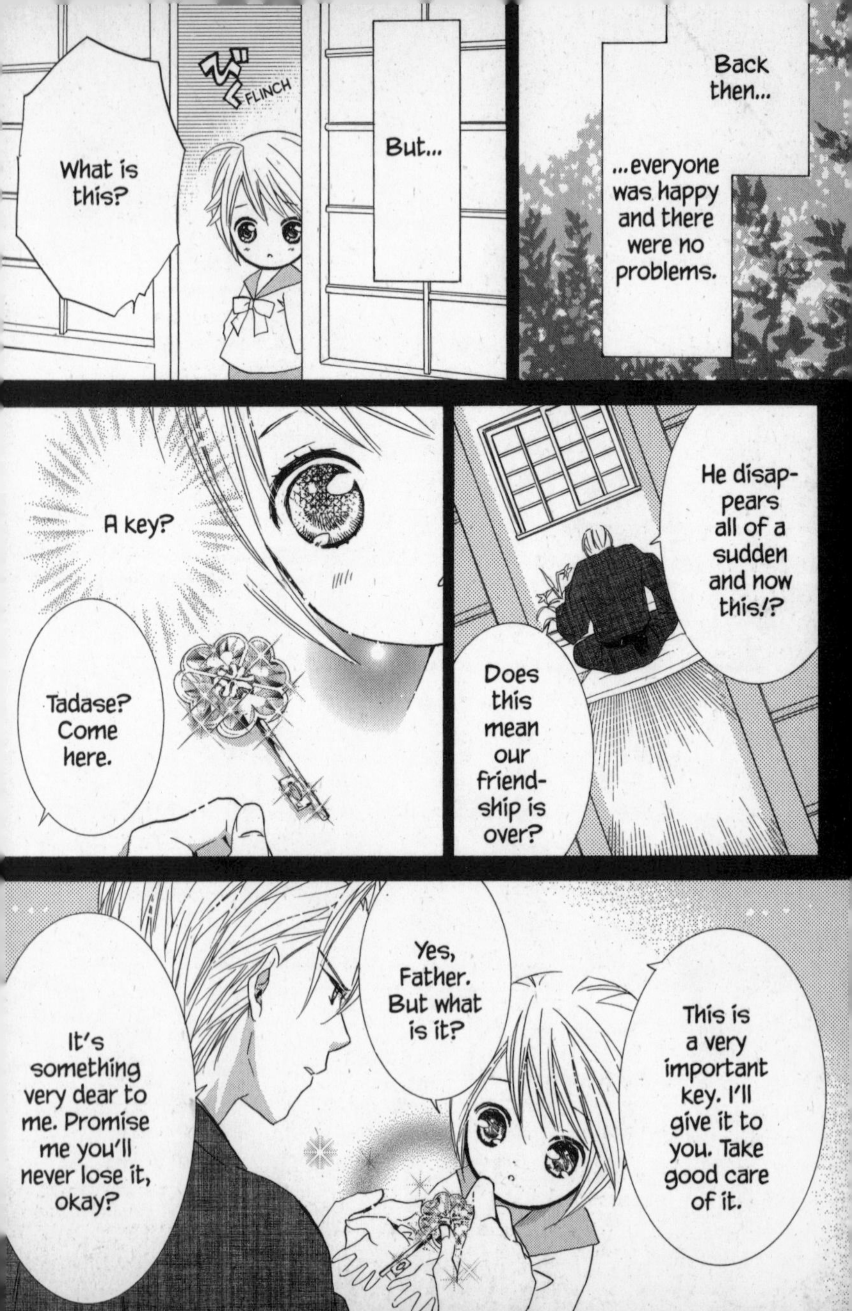
Back then...
...everyone was happy and there were no problems.
But...
FLINCH
What is this?
He disap-pears all of a sudden and now this!?
Does this mean our friend-ship is over?
A key?
Tadase? Come here.
This is a very important key. I'll give it to you. Take good care of it.
Yes, Father. But what is it?
It's something very dear to me. Promise me you'll never lose it, okay?

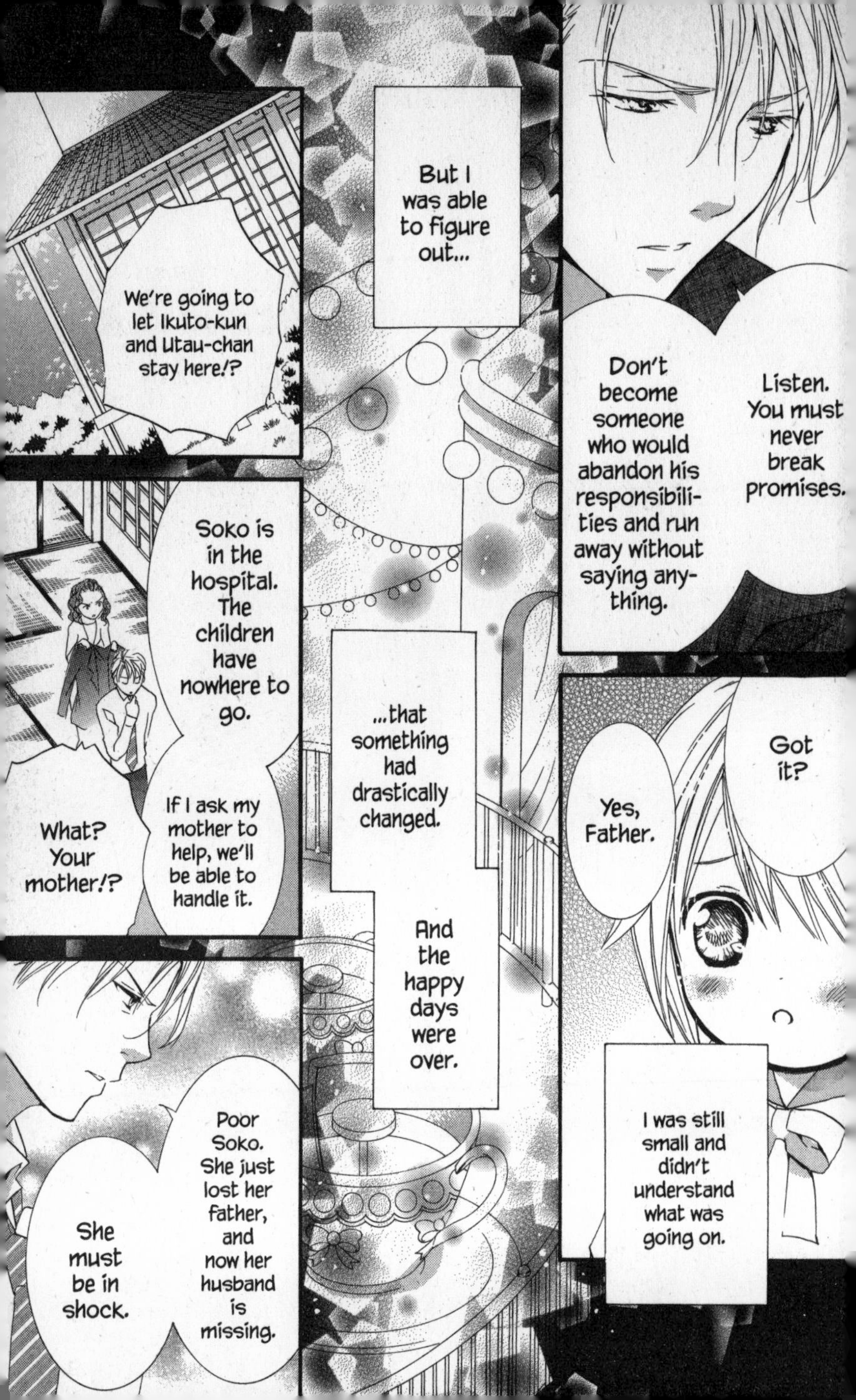
Listen. You must never break promises.
Don't become someone who would abandon his responsibili-ties and run away without saying any-thing.
Got it?
Yes, Father.
I was still small and didn't understand what was going on.
But I was able to figure out...
...that something had drastically changed.
And the happy days were over.
We're going to let Ikuto-kun and Utau-chan stay here!?
Soko is in the hospital. The children have nowhere to go.
If I ask my mother to help, we'll be able to handle it.
What? Your mother!?
Poor Soko. She just lost her father, and now her husband is missing.
She must be in shock.

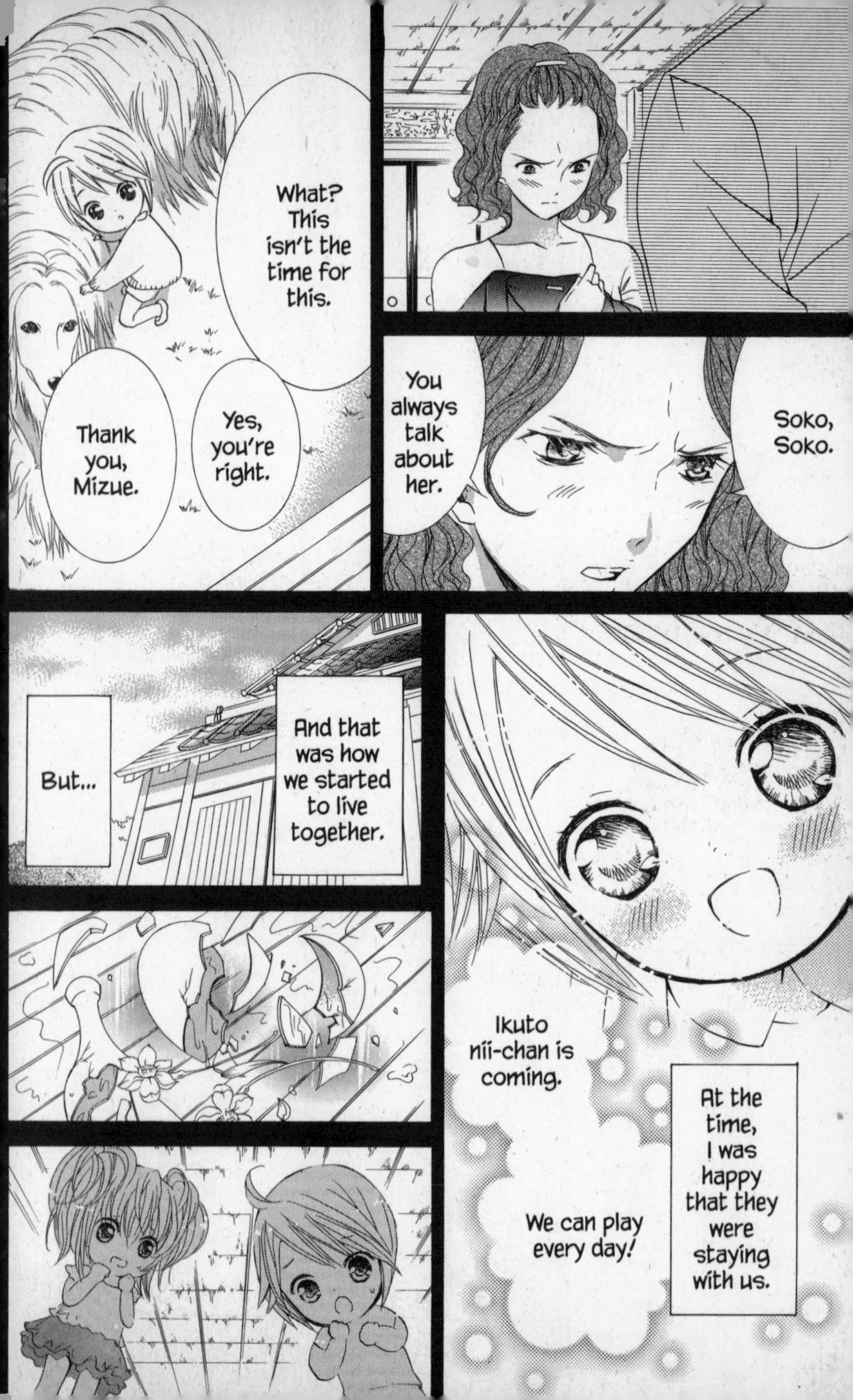
Soko, Soko.
You always talk about her.
What? This isn't the time for this.
Yes, you're right.
Thank you, Mizue.
Ikuto nii-chan is coming.
At the time, I was happy that they were staying with us.
We can play every day!
And that was how we started to live together.
But...

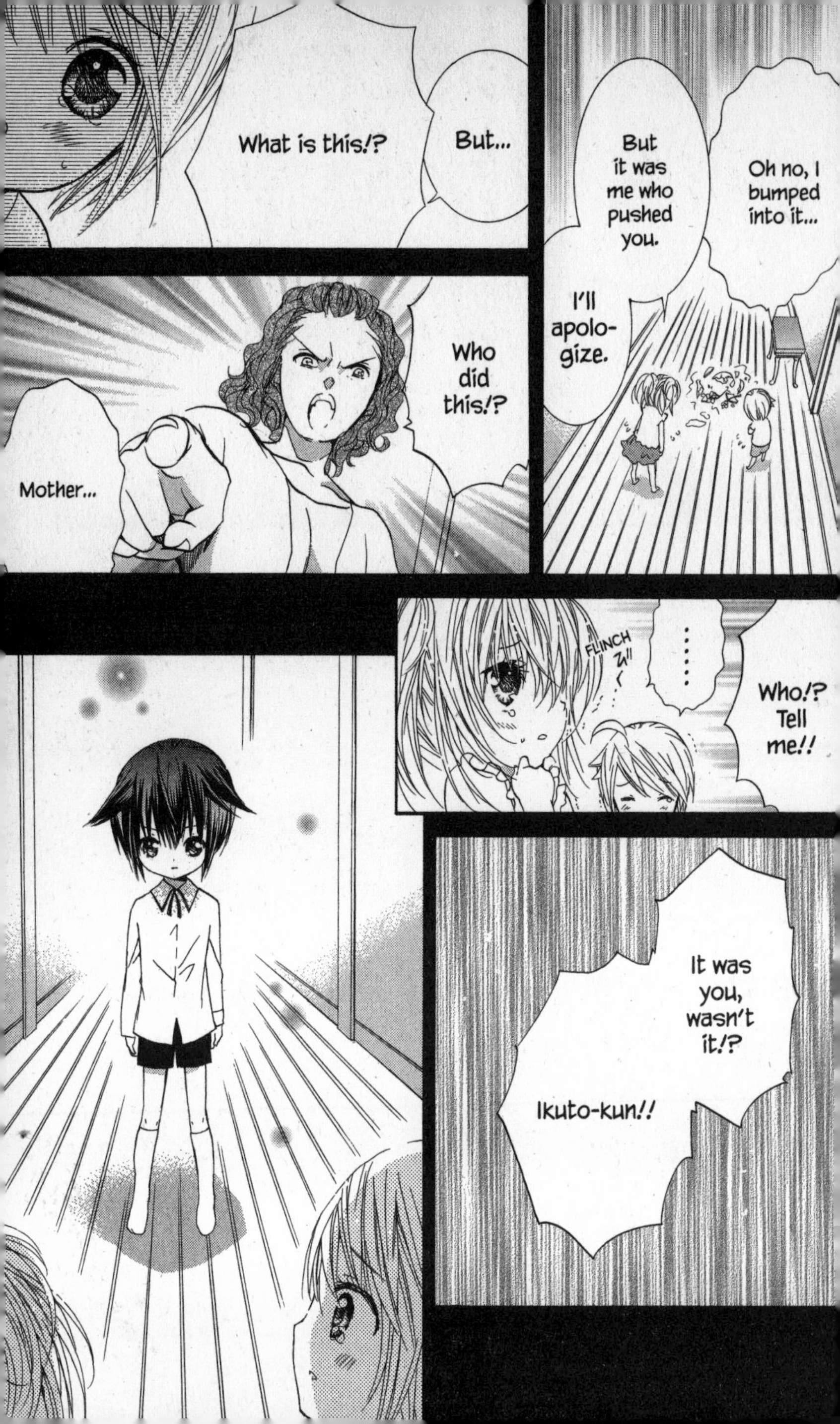
Oh no, I bumped into it...
But it was me who pushed you.
I'll apologize.
But...
What is this!?
Who did this!?
Mother...
Who!? Tell me!!
......
FLINCH
It was you, wasn't it!?
Ikuto-kun!!

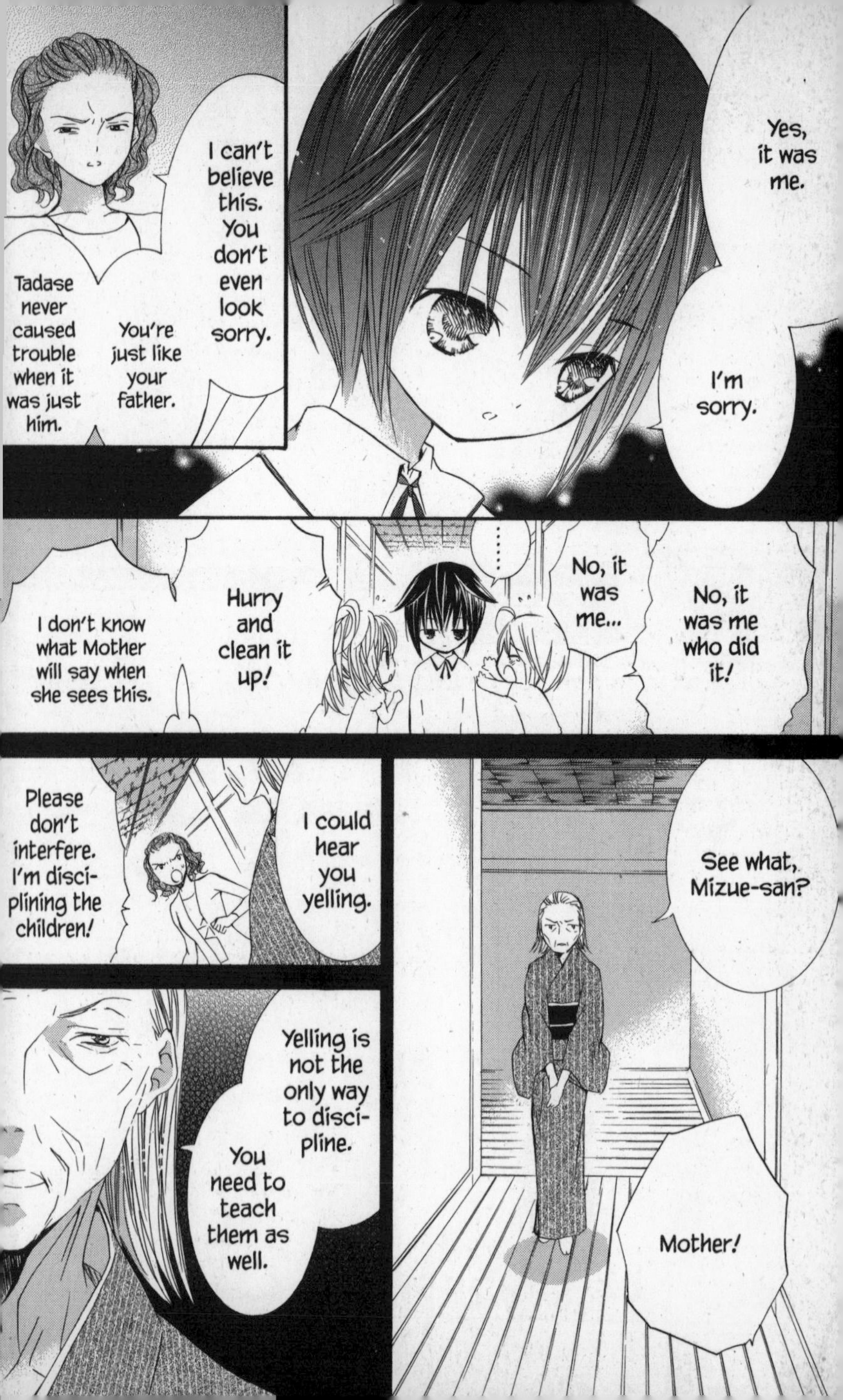

Yes, it was me.
I'm sorry.
I can't believe this. You don't even look sorry.
You're just like your father.
Tadase never caused trouble when it was just him.
No, it was me who did it!
No, it was me...
......
Hurry and clean it up!
I don't know what Mother will say when she sees this.
See what, Mizue-san?
Mother!
I could hear you yelling.
Please don't interfere. I'm disci-plining the children!
Yelling is not the only way to disci-pline.
You need to teach them as well.

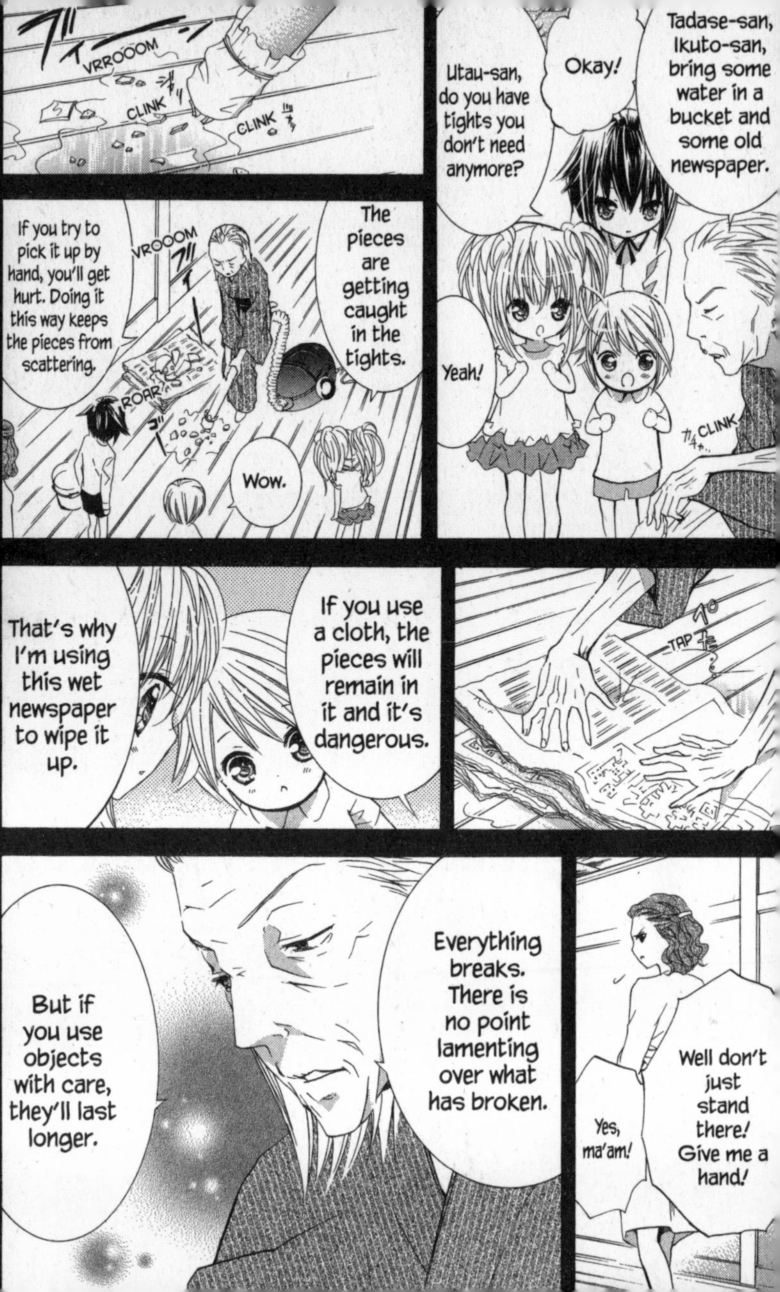
Tadase-san, Ikuto-san, bring some water in a bucket and some old newspaper.
Okay!
Utau-san, do you have tights you don't need anymore?
Yeah!
CLINK
VRROOOM
CLINK
CLINK
The pieces are getting caught in the tights.
VROOOM
If you try to pick it up by hand, you'll get hurt. Doing it this way keeps the pieces from scattering.
ROAR
Wow.
TAP
If you use a cloth, the pieces will remain in it and it's dangerous.
That's why I'm using this wet newspaper to wipe it up.
Well don't just stand there! Give me a hand!
Yes, ma'am!
Everything breaks. There is no point lamenting over what has broken.
But if you use objects with care, they'll last longer.

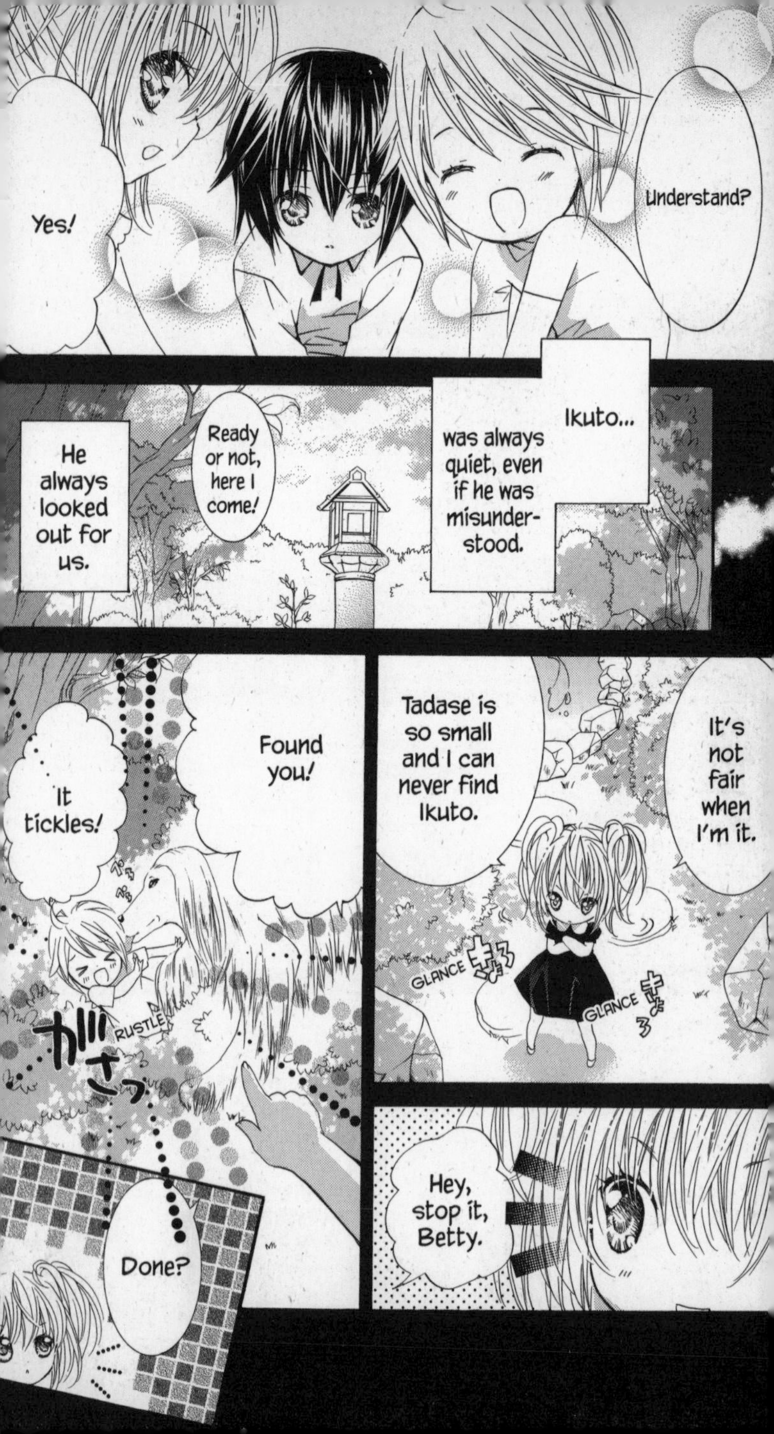
Understand?
Yes!
Ikuto...
was always quiet, even if he was misunderstood.
Ready or not, here I come!
He always looked out for us.
It's not fair when I'm it.
Tadase is so small and I can never find Ikuto.
GLANCE
GLANCE
Hey, stop it, Betty.
Found you!
It tickles!
RUSTLE
Done?

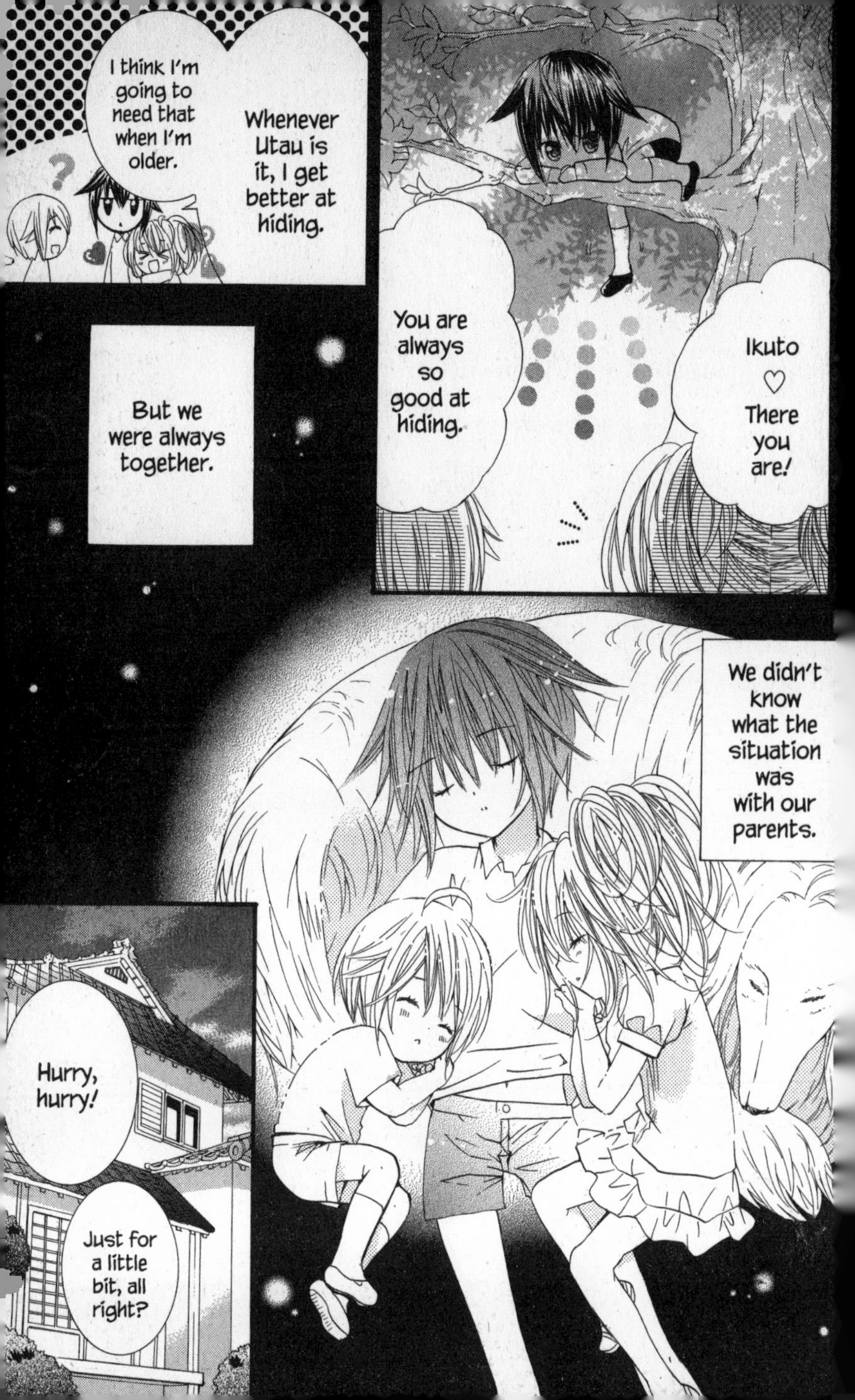
Ikuto ♡ There you are!
You are always so good at hiding.
Whenever Utau is it, I get better at hiding.
I think I'm going to need that when I'm older.
But we were always together.
We didn't know what the situation was with our parents.
Hurry, hurry!
Just for a little bit, all right?

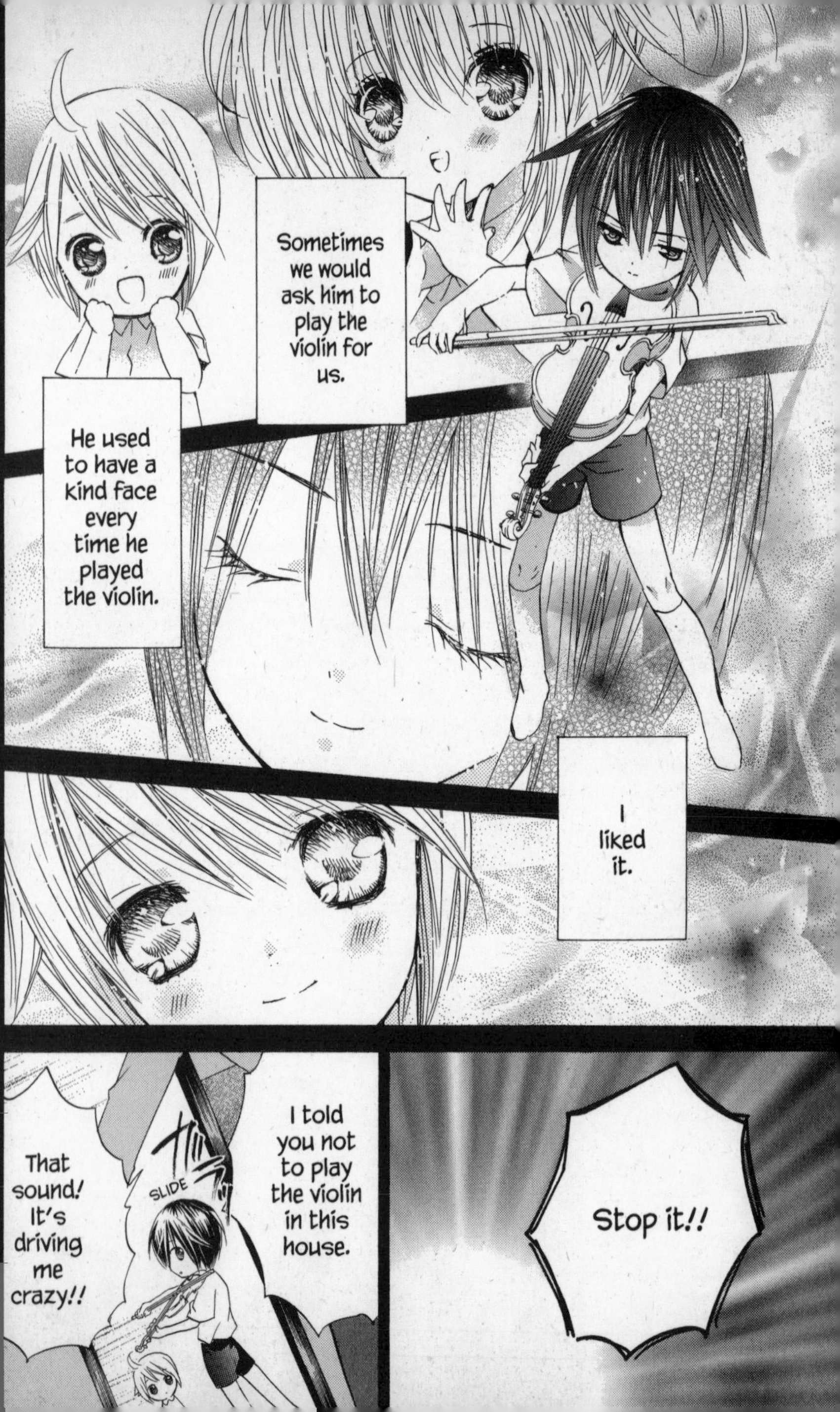
Sometimes we would ask him to play the violin for us.
He used to have a kind face every time he played the violin.
I liked it.
Stop it!!
I told you not to play the violin in this house.
SLIDE
That sound! It's driving me crazy!!

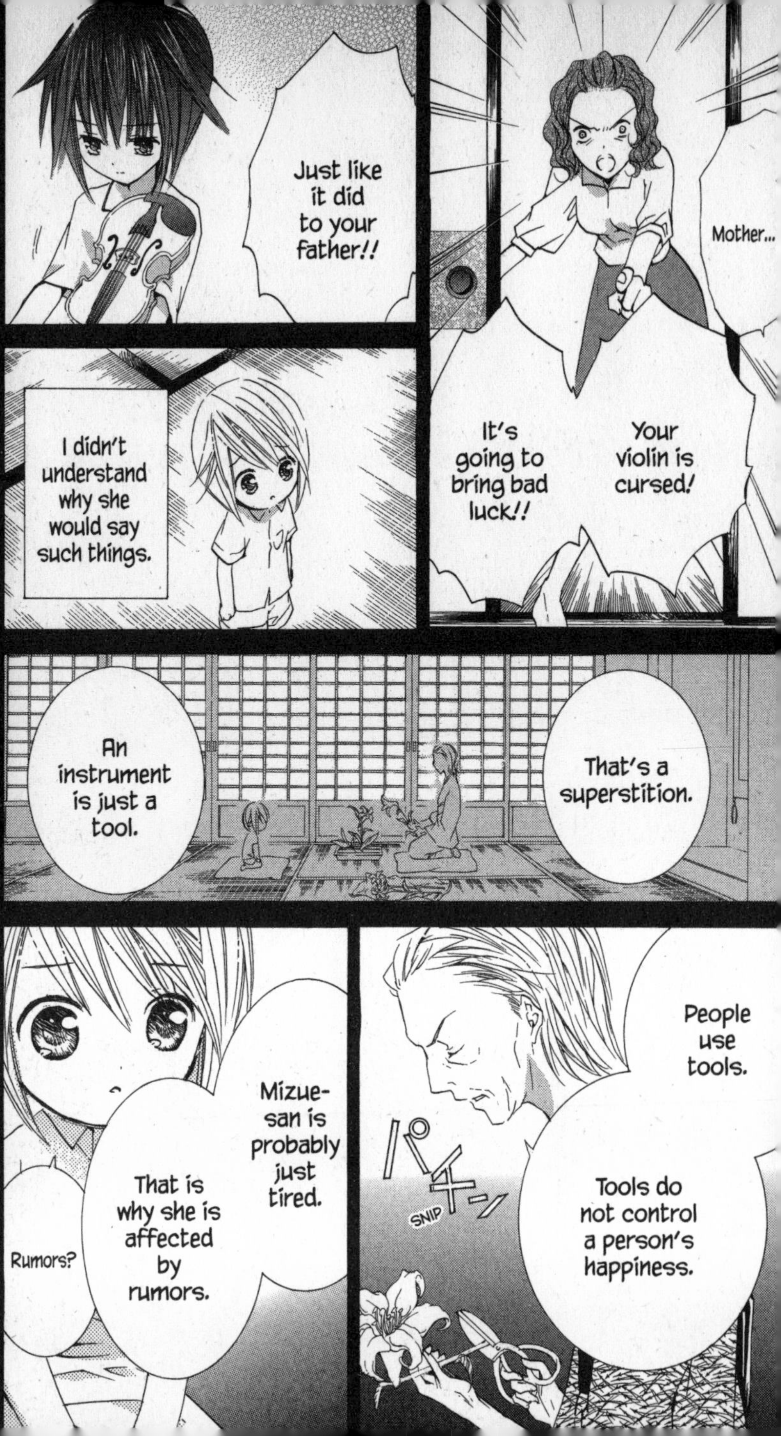
Mother...
Your violin is cursed!
It's going to bring bad luck!!
Just like it did to your father!!
I didn't understand why she would say such things.
That's a superstition.
An instrument is just a tool.
People use tools.
Tools do not control a person's happiness.
SNIP
Mizue-san is probably just tired.
That is why she is affected by rumors.
Rumors?

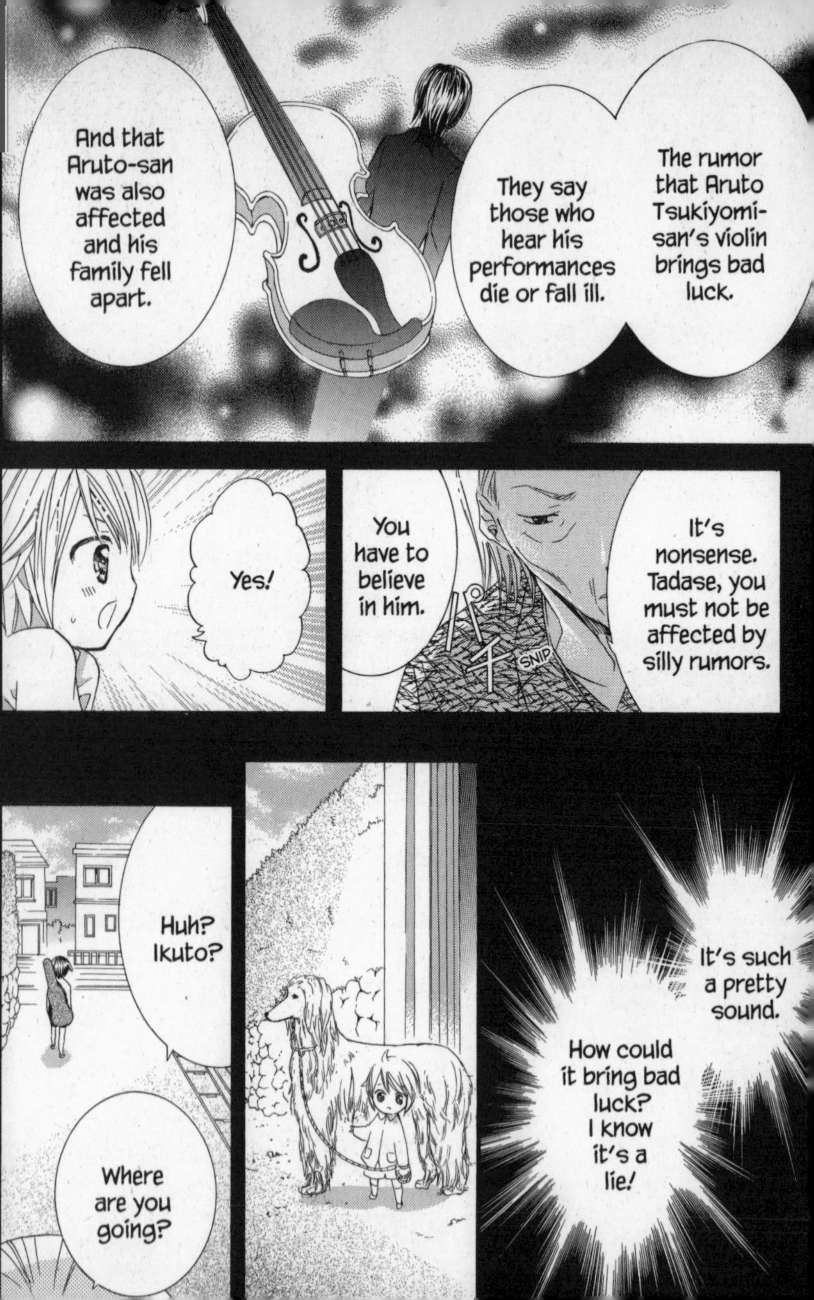
The rumor that Aruto Tsukiyomi-san's violin brings bad luck.
They say those who hear his performances die or fall ill.
And that Aruto-san was also affected and his family fell apart.
It's nonsense. Tadase, you must not be affected by silly rumors.
パチ
SNIP
You have to believe in him.
Yes!
It's such a pretty sound.
How could it bring bad luck? I know it's a lie!
Huh? Ikuto?
Where are you going?

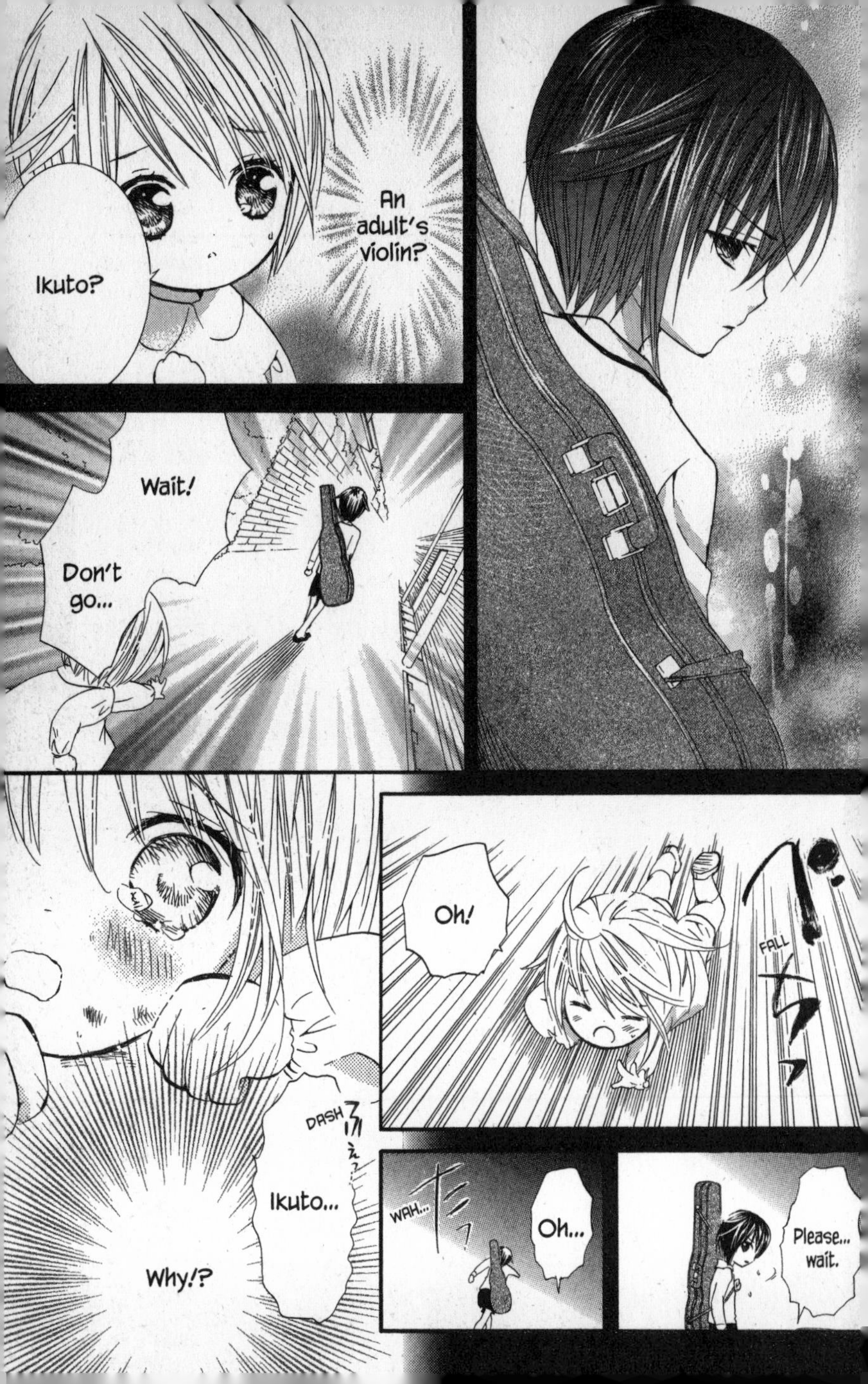
An adult's violin?
Ikuto?
Wait!
Don't go...
Oh!
FALL
Please... wait.
Oh...
WAH...
DASH
Ikuto...
Why!?

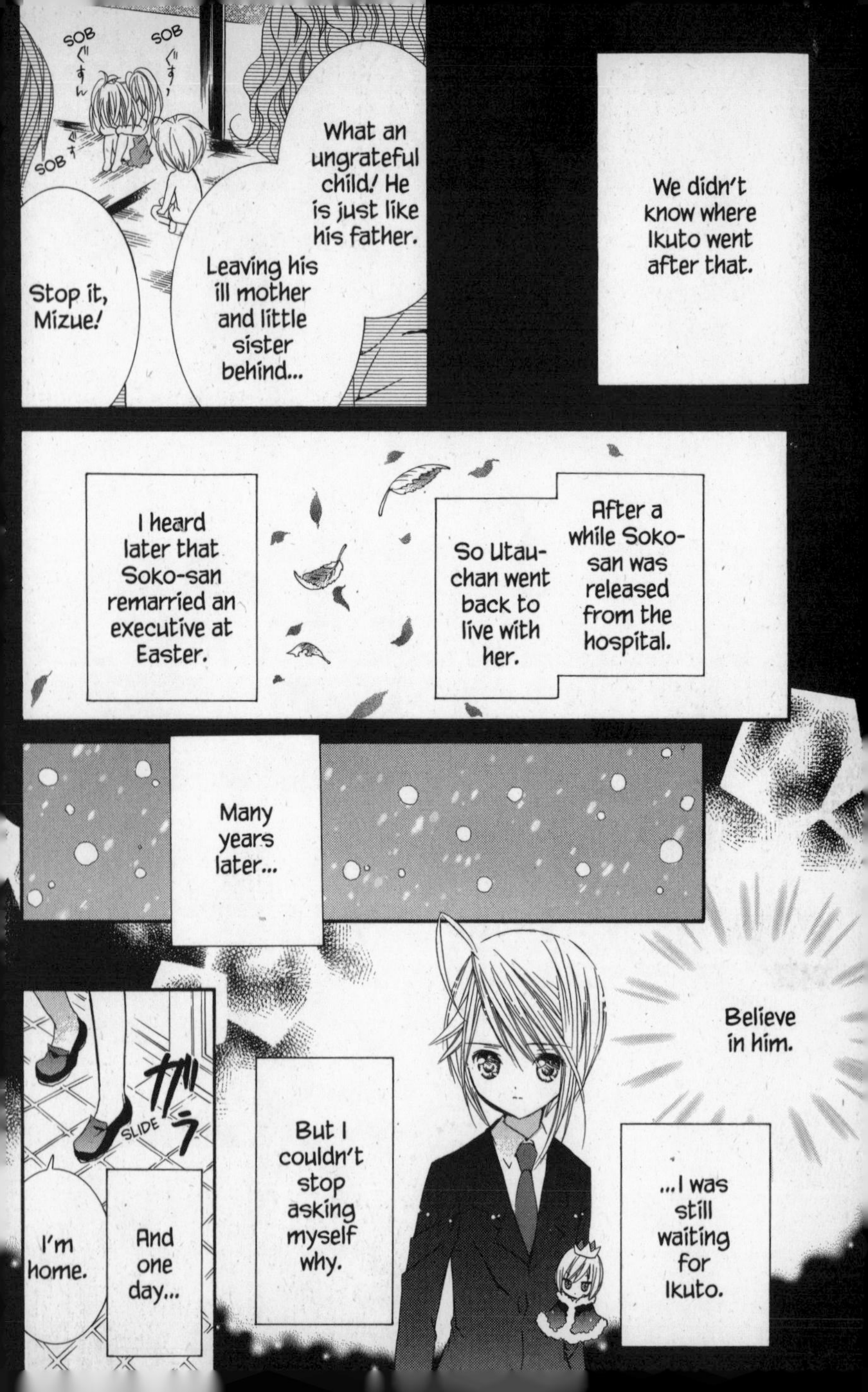
We didn't know where Ikuto went after that.
SOB
SOB
SOB
What an ungrateful child! He is just like his father.
Leaving his ill mother and little sister behind...
Stop it, Mizue!
After a while Soko-san was released from the hospital.
So Utau-chan went back to live with her.
I heard later that Soko-san remarried an executive at Easter.
Many years later...
Believe in him.
...I was still waiting for Ikuto.
But I couldn't stop asking myself why.
SLIDE
And one day...
I'm home.

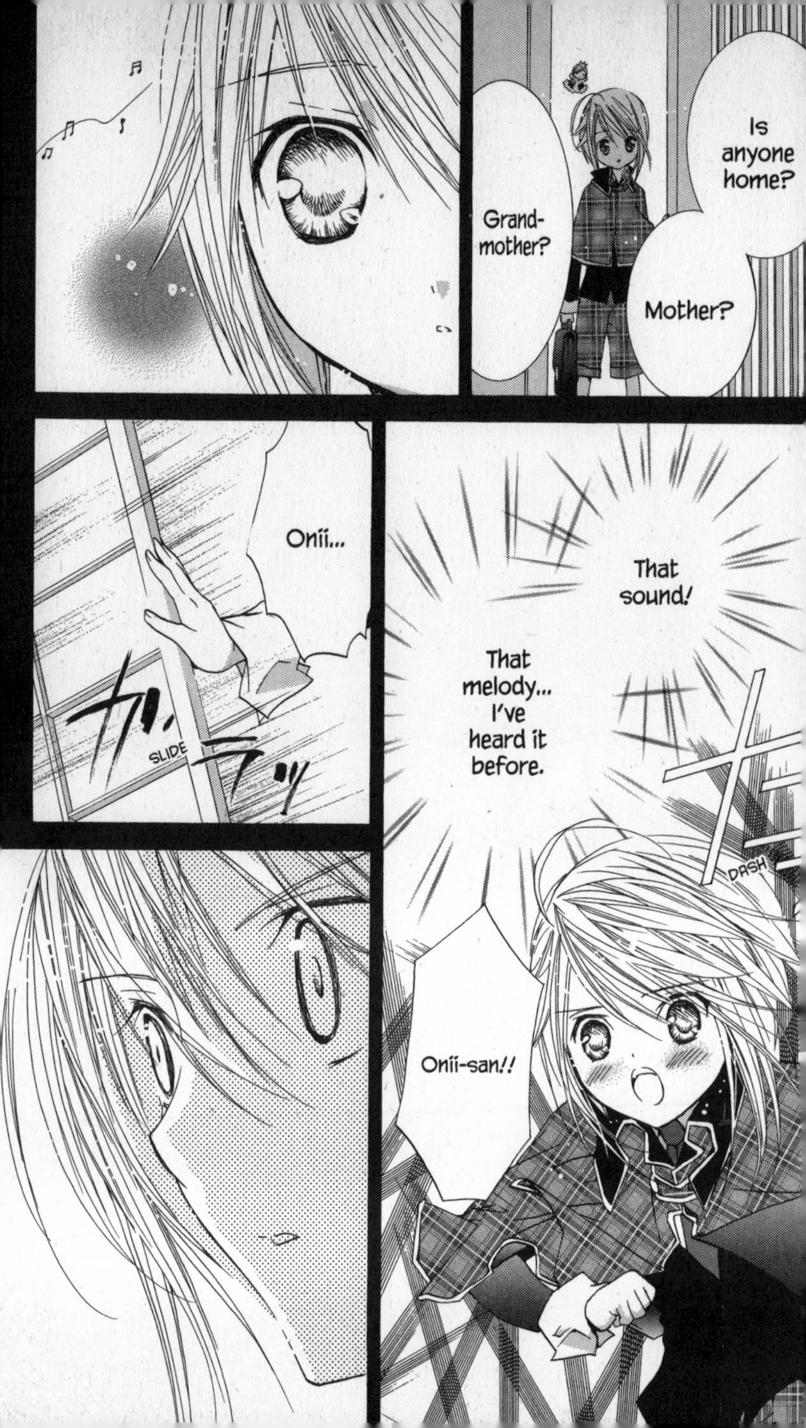
Is anyone home?
Mother?
Grand-mother?
That sound!
That melody... I've heard it before.
DASH
Onii-san!!
Onii...
SLIDE

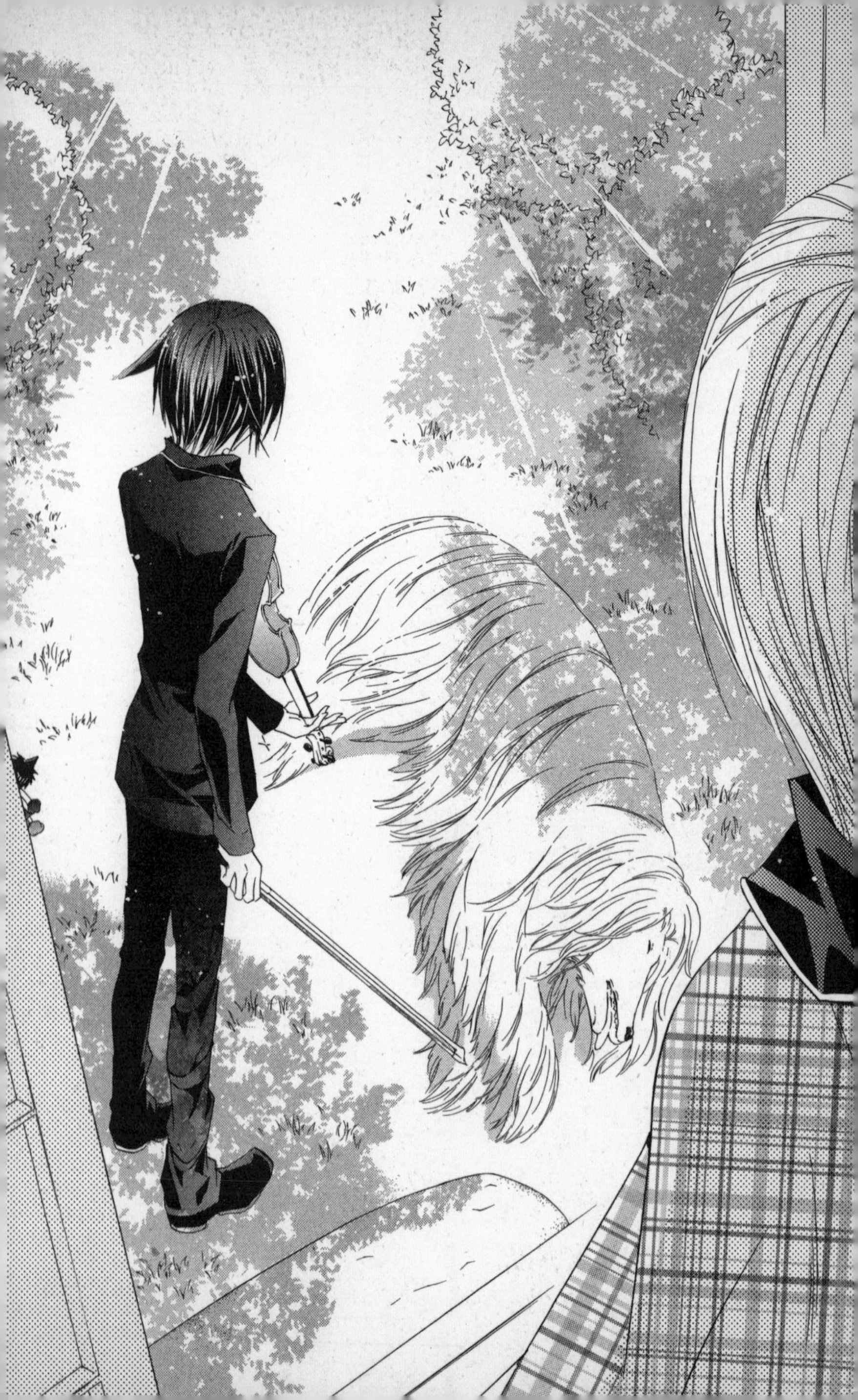

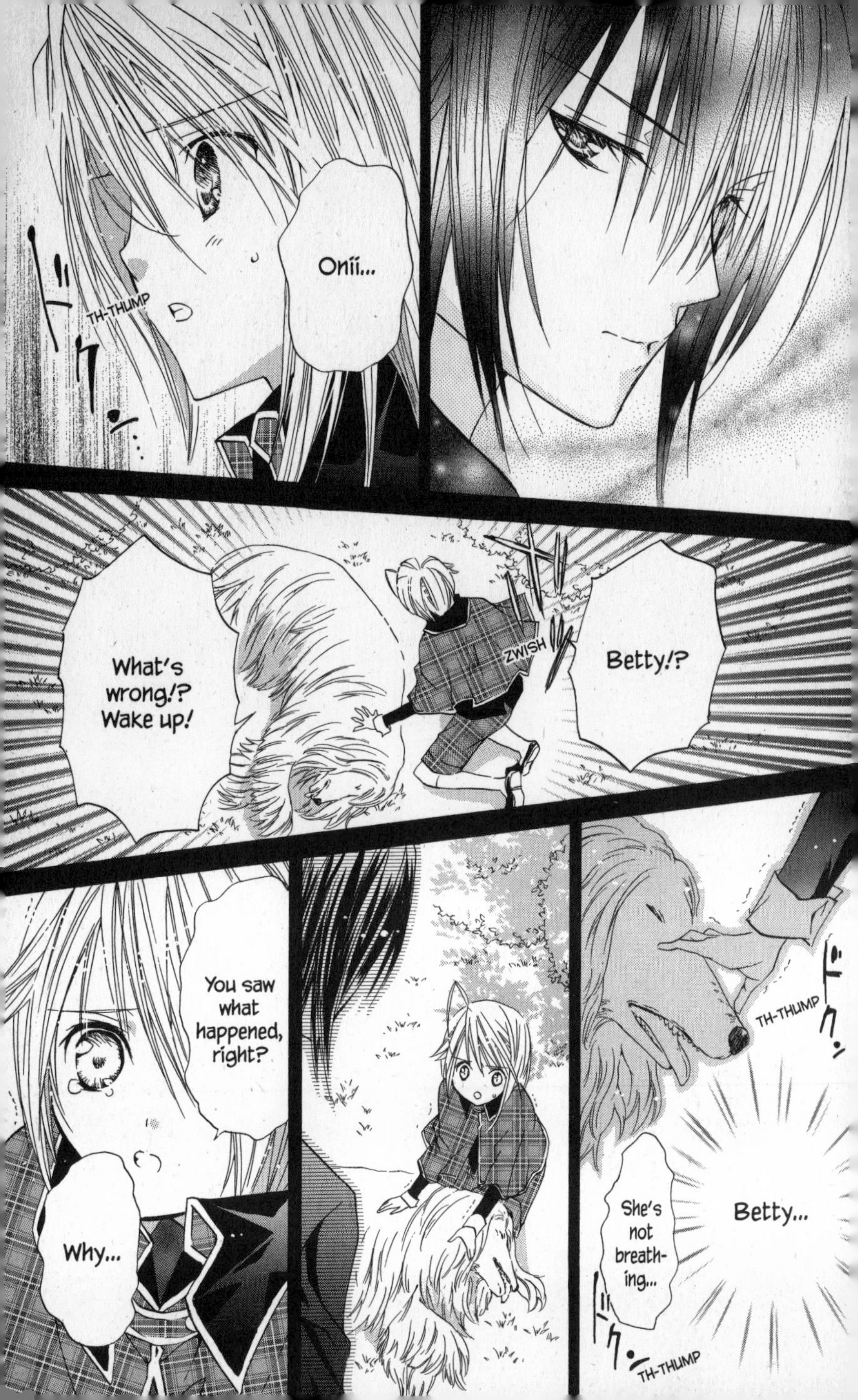
Onii...
TH-THUMP
Betty!?
ZWISH
What's wrong!? Wake up!
TH-THUMP
Betty...
She's not breathing...
TH-THUMP
You saw what happened, right?
Why...

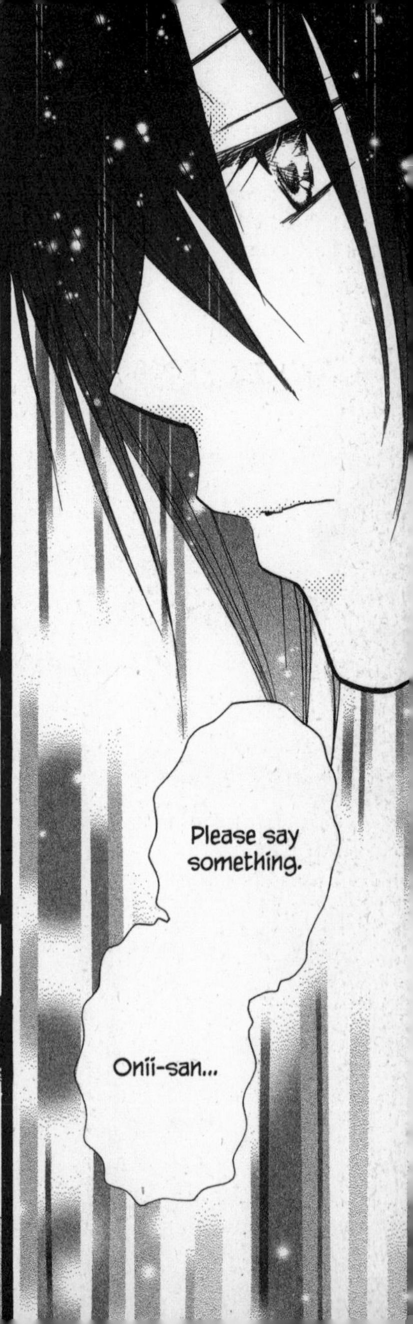
Please say something.
Onii-san...

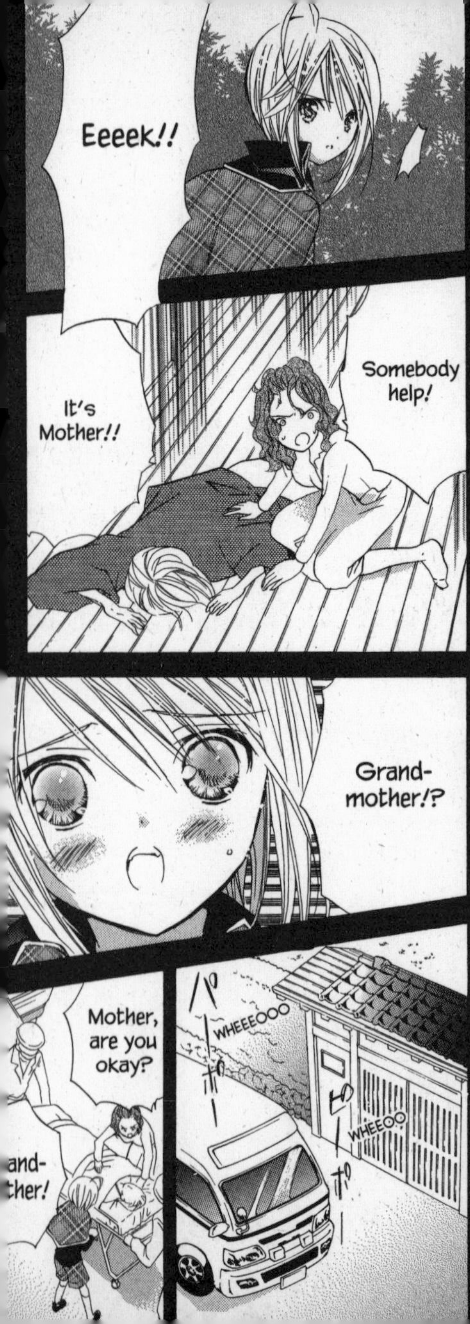
Eeeek!!
Somebody help!
It's Mother!!
Grand-mother!?
WHEEEOOO
WHEEOO
Mother, are you okay?

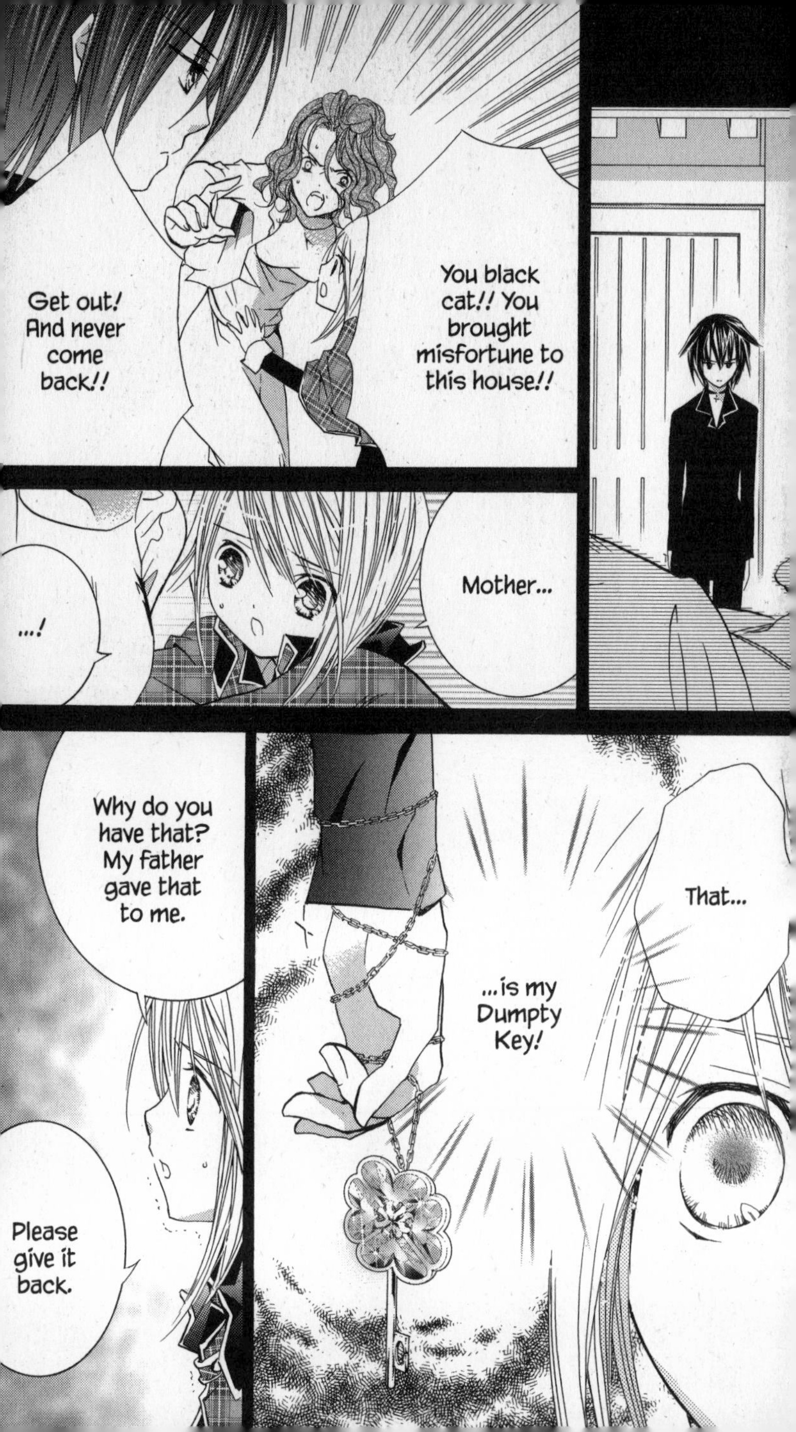
You black cat!! You brought misfortune to this house!!
Get out! And never come back!!
Mother...
...!
That...
...is my Dumpty Key!
Why do you have that? My father gave that to me.
Please give it back.

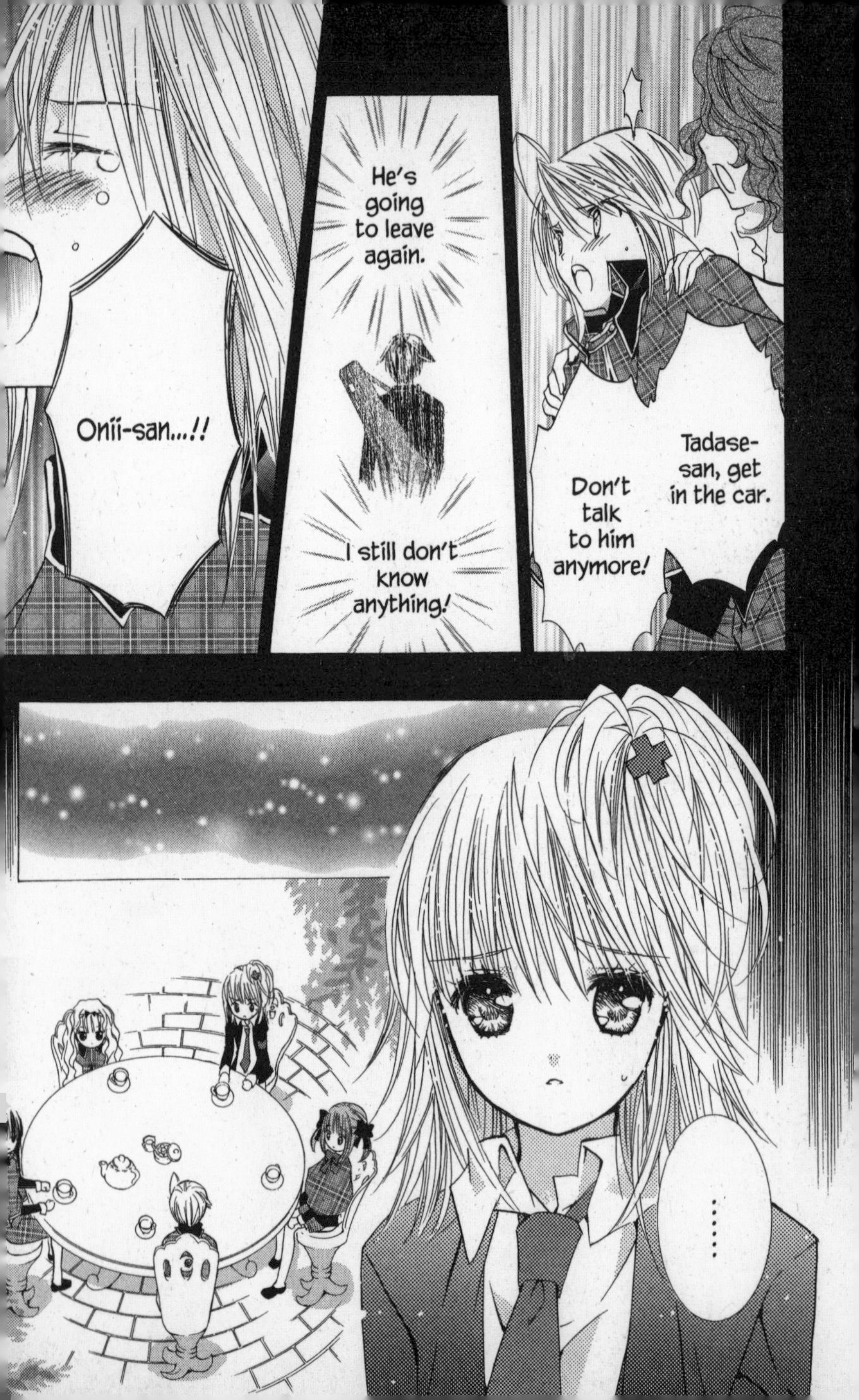
Tadase-san, get in the car.
Don't talk to him anymore!
He's going to leave again.
I still don't know anything!
Onii-san...!!
......

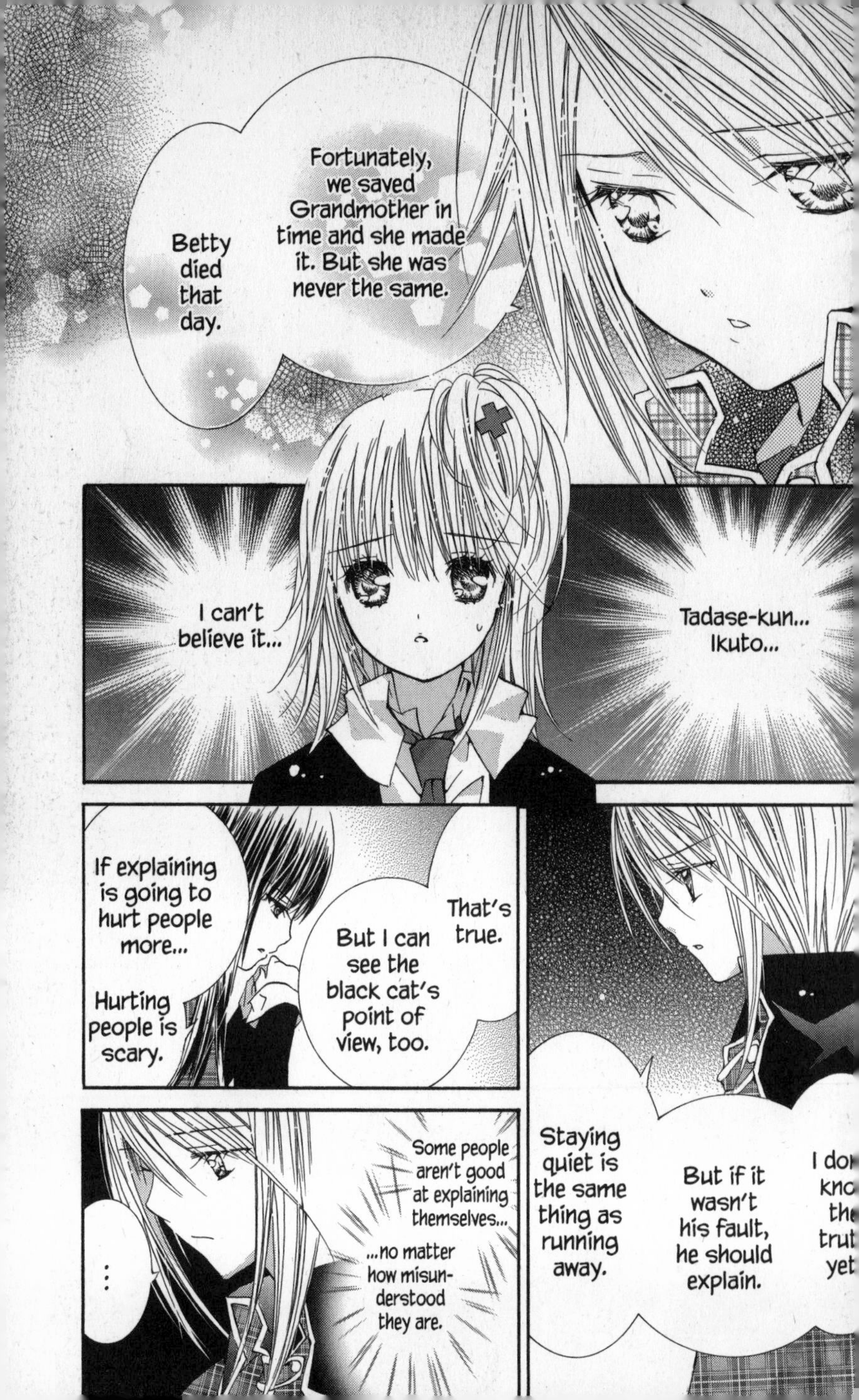
Fortunately, we saved Grandmother in time and she made it. But she was never the same.
Betty died that day.
Tadase-kun... Ikuto...
I can't believe it...
I don kno the trut yet
But if it wasn't his fault, he should explain.
Staying quiet is the same thing as running away.
That's true.
But I can see the black cat's point of view, too.
If explaining is going to hurt people more...
Hurting people is scary.
Some people aren't good at explaining themselves...
...no matter how misunderstood they are.
...

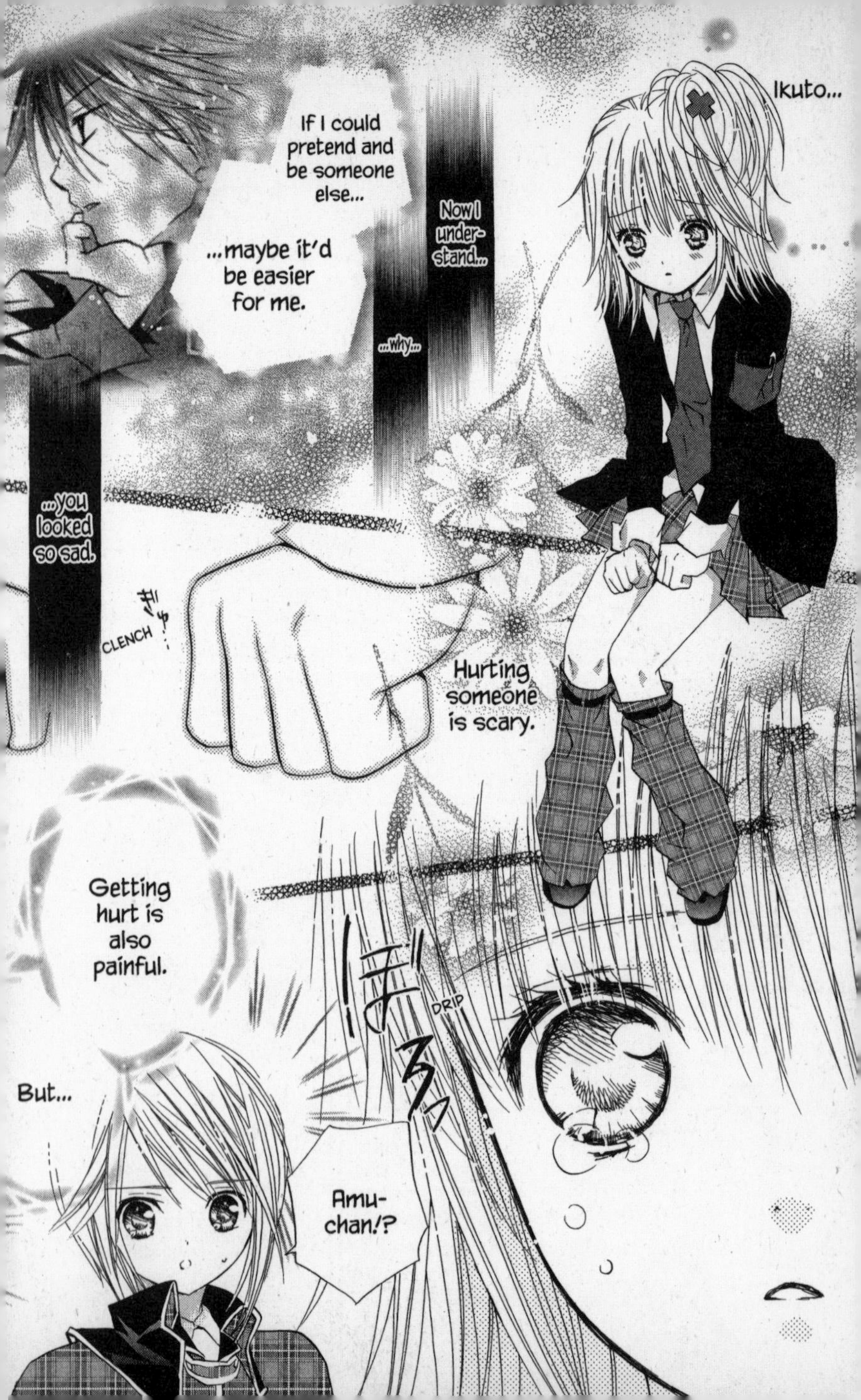

Ikuto...
Now I under-stand...
...why...
...you looked so sad.
If I could pretend and be someone else...
...maybe it'd be easier for me.
CLENCH
Hurting someone is scary.
Getting hurt is also painful.
DRIP
But...
Amu-chan!?

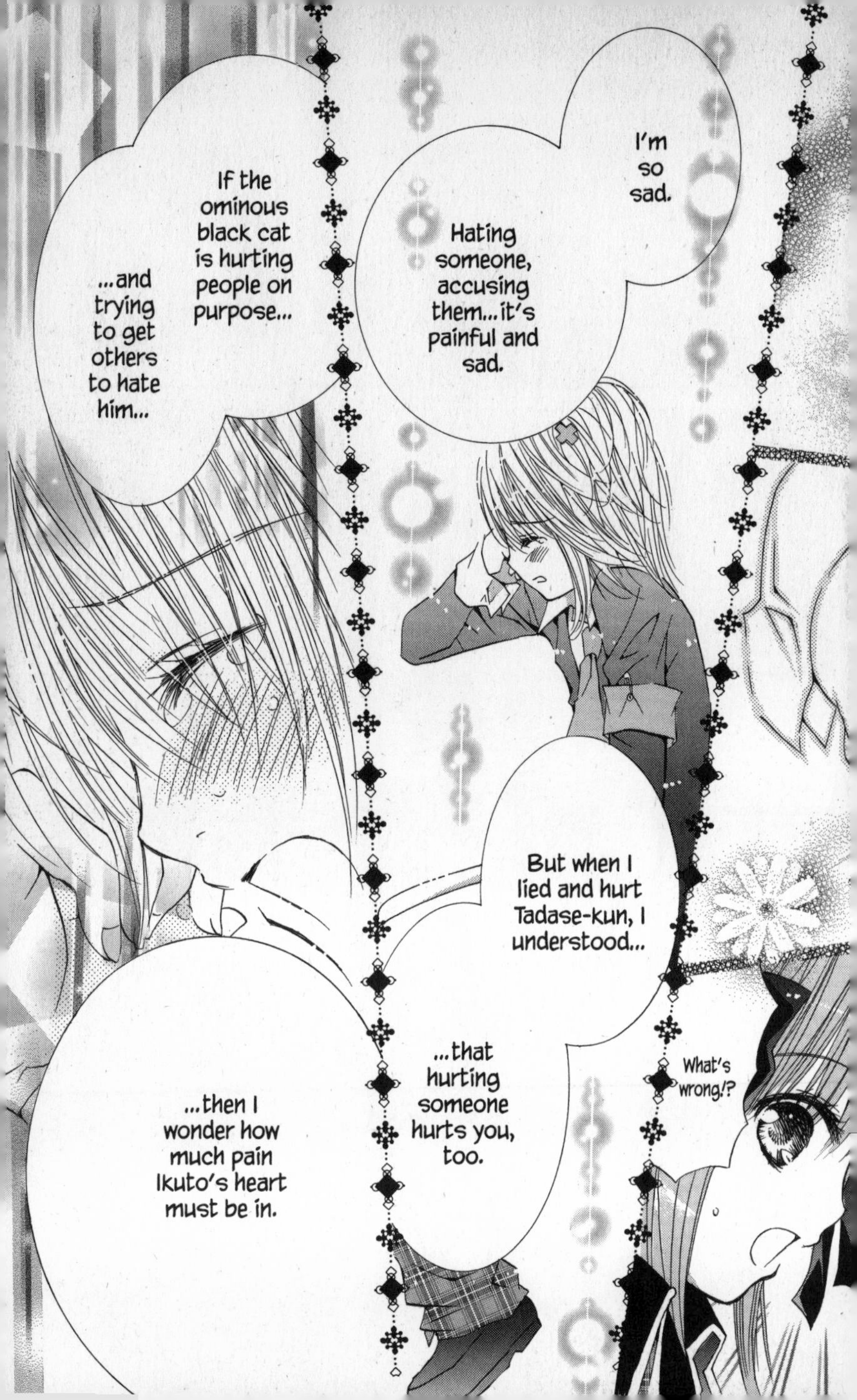
I'm so sad.
Hating someone, accusing them...it's painful and sad.
If the ominous black cat is hurting people on purpose...
...and trying to get others to hate him...
But when I lied and hurt Tadase-kun, I understood...
...that hurting someone hurts you, too.
...then I wonder how much pain Ikuto's heart must be in.
What's wrong!?

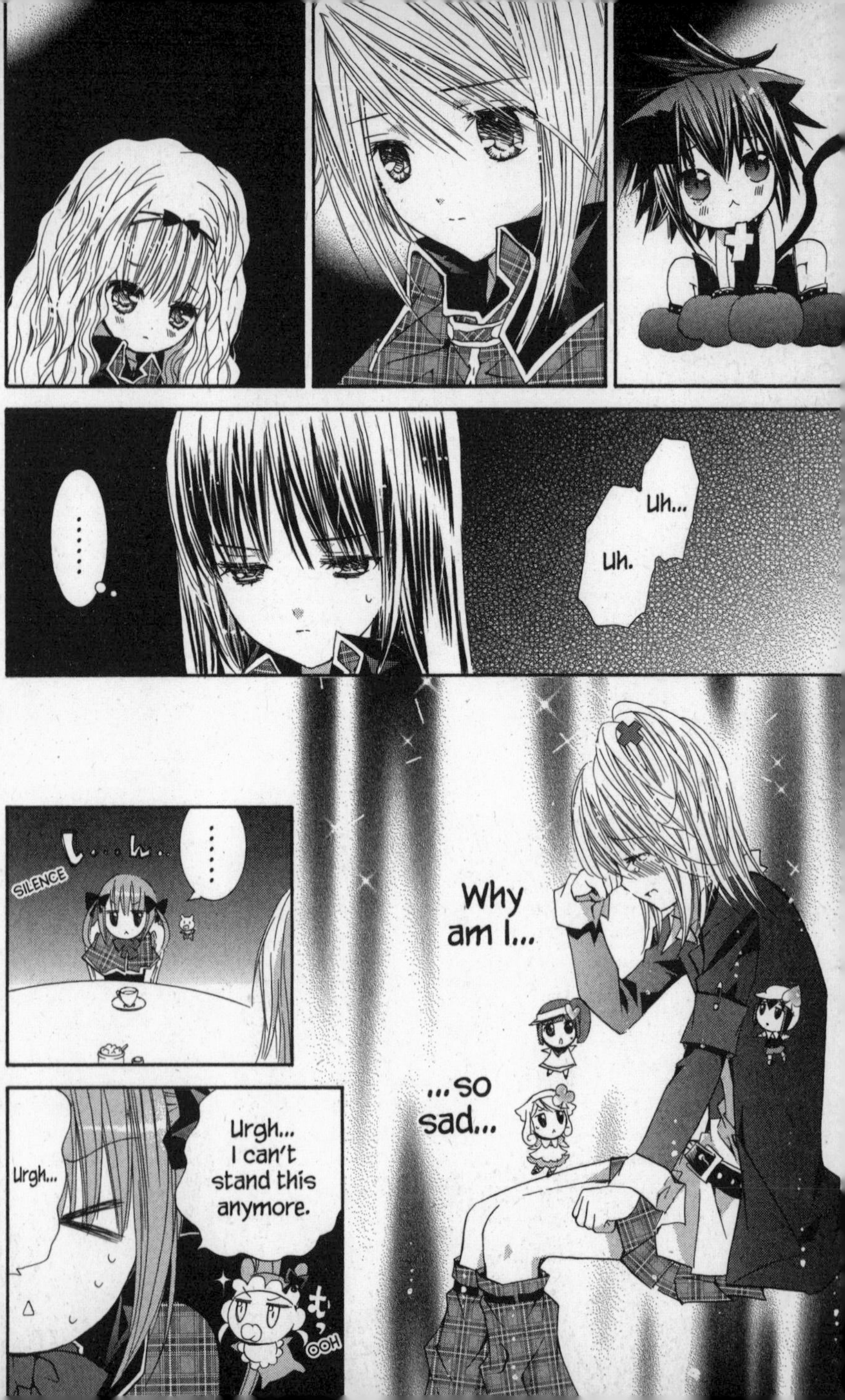

Uh...
Uh.
......
Why am I...
...so sad...
SILENCE
......
Urgh... I can't stand this anymore.
Urgh...
OOH

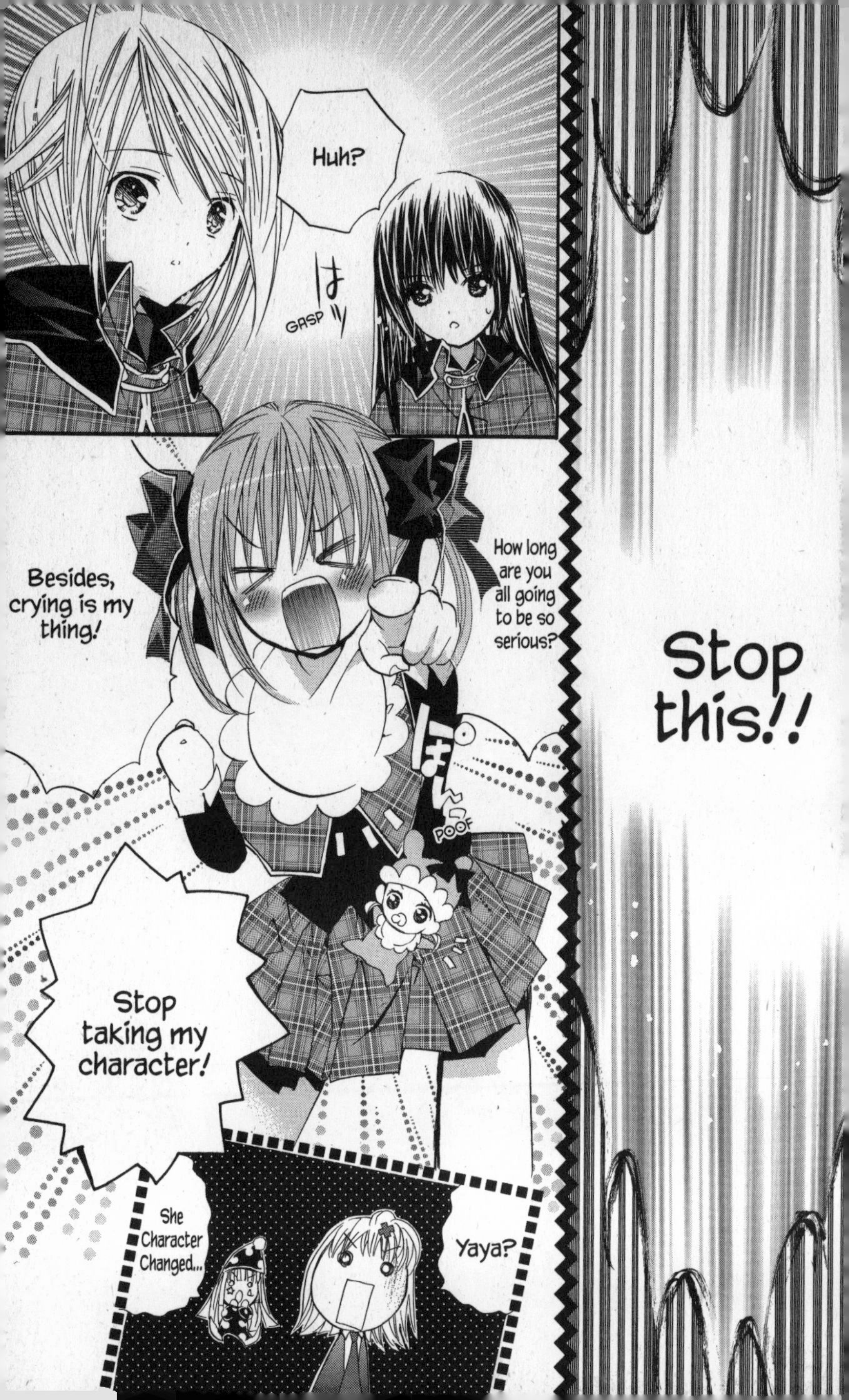
Stop this!!
Huh?
はッ
GASP
How long are you all going to be so serious?
Besides, crying is my thing!
ぽんっ
POOF
Stop taking my character!
Yaya?
She Character Changed...

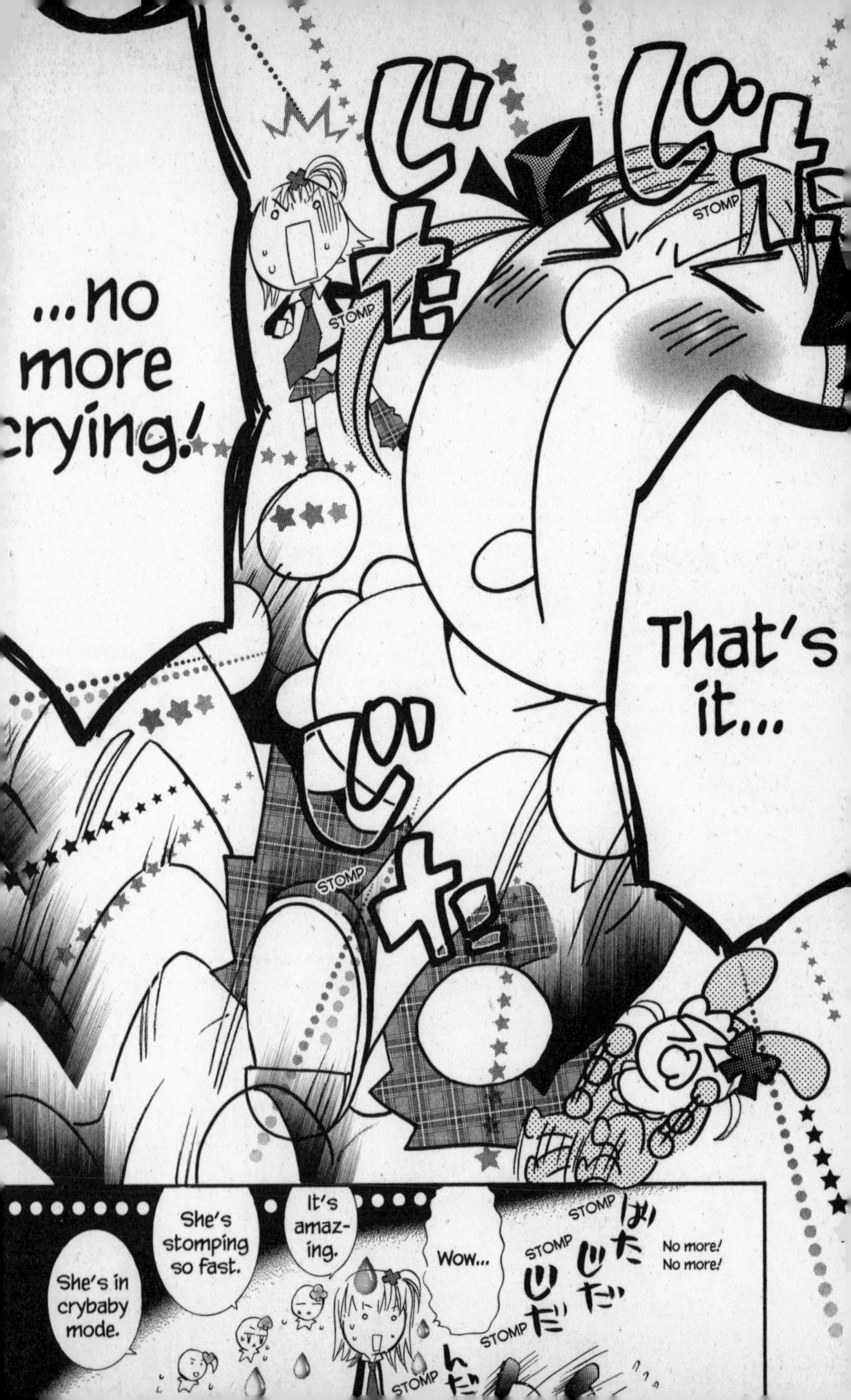
STOMP
STOMP
That's it...
...no more crying!
STOMP
No more! No more!
STOMP
STOMP
STOMP
STOMP
Wow...
It's amazing.
She's stomping so fast.
She's in crybaby mode.

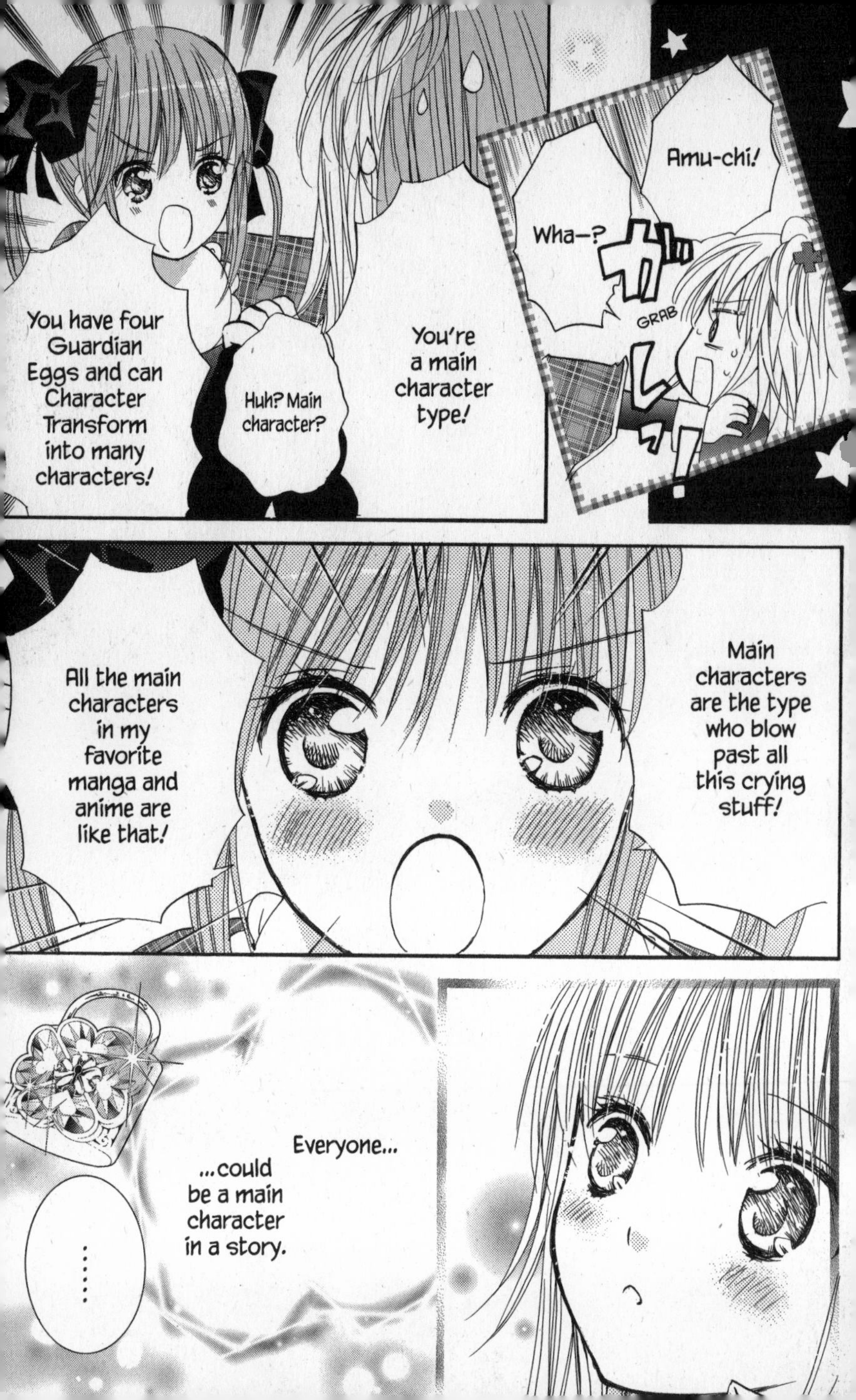
Amu-chi!
Wha-?
GRAB
You're a main character type!
Huh? Main character?
You have four Guardian Eggs and can Character Transform into many characters!
Main characters are the type who blow past all this crying stuff!
All the main characters in my favorite manga and anime are like that!
Everyone...
...could be a main character in a story.
......

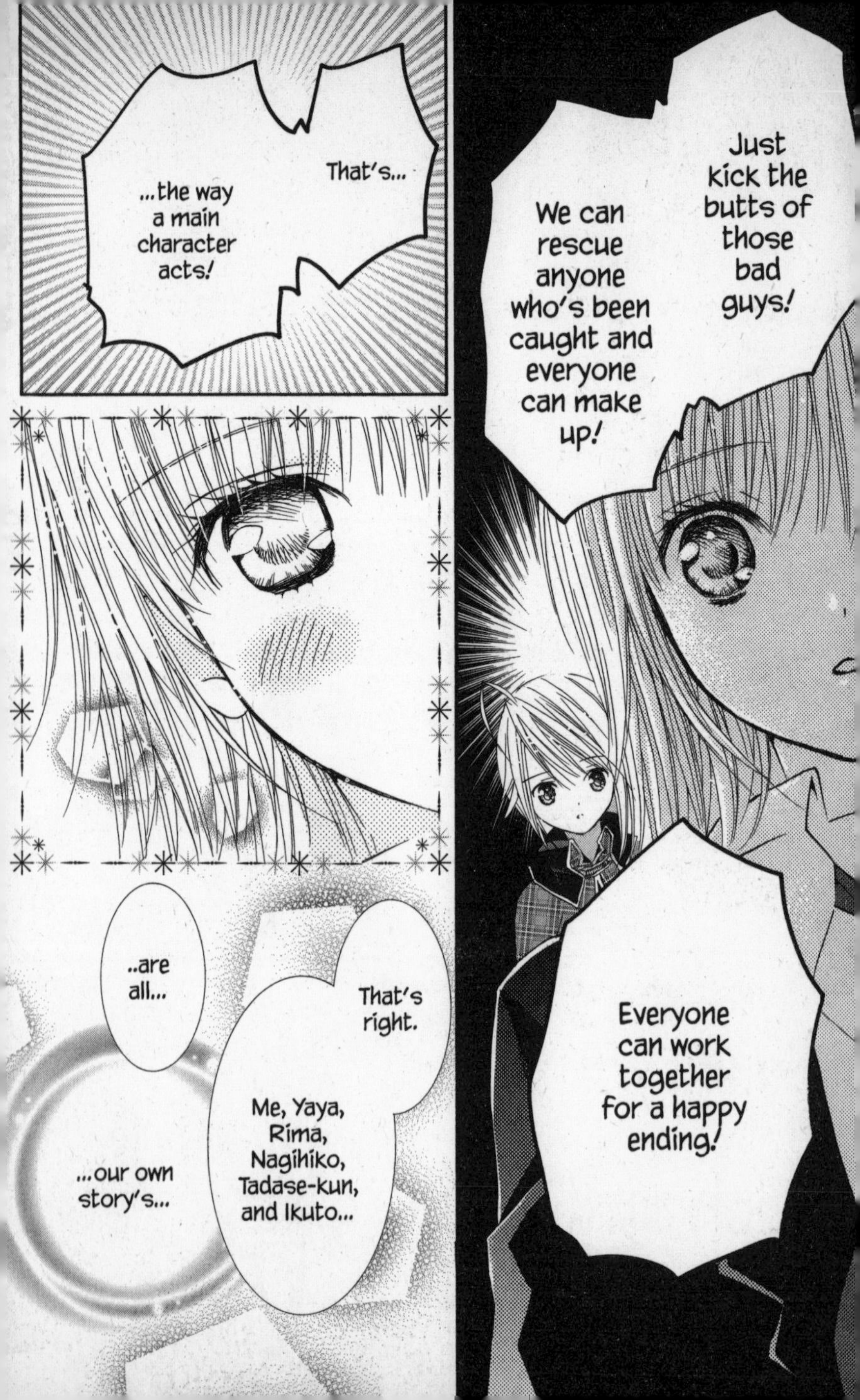
Just kick the butts of those bad guys!
We can rescue anyone who's been caught and everyone can make up!
Everyone can work together for a happy ending!
That's...
...the way a main character acts!
That's right.
..are all...
Me, Yaya, Rima, Nagihiko, Tadase-kun, and Ikuto...
...our own story's...

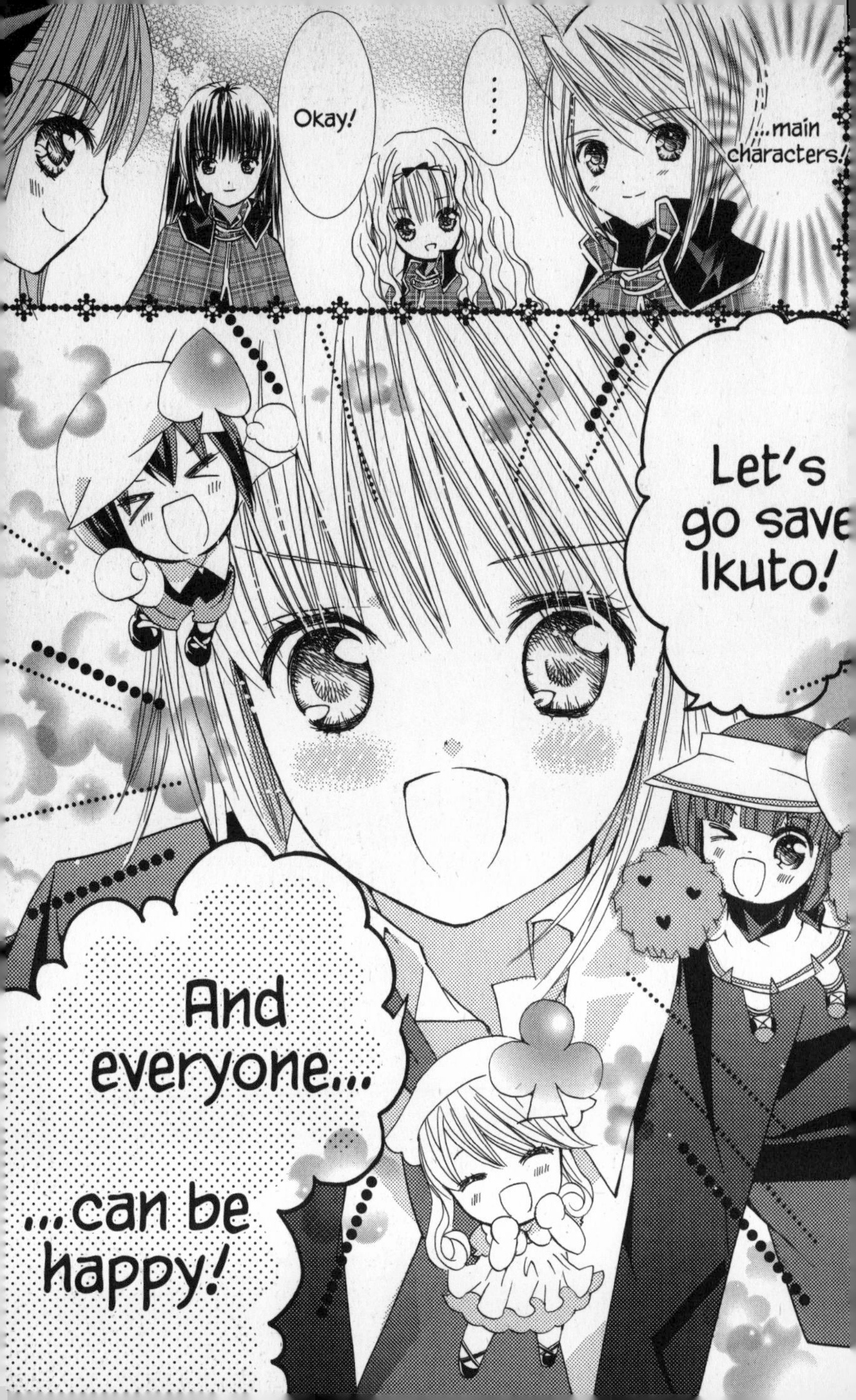
...main characters!
......
Okay!
Let's go save Ikuto!
And everyone...
...can be happy!

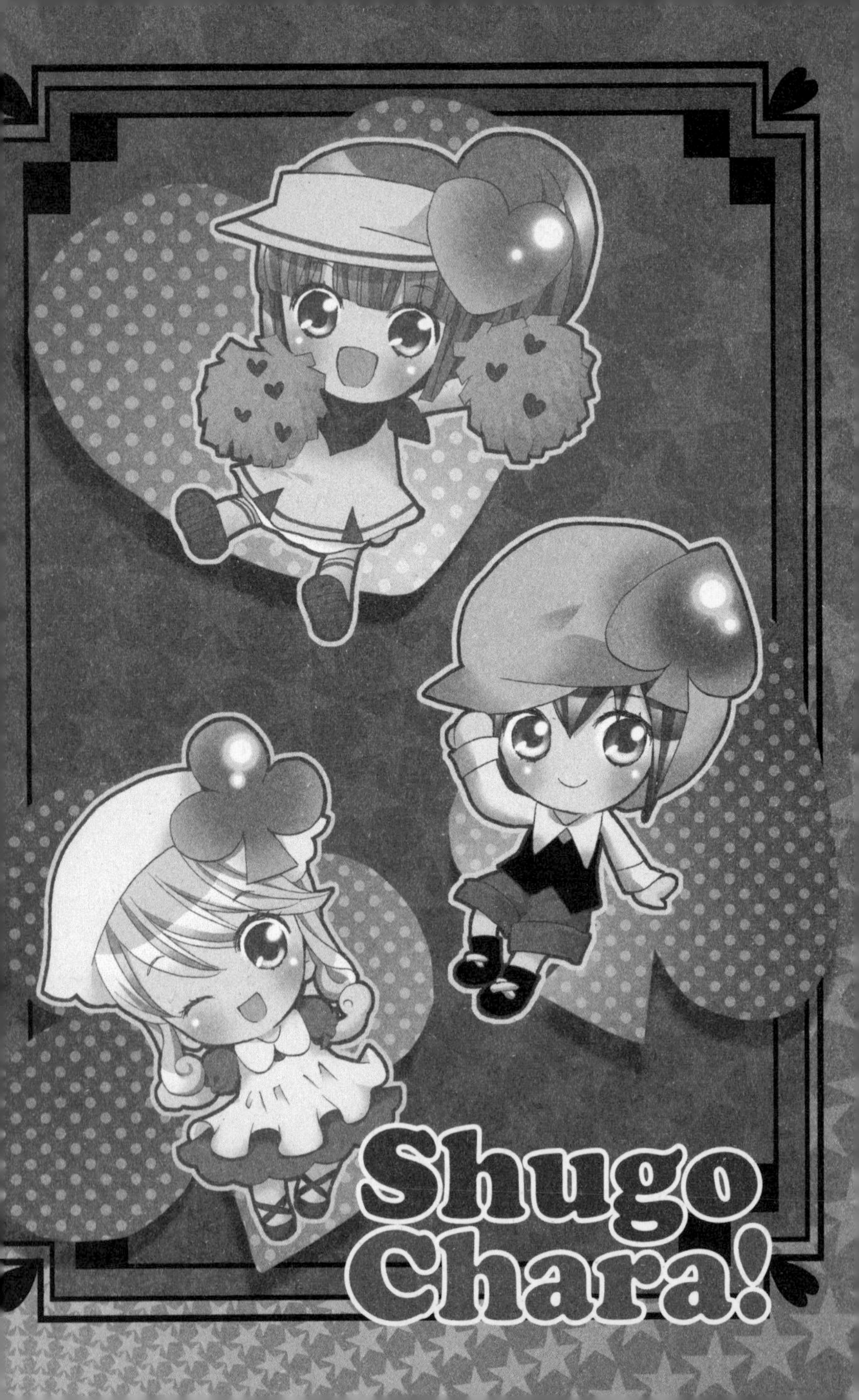
Shugo
Chara!

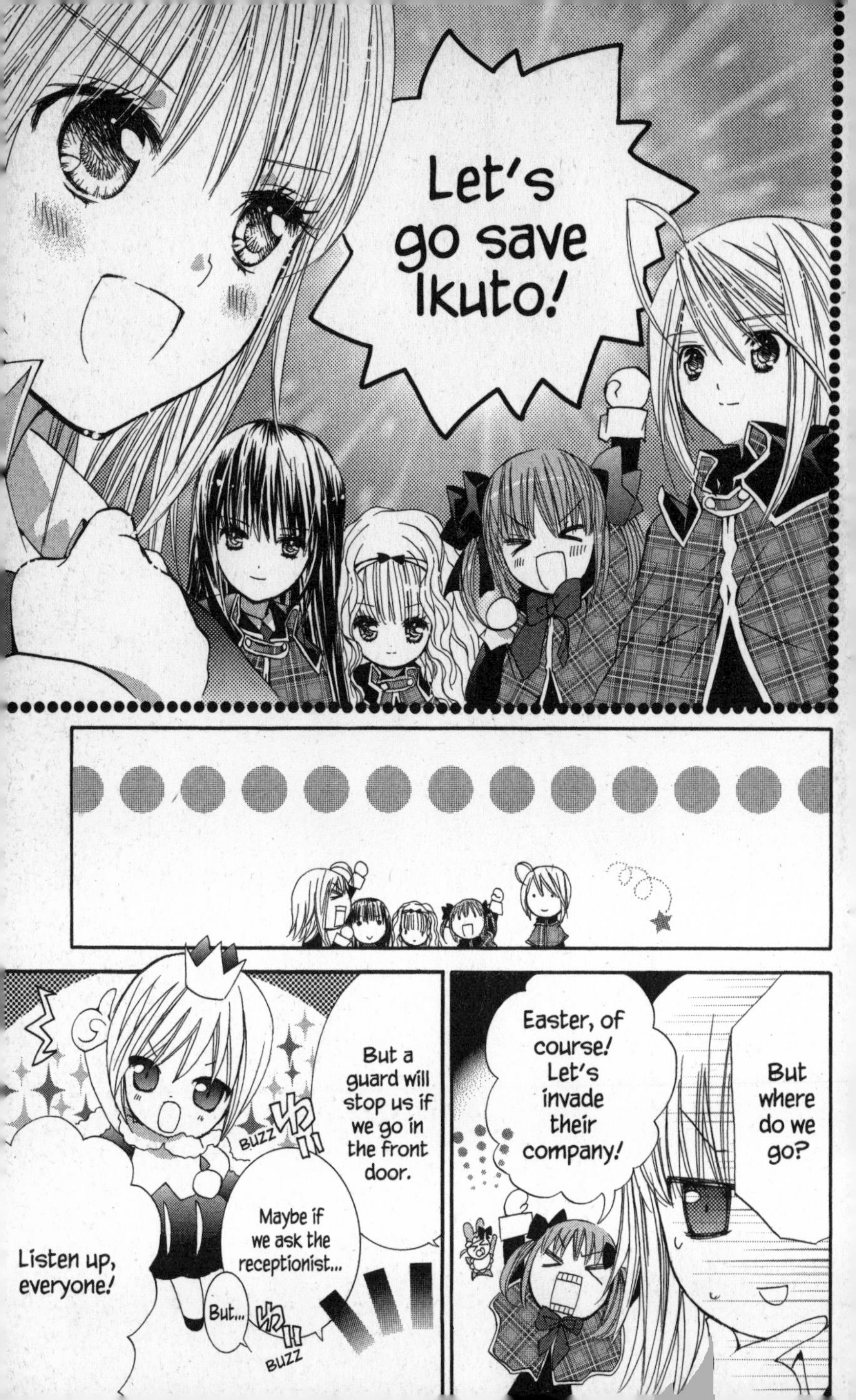
Let's go save Ikuto!
But where do we go?
Easter, of course! Let's invade their company!
But a guard will stop us if we go in the front door.
BUZZ
Maybe if we ask the receptionist...
But...
BUZZ
Listen up, everyone!

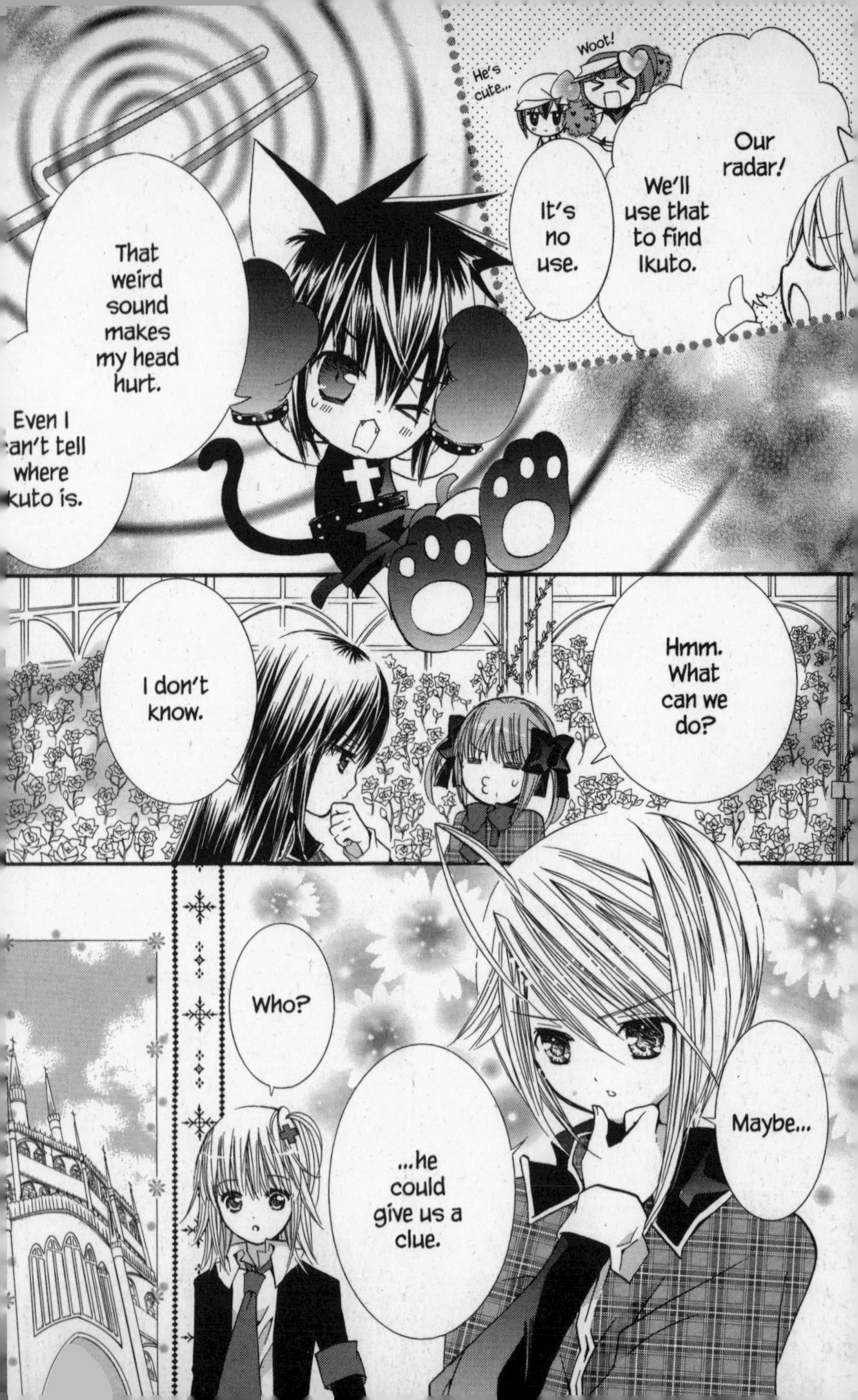

Our radar!
We'll use that to find Ikuto.
Woot!
He's cute...
It's no use.
That weird sound makes my head hurt.
Even I an't tell where kuto is.
Hmm. What can we do?
I don't know.
Maybe...
...he could give us a clue.
Who?

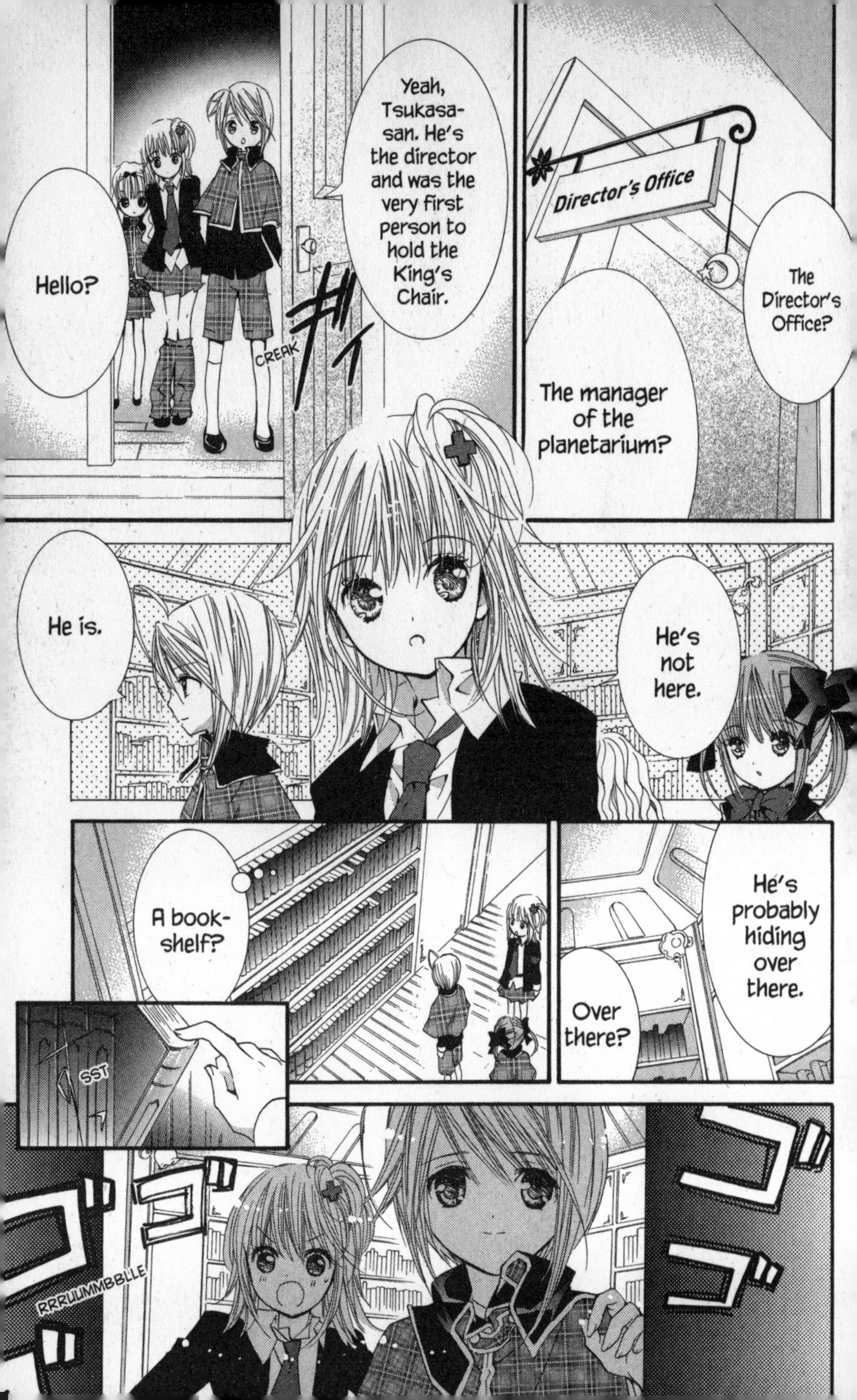
Director's Office
The Director's Office?
The manager of the planetarium?
Yeah, Tsukasa-san. He's the director and was the very first person to hold the King's Chair.
CREAK
Hello?
He's not here.
He is.
He's probably hiding over there.
Over there?
A book-shelf?
SST
RRRUUMMBBLLE

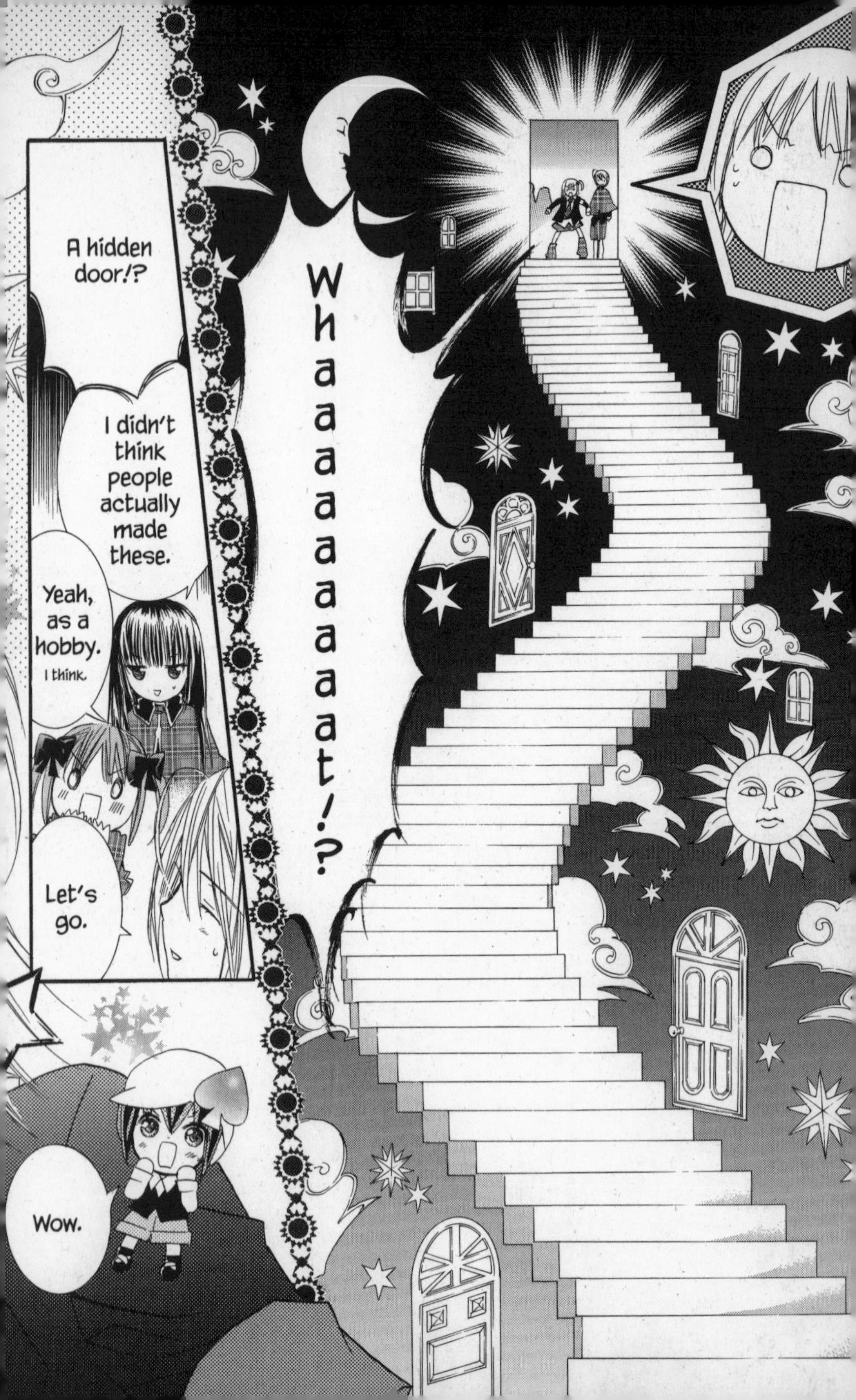
Whaaaaaaaat!?
A hidden door!?
I didn't think people actually made these.
Yeah, as a hobby.
I think.
Let's go.
Wow.

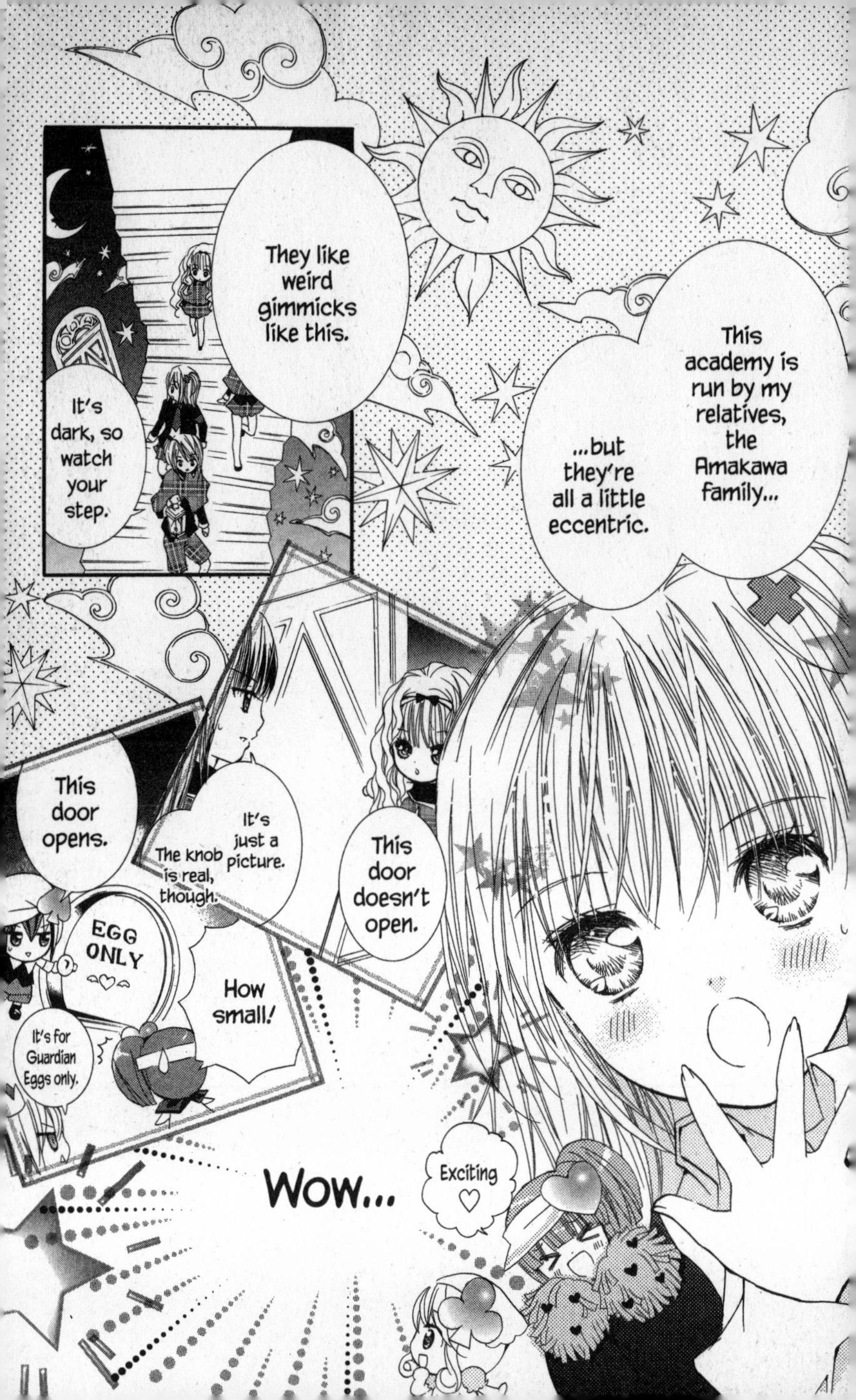
This academy is run by my relatives, the Amakawa family...
...but they're all a little eccentric.
They like weird gimmicks like this.
It's dark, so watch your step.
This door doesn't open.
It's just a picture.
The knob is real, though.
This door opens.
EGG ONLY
How small!
It's for Guardian Eggs only.
Exciting ♡
Wow...

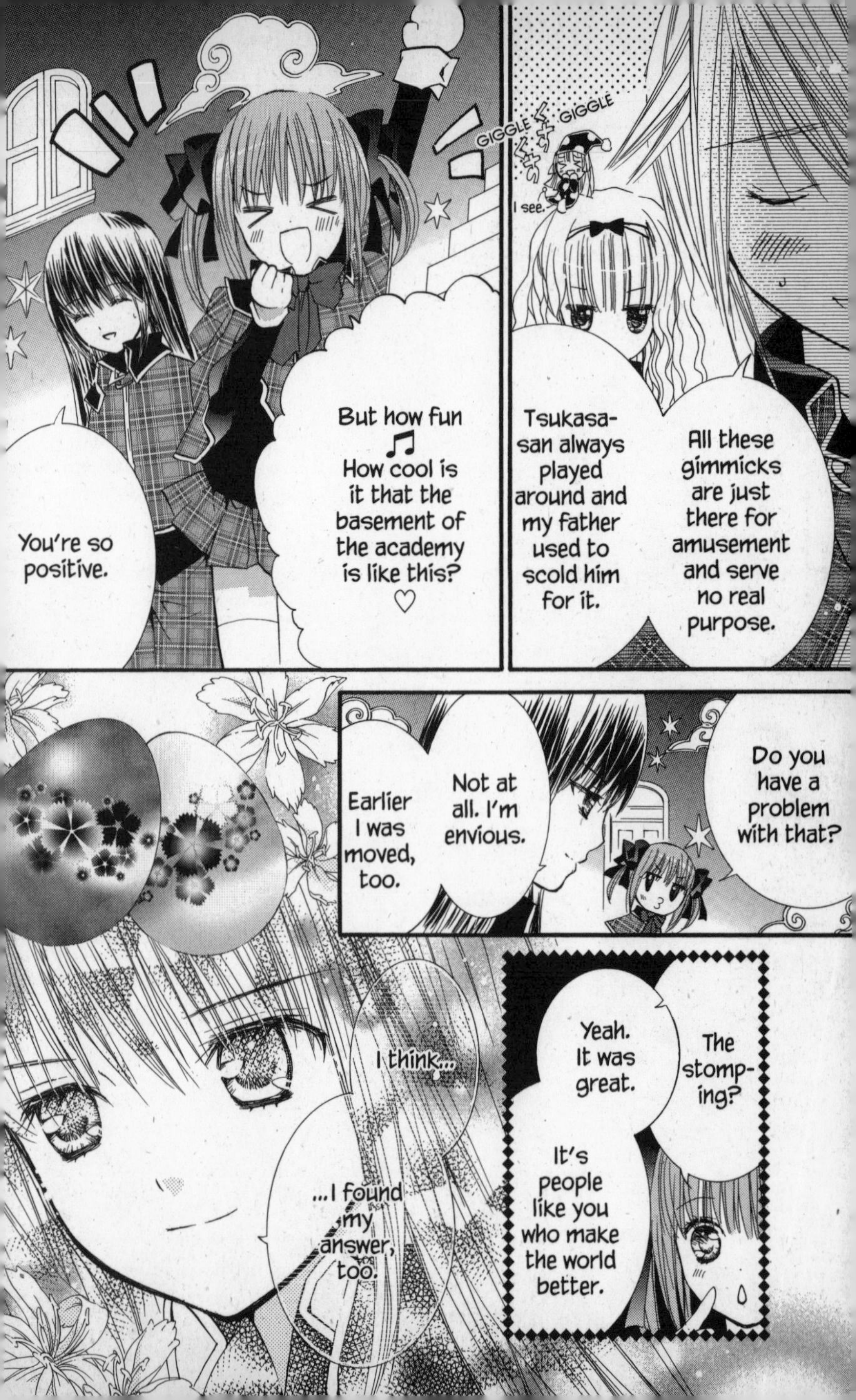
GIGGLE GIGGLE
I see.
All these gimmicks are just there for amusement and serve no real purpose.
Tsukasa-san always played around and my father used to scold him for it.
But how fun ♫ How cool is it that the basement of the academy is like this? ♡
You're so positive.
Do you have a problem with that?
Not at all. I'm envious.
Earlier I was moved, too.
The stomp-ing?
Yeah. It was great.
It's people like you who make the world better.
I think...
...I found my answer, too.

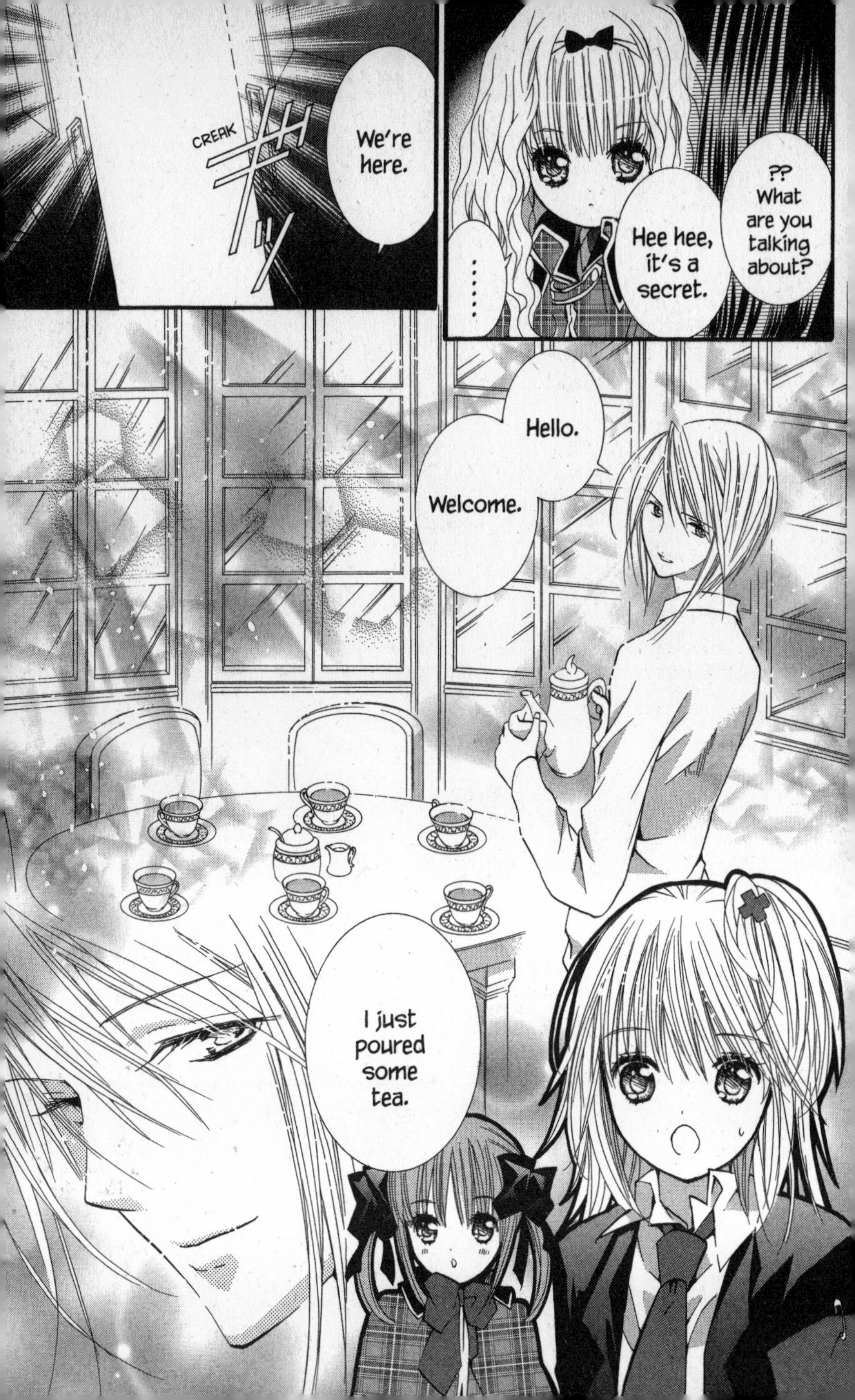
?? What are you talking about?
Hee hee, it's a secret.
......
CREAK
We're here.
Hello.
Welcome.
I just poured some tea.

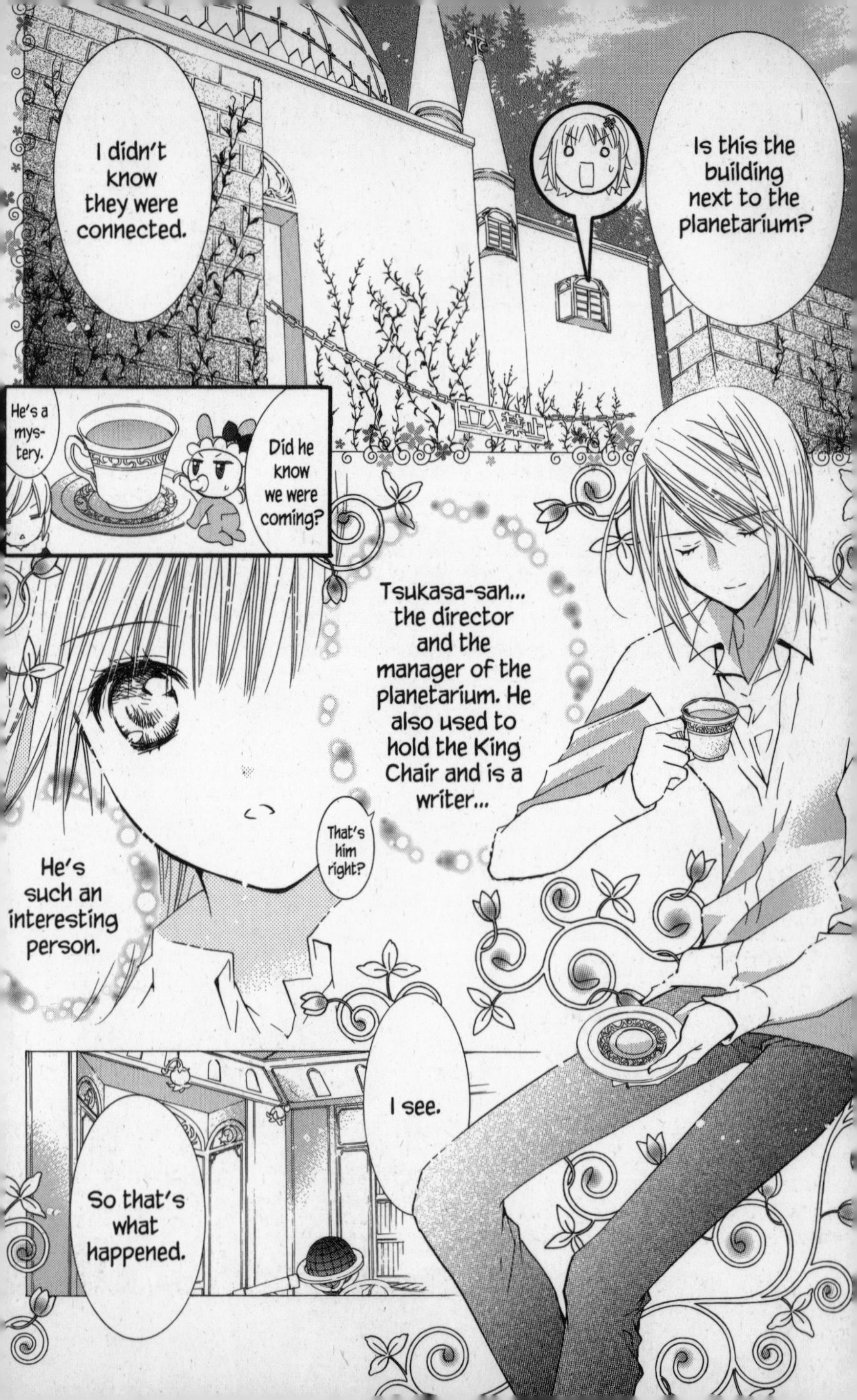
Is this the building next to the planetarium?
I didn't know they were connected.
立入禁止
Did he know we were coming?
He's a mys-tery.
Tsukasa-san... the director and the manager of the planetarium. He also used to hold the King Chair and is a writer...
That's him right?
He's such an interesting person.
I see.
So that's what happened.

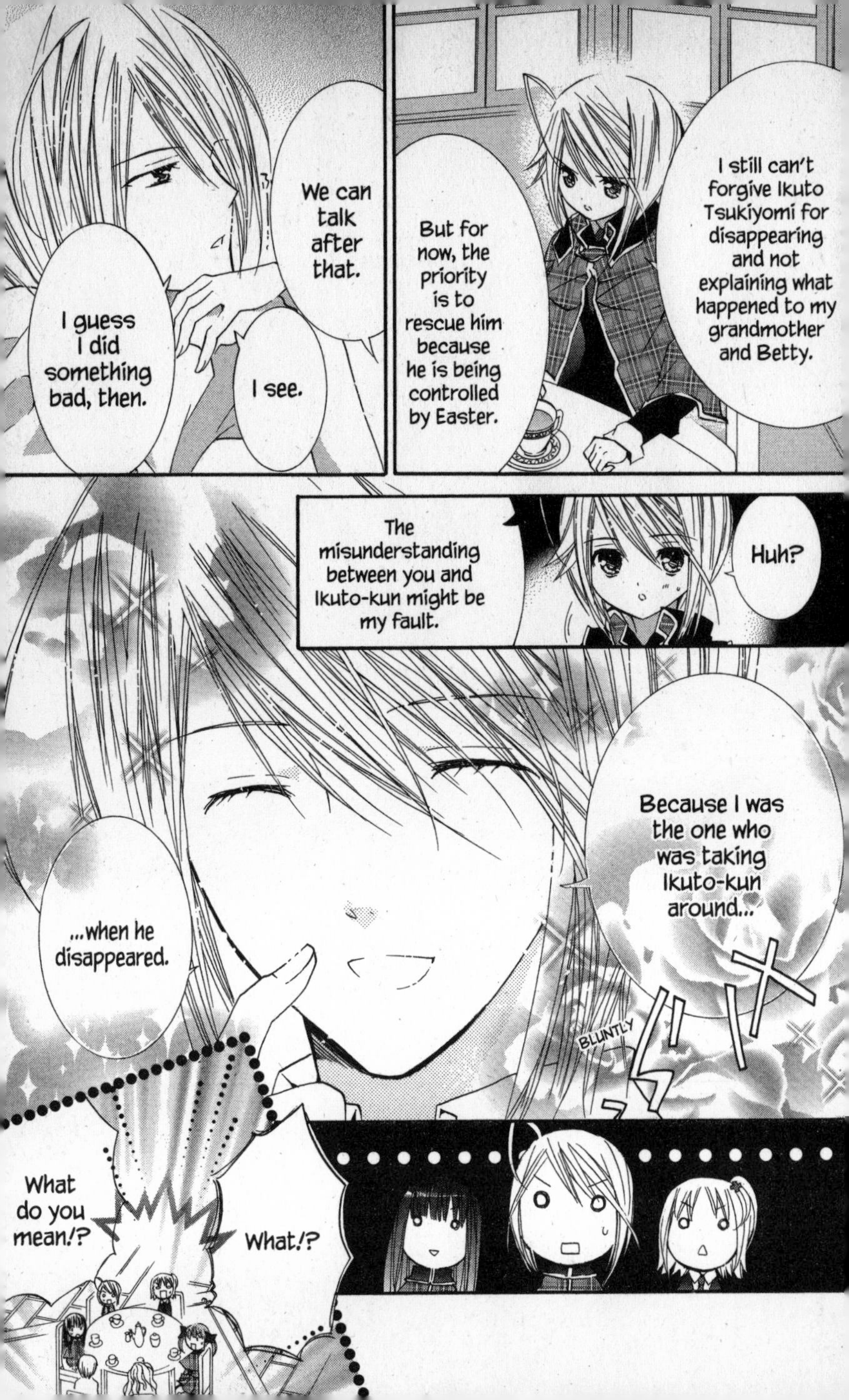
I still can't forgive Ikuto Tsukiyomi for disappearing and not explaining what happened to my grandmother and Betty.
But for now, the priority is to rescue him because he is being controlled by Easter.
We can talk after that.
I see.
I guess I did something bad, then.
The misunderstanding between you and Ikuto-kun might be my fault.
Huh?
Because I was the one who was taking Ikuto-kun around...
...when he disappeared.
BLUNTLY
What!?
What do you mean!?

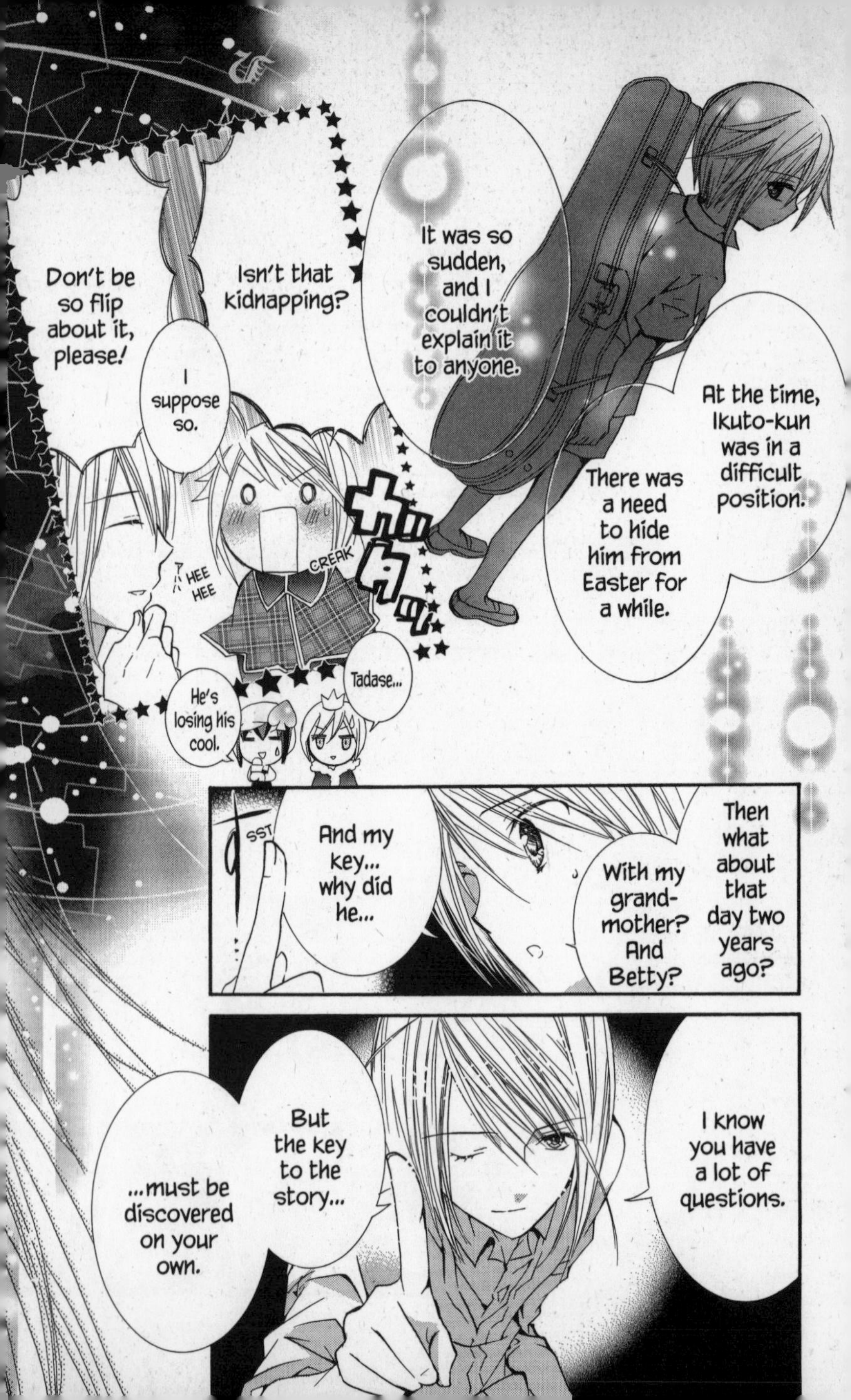
At the time, Ikuto-kun was in a difficult position.
There was a need to hide him from Easter for a while.
It was so sudden, and I couldn't explain it to anyone.
Isn't that kidnapping?
Don't be so flip about it, please!
I suppose so.
HEE HEE
CREAK
Tadase...
He's losing his cool.
Then what about that day two years ago?
With my grandmother? And Betty?
SST
And my key... why did he...
I know you have a lot of questions.
But the key to the story...
...must be discovered on your own.

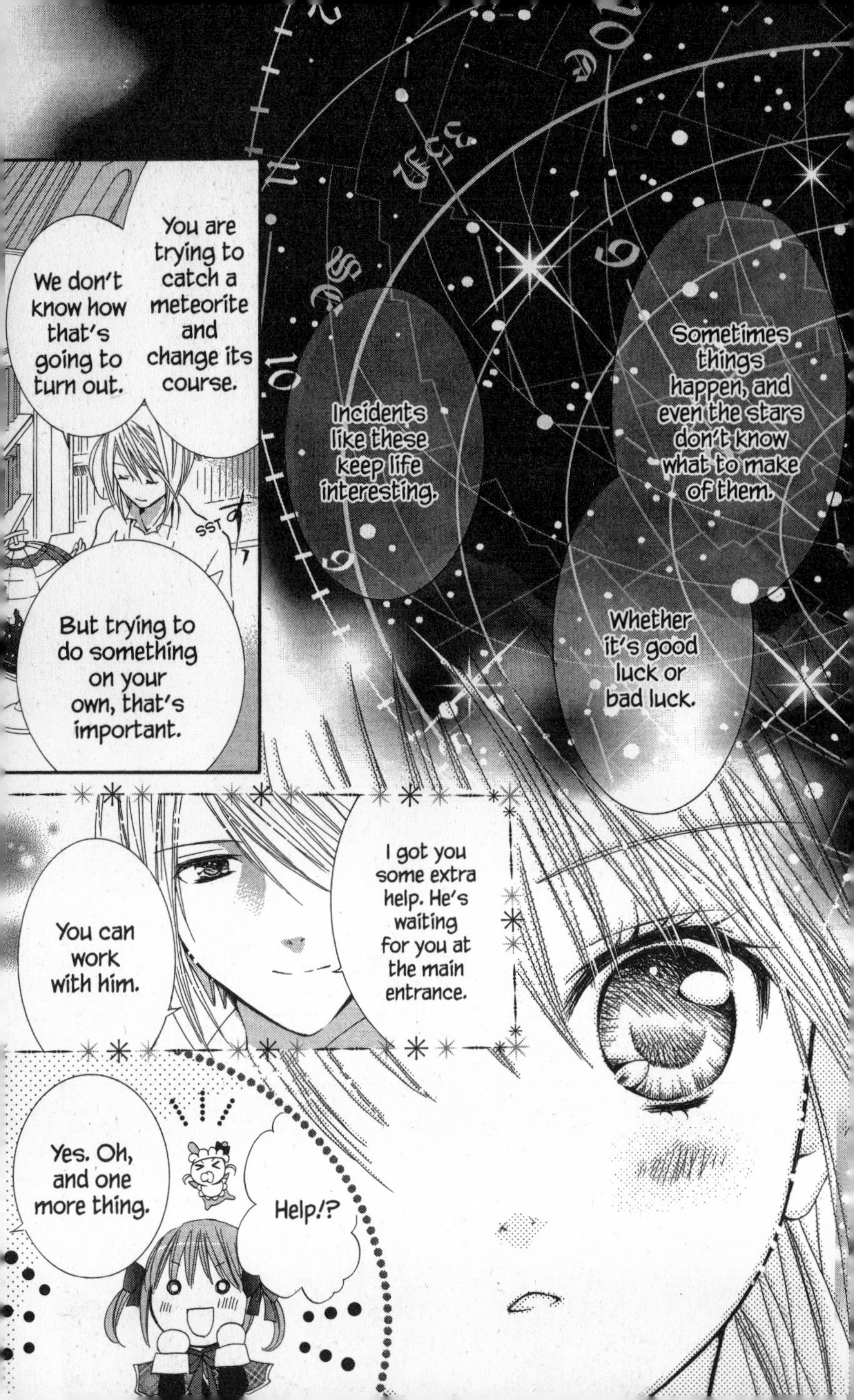
Sometimes things happen, and even the stars don't know what to make of them.
Whether it's good luck or bad luck.
Incidents like these keep life interesting.
You are trying to catch a meteorite and change its course.
We don't know how that's going to turn out.
SST
But trying to do something on your own, that's important.
I got you some extra help. He's waiting for you at the main entrance.
You can work with him.
Help!?
Yes. Oh, and one more thing.

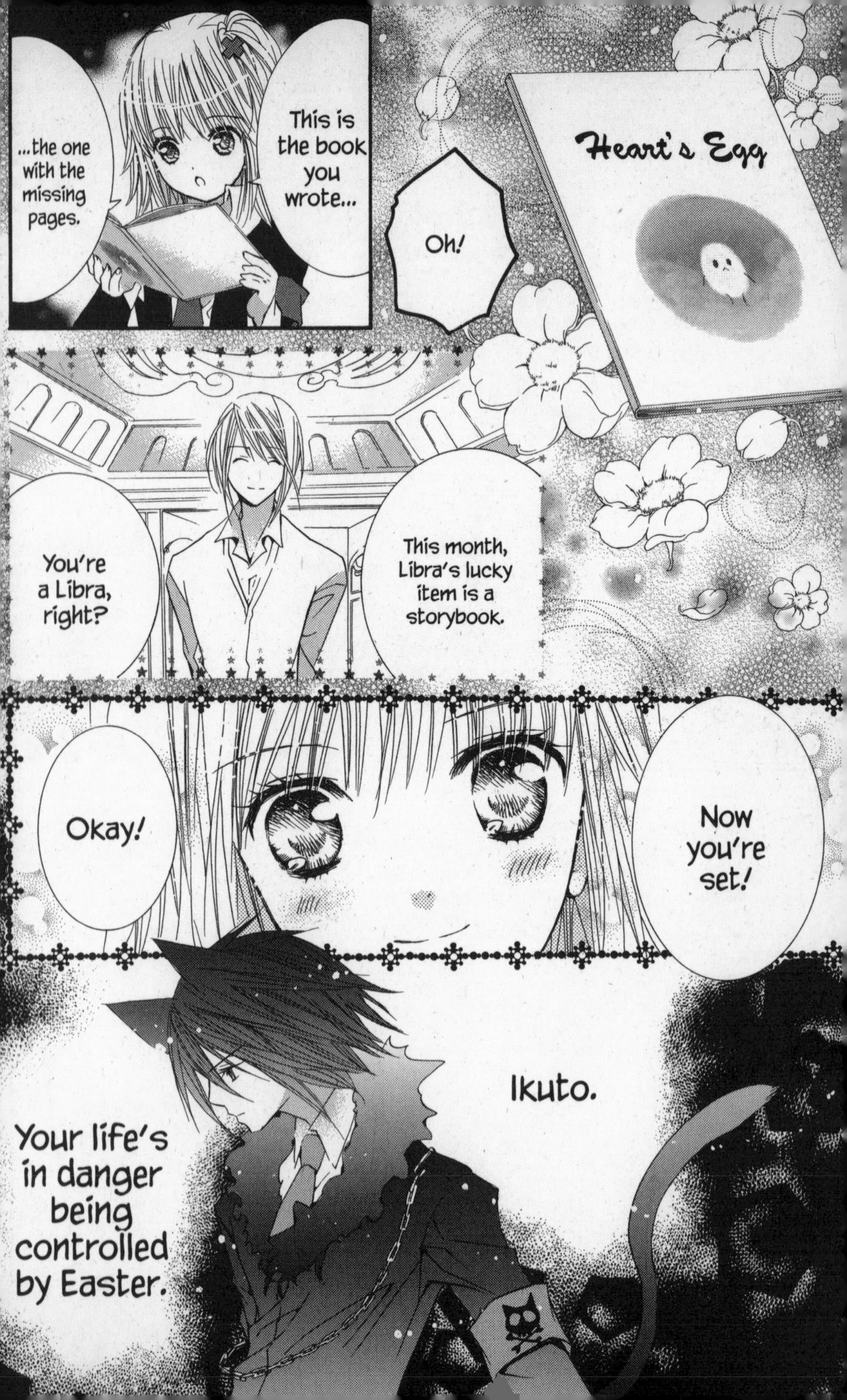

Heart's Egg
Oh!
This is the book you wrote...
...the one with the missing pages.
This month, Libra's lucky item is a storybook.
You're a Libra, right?
Now you're set!
Okay!
Ikuto.
Your life's in danger being controlled by Easter.

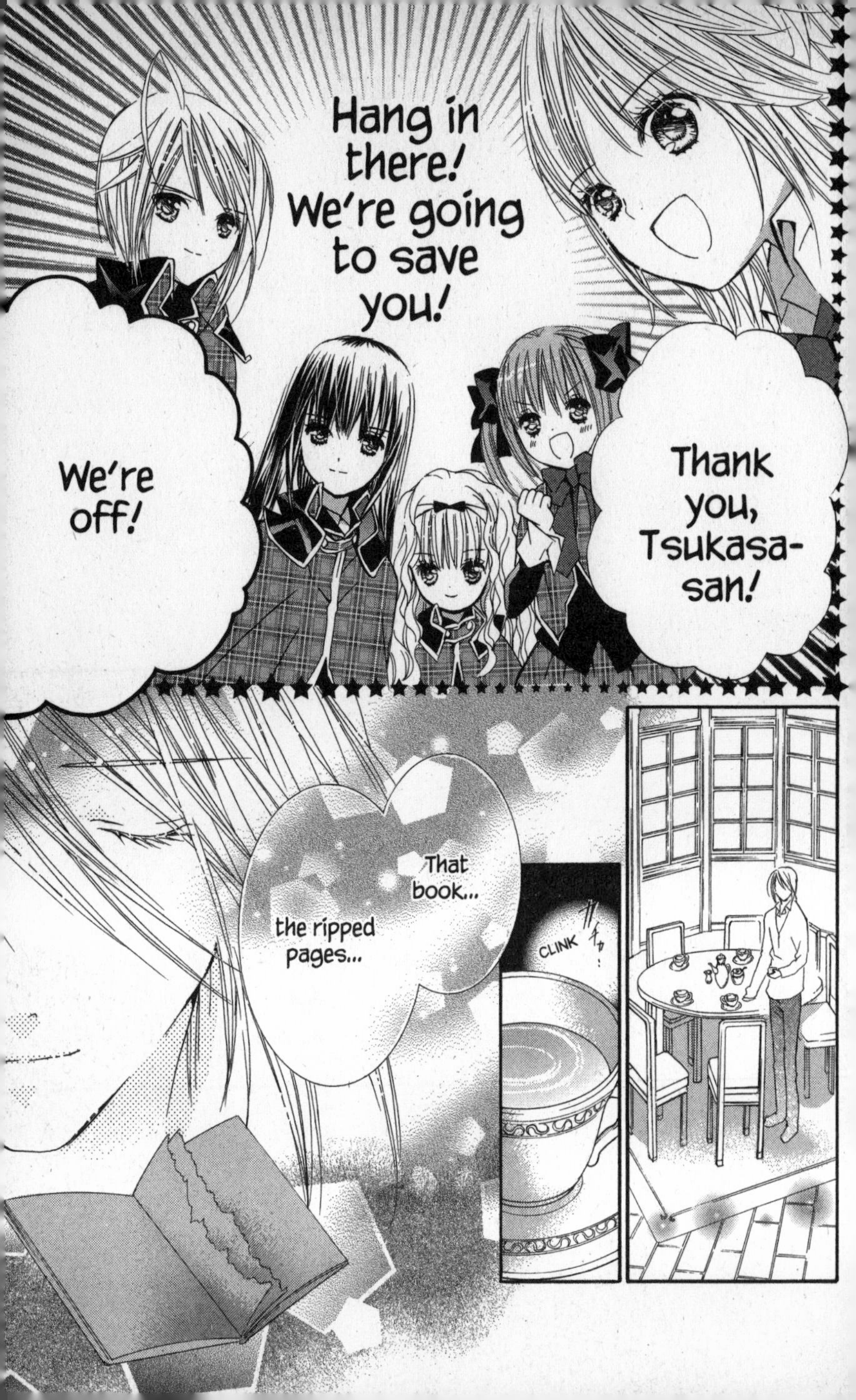

Hang in there! We're going to save you!
Thank you, Tsukasa-san!
We're off!
CLINK
That book...
the ripped pages...

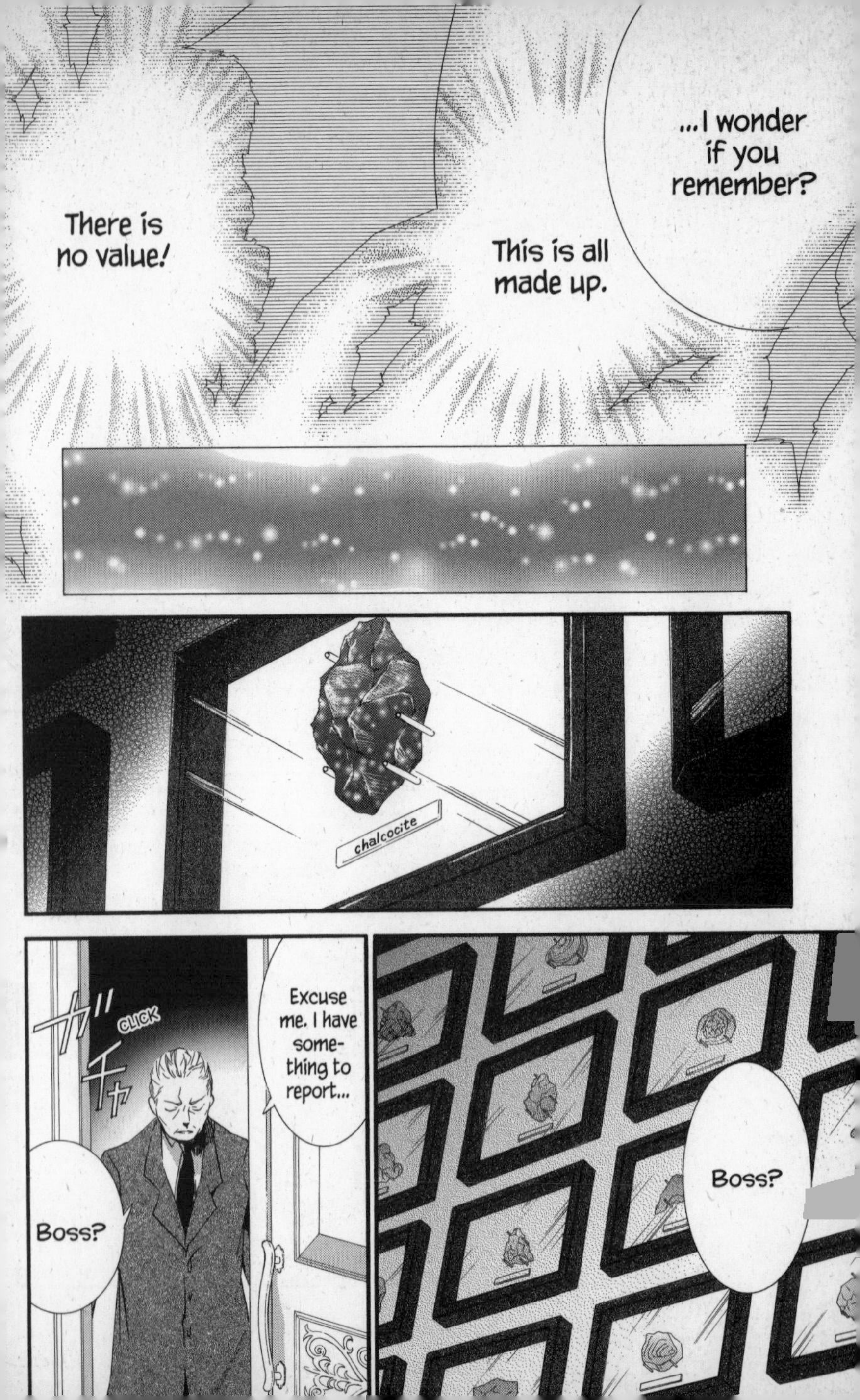
...I wonder if you remember?
This is all made up.
There is no value!
chalcocite
Boss?
Excuse me. I have something to report...
ガチャ
CLICK
Boss?

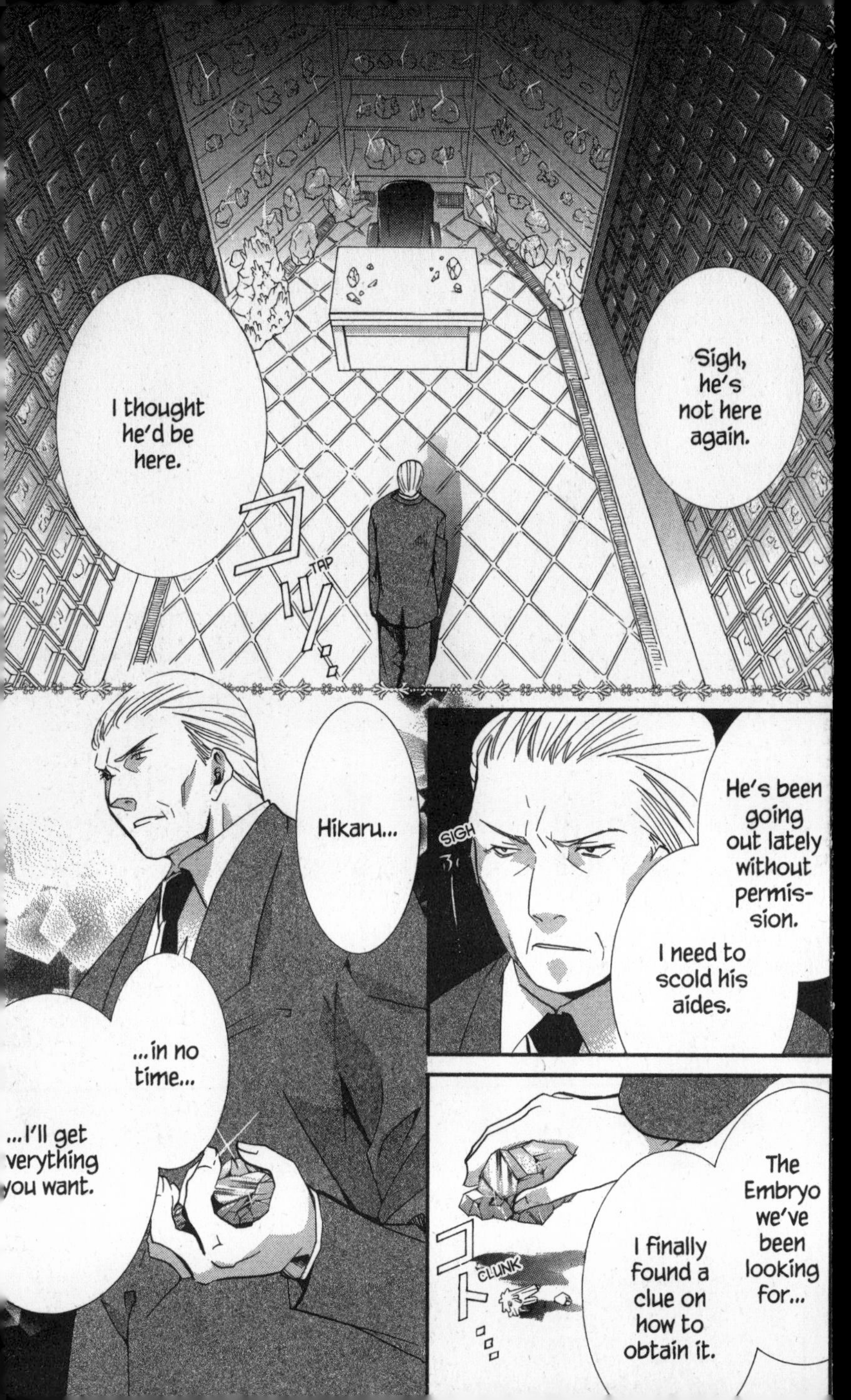
Sigh, he's not here again.
I thought he'd be here.
TAP
He's been going out lately without permission.
SIGH
I need to scold his aides.
The Embryo we've been looking for...
I finally found a clue on how to obtain it.
CLUNK
Hikaru...
...in no time...
...I'll get verything you want.

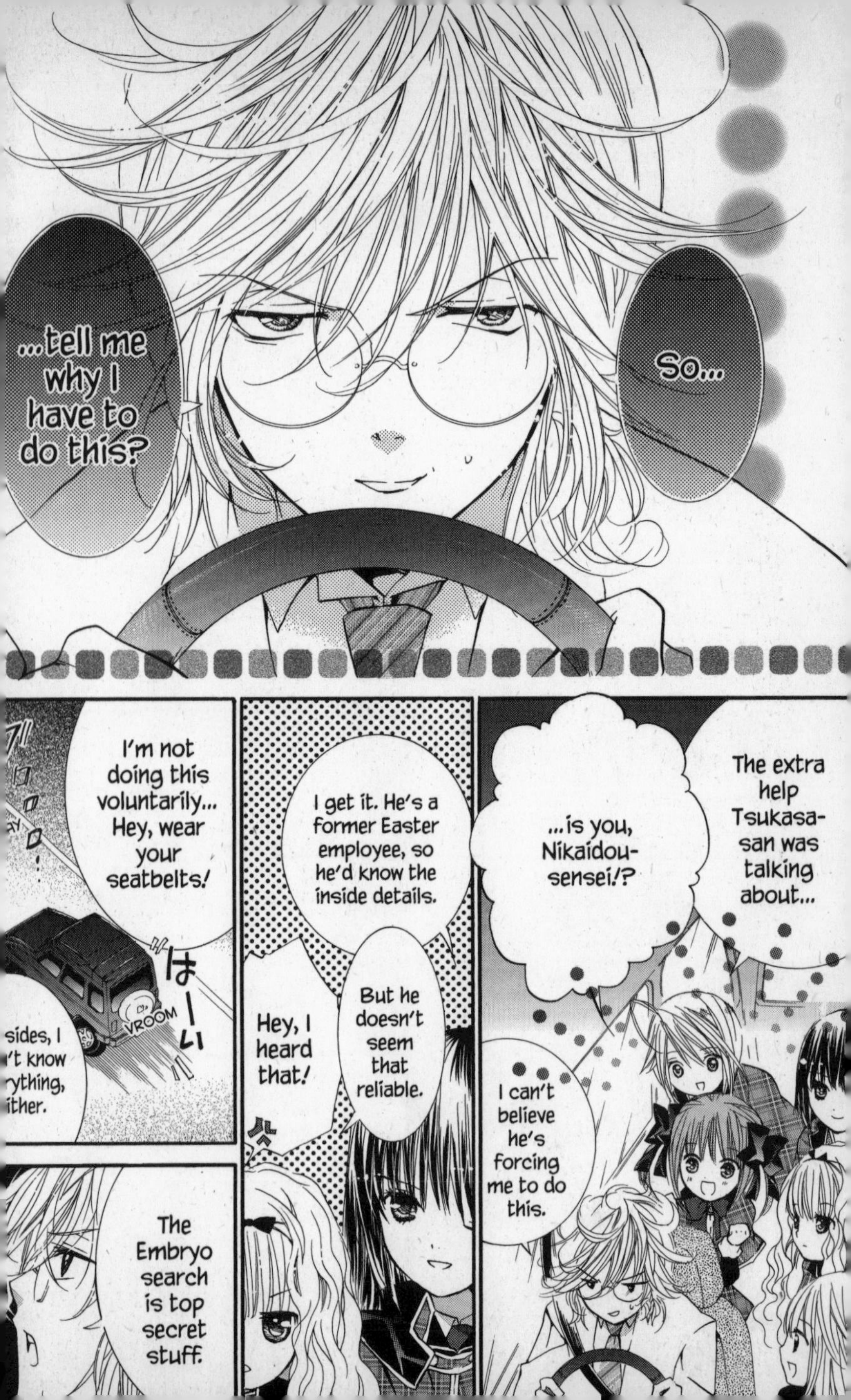
So...
...tell me why I have to do this?
The extra help Tsukasa-san was talking about...
...is you, Nikaidou-sensei!?
I can't believe he's forcing me to do this.
I get it. He's a former Easter employee, so he'd know the inside details.
But he doesn't seem that reliable.
Hey, I heard that!
I'm not doing this voluntarily... Hey, wear your seatbelts!
はーい
VROOM
sides, I 't know ything, ither.
The Embryo search is top secret stuff.

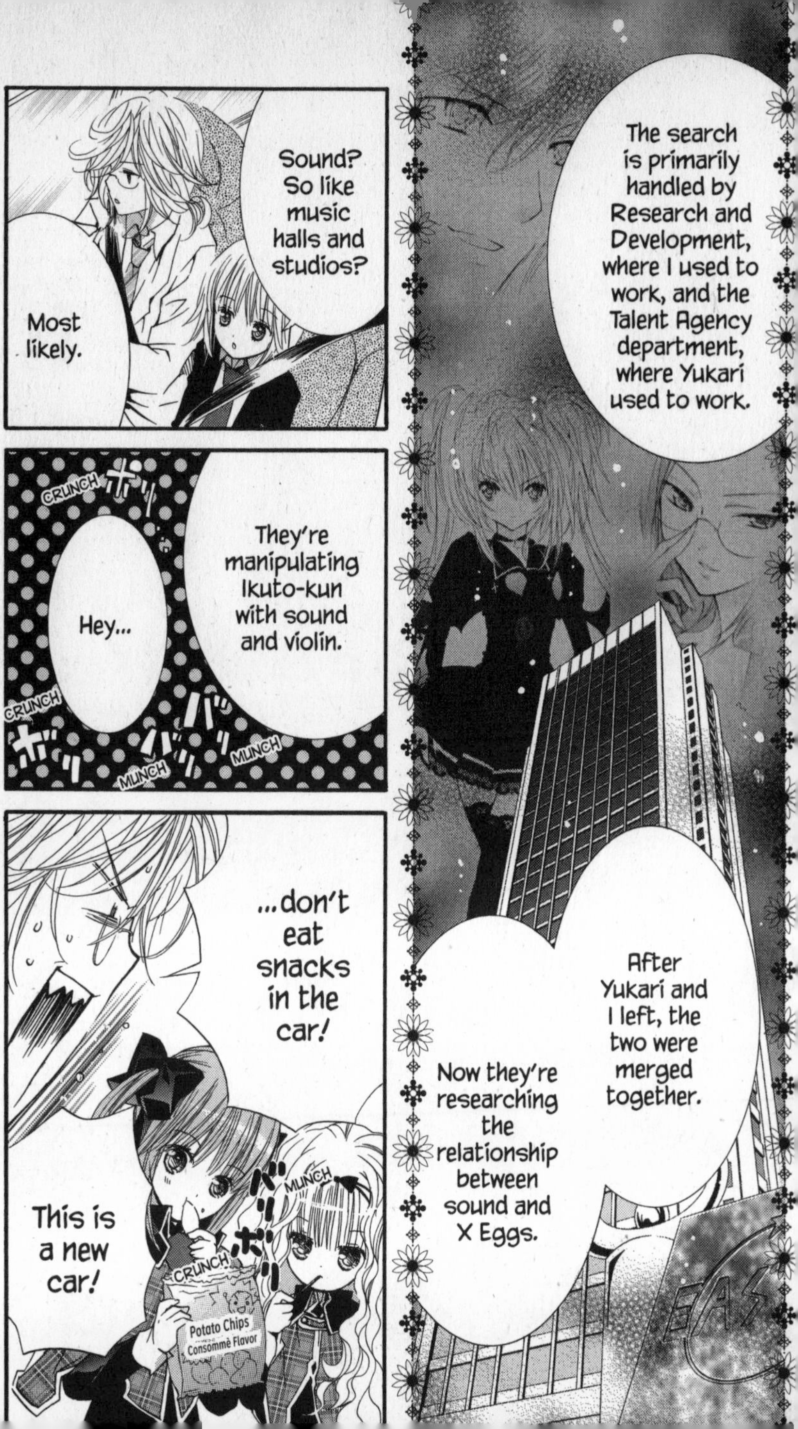

The search is primarily handled by Research and Development, where I used to work, and the Talent Agency department, where Yukari used to work.
After Yukari and I left, the two were merged together.
Now they're researching the relationship between sound and X Eggs.
Sound? So like music halls and studios?
Most likely.
CRUNCH
They're manipulating Ikuto-kun with sound and violin.
Hey...
CRUNCH
MUNCH
MUNCH
...don't eat snacks in the car!
MUNCH
CRUNCH
This is a new car!
Potato Chips
Consommé Flavor

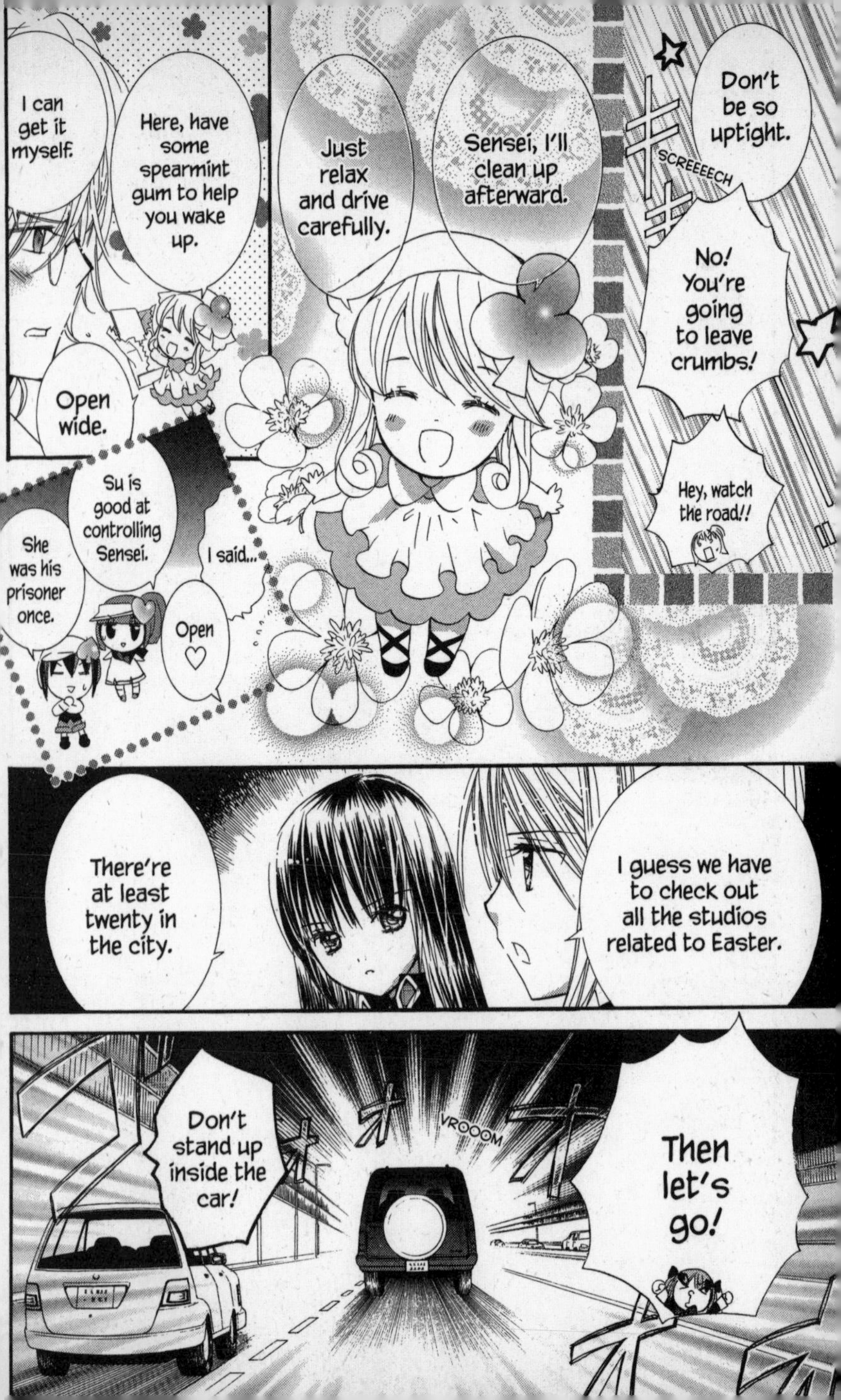
Don't be so uptight.
SCREEEECH
No! You're going to leave crumbs!
Hey, watch the road!!
Sensei, I'll clean up afterward.
Just relax and drive carefully.
Here, have some spearmint gum to help you wake up.
I can get it myself.
Open wide.
I said...
Open ♡
Su is good at controlling Sensei.
She was his prisoner once.
I guess we have to check out all the studios related to Easter.
There're at least twenty in the city.
Then let's go!
VROOOM
Don't stand up inside the car!

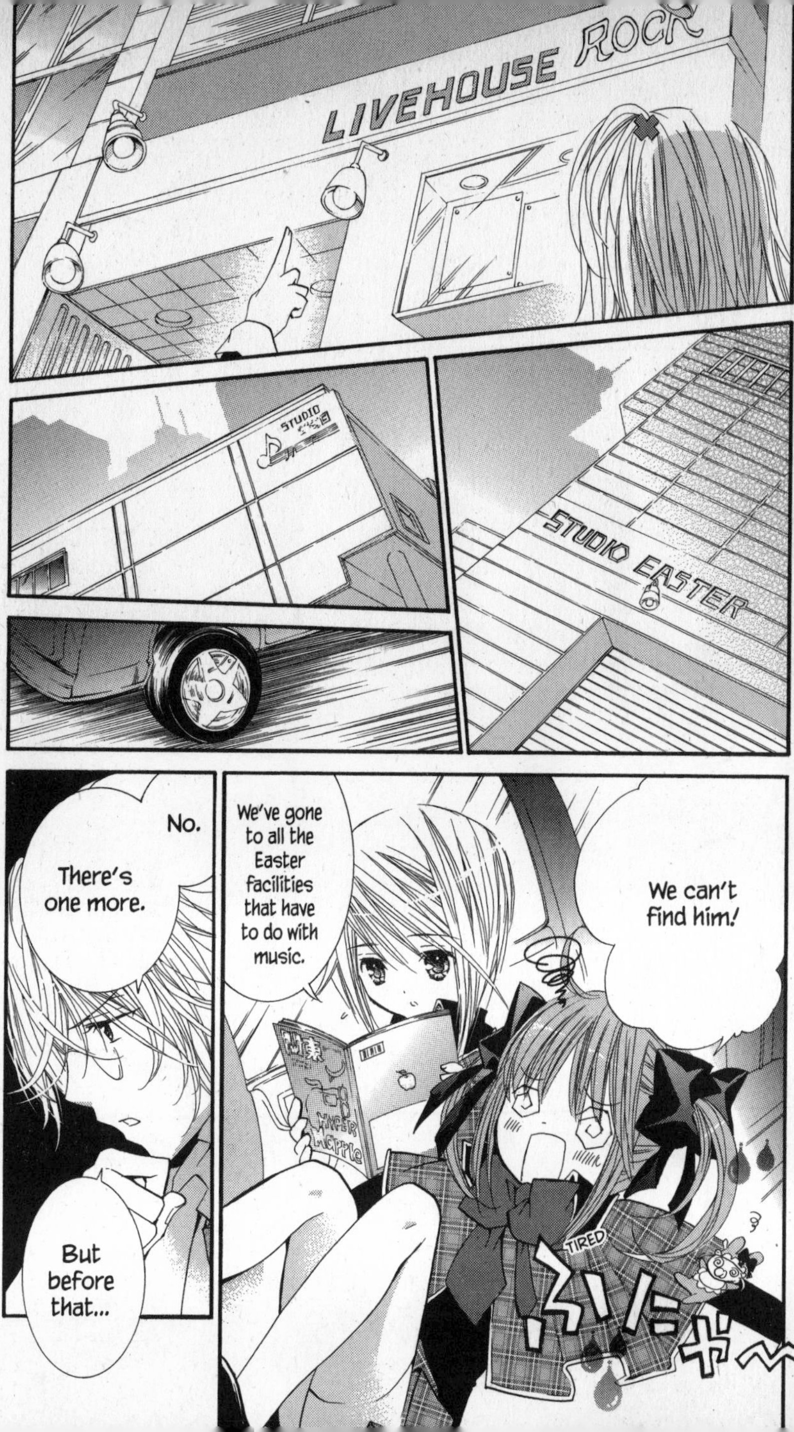
LIVEHOUSE ROCK
STUDIO EASTER
STUDIO
We can't find him!
TIRED
We've gone to all the Easter facilities that have to do with music.
No.
There's one more.
But before that...

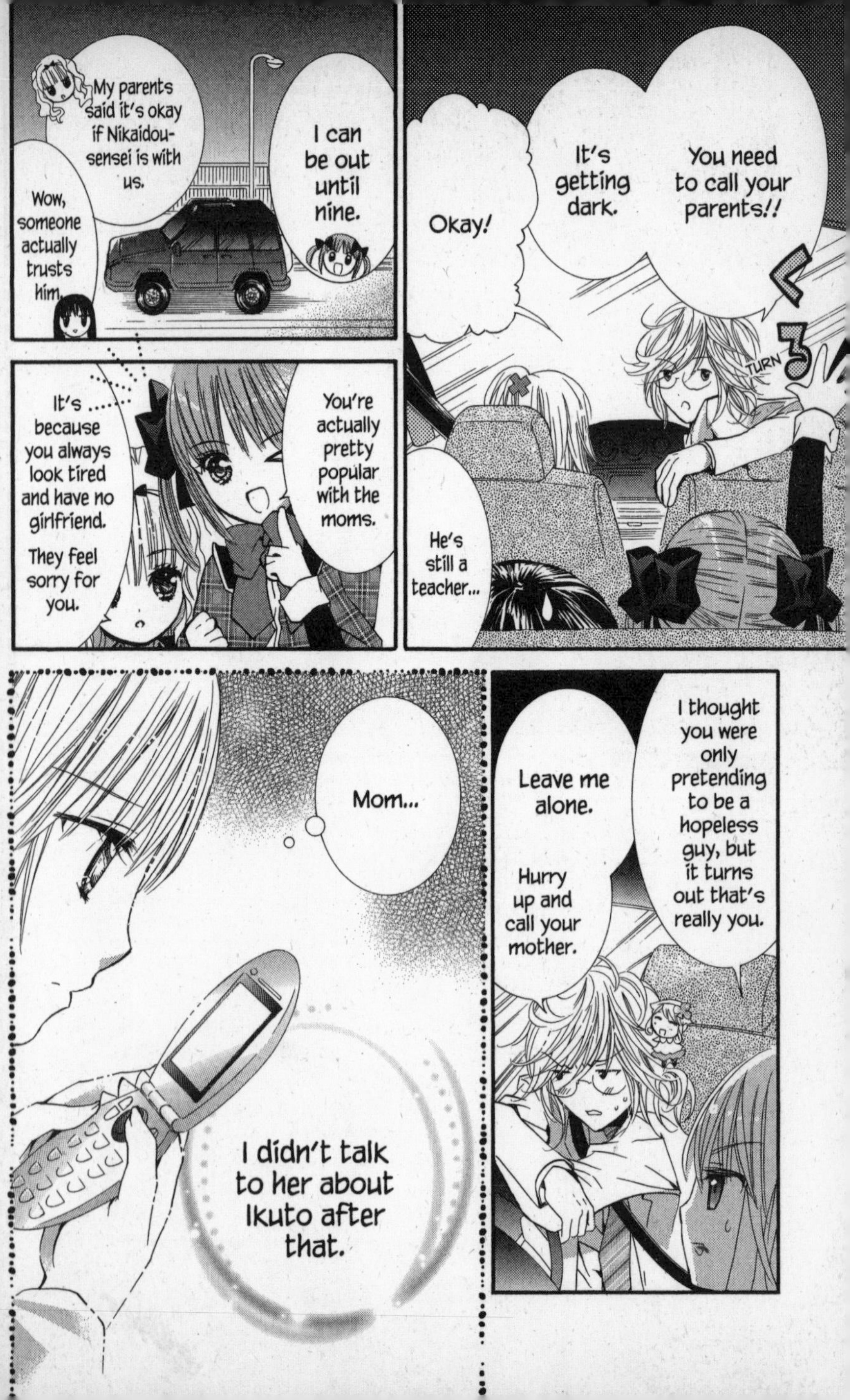
You need to call your parents!!
It's getting dark.
Okay!
TURN
He's still a teacher...
I can be out until nine.
My parents said it's okay if Nikaidou-sensei is with us.
Wow, someone actually trusts him.
You're actually pretty popular with the moms.
It's ...because you always look tired and have no girlfriend.
They feel sorry for you.
I thought you were only pretending to be a hopeless guy, but it turns out that's really you.
Leave me alone.
Hurry up and call your mother.
Mom...
I didn't talk to her about Ikuto after that.

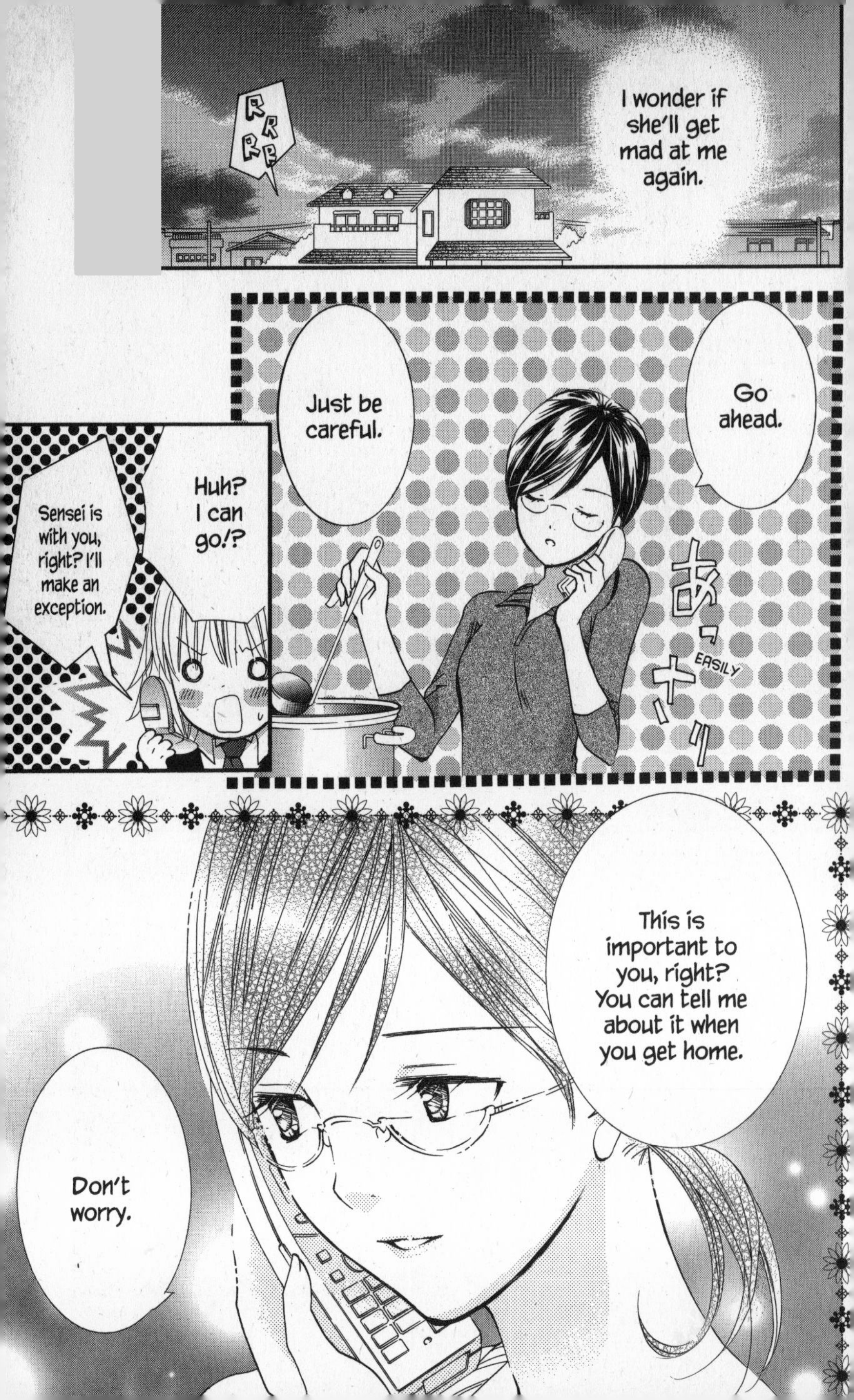
I wonder if she'll get mad at me again.
RRRR
Go ahead.
Just be careful.
あっサリ
EASILY
Huh? I can go!?
Sensei is with you, right? I'll make an exception.
This is important to you, right? You can tell me about it when you get home.
Don't worry.

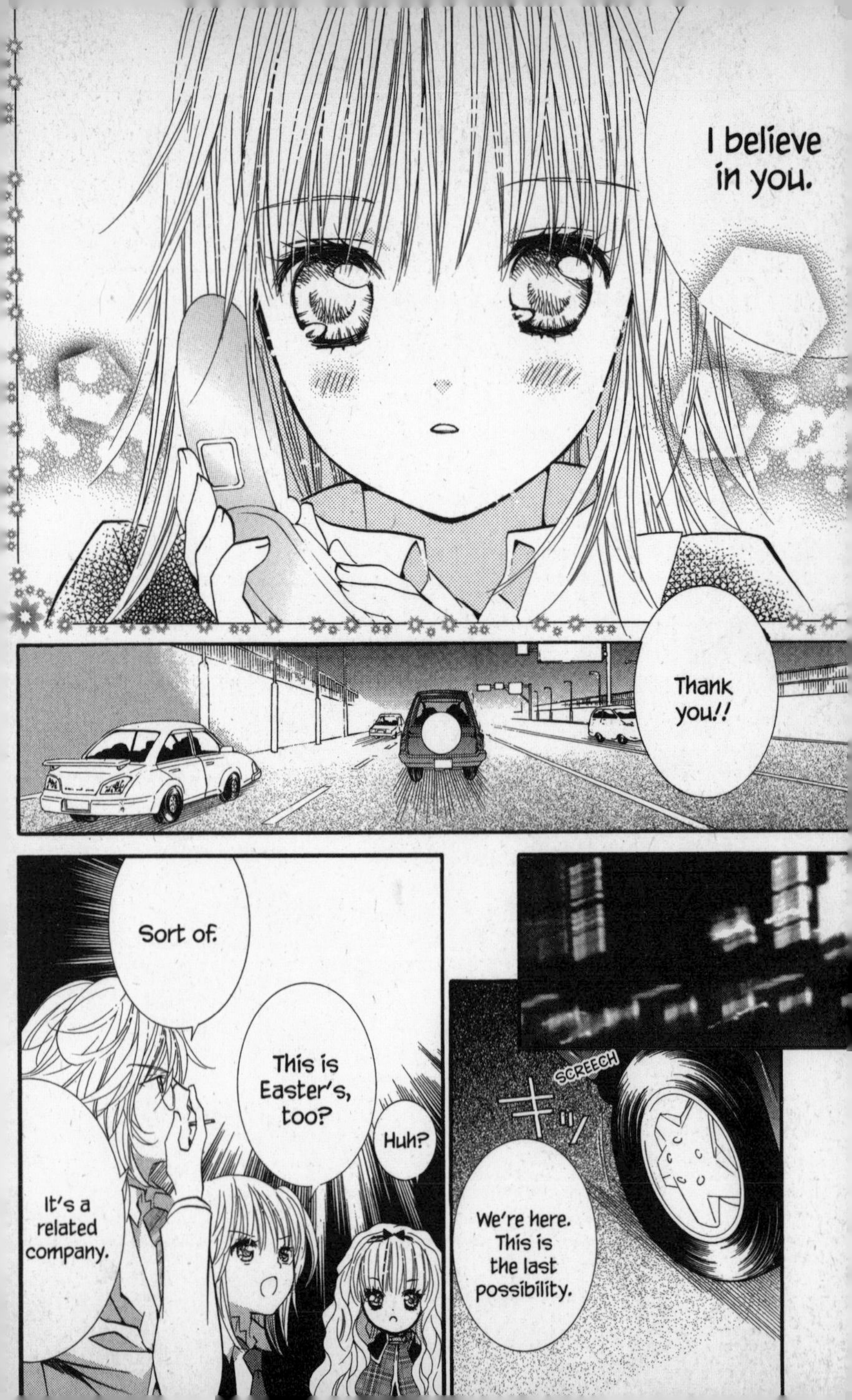
I believe in you.
Thank you!!
SCREECH
We're here. This is the last possibility.
Huh?
This is Easter's, too?
Sort of.
It's a related company.

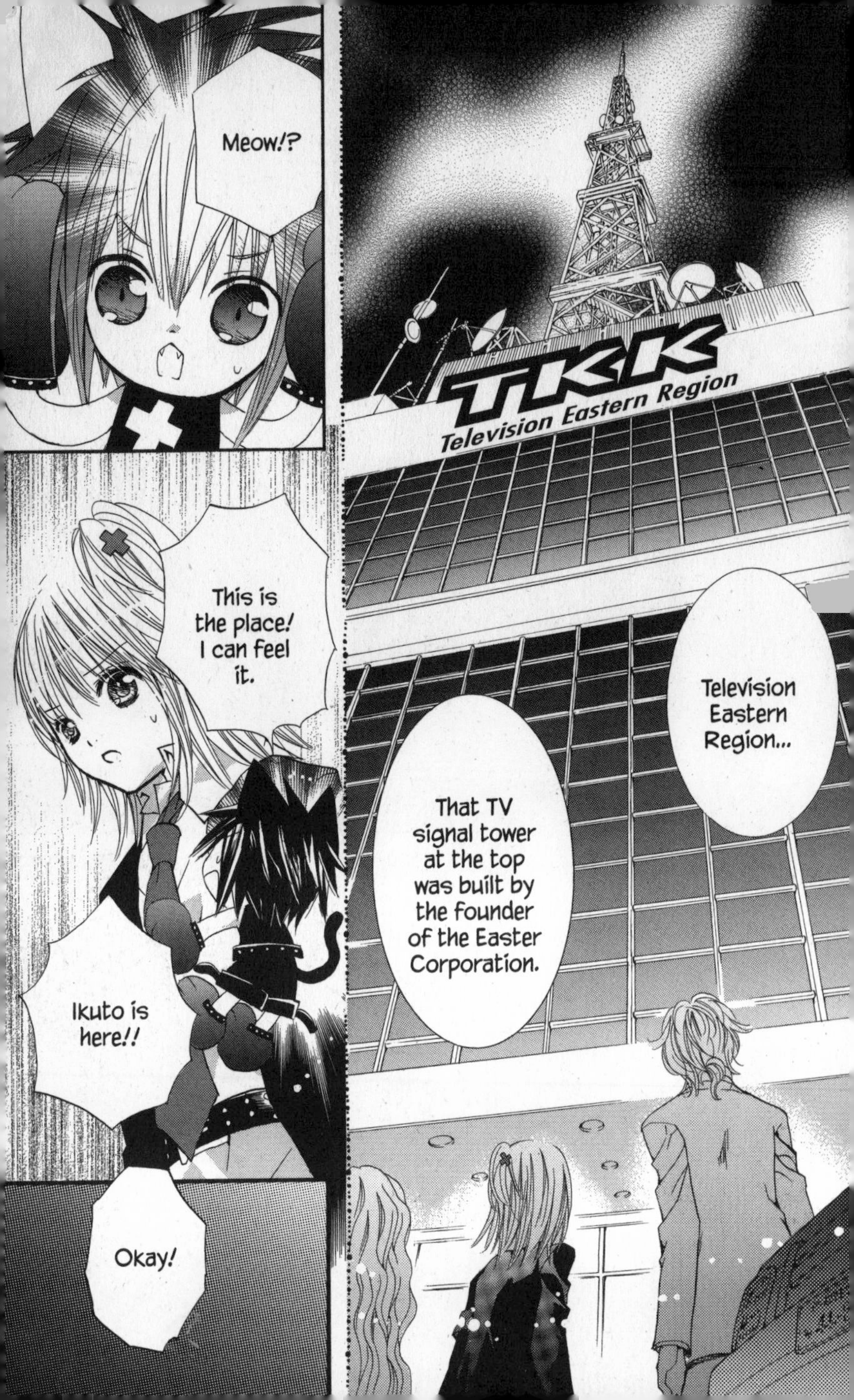
TKK
Television Eastern Region
Television Eastern Region...
That TV signal tower at the top was built by the founder of the Easter Corporation.
Meow!?
This is the place! I can feel it.
Ikuto is here!!
Okay!

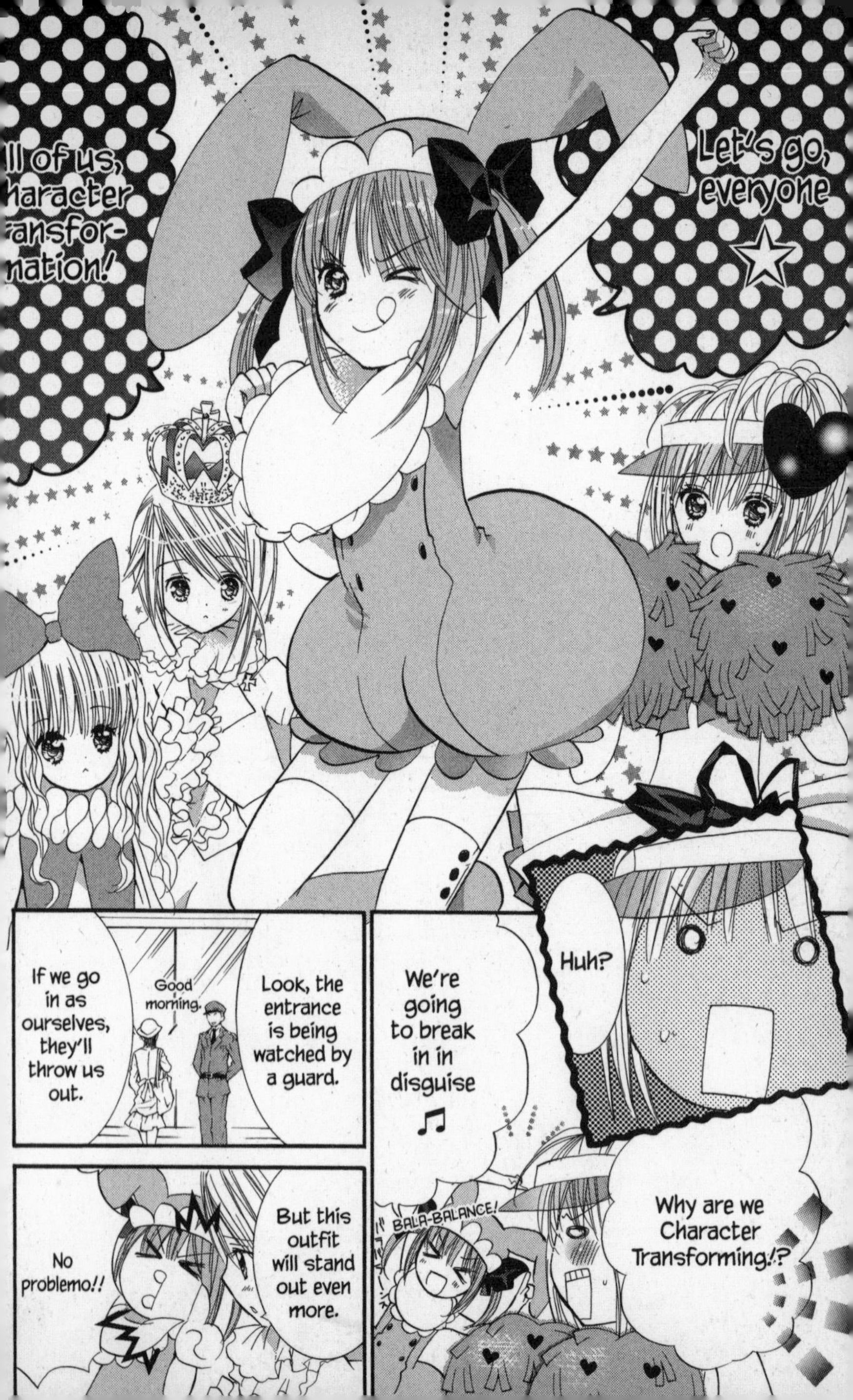
Let's go, everyone ☆
ll of us, haracter ransfor- nation!
We're going to break in in disguise ♪
Huh?
BALA-BALANCE!
Why are we Character Transforming!?
Look, the entrance is being watched by a guard.
Good morning.
If we go in as ourselves, they'll throw us out.
But this outfit will stand out even more.
No problemo!!

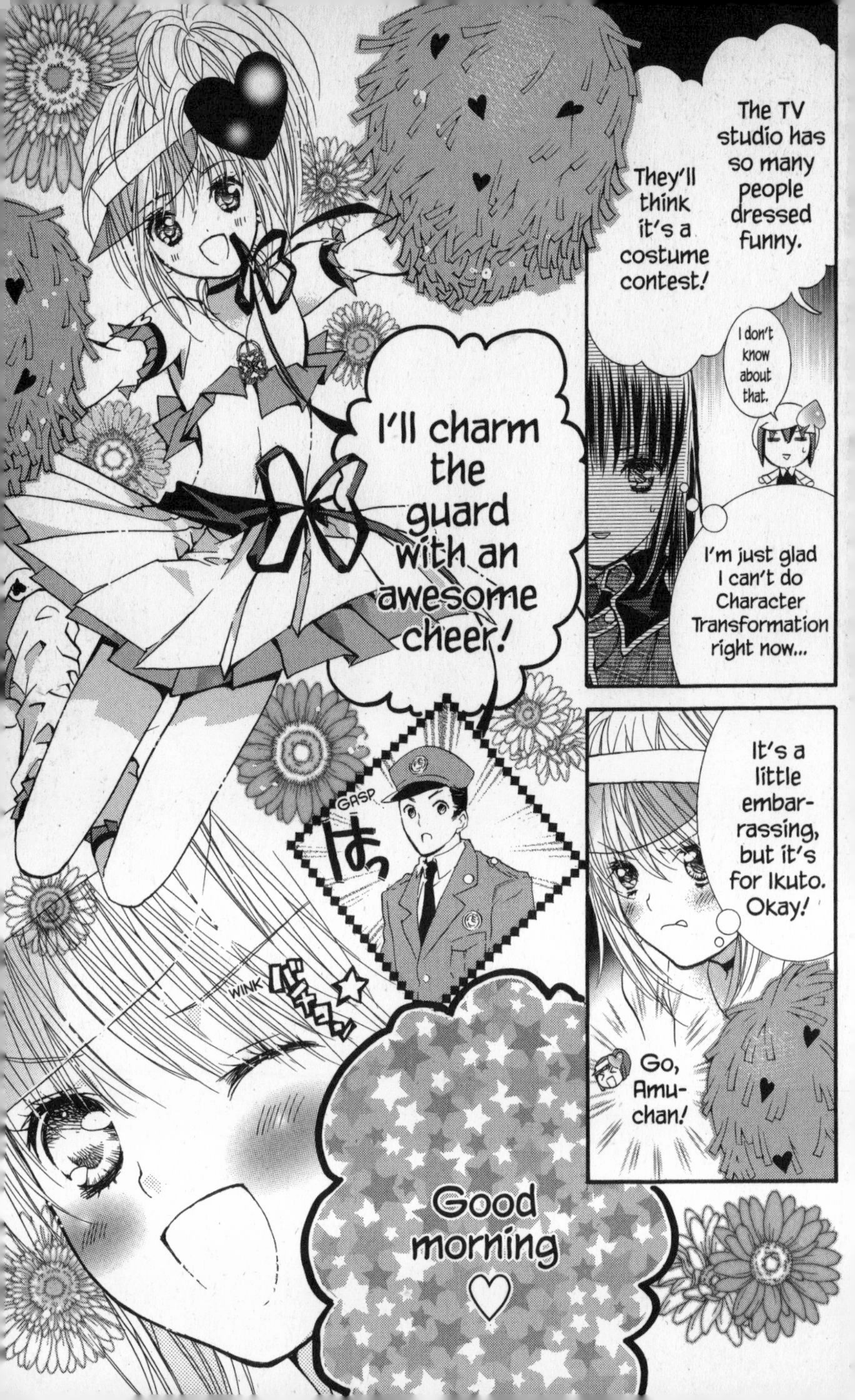
The TV studio has so many people dressed funny.
They'll think it's a costume contest!
I don't know about that.
I'm just glad I can't do Character Transformation right now...
It's a little embarrassing, but it's for Ikuto. Okay!
Go, Amu-chan!
I'll charm the guard with an awesome cheer!
GASP
はっ
WINK
Good morning ♡

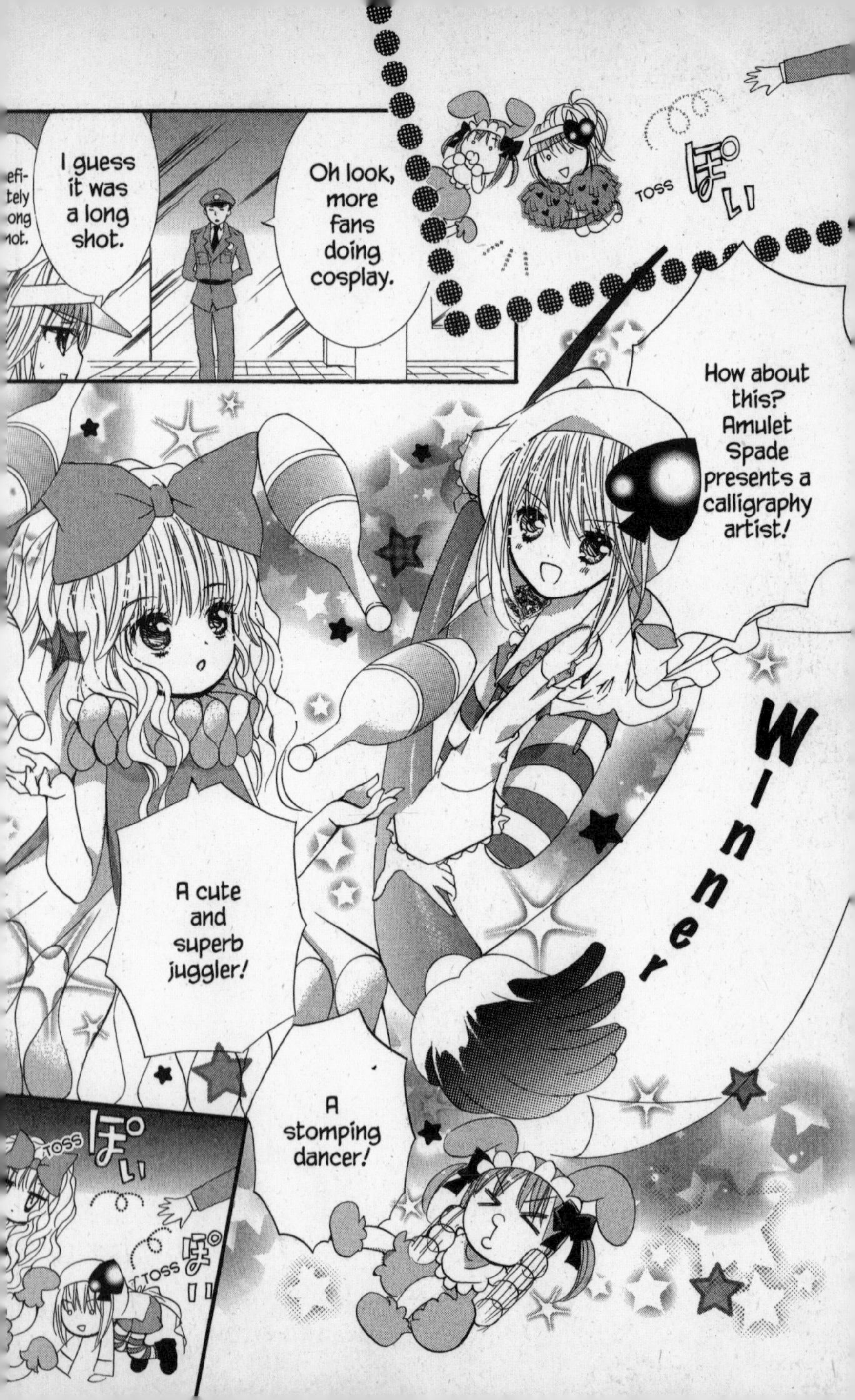

TOSS ぽい
Oh look, more fans doing cosplay.
I guess it was a long shot.
How about this? Amulet Spade presents a calligraphy artist!
Winner
A cute and superb juggler!
A stomping dancer!
TOSS ぽい
TOSS ぽい

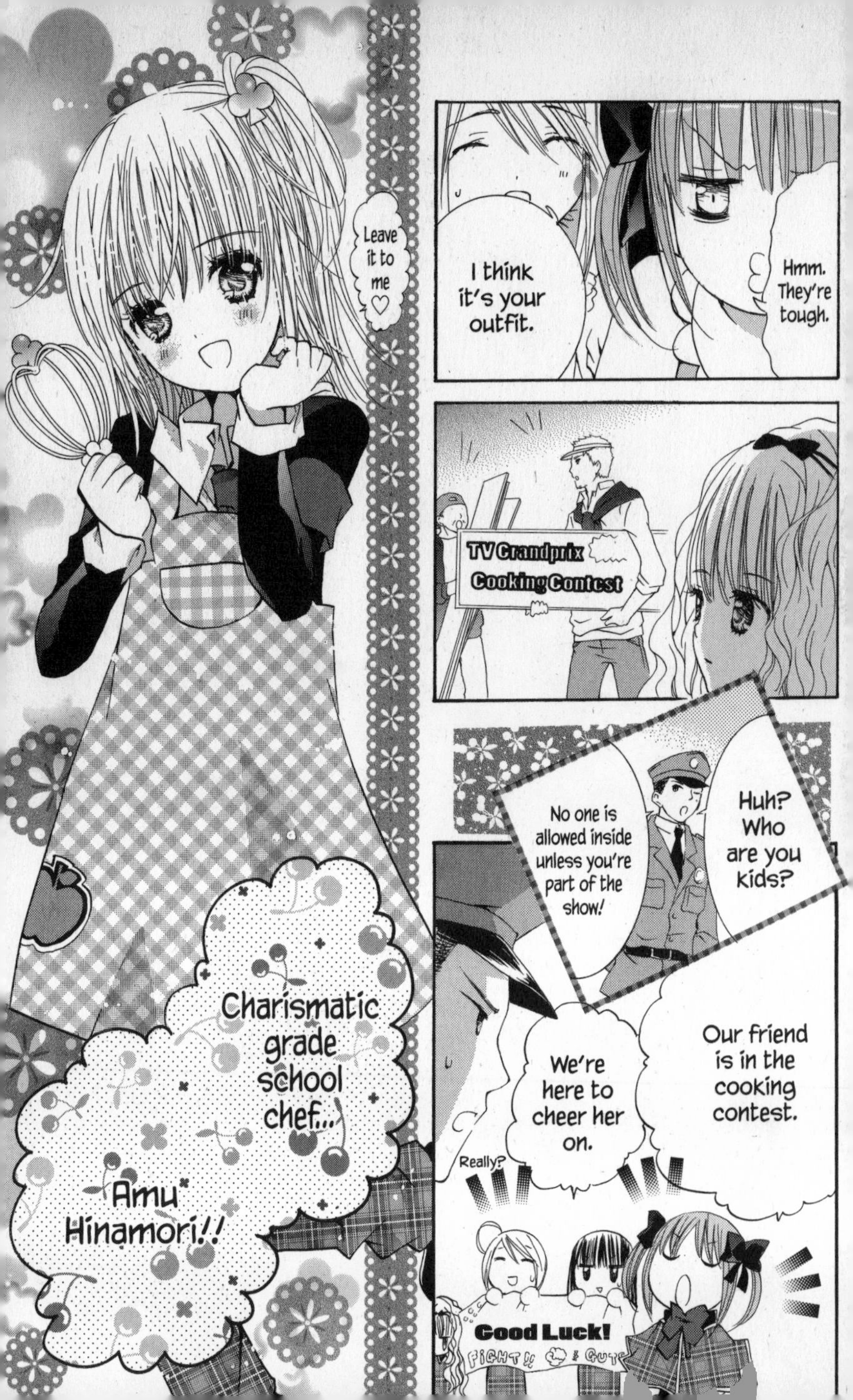
Hmm. They're tough.
I think it's your outfit.
TV Grandprix Cooking Contest
Huh? Who are you kids?
No one is allowed inside unless you're part of the show!
Our friend is in the cooking contest.
We're here to cheer her on.
Really?
Good Luck!
FIGHT!!
Leave it to me ♡
Charismatic grade school chef...
Amu Hinamori!!

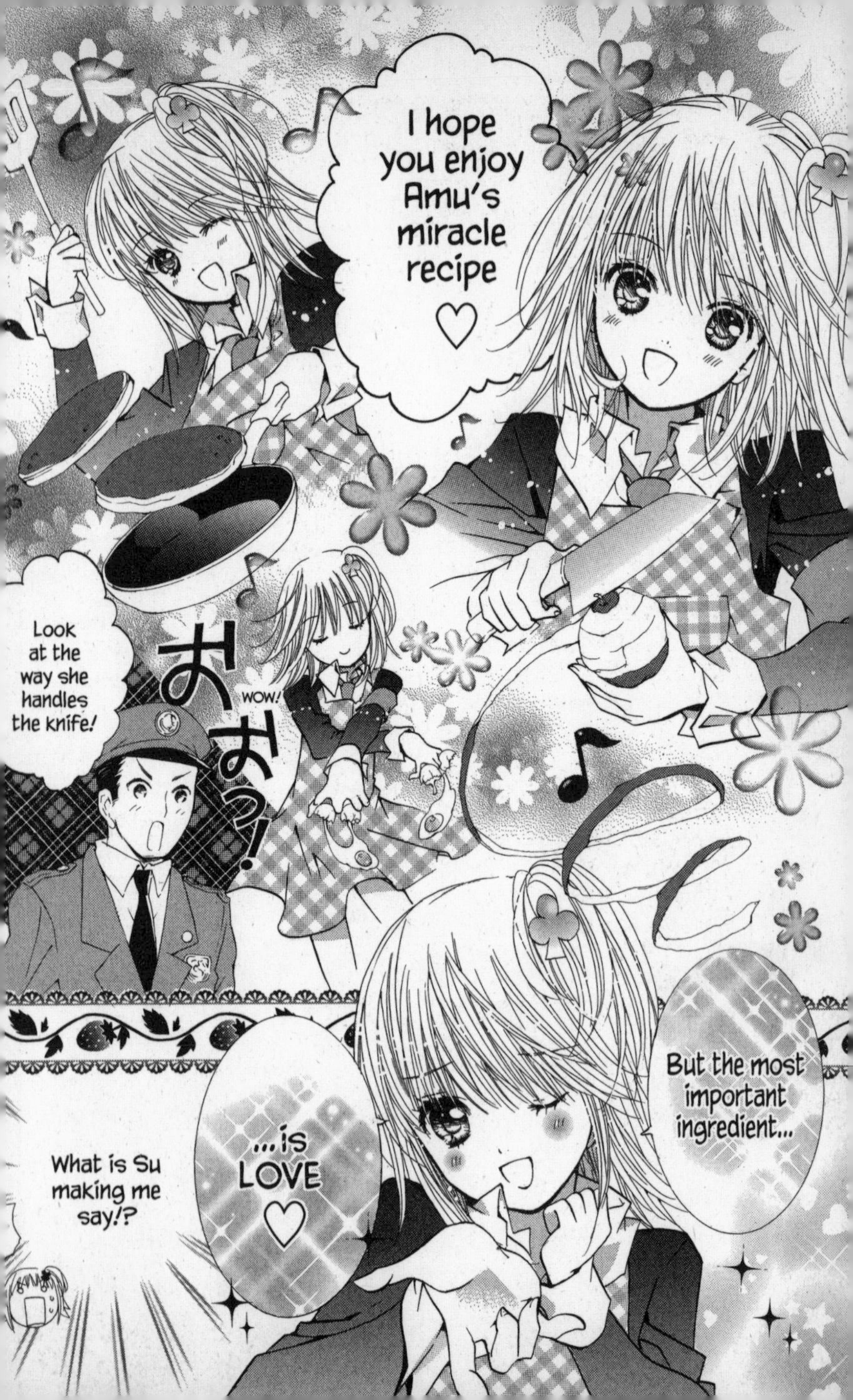

I hope you enjoy Amu's miracle recipe ♡
おおっ!
WOW!
Look at the way she handles the knife!
But the most important ingredient...
...is LOVE ♡
What is Su making me say!?

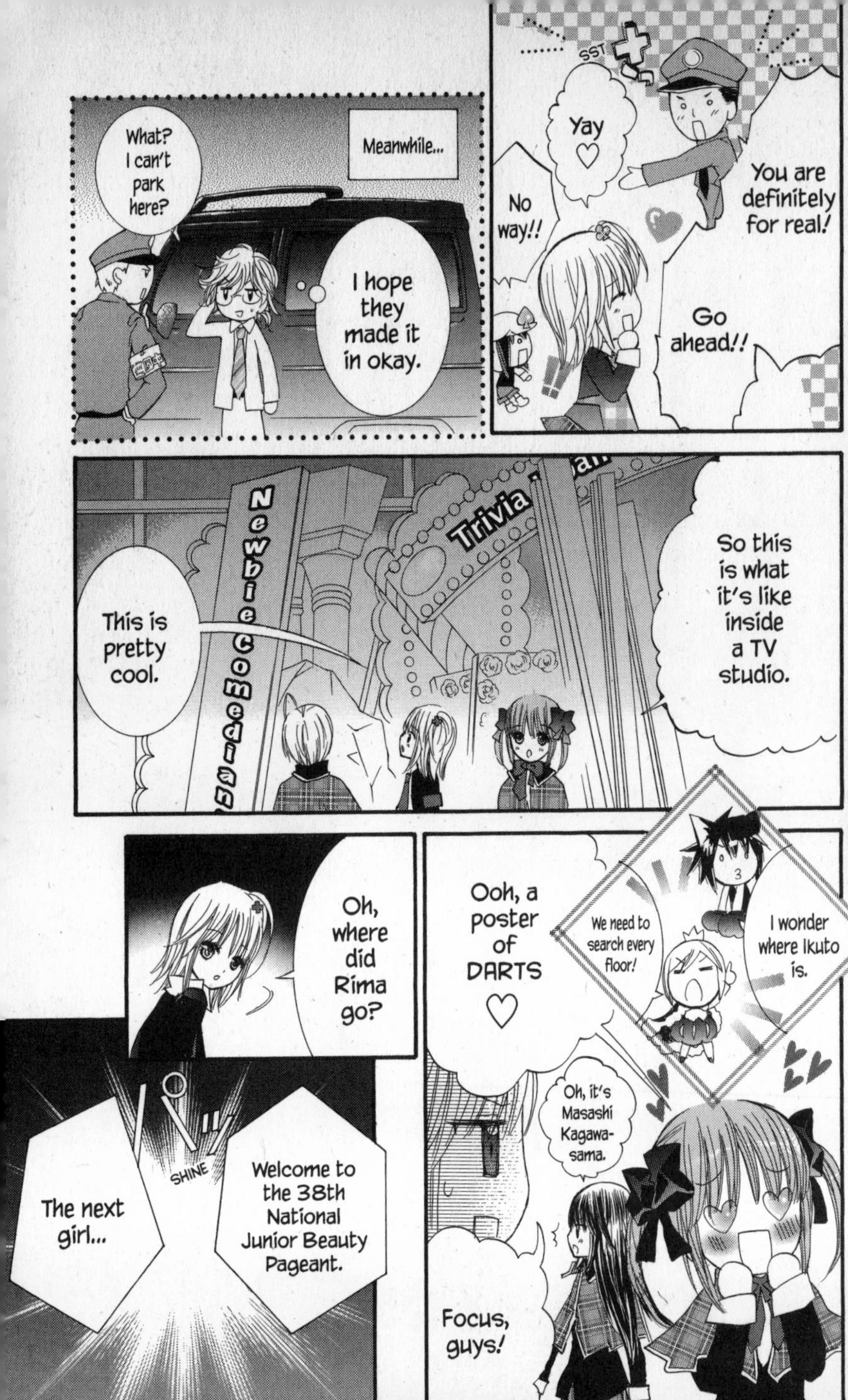
......
You are definitely for real!
SST
Yay ♡
No way!!
Go ahead!!
Meanwhile...
What? I can't park here?
I hope they made it in okay.
So this is what it's like inside a TV studio.
Trivia
Newbie Comedian
This is pretty cool.
I wonder where Ikuto is.
We need to search every floor!
Ooh, a poster of DARTS ♡
Oh, it's Masashi Kagawa-sama.
Focus, guys!
Oh, where did Rima go?
Welcome to the 38th National Junior Beauty Pageant.
SHINE
The next girl...

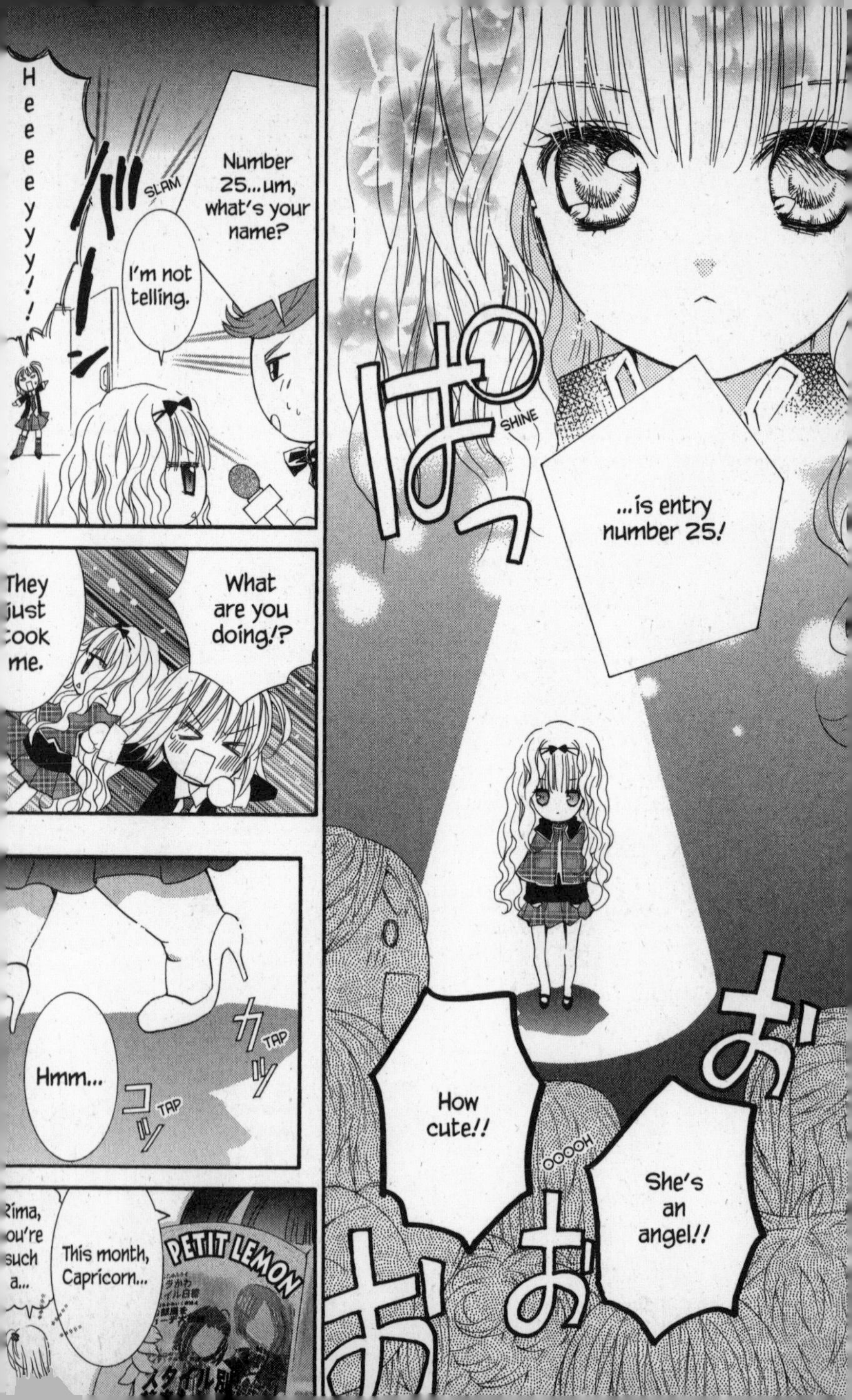
ぱっ
SHINE
...is entry number 25!
おおお
OOOOH
She's an angel!!
How cute!!
Number 25...um, what's your name?
SLAM
I'm not telling.
Heeeeyyyy!!
What are you doing!?
They just took me.
カッ
TAP
コッ
TAP
Hmm...
PETIT LEMON
This month, Capricorn...
Rima, you're such a...

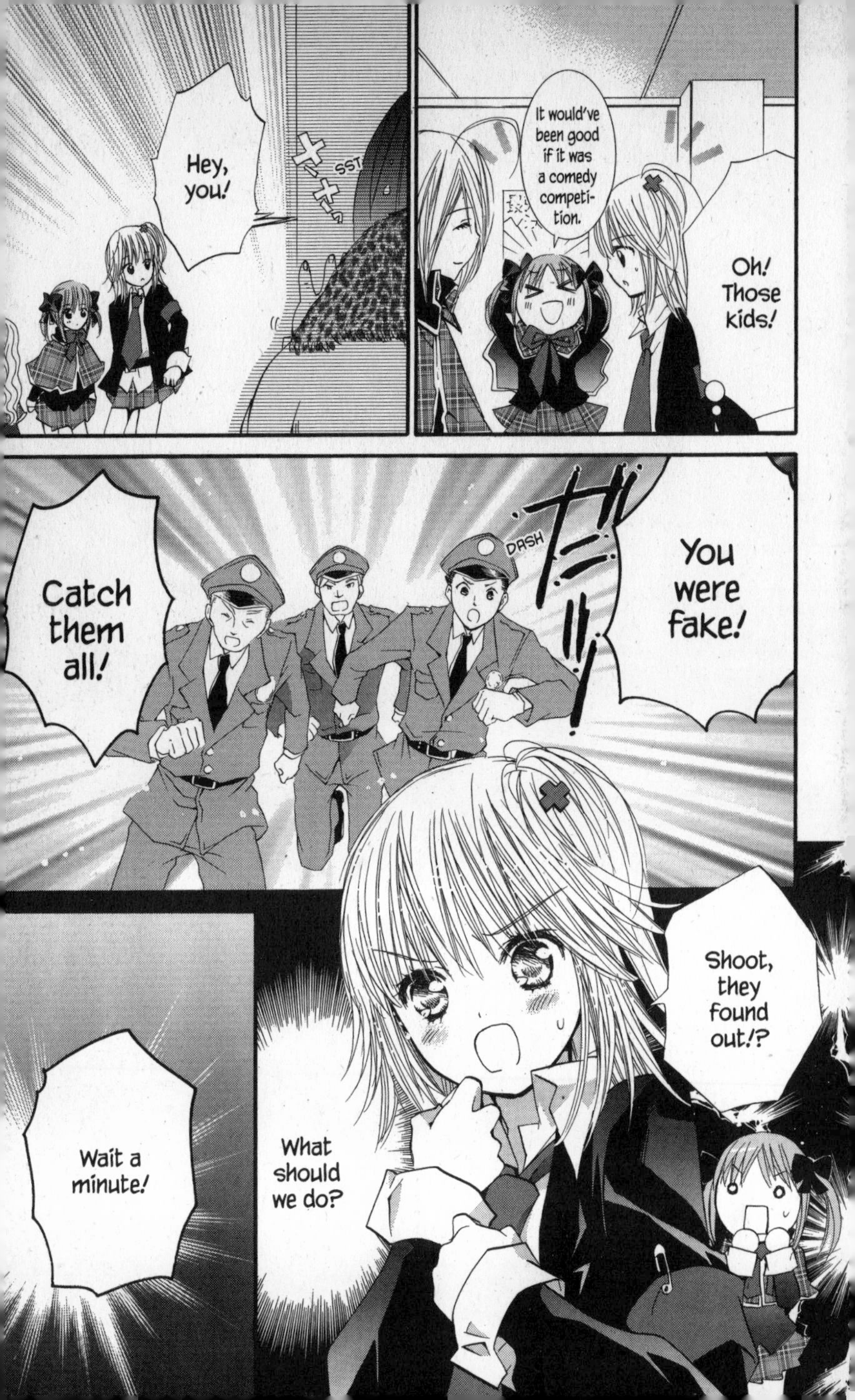
It would've been good if it was a comedy competition.
Oh! Those kids!
SST
Hey, you!
You were fake!
DASH
Catch them all!
Shoot, they found out!?
What should we do?
Wait a minute!

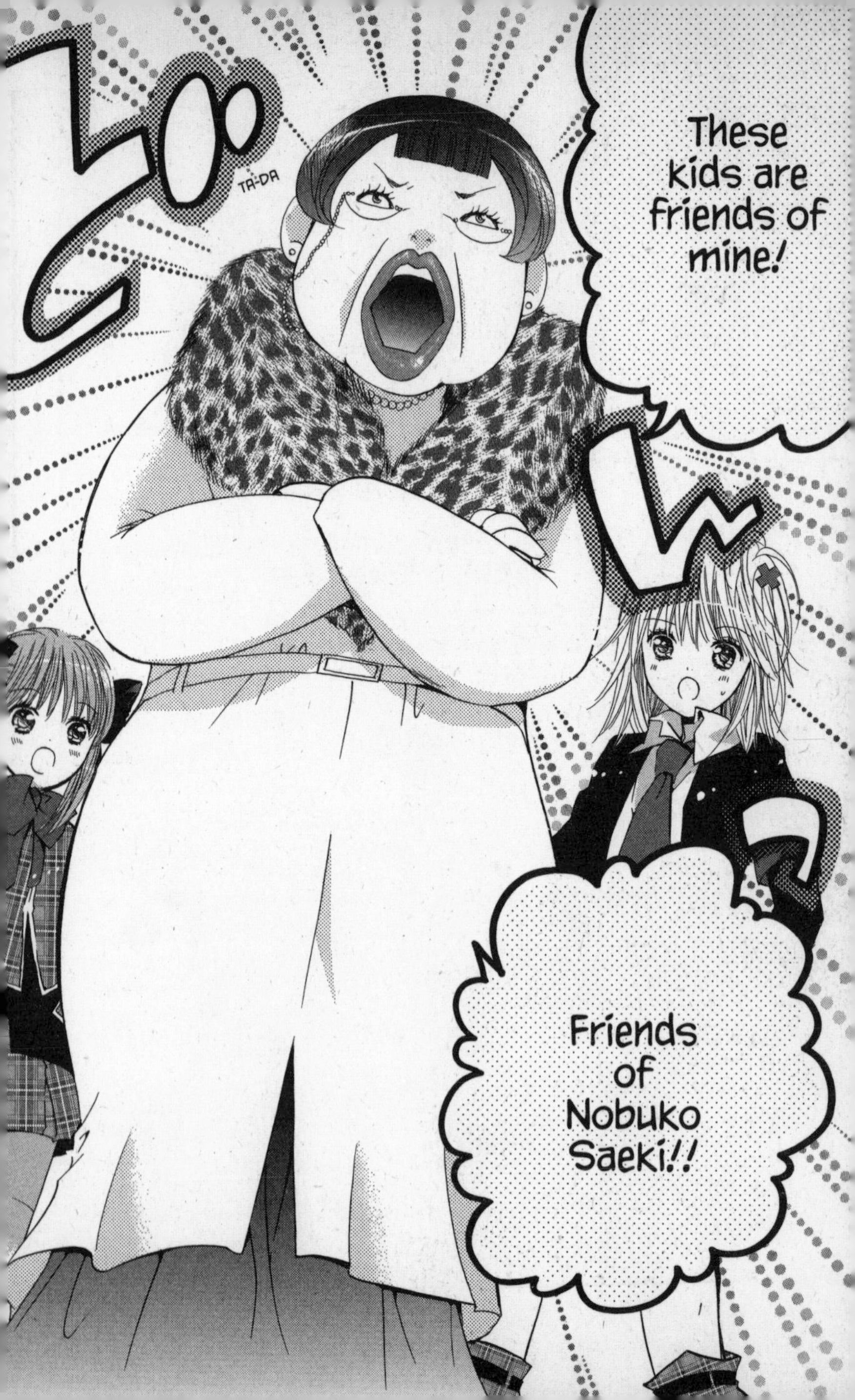
These kids are friends of mine!
TA-DA
Friends of Nobuko Saeki!!

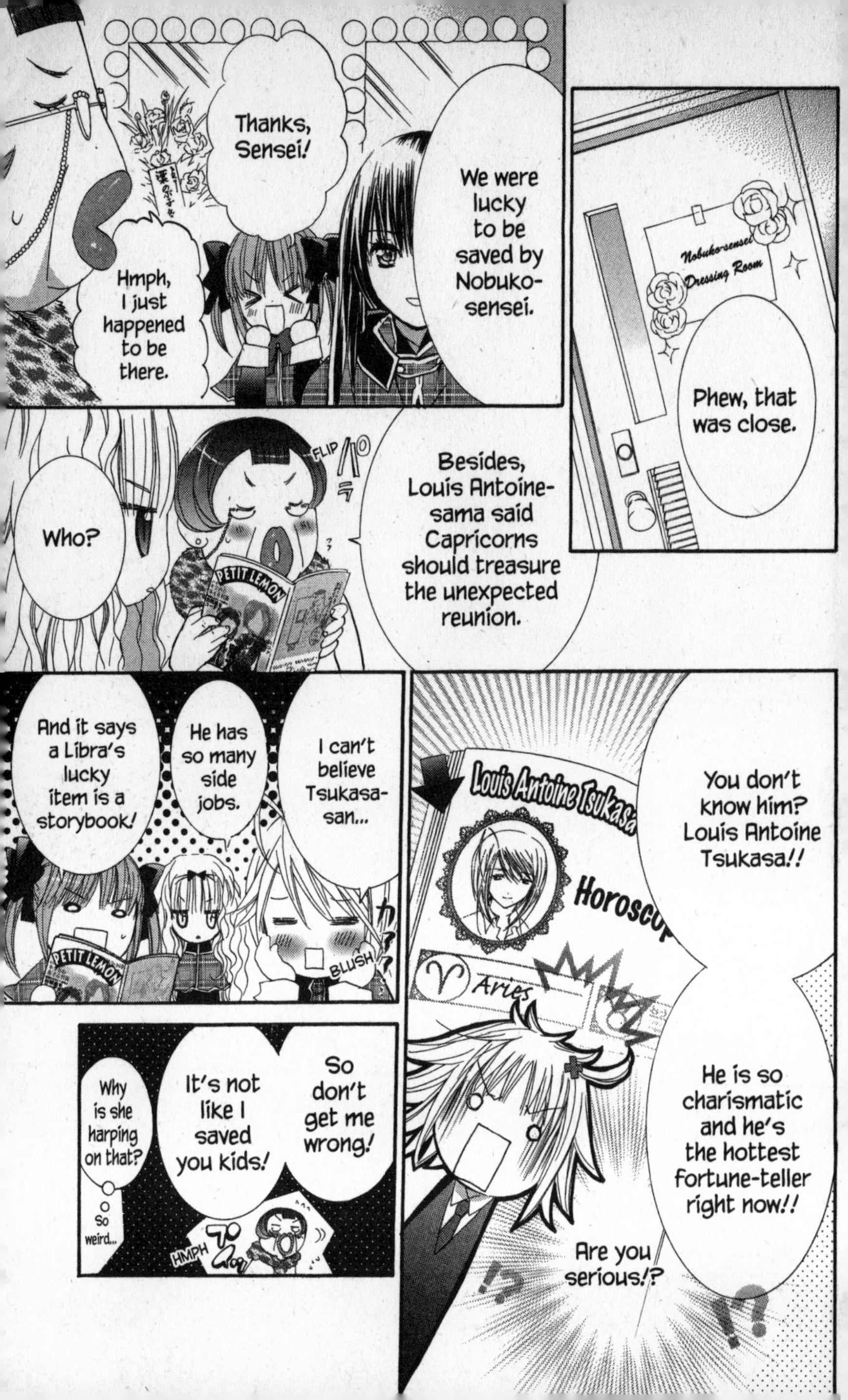
Nobuko-sensei Dressing Room
Phew, that was close.
We were lucky to be saved by Nobuko-sensei.
Thanks, Sensei!
Hmph, I just happened to be there.
Besides, Louis Antoine-sama said Capricorns should treasure the unexpected reunion.
FLIP
PETIT LEMON
Who?
You don't know him? Louis Antoine Tsukasa!!
Louis Antoine Tsukasa
Horoscop
Aries
He is so charismatic and he's the hottest fortune-teller right now!!
Are you serious!?
I can't believe Tsukasa-san...
He has so many side jobs.
And it says a Libra's lucky item is a storybook!
BLUSH
PETIT LEMON
So don't get me wrong!
It's not like I saved you kids!
Why is she harping on that?
So weird...
HMPH

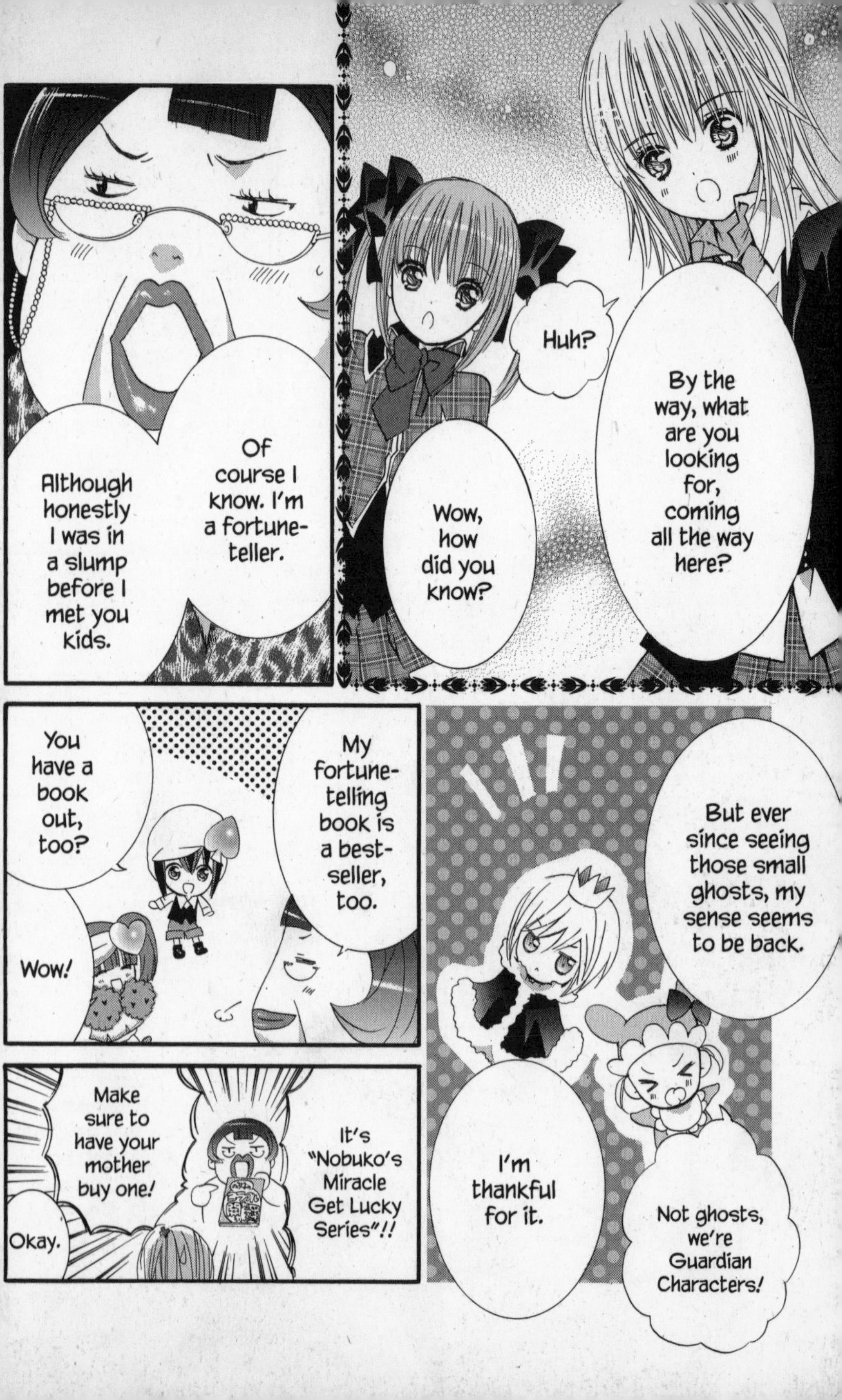
By the way, what are you looking for, coming all the way here?
Huh?
Wow, how did you know?
Of course I know. I'm a fortune-teller.
Although honestly I was in a slump before I met you kids.
But ever since seeing those small ghosts, my sense seems to be back.
I'm thankful for it.
Not ghosts, we're Guardian Characters!
My fortune-telling book is a best-seller, too.
You have a book out, too?
Wow!
It's "Nobuko's Miracle Get Lucky Series"!!
Make sure to have your mother buy one!
Okay.

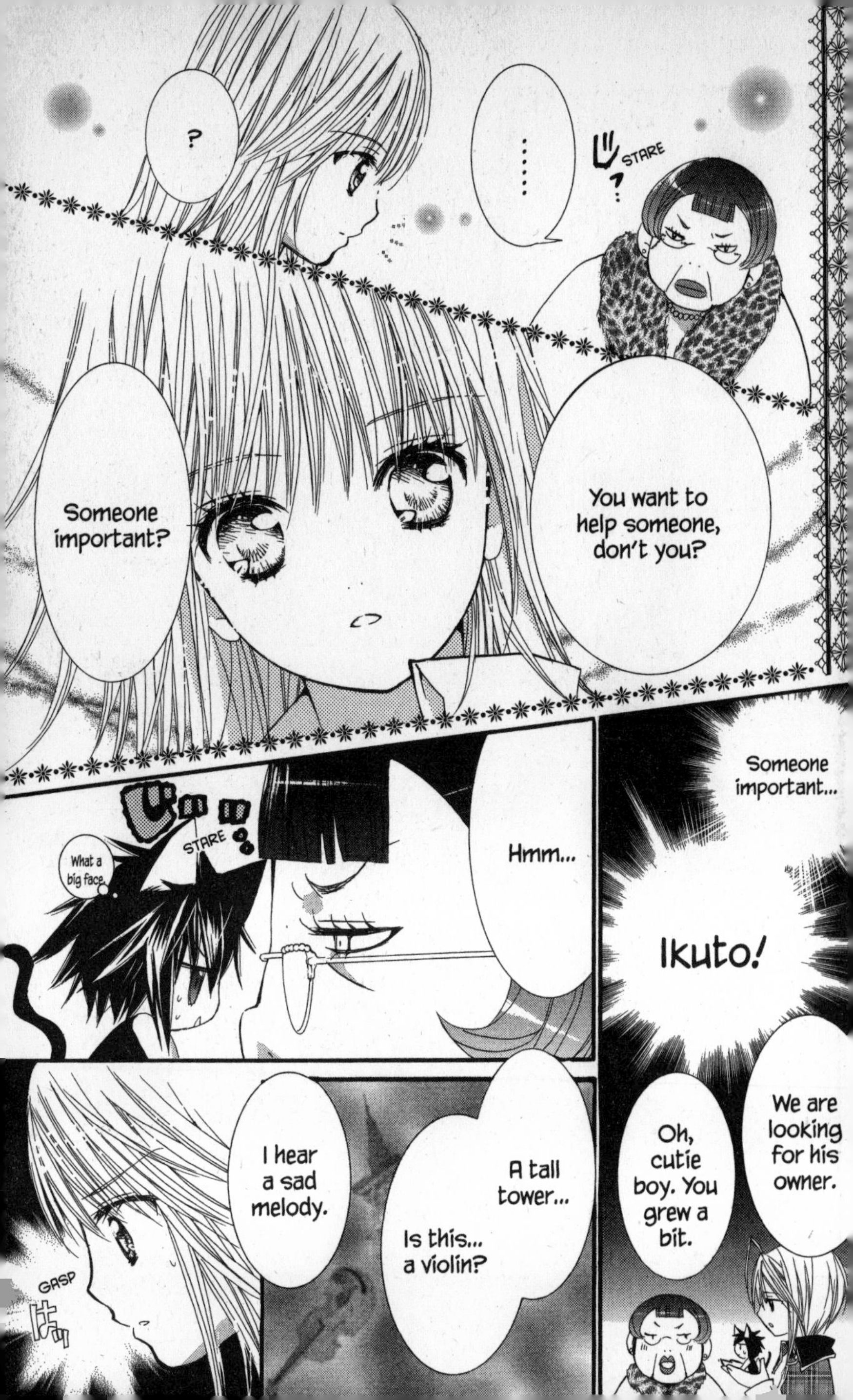
STARE
......
?
You want to help someone, don't you?
Someone important?
Someone important...
Ikuto!
Hmm...
STARE
What a big face.
We are looking for his owner.
Oh, cutie boy. You grew a bit.
A tall tower...
Is this... a violin?
I hear a sad melody.
GASP

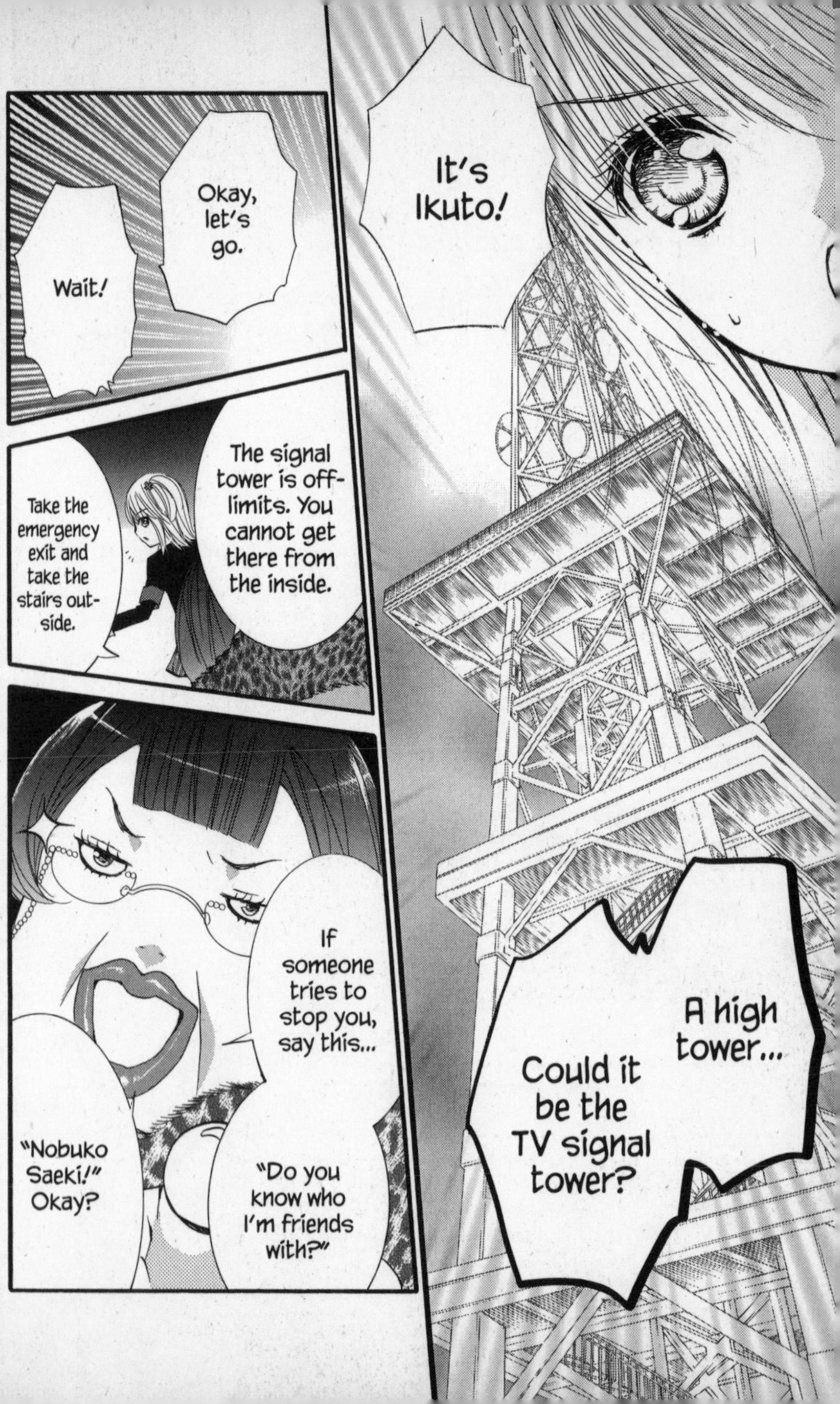
It's Ikuto!
A high tower...
Could it be the TV signal tower?
Okay, let's go.
Wait!
The signal tower is off-limits. You cannot get there from the inside.
Take the emergency exit and take the stairs outside.
If someone tries to stop you, say this...
"Do you know who I'm friends with?"
"Nobuko Saeki!" Okay?

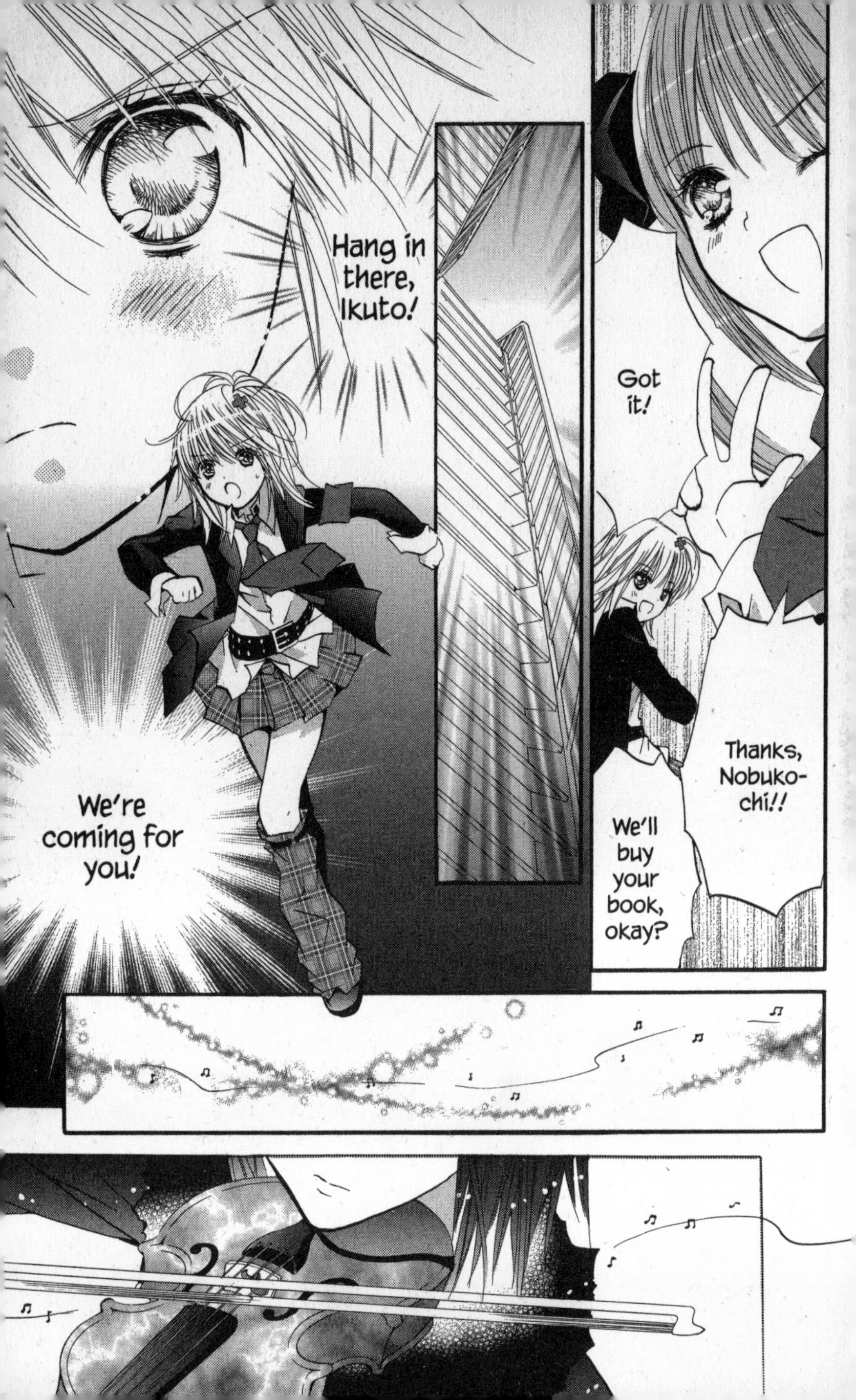
Got it!
Thanks, Nobuko-chi!!
We'll buy your book, okay?
Hang in there, Ikuto!
We're coming for you!

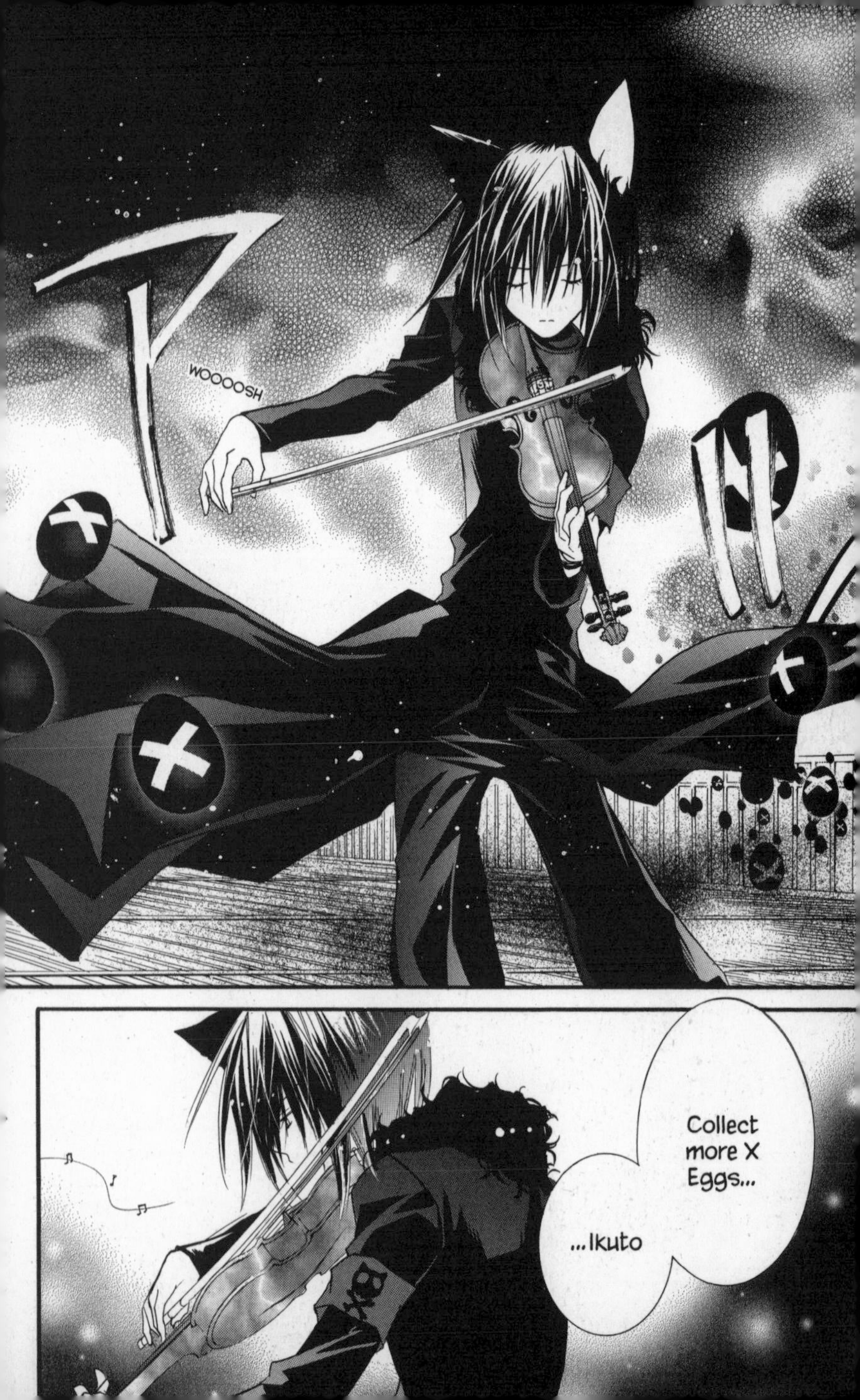
WOOOOSH
Collect more X Eggs...
...Ikuto

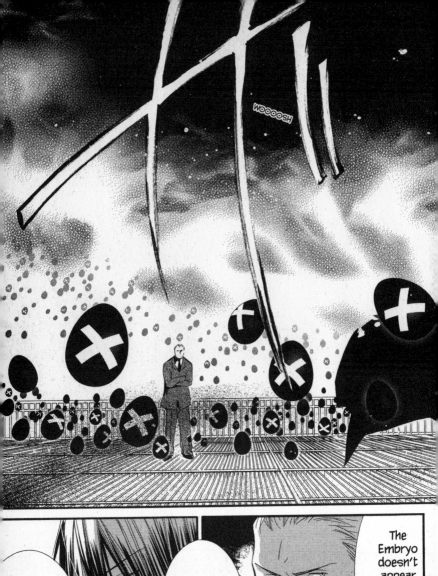

WOOOOSH

The Embryo doesn't appear just because there are a lot of X Eggs...

It appears when the X gets taken off!

I'll make those Guardian brats do my work for me.

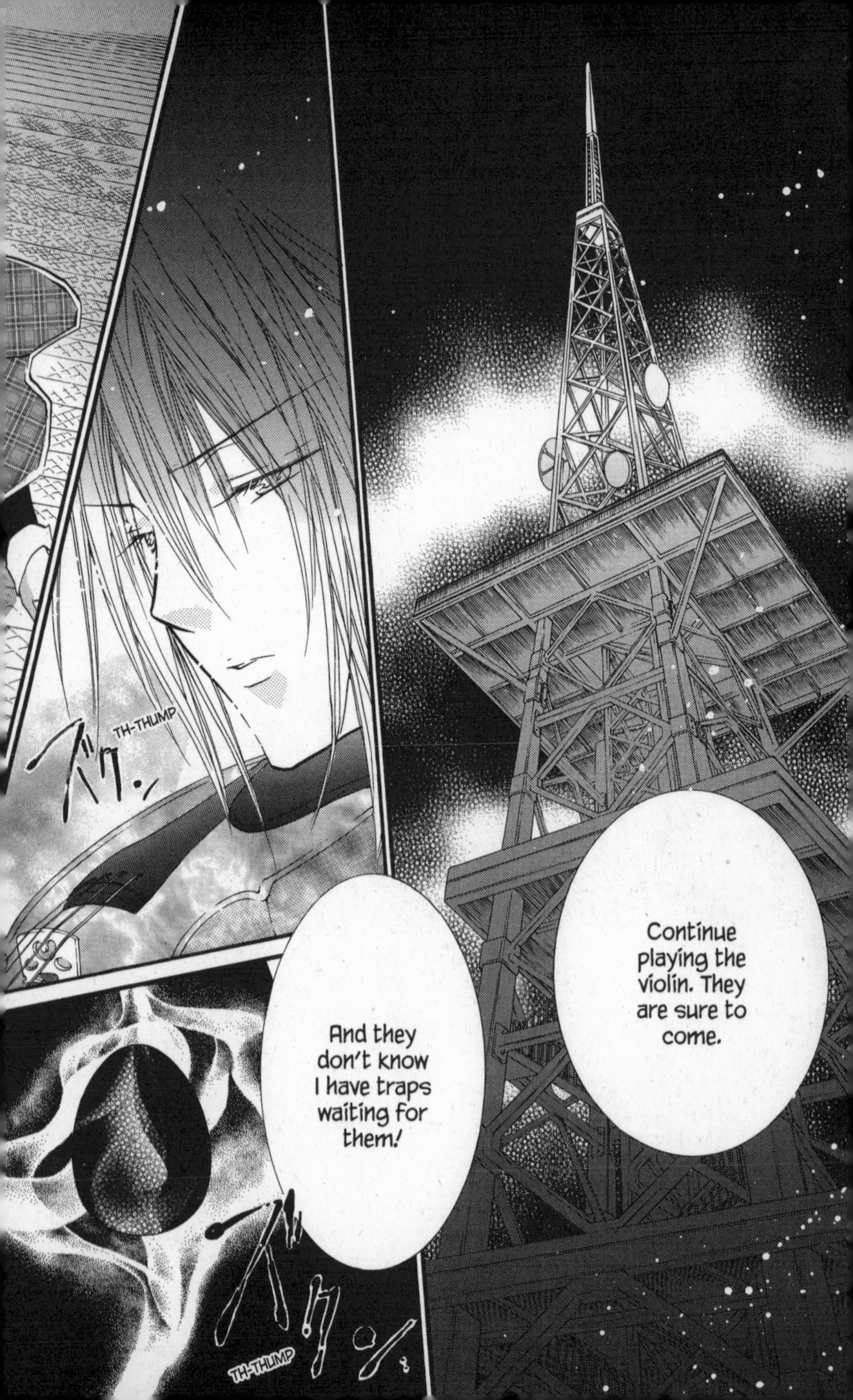
Continue playing the violin. They are sure to come.
And they don't know I have traps waiting for them!
TH-THUMP
TH-THUMP

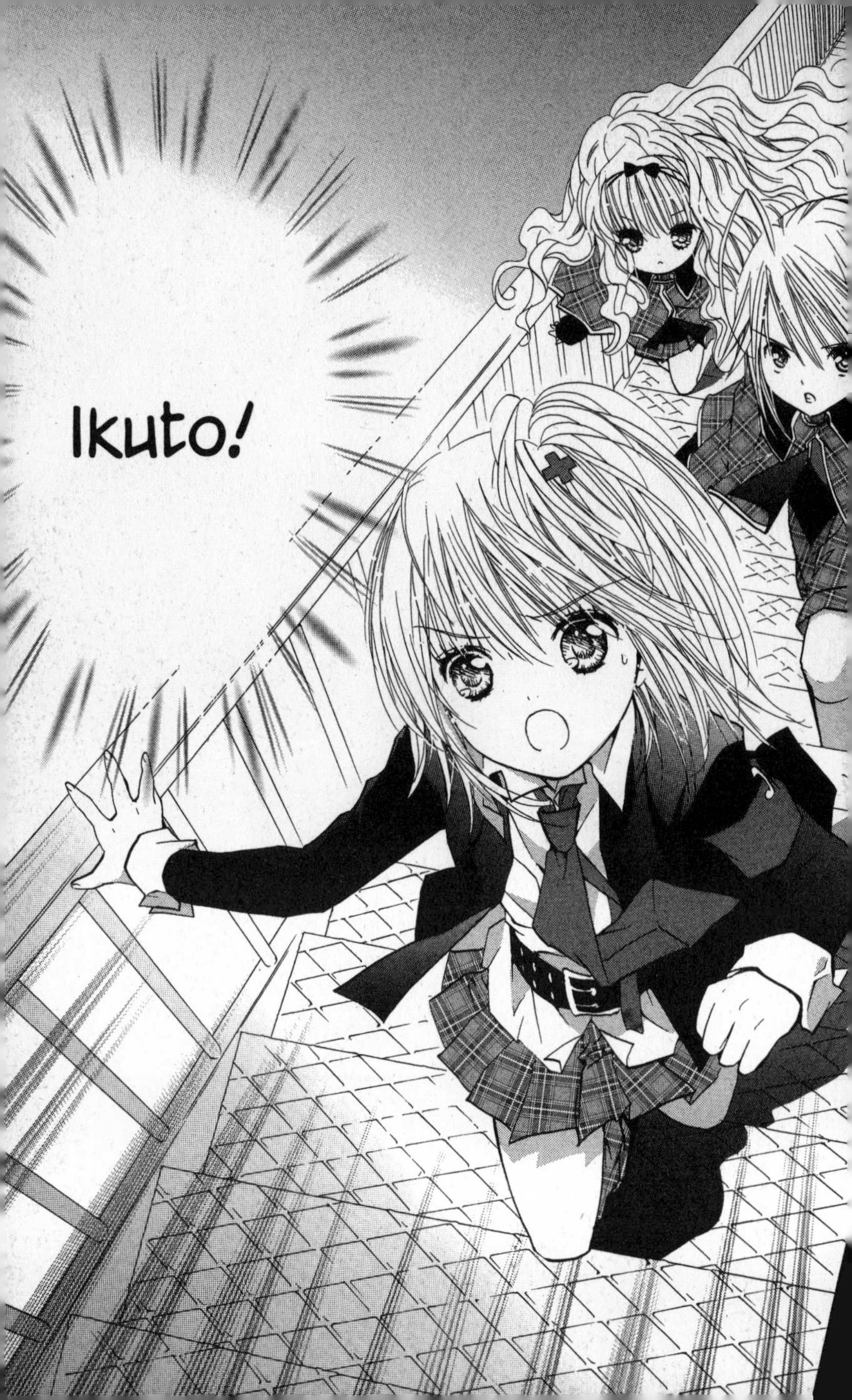
Ikuto!

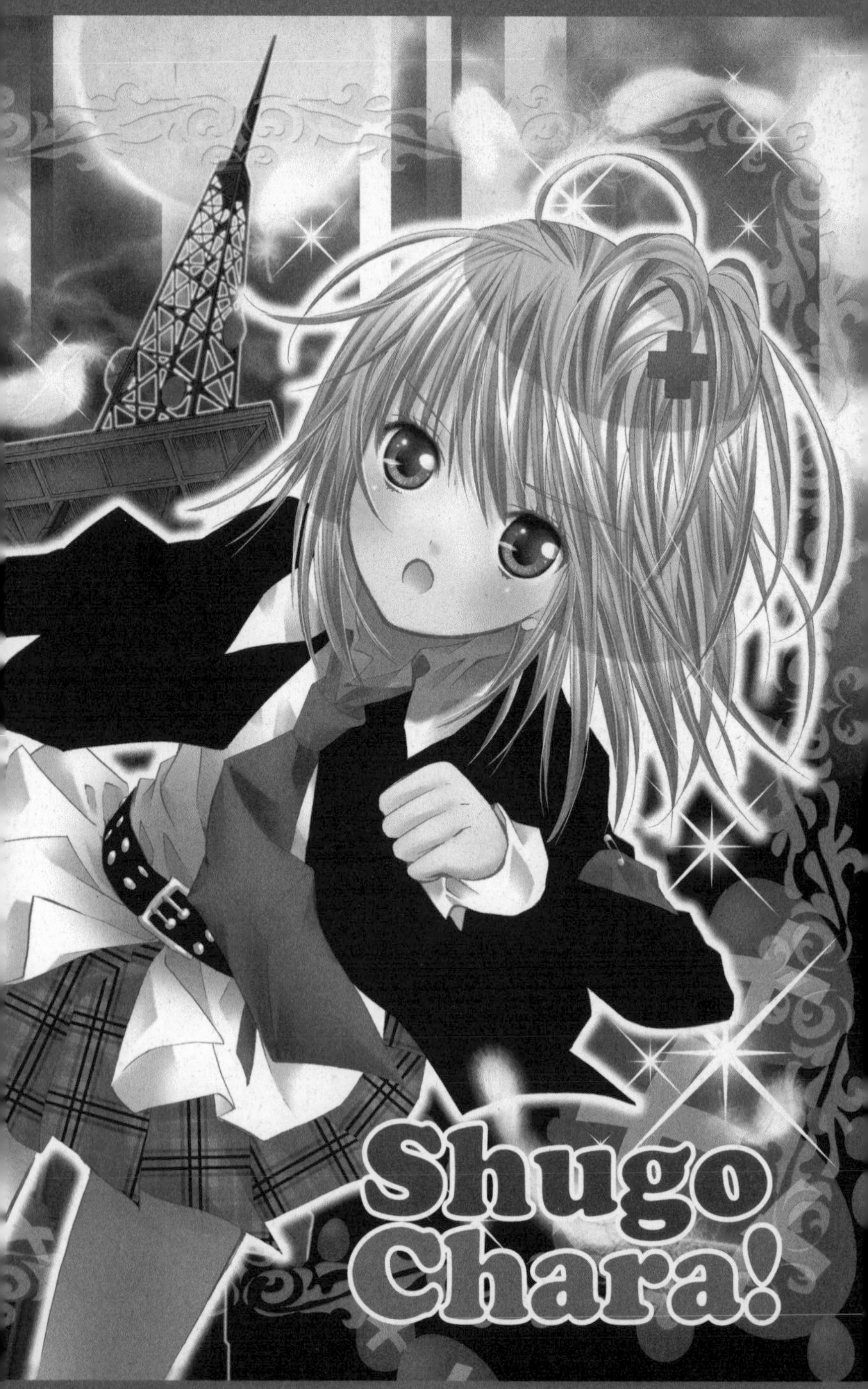
Shugo
Chara!

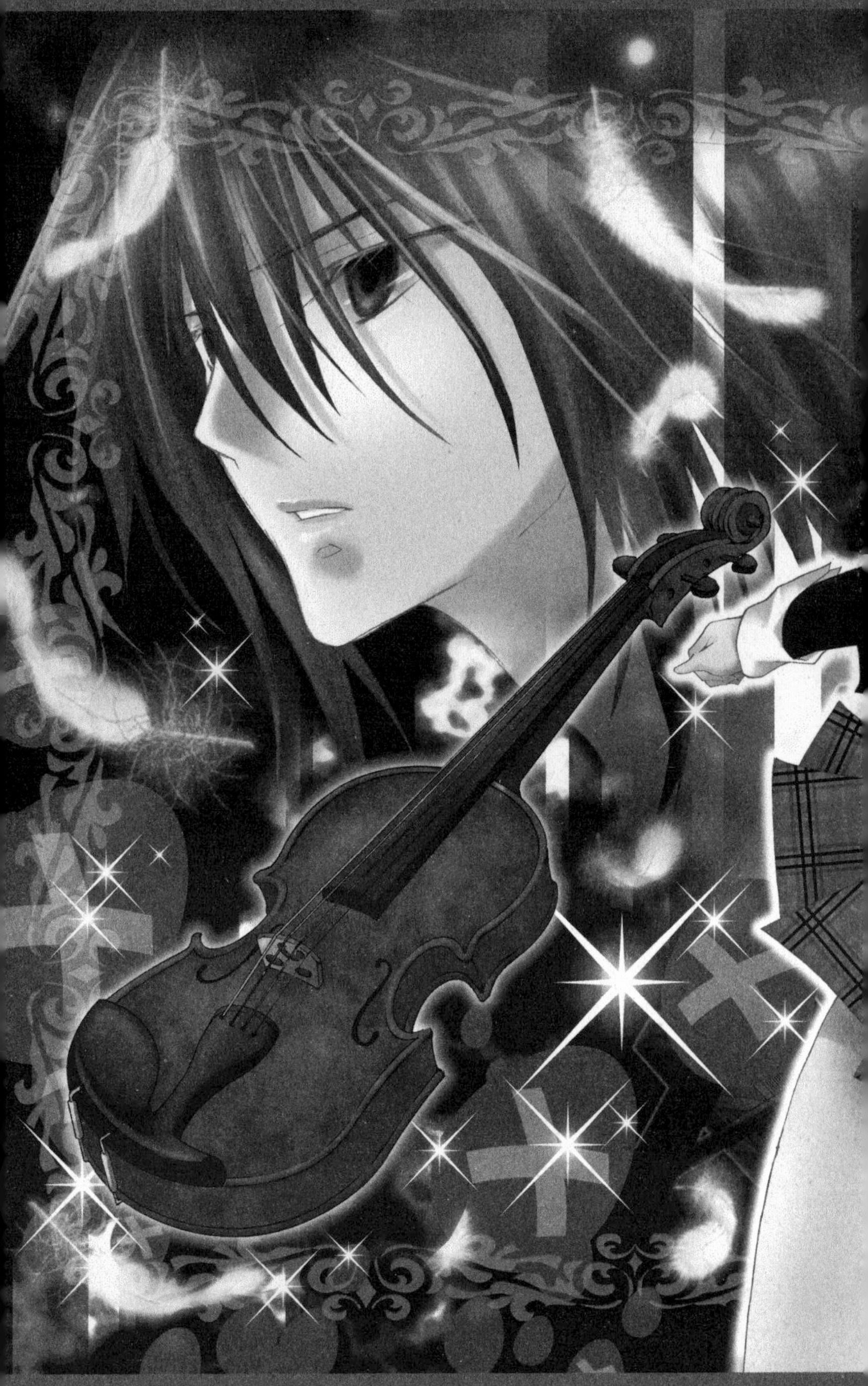

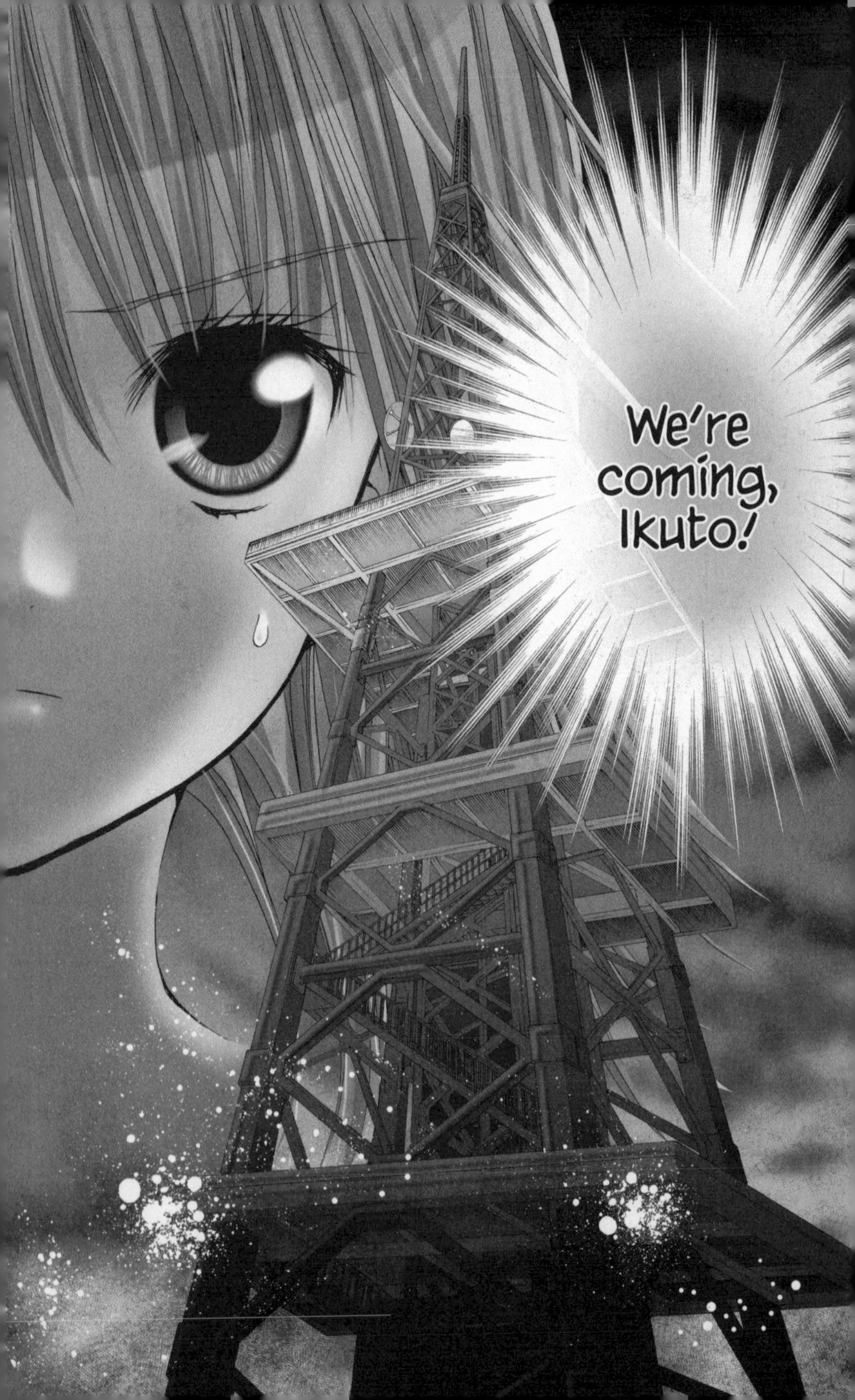
We're coming, Ikuto!

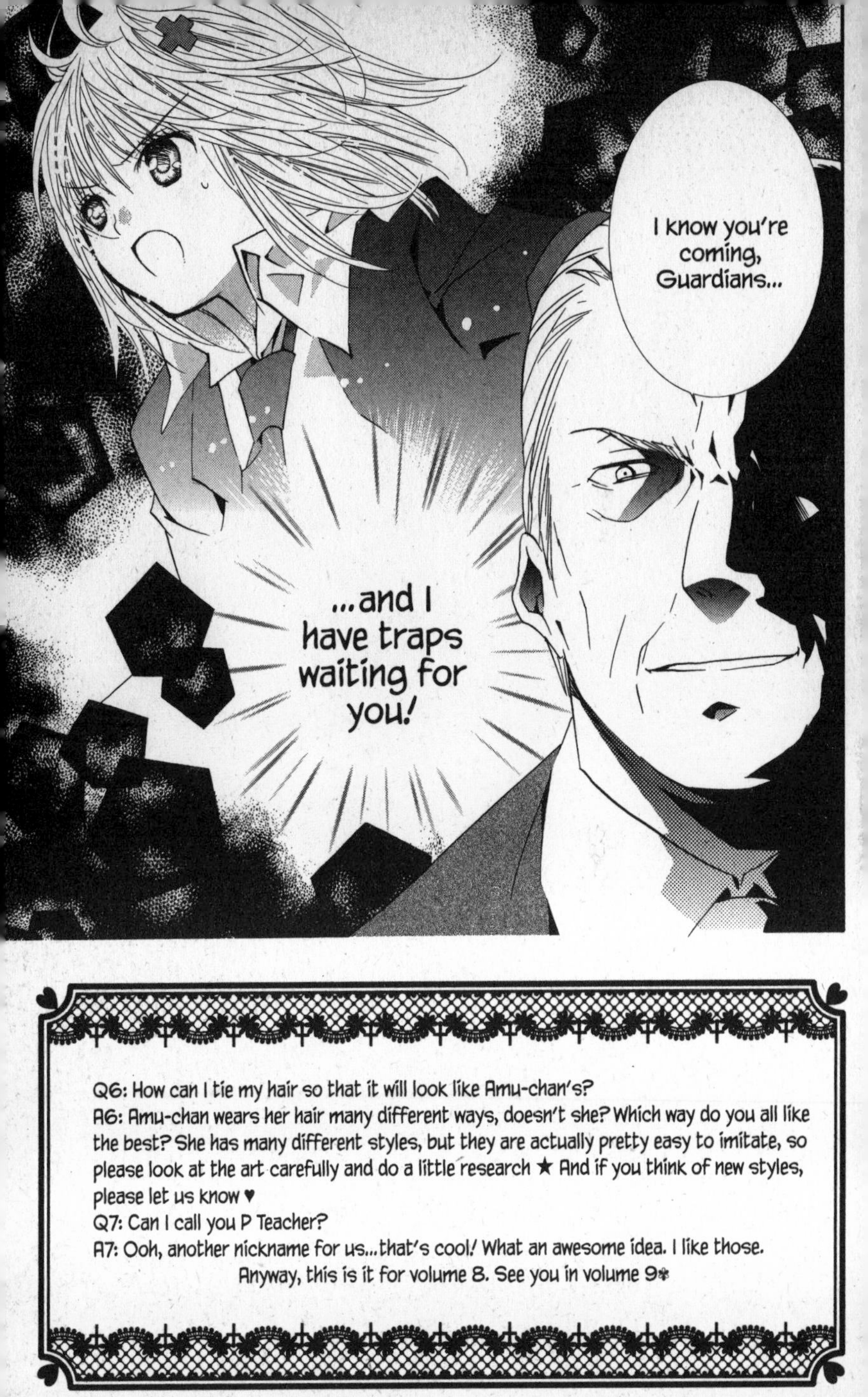
I know you're coming, Guardians...
...and I have traps waiting for you!

Q6: How can I tie my hair so that it will look like Amu-chan's?
A6: Amu-chan wears her hair many different ways, doesn't she? Which way do you all like the best? She has many different styles, but they are actually pretty easy to imitate, so please look at the art carefully and do a little research ★ And if you think of new styles, please let us know ♥
Q7: Can I call you P Teacher?
A7: Ooh, another nickname for us...that's cool! What an awesome idea. I like those.
Anyway, this is it for volume 8. See you in volume 9✽

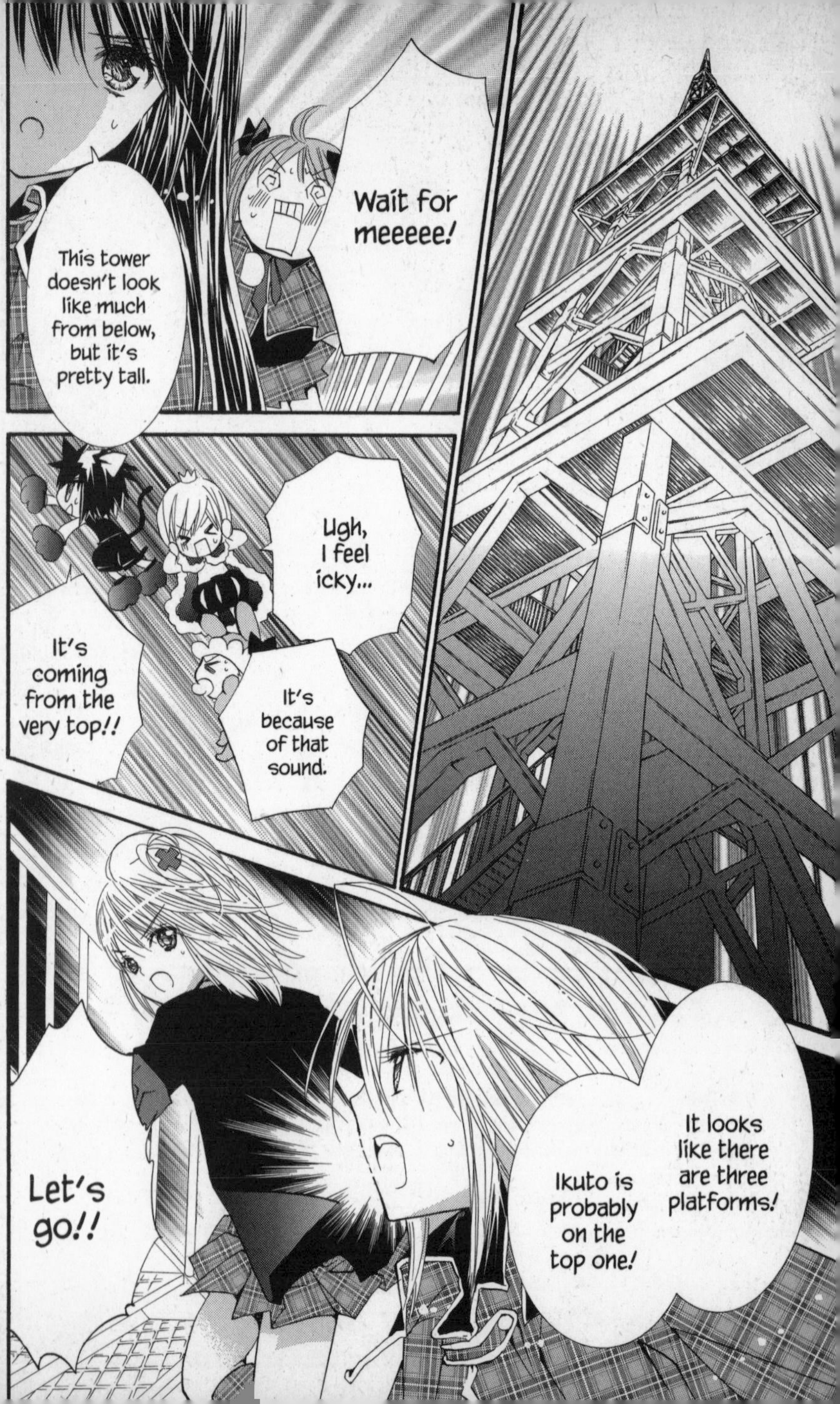
Wait for meeeee!
This tower doesn't look like much from below, but it's pretty tall.
Ugh, I feel icky...
It's because of that sound.
It's coming from the very top!!
It looks like there are three platforms!
Ikuto is probably on the top one!
Let's go!!

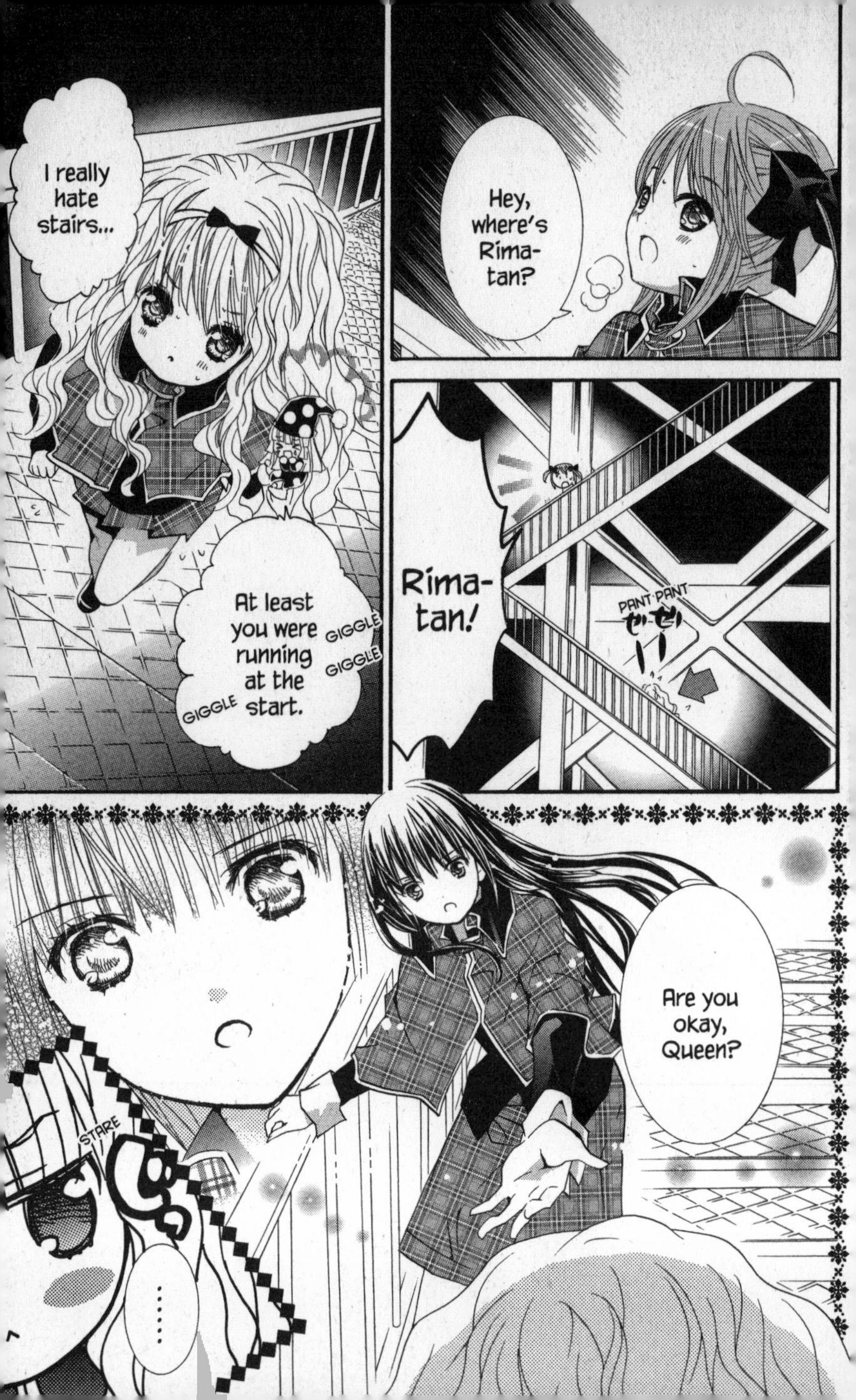
Hey, where's Rima-tan?
Rima-tan!
PANT PANT
I really hate stairs...
At least you were running at the start.
GIGGLE GIGGLE GIGGLE
Are you okay, Queen?
STARE
......

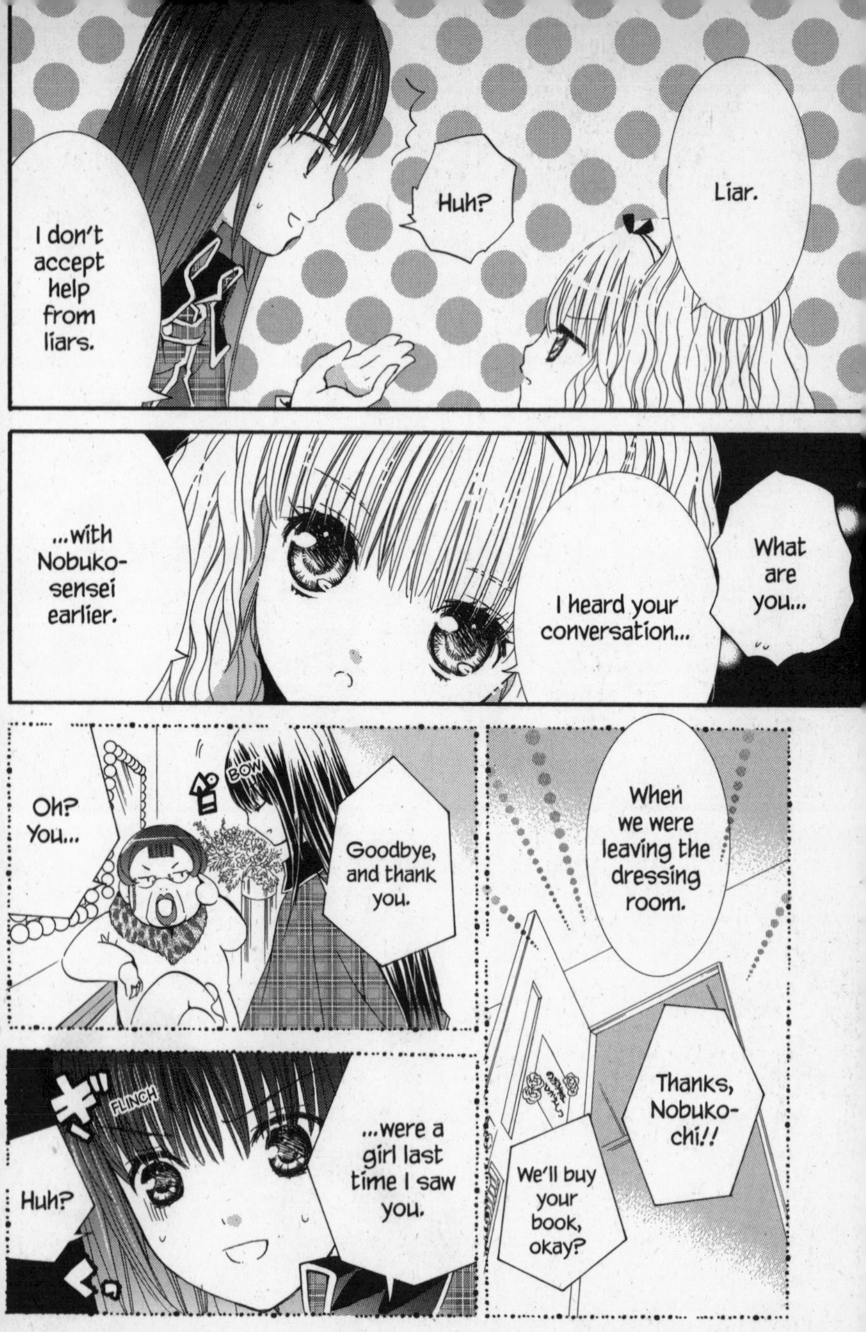
Liar.
Huh?
I don't accept help from liars.
What are you...
I heard your conversation...
...with Nobuko-sensei earlier.
When we were leaving the dressing room.
Thanks, Nobuko-chi!!
We'll buy your book, okay?
Goodbye, and thank you.
BOW
Oh? You...
...were a girl last time I saw you.
FLINCH
Huh?

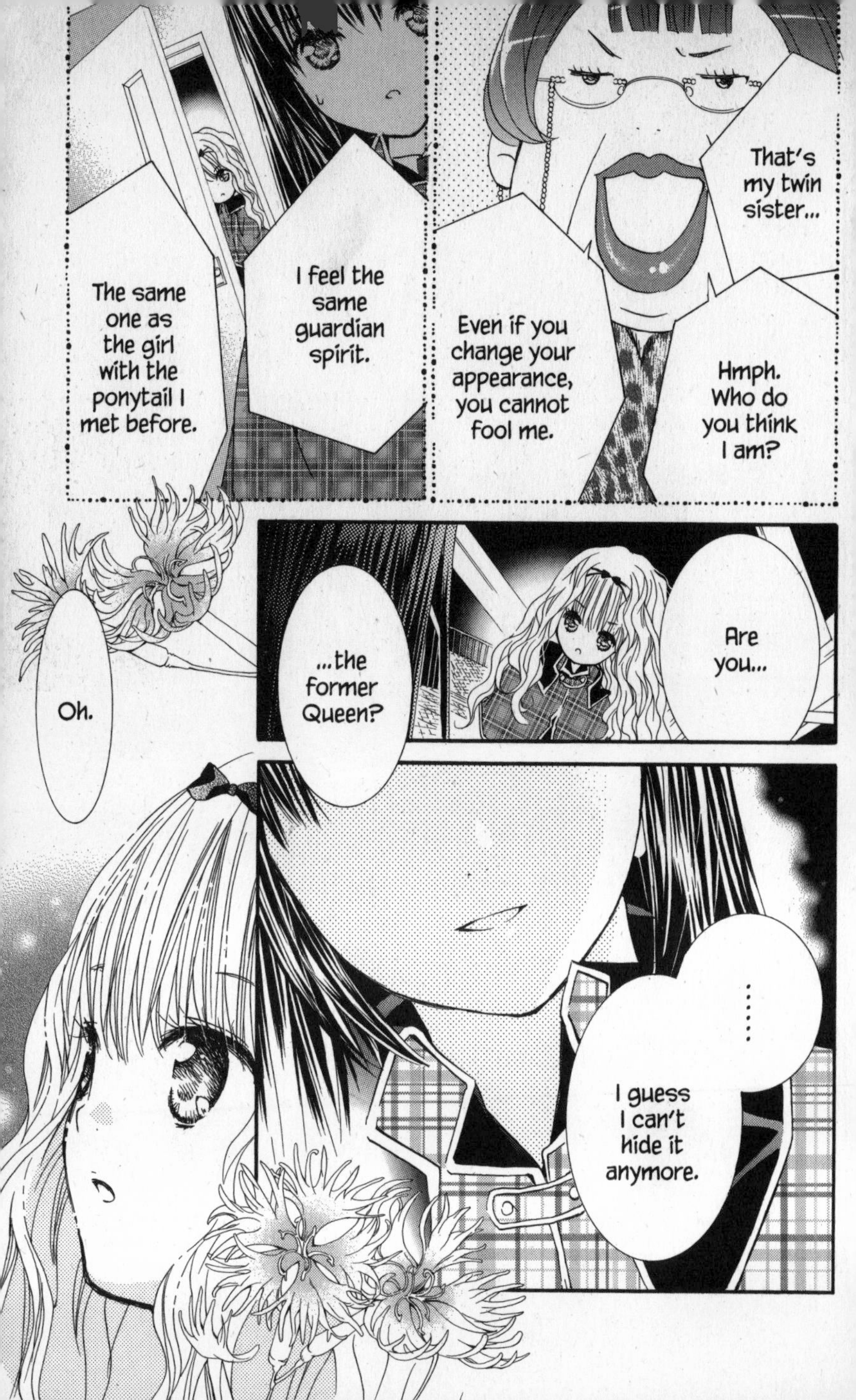
That's my twin sister...
Hmph. Who do you think I am?
Even if you change your appearance, you cannot fool me.
I feel the same guardian spirit.
The same one as the girl with the ponytail I met before.
Are you...
...the former Queen?
Oh.
......
I guess I can't hide it anymore.

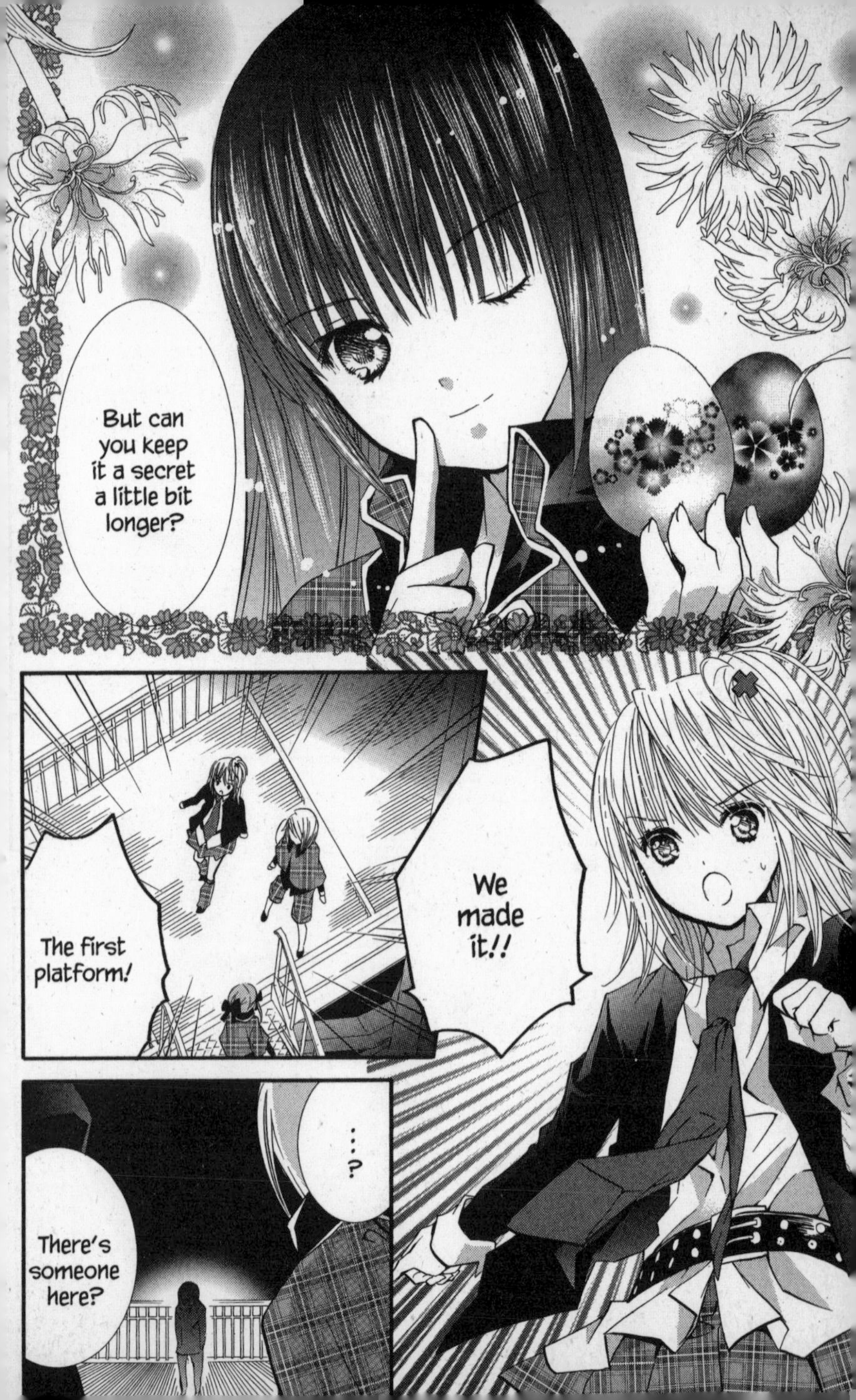
But can you keep it a secret a little bit longer?
We made it!!
The first platform!
...?
There's someone here?

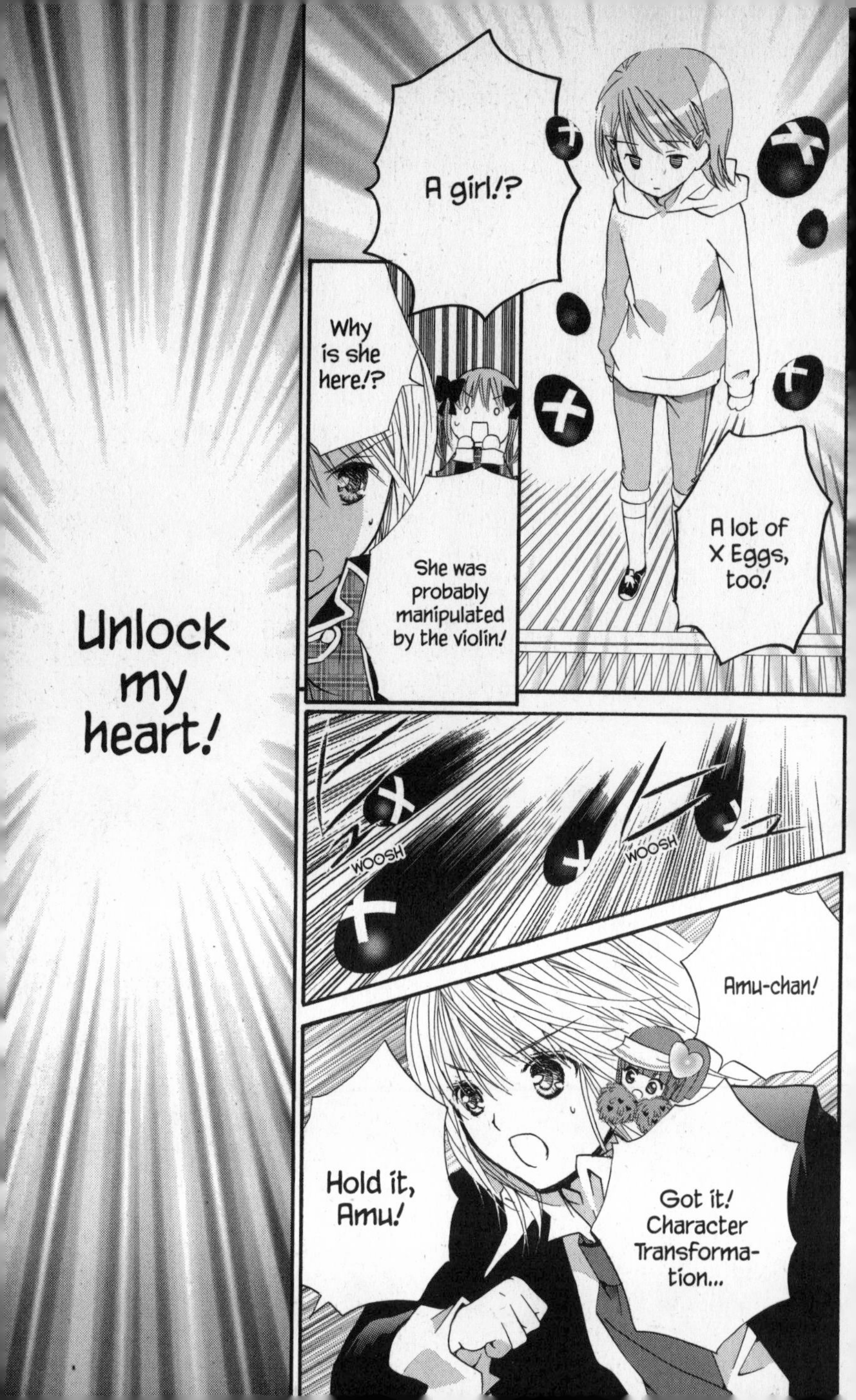
A girl!?
A lot of X Eggs, too!
Why is she here!?
She was probably manipulated by the violin!
WOOSH
WOOSH
Amu-chan!
Got it! Character Transforma-tion...
Hold it, Amu!
Unlock my heart!

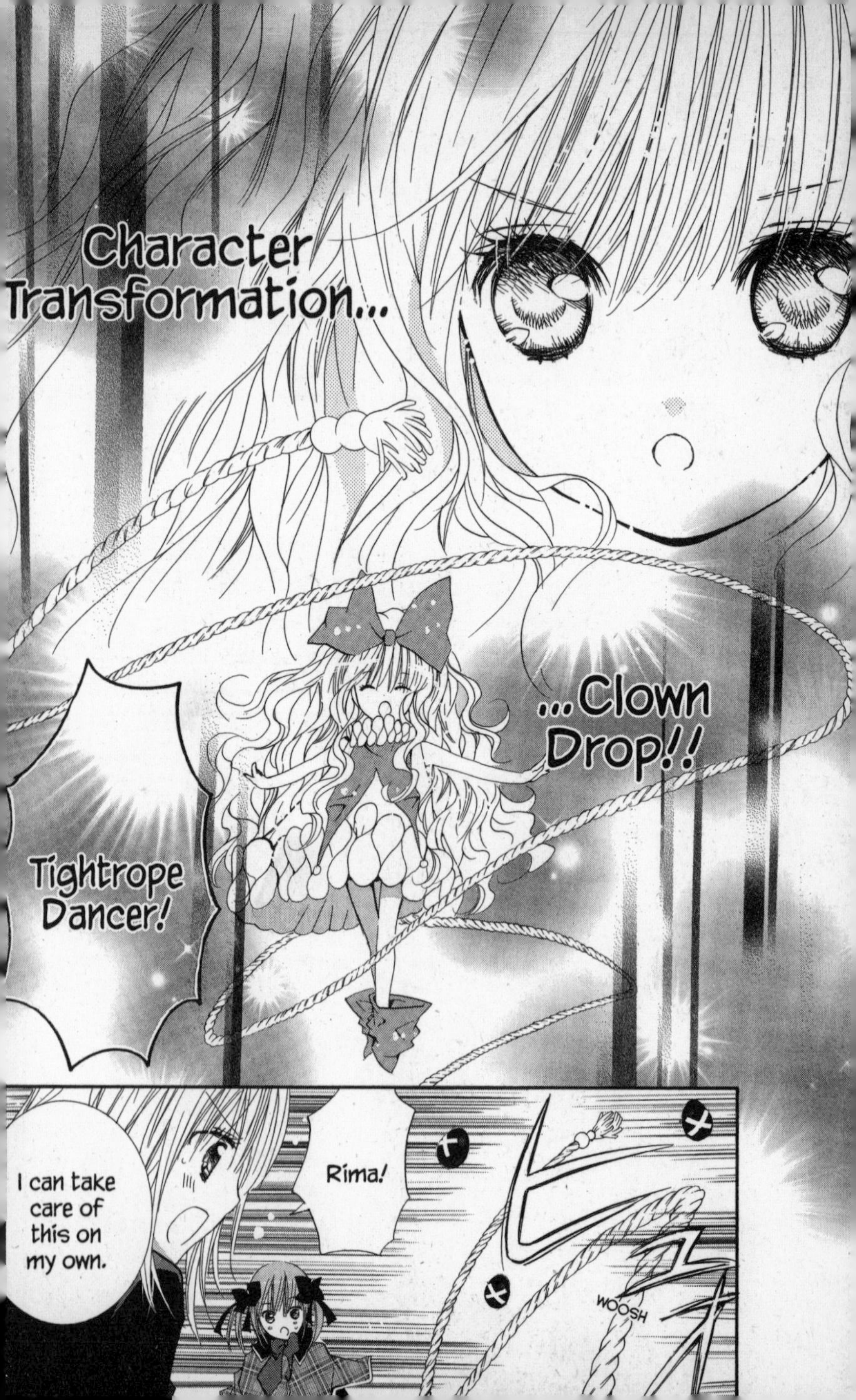
Character Transformation...
...Clown Drop!!
Tightrope Dancer!
WOOSH
Rima!
I can take care of this on my own.

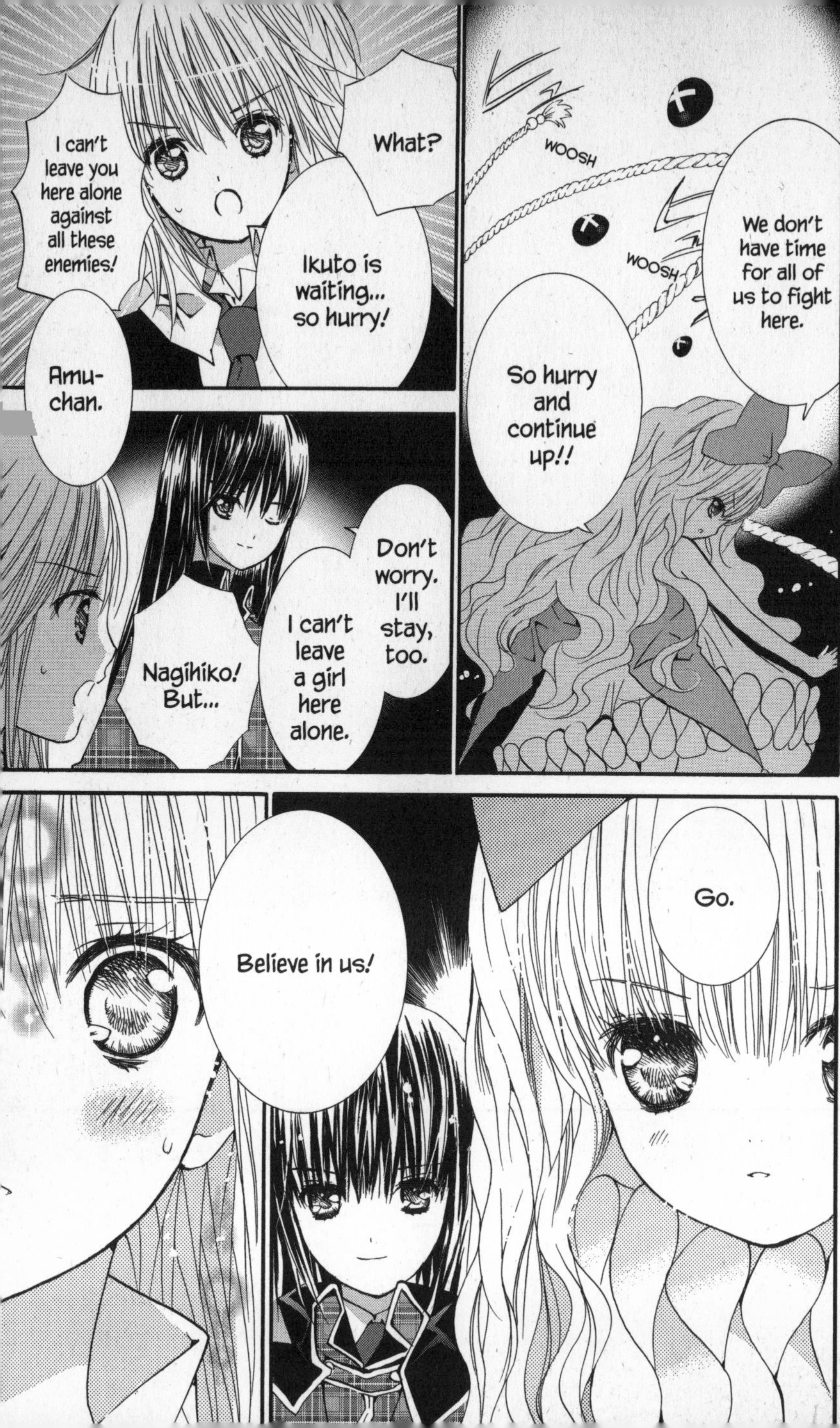
WOOSH
WOOSH
We don't have time for all of us to fight here.
So hurry and continue up!!
What?
I can't leave you here alone against all these enemies!
Ikuto is waiting... so hurry!
Amu-chan.
Don't worry. I'll stay, too.
I can't leave a girl here alone.
Nagihiko! But...
Go.
Believe in us!

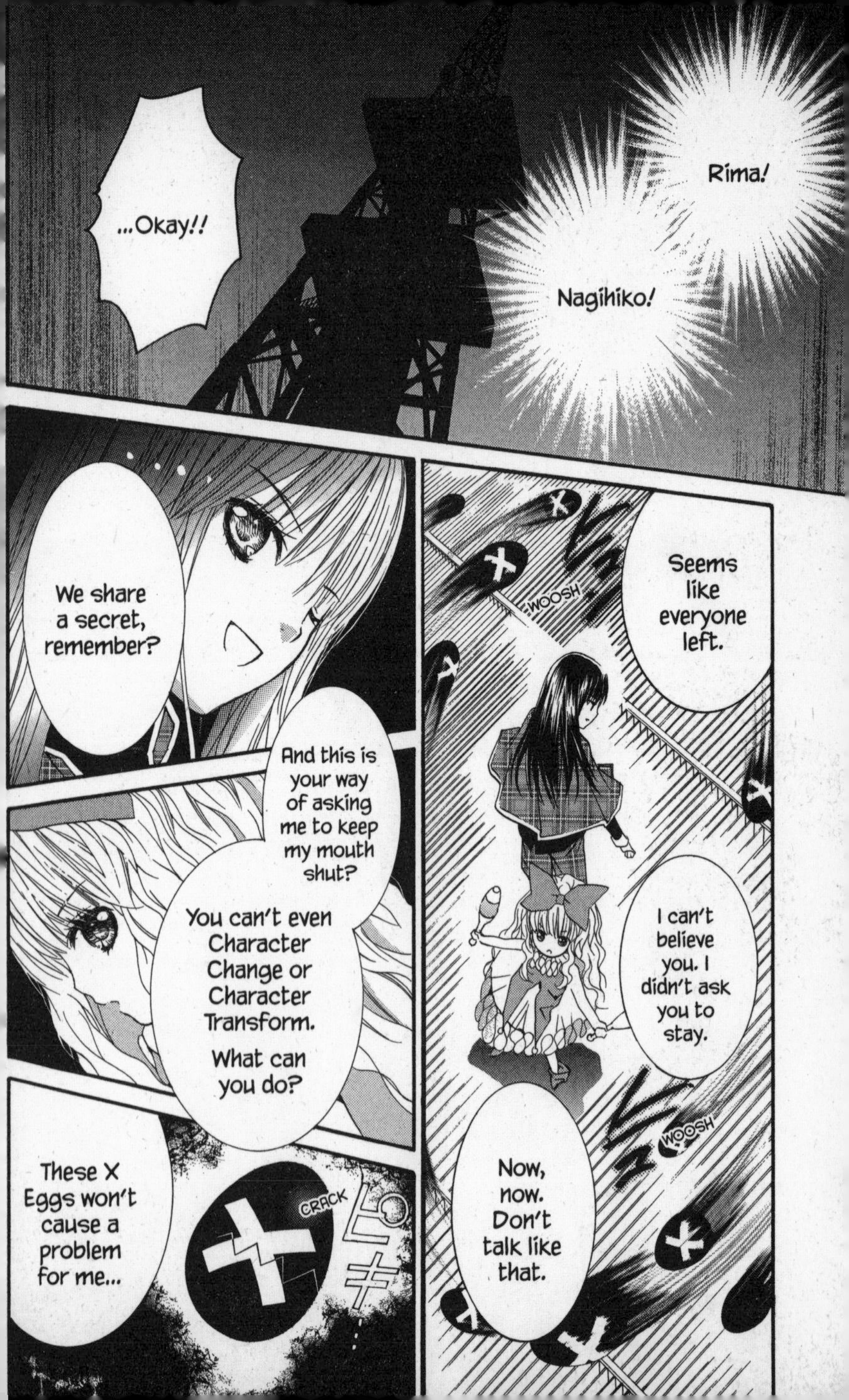
Rima!
Nagihiko!
...Okay!!
Seems like everyone left.
WOOSH
I can't believe you. I didn't ask you to stay.
Now, now. Don't talk like that.
WOOSH
We share a secret, remember?
And this is your way of asking me to keep my mouth shut?
You can't even Character Change or Character Transform.
What can you do?
These X Eggs won't cause a problem for me...
CRACK

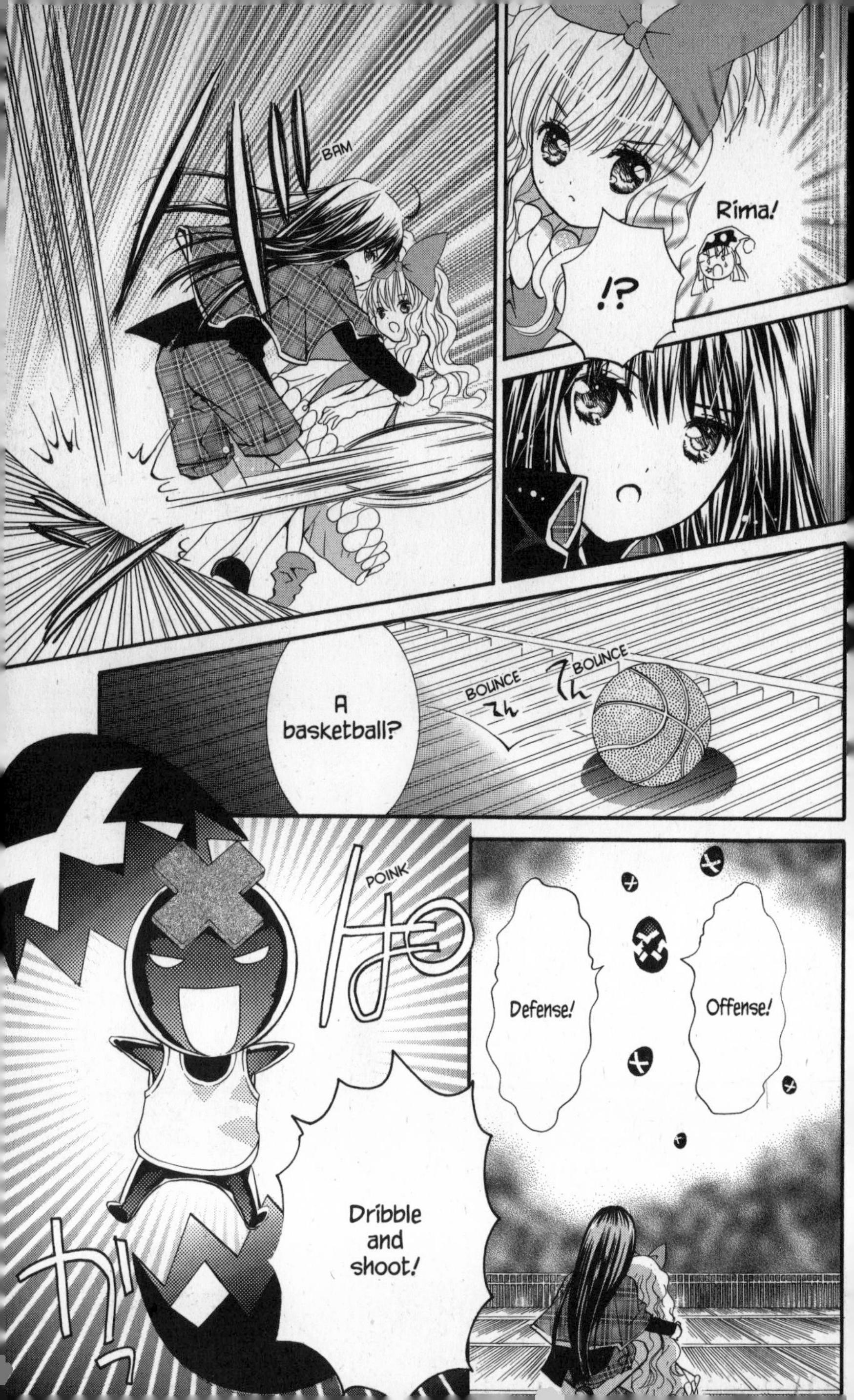
Rima!
!?
BAM
BOUNCE
BOUNCE
A basketball?
Offense!
Defense!
POINK
Dribble and shoot!

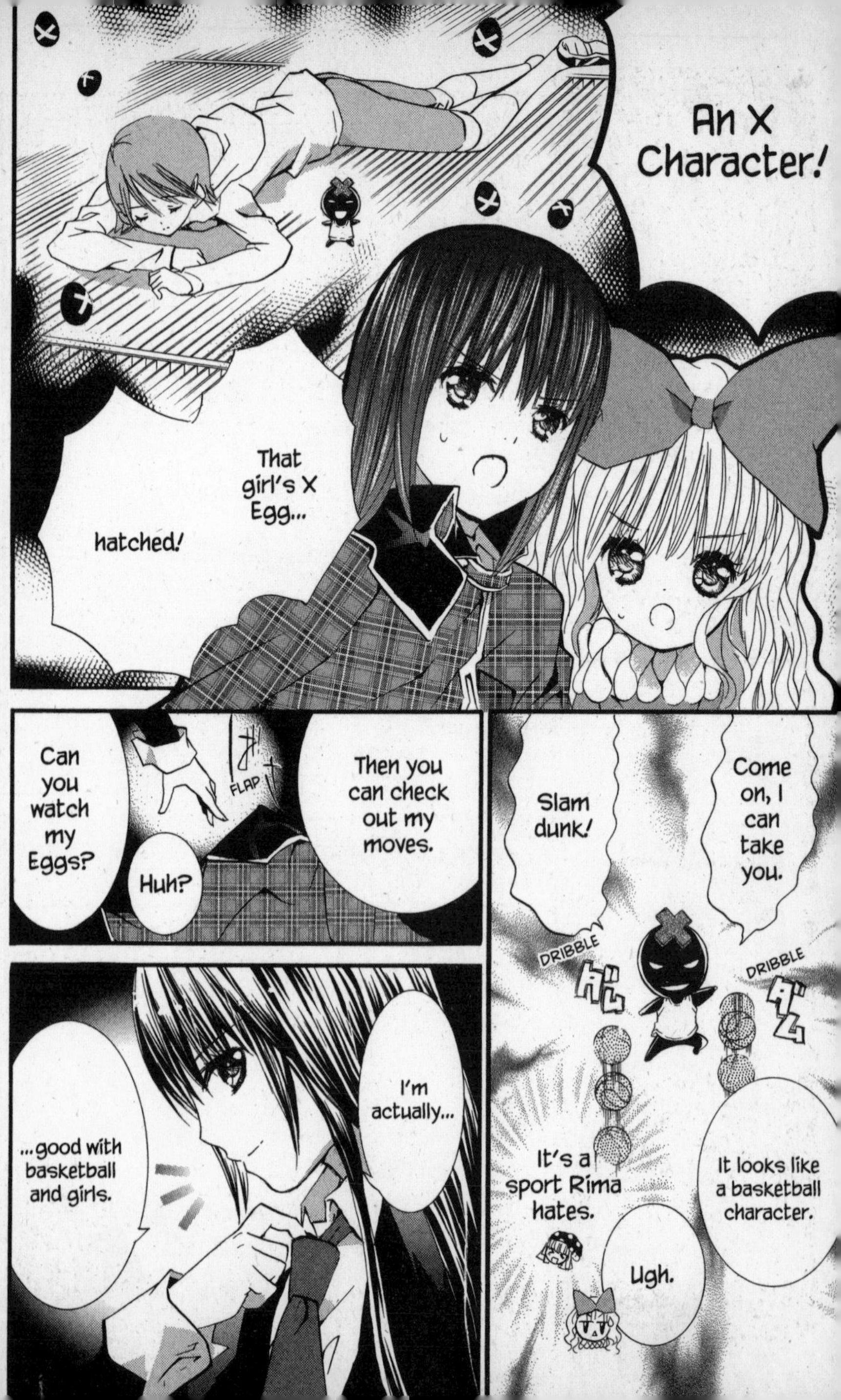
An X Character!
That girl's X Egg...
hatched!
Come on, I can take you.
Slam dunk!
DRIBBLE
DRIBBLE
It looks like a basketball character.
It's a sport Rima hates.
Ugh.
Then you can check out my moves.
FLAP
Huh?
Can you watch my Eggs?
I'm actually...
...good with basketball and girls.

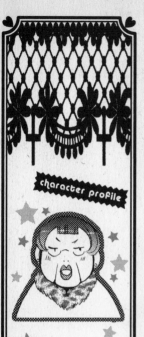

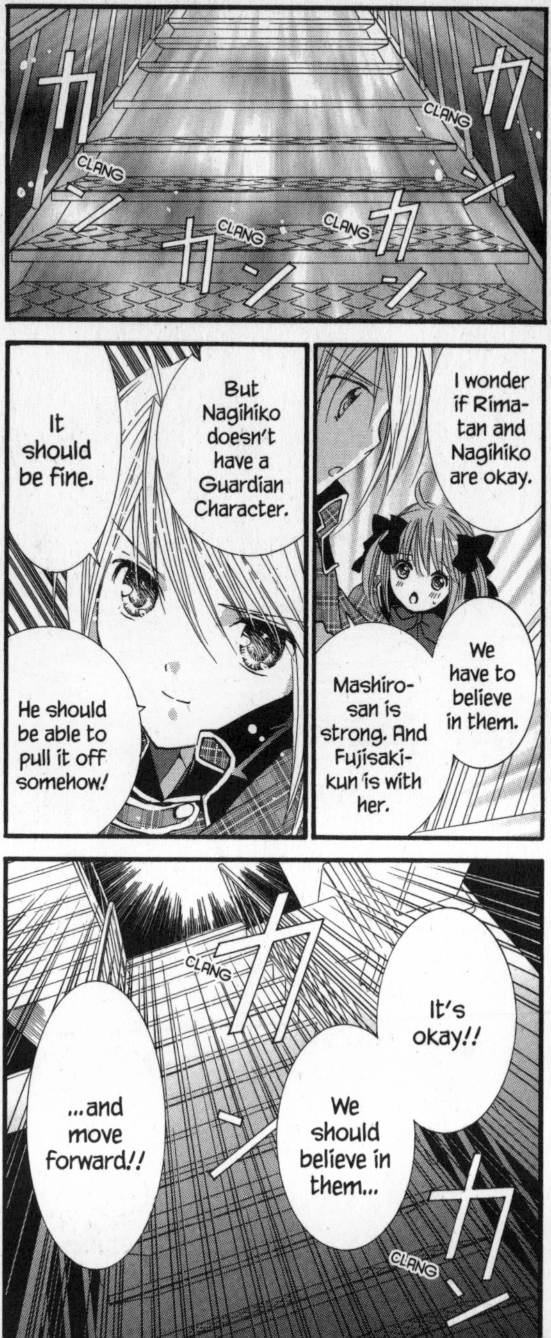
CLANG
CLANG
CLANG
CLANG
I wonder if Rima-tan and Nagihiko are okay.
We have to believe in them.
Mashiro-san is strong. And Fujisaki-kun is with her.
But Nagihiko doesn't have a Guardian Character.
It should be fine.
He should be able to pull it off somehow!
CLANG
It's okay!!
We should believe in them...
...and move forward!!
CLANG

character profile

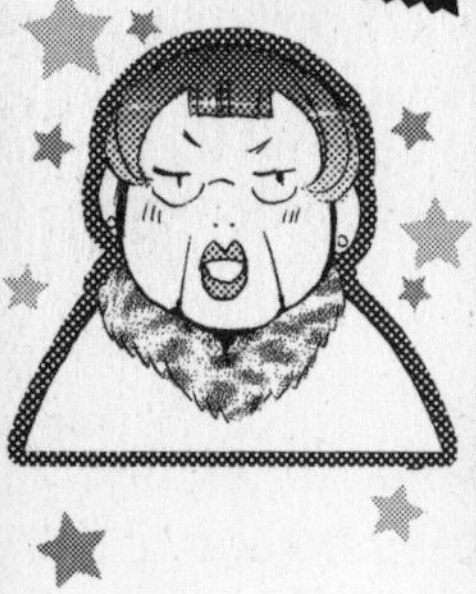

Nobuko Saeki

Birthday: 1/5
Blood Type: B
Sign: Capricorn

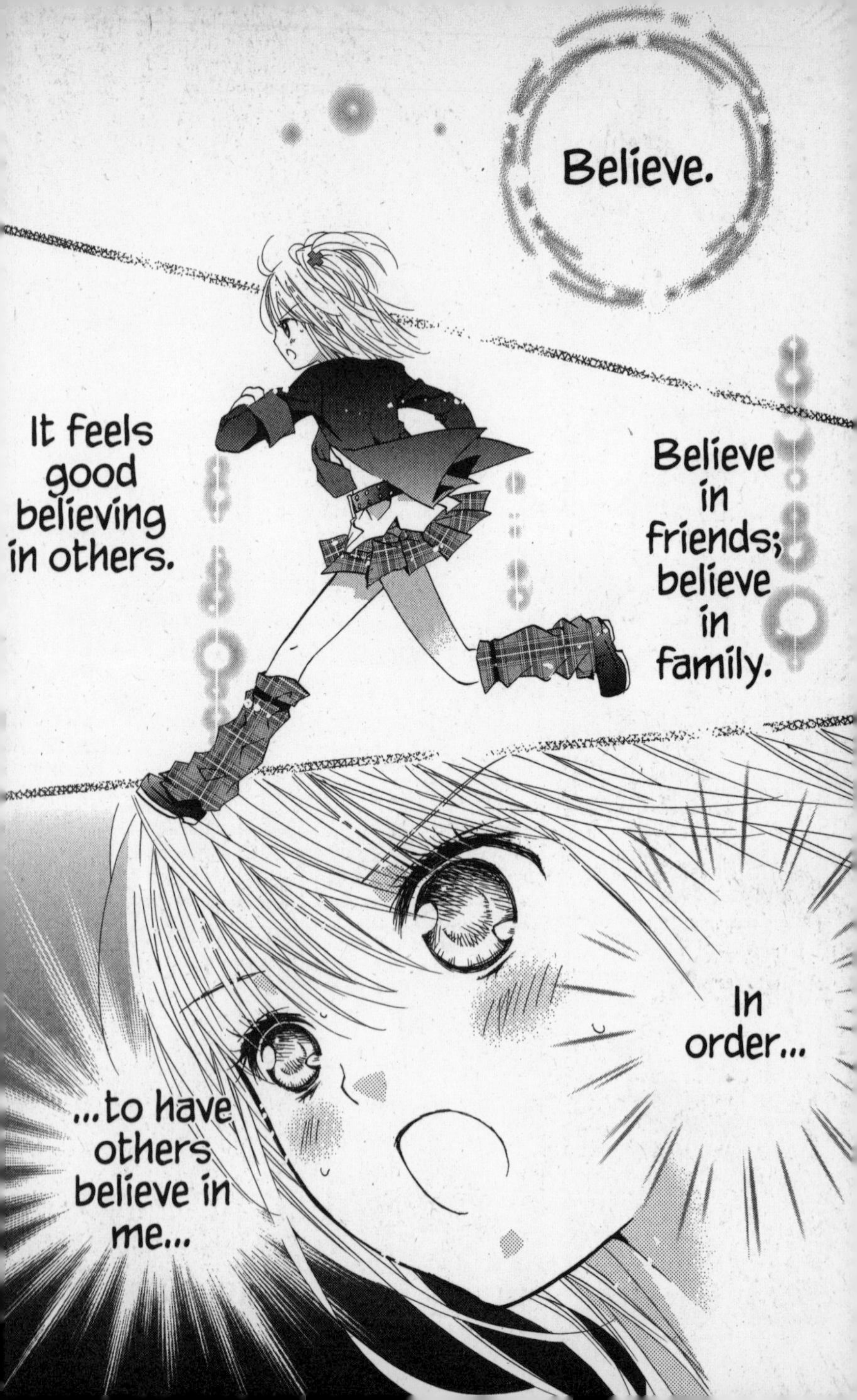
Believe.
Believe in friends; believe in family.
It feels good believing in others.
In order...
...to have others believe in me...

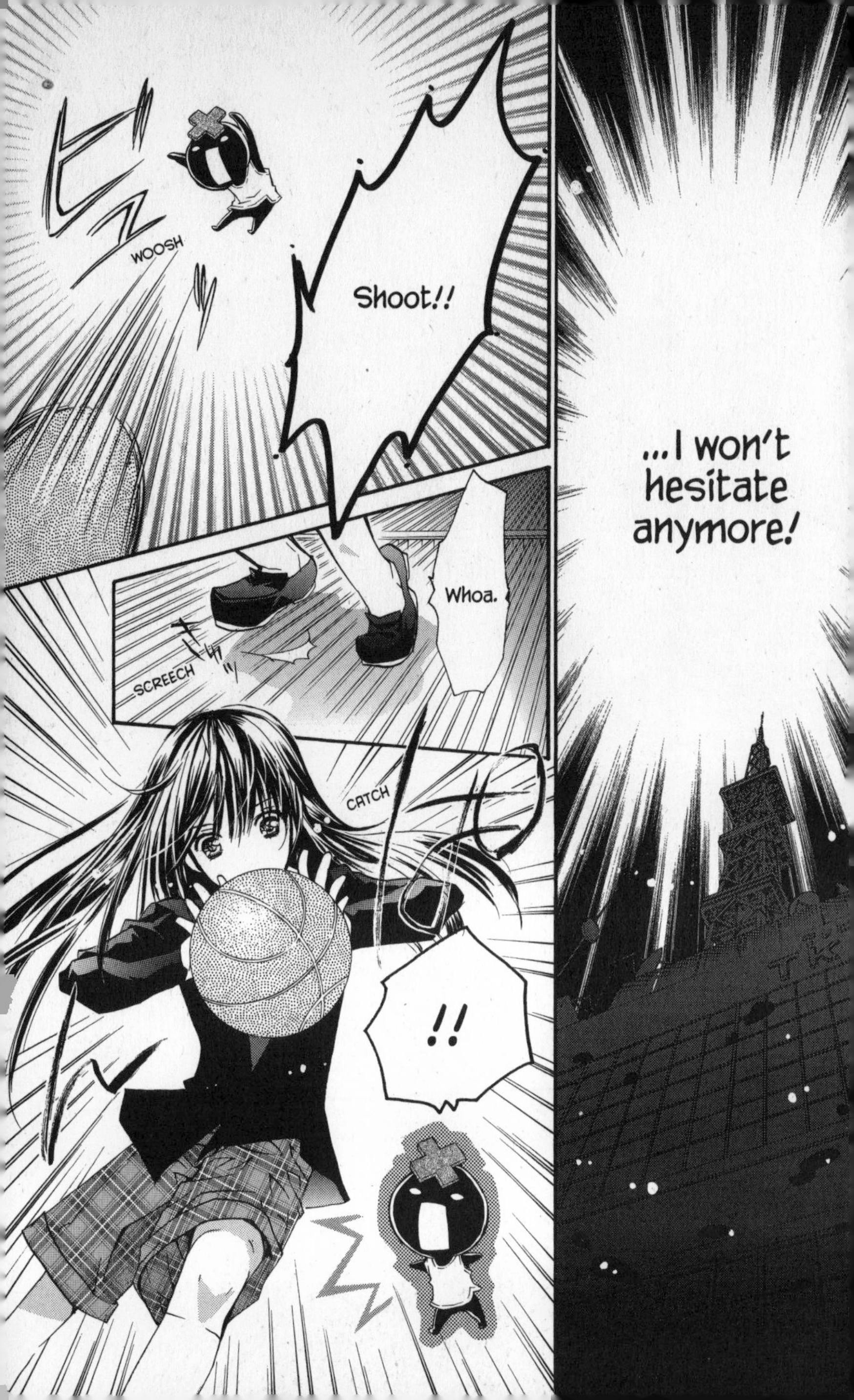
...I won't hesitate anymore!
Shoot!!
WOOSH
Whoa.
SCREECH
CATCH
!!

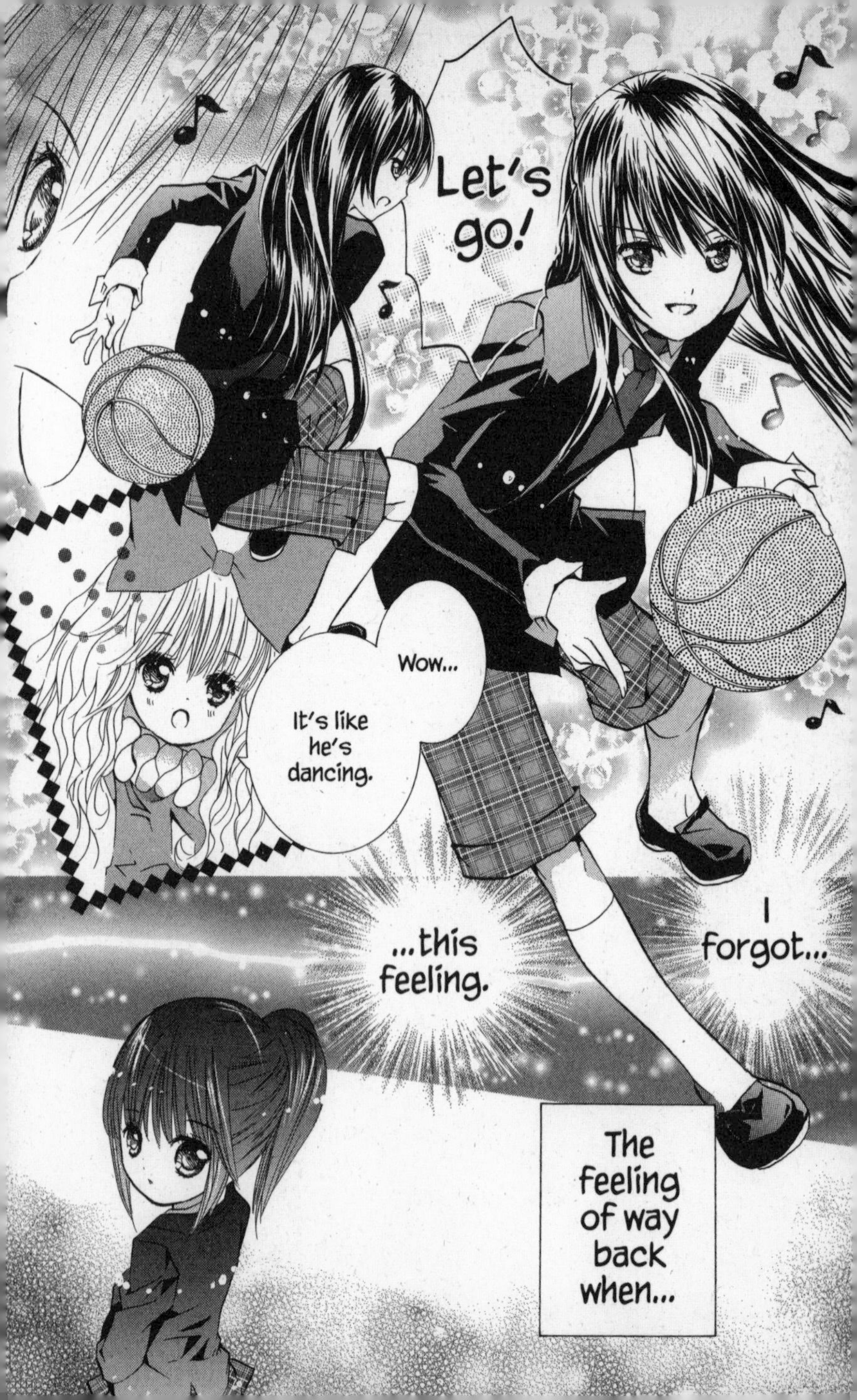
Let's go!
Wow... It's like he's dancing.
I forgot...
...this feeling.
The feeling of way back when...

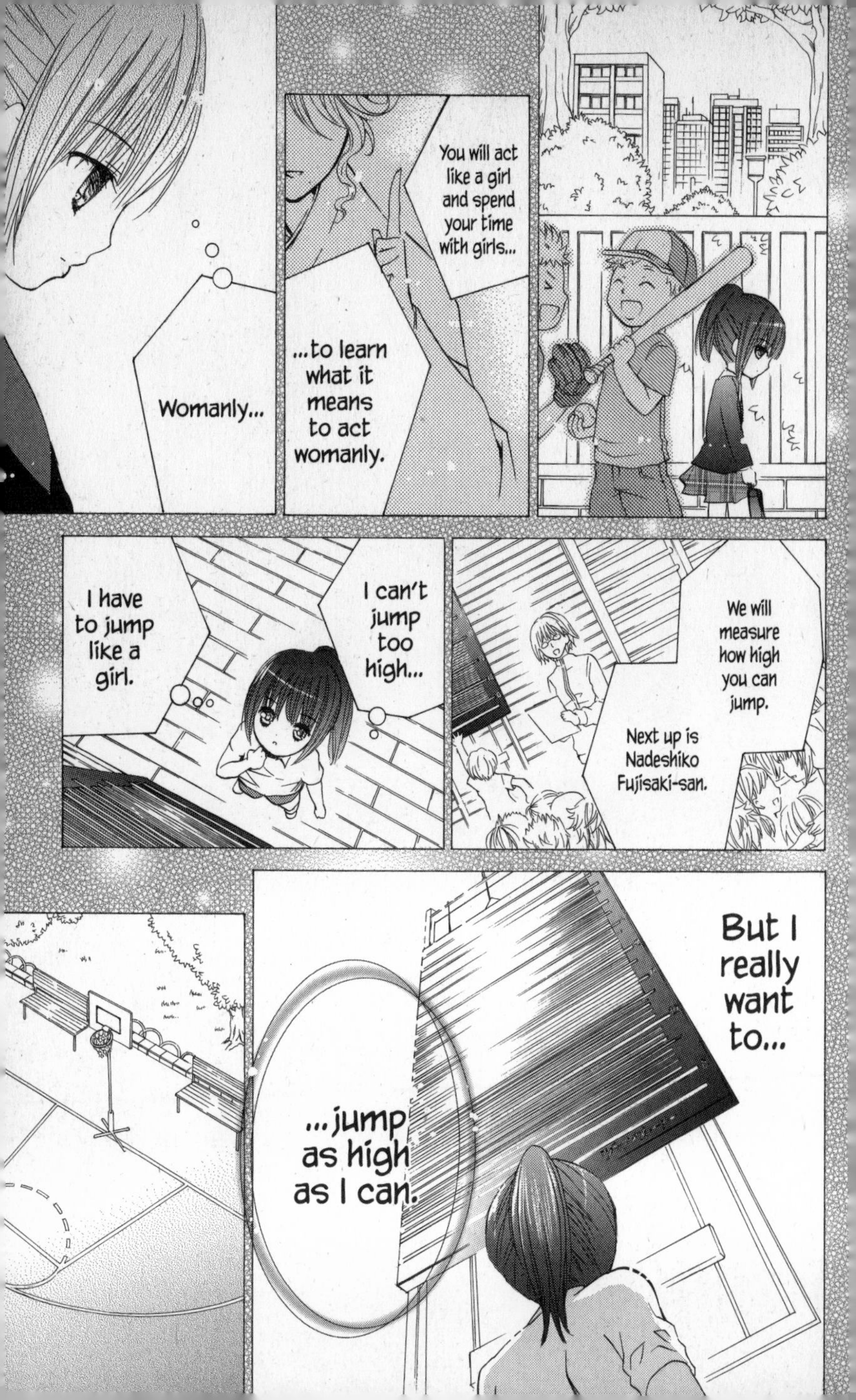
You will act like a girl and spend your time with girls...
...to learn what it means to act womanly.
Womanly...
We will measure how high you can jump.
Next up is Nadeshiko Fujisaki-san.
I can't jump too high...
I have to jump like a girl.
But I really want to...
...jump as high as I can.

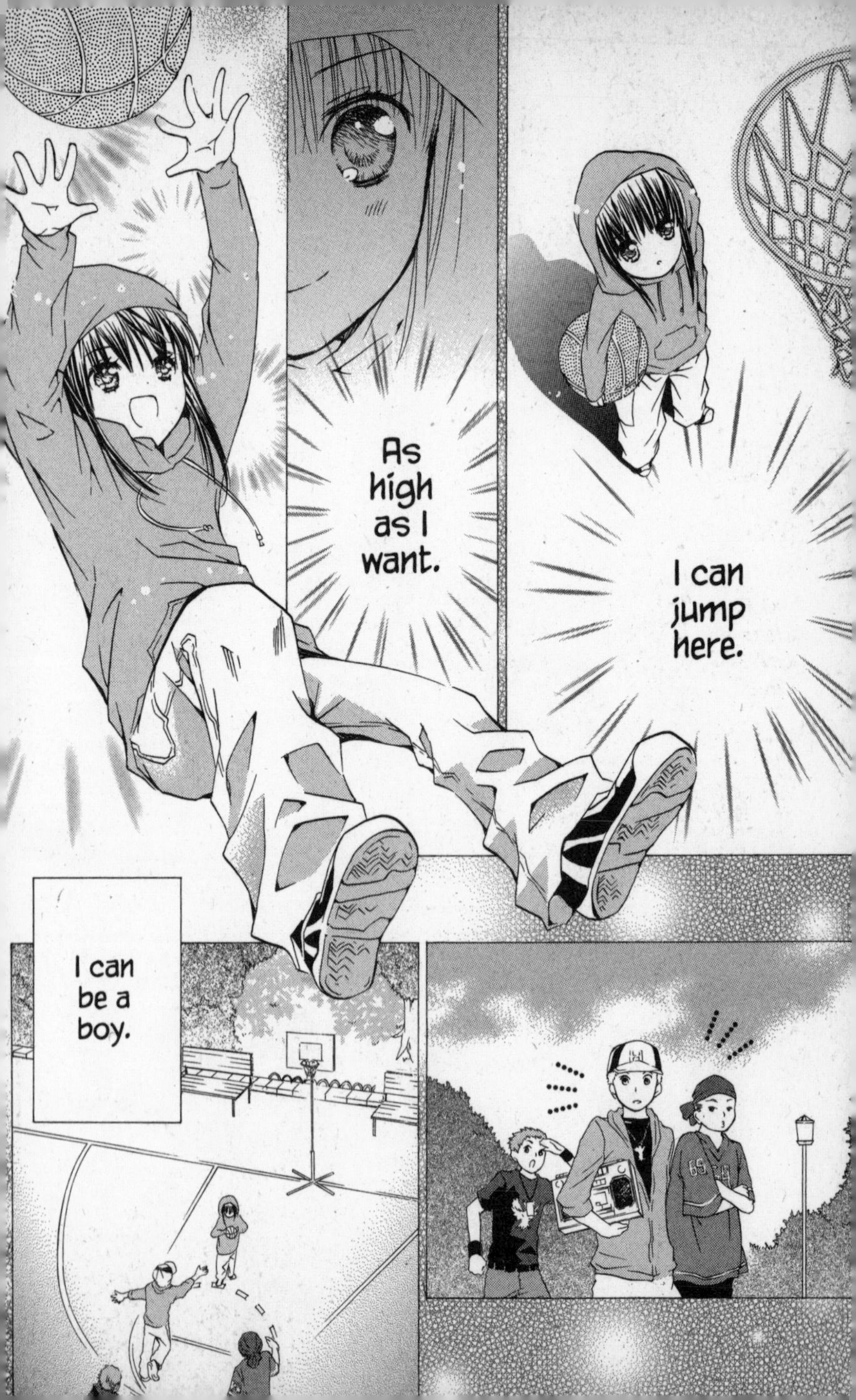
I can jump here.
As high as I want.
I can be a boy.

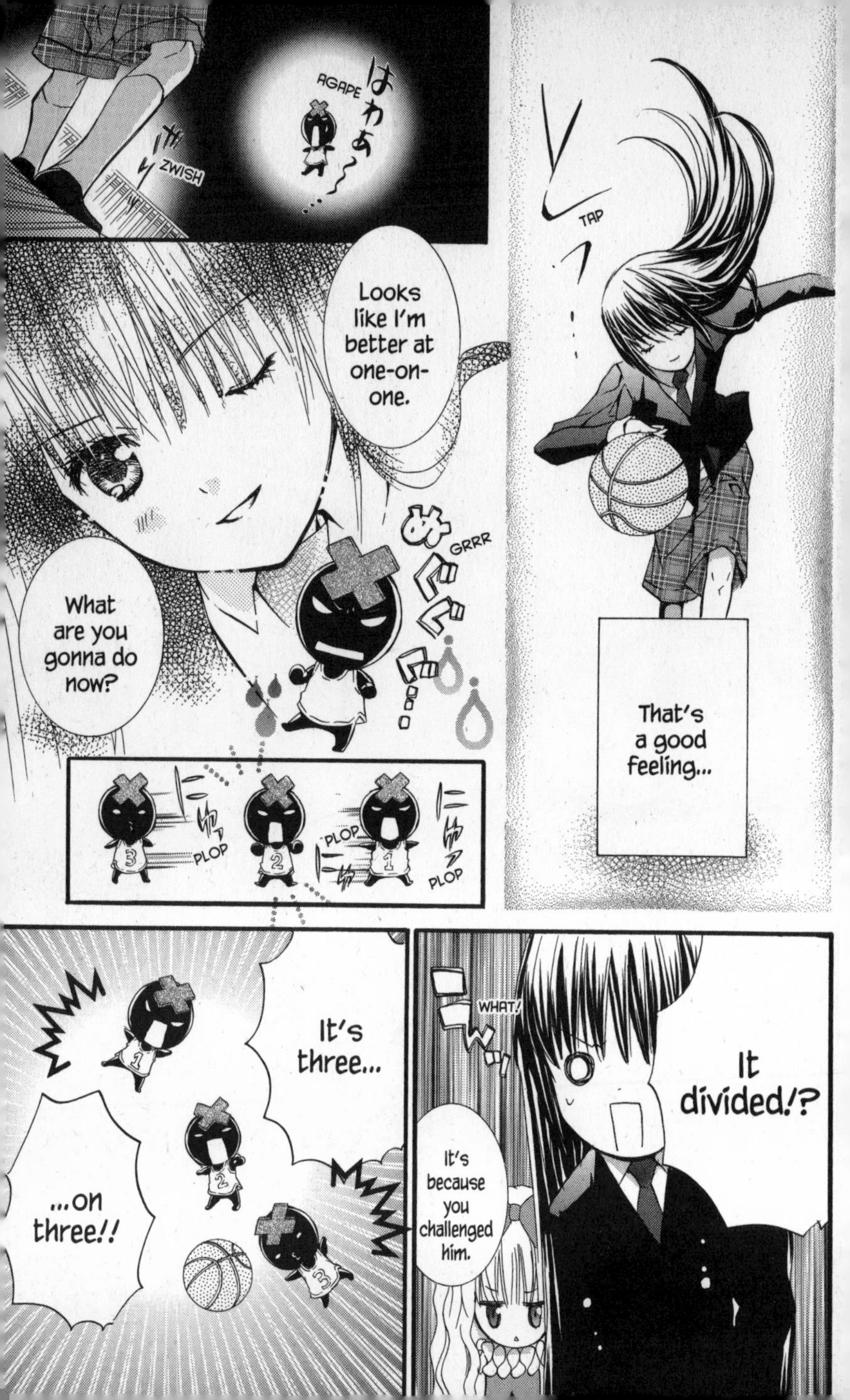
TAP
That's a good feeling...
はわあ〜
AGAPE
ZWISH
Looks like I'm better at one-on-one.
GRRR
What are you gonna do now?
PLOP
PLOP
PLOP
WHAT!
It divided!?
It's because you challenged him.
It's three...
...on three!!

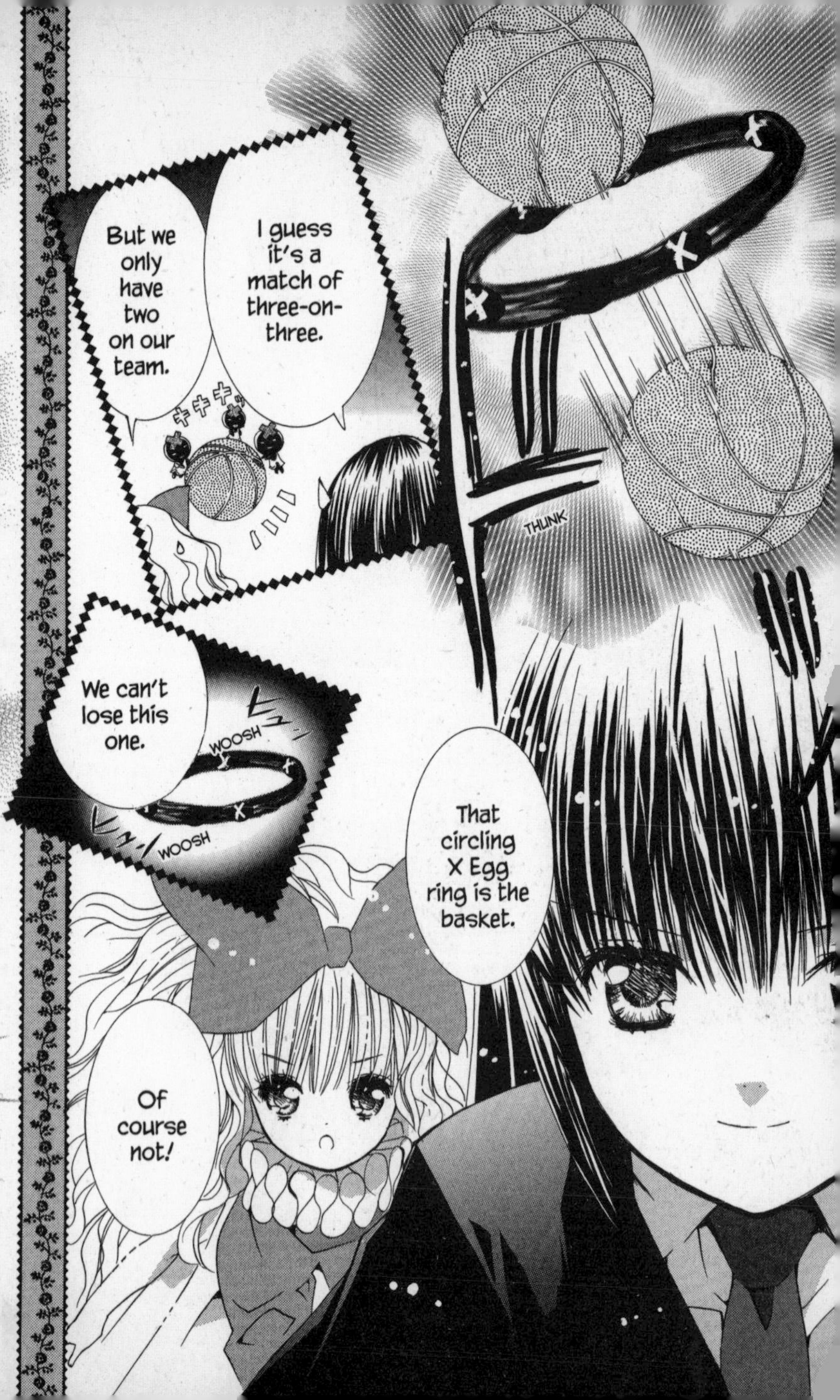
THUNK
I guess it's a match of three-on-three.
But we only have two on our team.
We can't lose this one.
WOOSH
WOOSH
That circling X Egg ring is the basket.
Of course not!

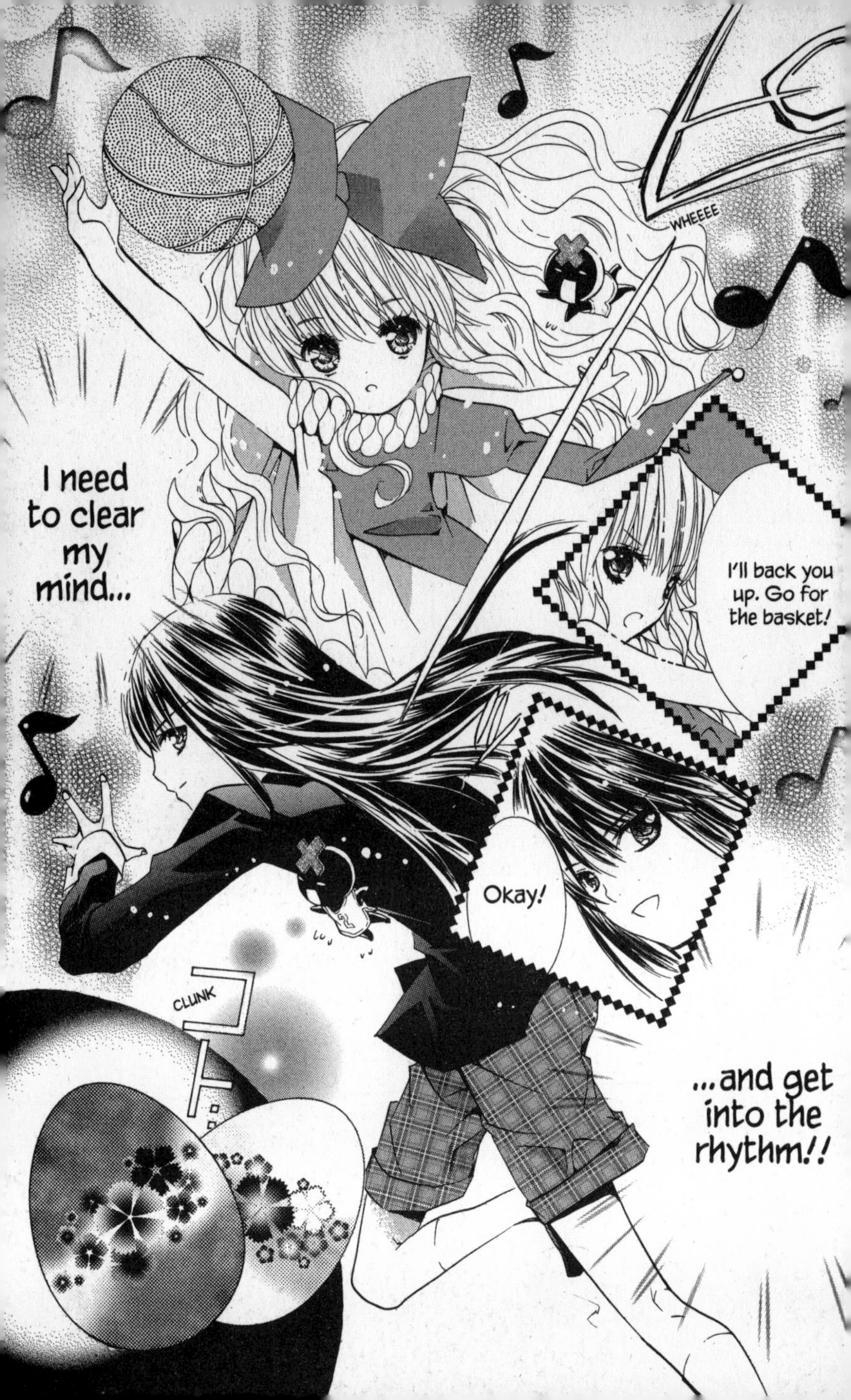
WHEEEE
I need to clear my mind...
I'll back you up. Go for the basket!
Okay!
CLUNK
...and get into the rhythm!!

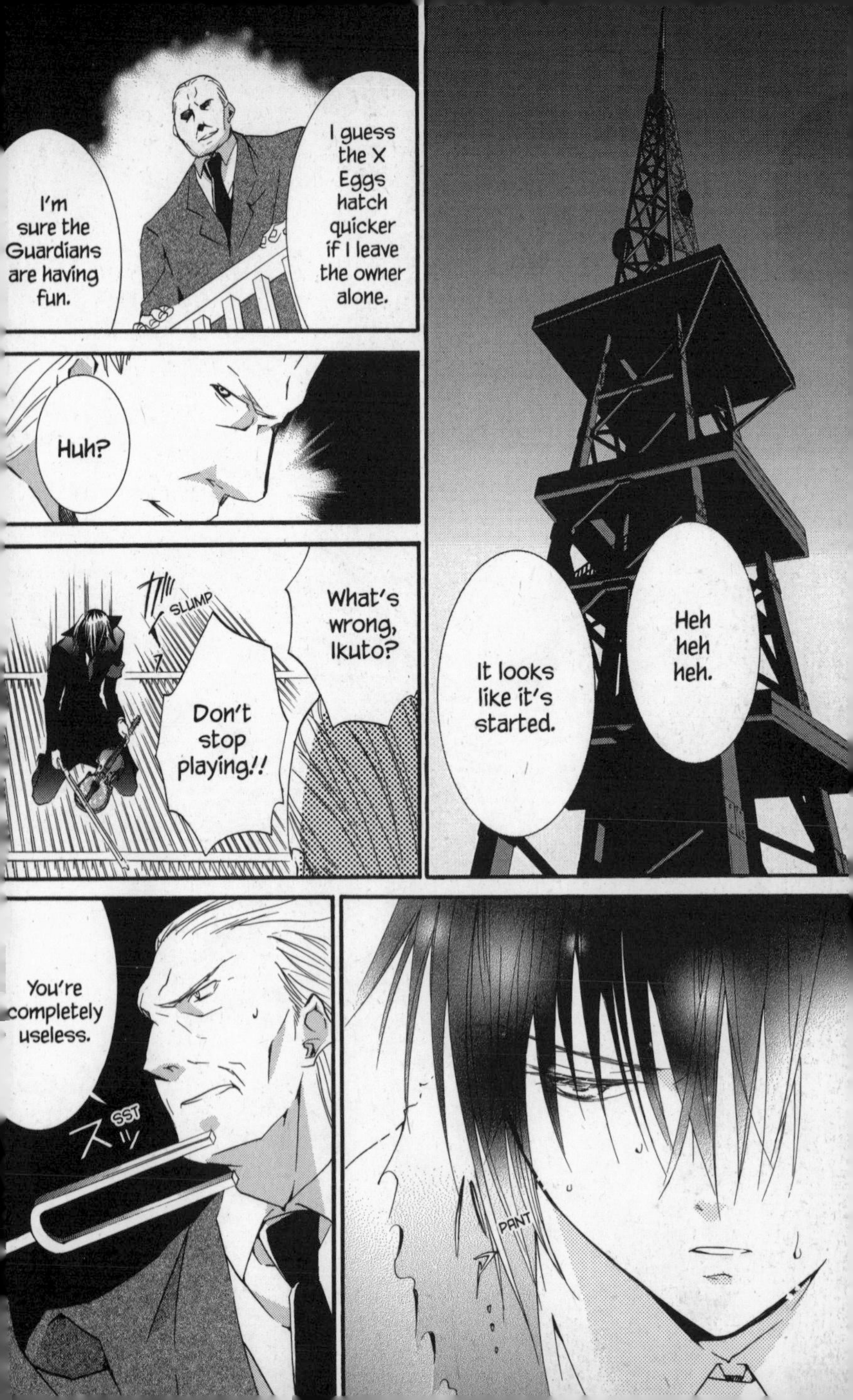
Heh heh heh.
It looks like it's started.
I guess the X Eggs hatch quicker if I leave the owner alone.
I'm sure the Guardians are having fun.
Huh?
What's wrong, Ikuto?
SLUMP
Don't stop playing!!
PANT
You're completely useless.
SST

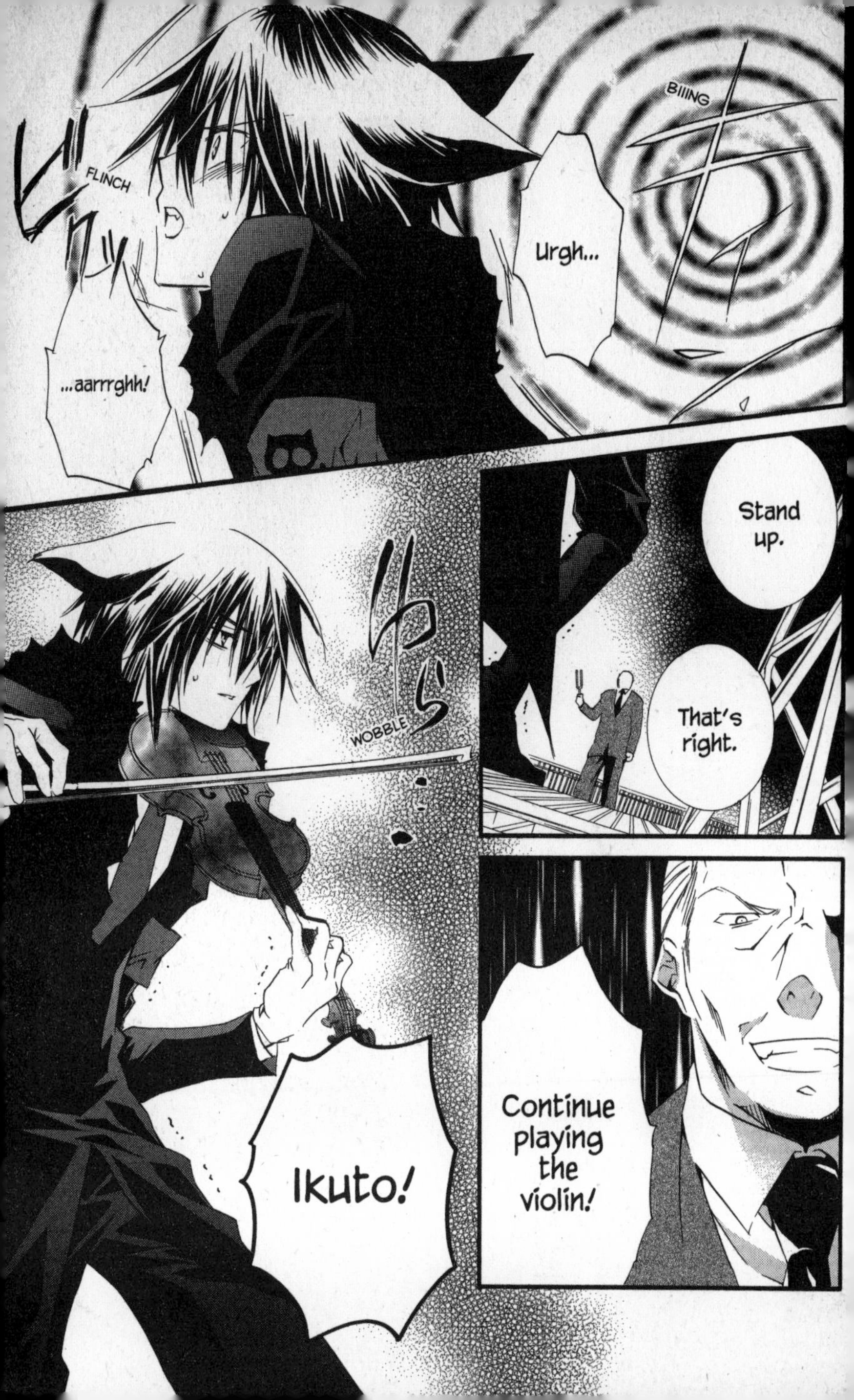
BIING
Urgh...
FLINCH
...aarrrghh!
Stand up.
That's right.
Continue playing the violin!
WOBBLE
Ikuto!

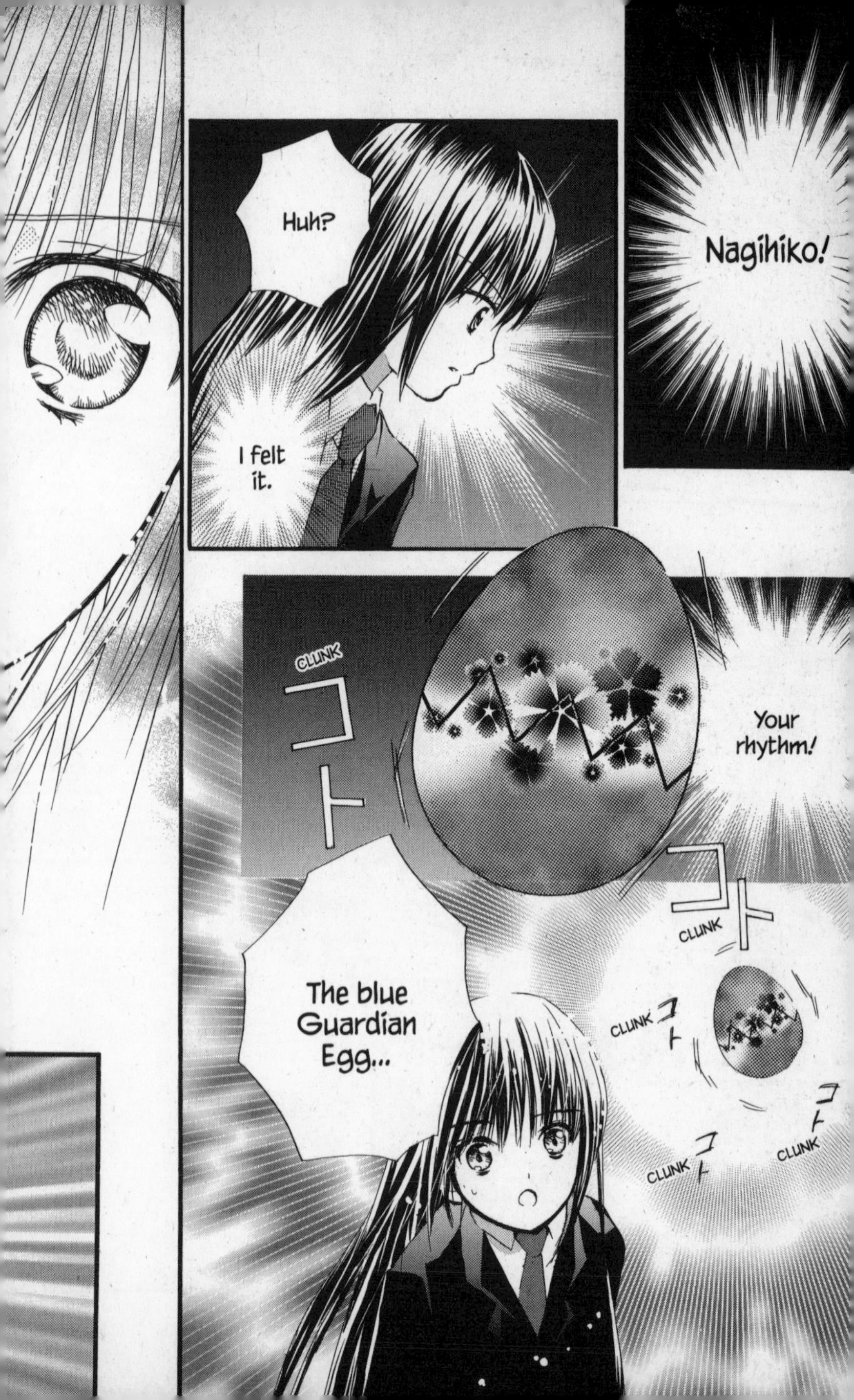

Nagihiko!
Huh?
I felt it.
Your rhythm!
CLUNK コト
CLUNK コト
The blue Guardian Egg...
CLUNK コト
CLUNK コト
CLUNK コト

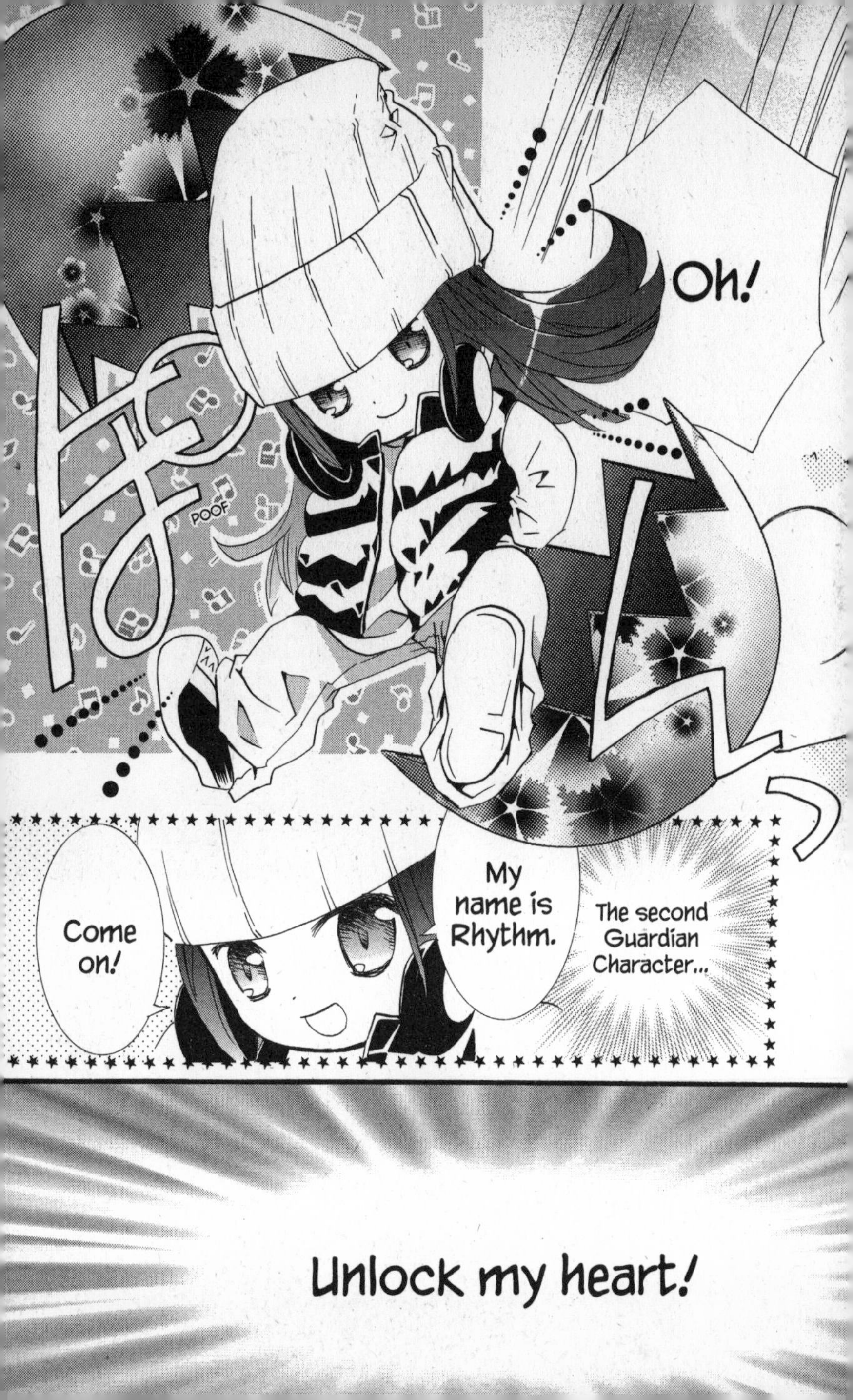
Oh!
POOF
The second Guardian Character...
My name is Rhythm.
Come on!
Unlock my heart!

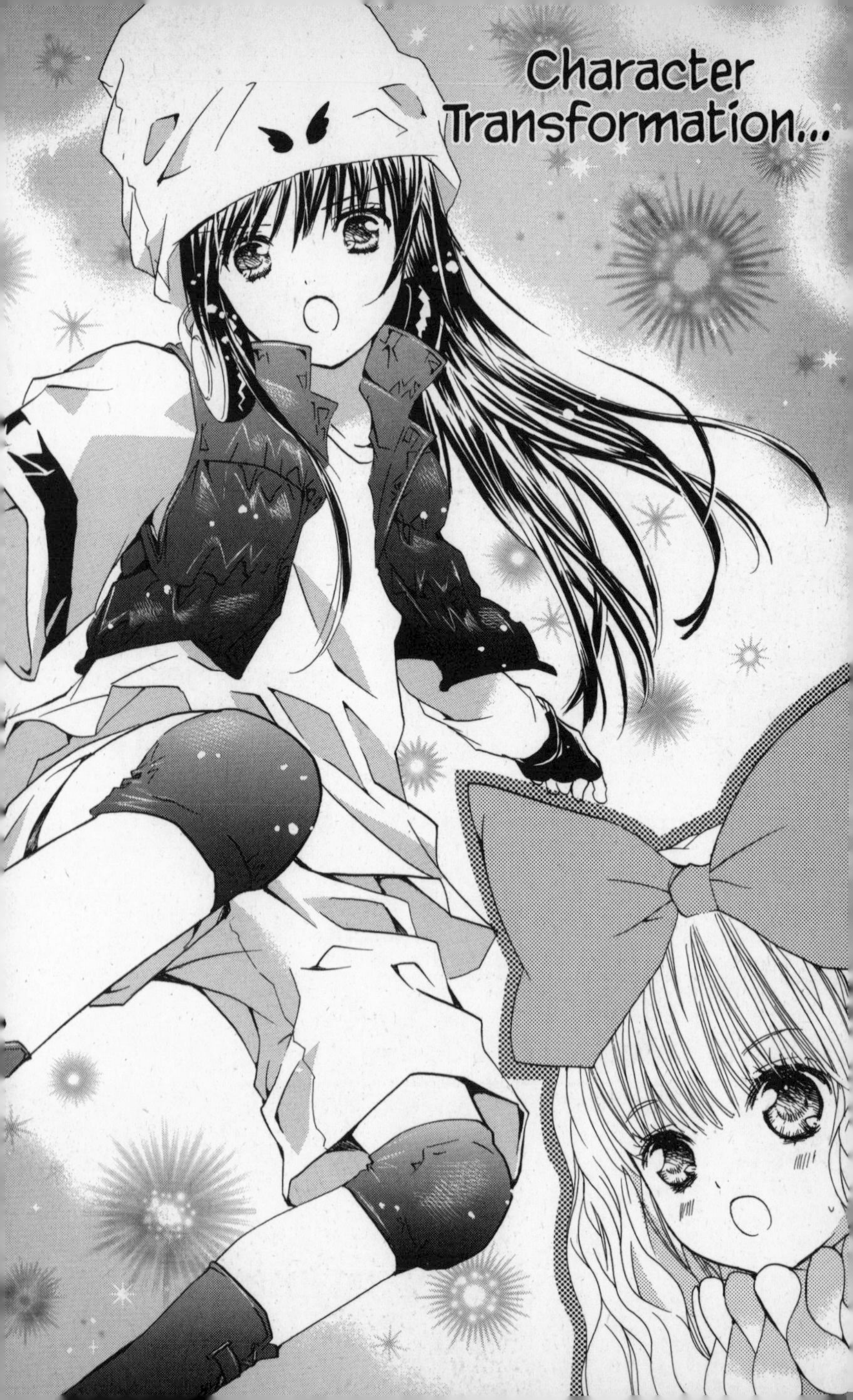
Character Transformation...

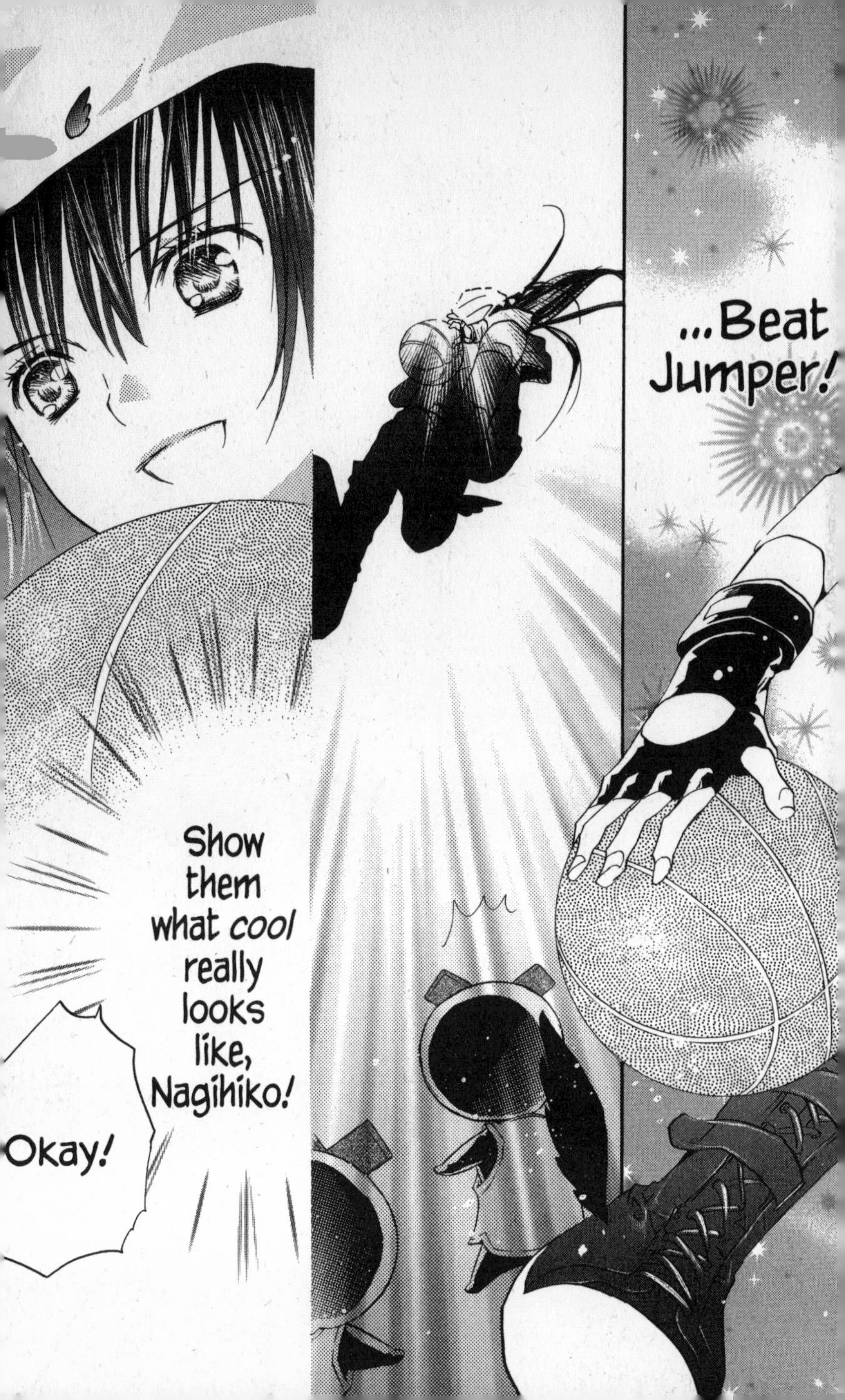
...Beat Jumper!
Show them what cool really looks like, Nagihiko!
Okay!

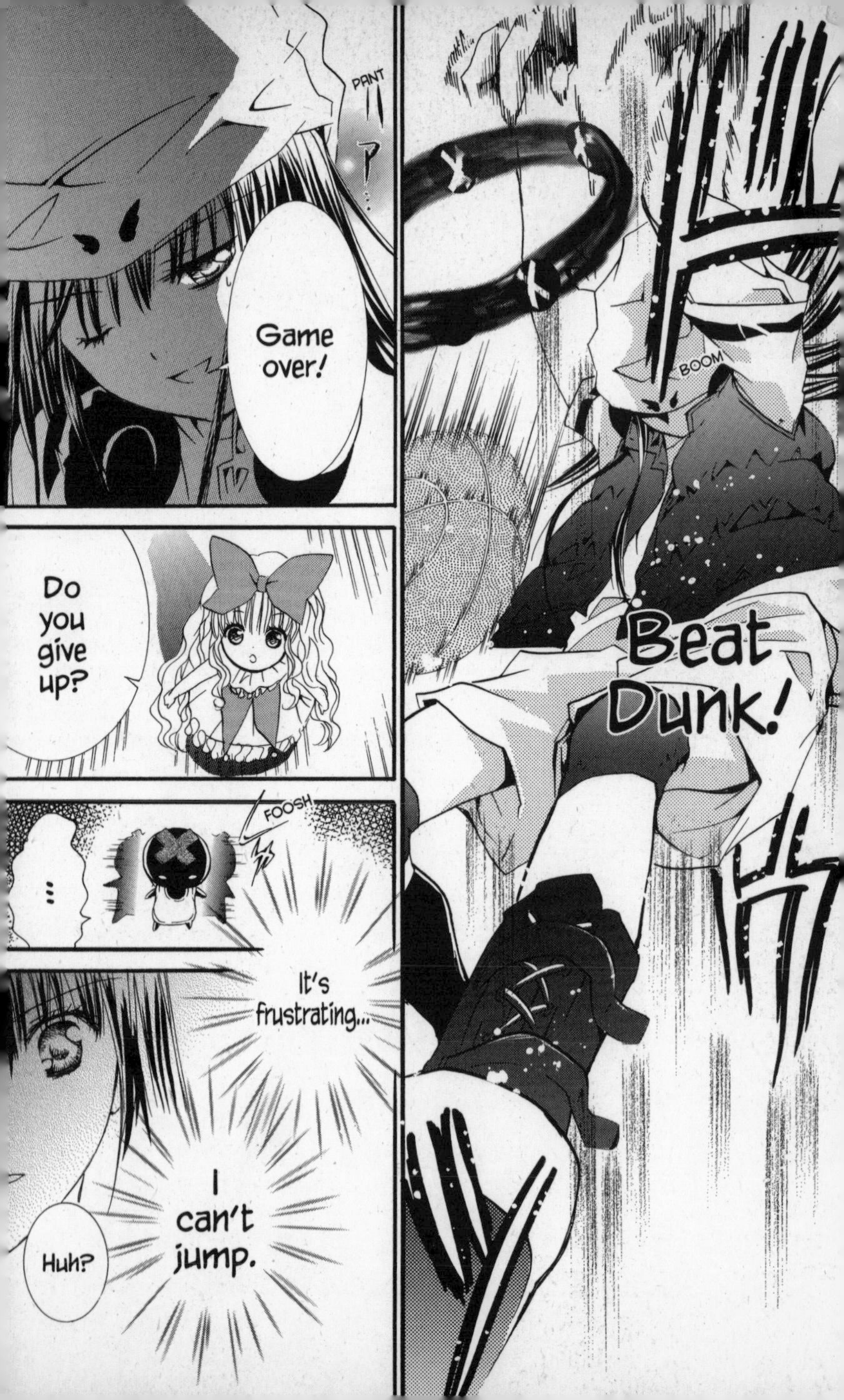
BOOM
Beat Dunk!
PANT
Game over!
Do you give up?
FOOSH
...
It's frustrating...
I can't jump.
Huh?

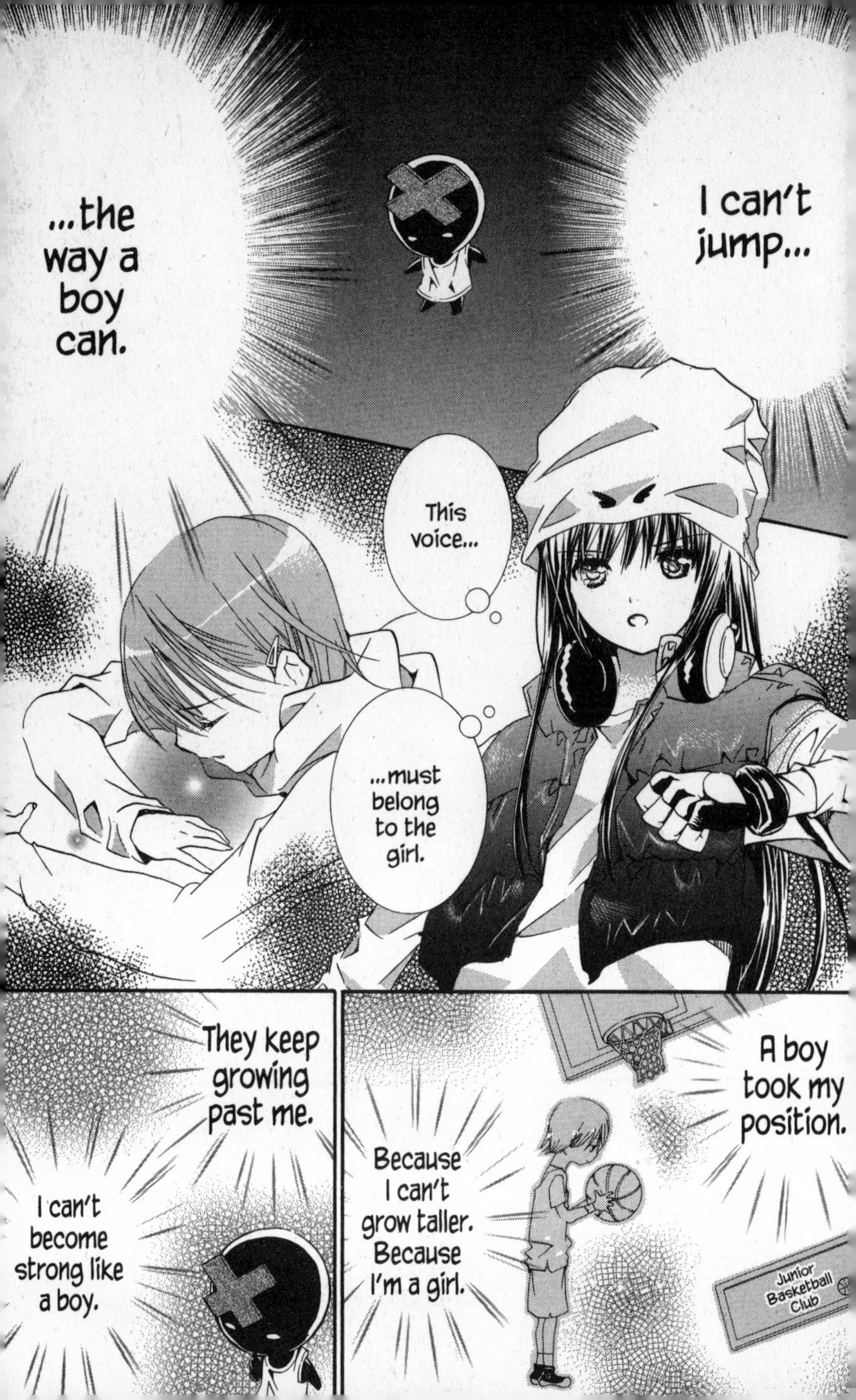
I can't jump...
...the way a boy can.
This voice...
...must belong to the girl.
A boy took my position.
Because I can't grow taller. Because I'm a girl.
Junior Basketball Club
They keep growing past me.
I can't become strong like a boy.

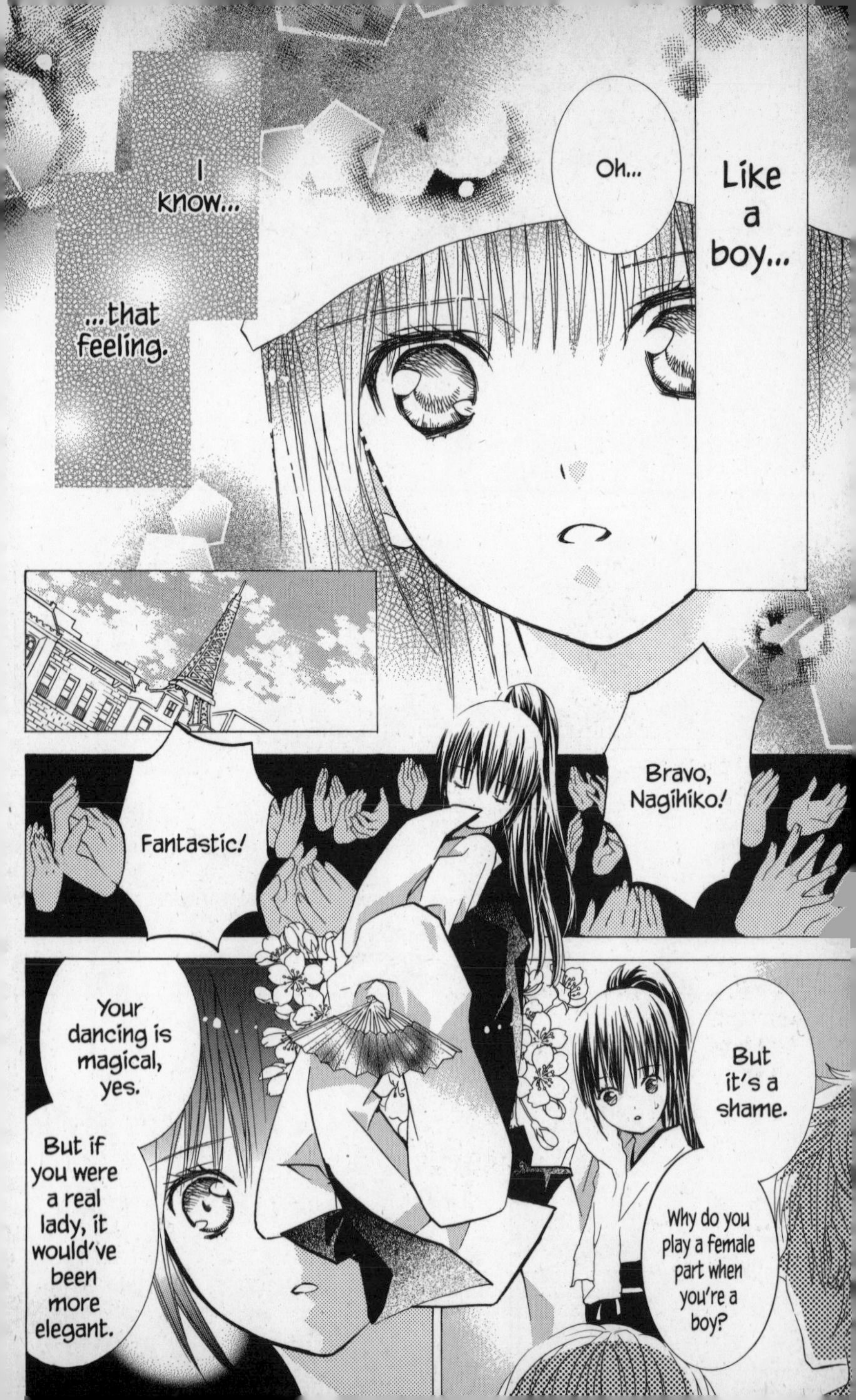
Like a boy...
Oh...
I know...
...that feeling.
Bravo, Nagihiko!
Fantastic!
But it's a shame.
Why do you play a female part when you're a boy?
Your dancing is magical, yes.
But if you were a real lady, it would've been more elegant.

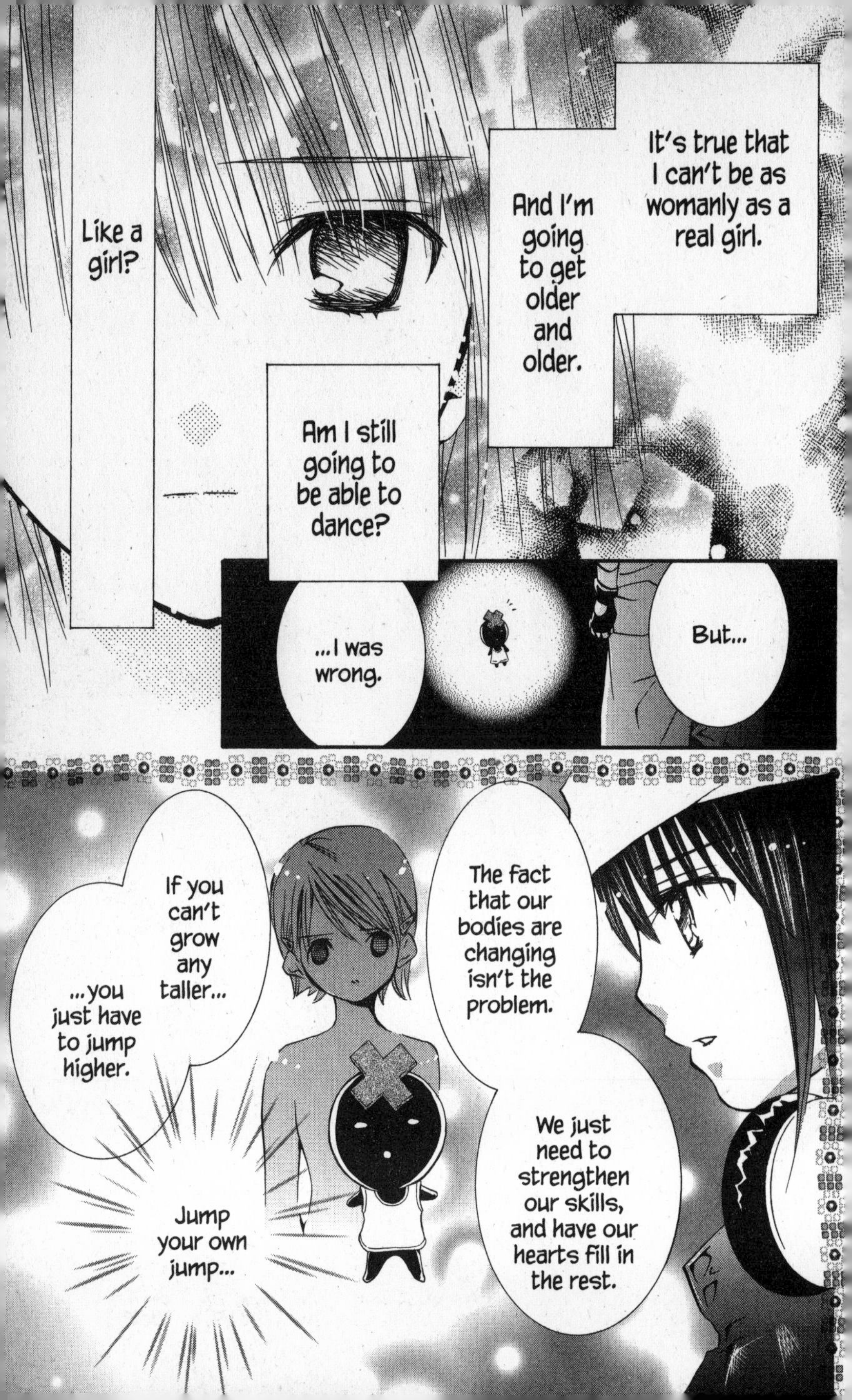
It's true that I can't be as womanly as a real girl.
And I'm going to get older and older.
Am I still going to be able to dance?
Like a girl?
But...
...I was wrong.
The fact that our bodies are changing isn't the problem.
We just need to strengthen our skills, and have our hearts fill in the rest.
If you can't grow any taller...
...you just have to jump higher.
Jump your own jump...

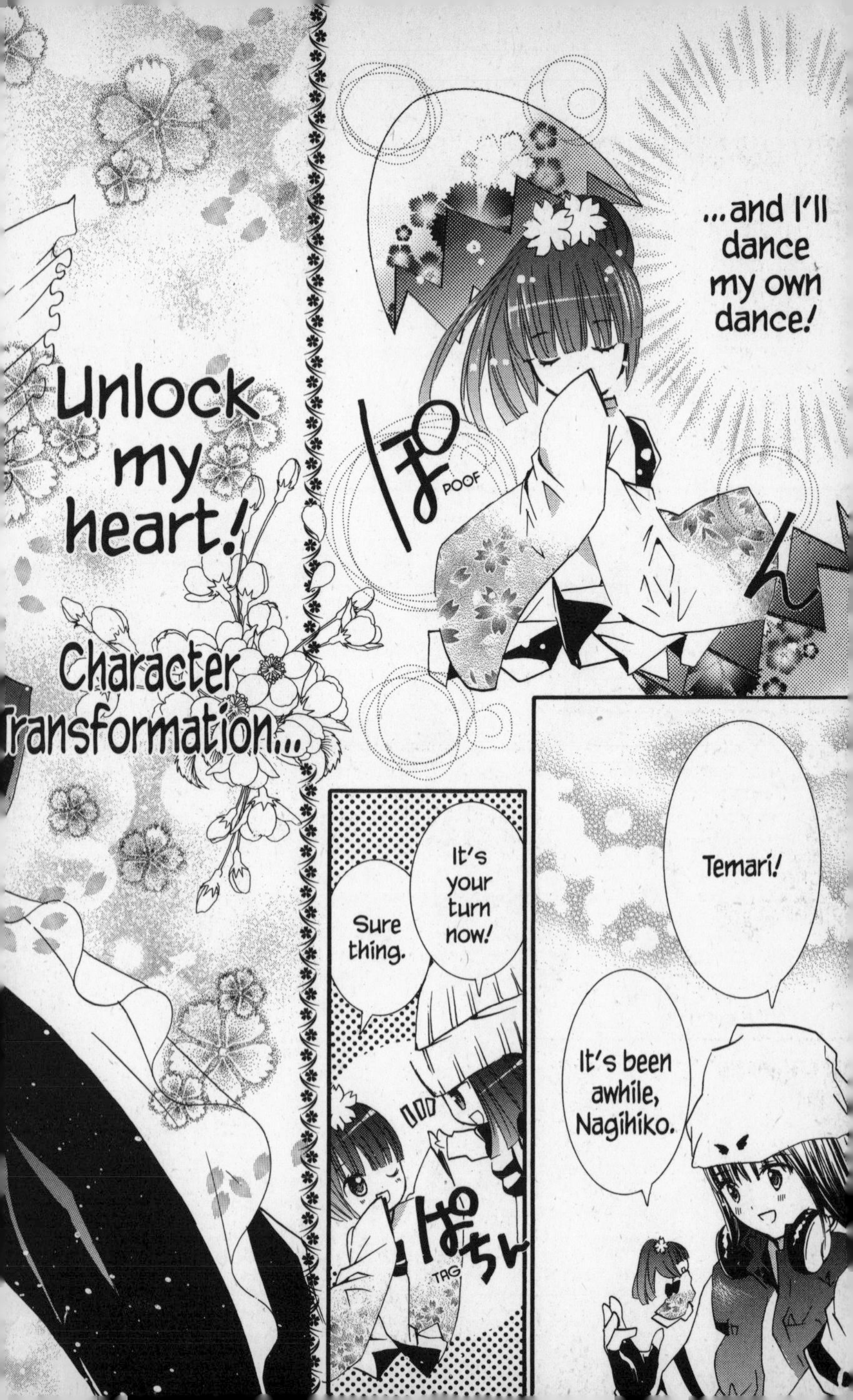
...and I'll dance my own dance!
POOF
Temari!
It's been awhile, Nagihiko.
It's your turn now!
Sure thing.
TAG
Unlock my heart!
Character Transformation...

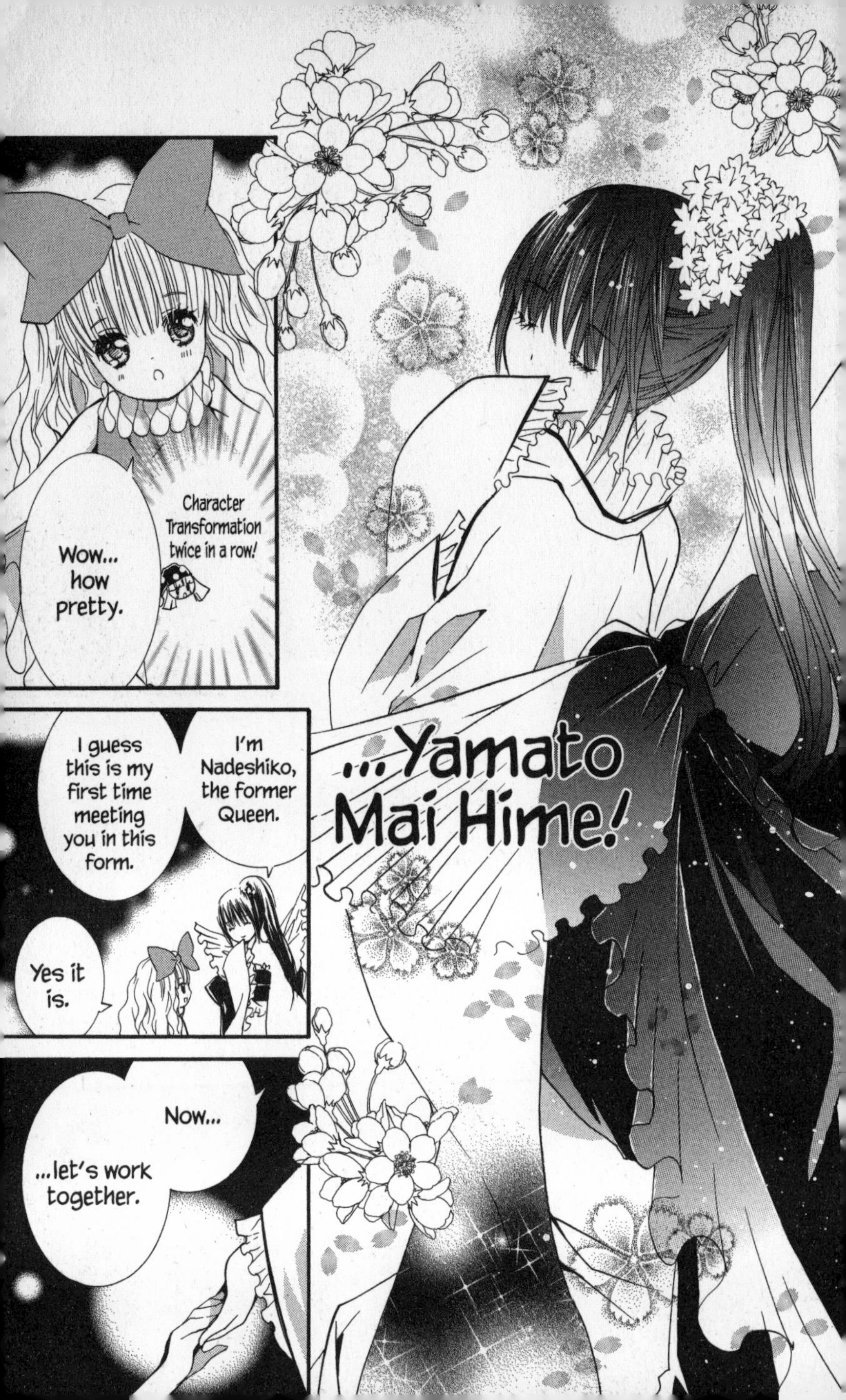
...Yamato Mai Hime!
Character Transformation twice in a row!
Wow... how pretty.
I'm Nadeshiko, the former Queen.
I guess this is my first time meeting you in this form.
Yes it is.
Now...
...let's work together.

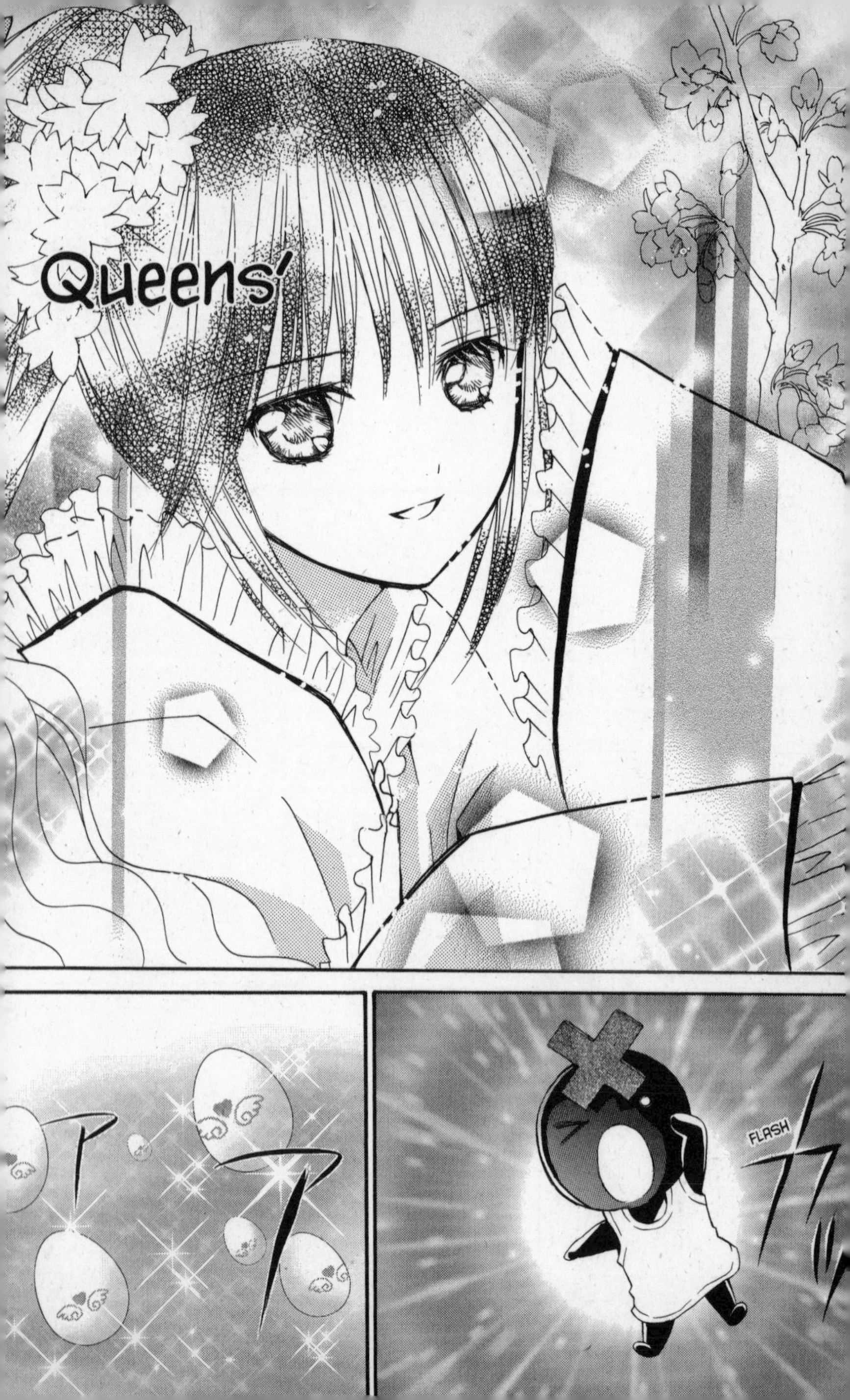
Queens'
FLASH

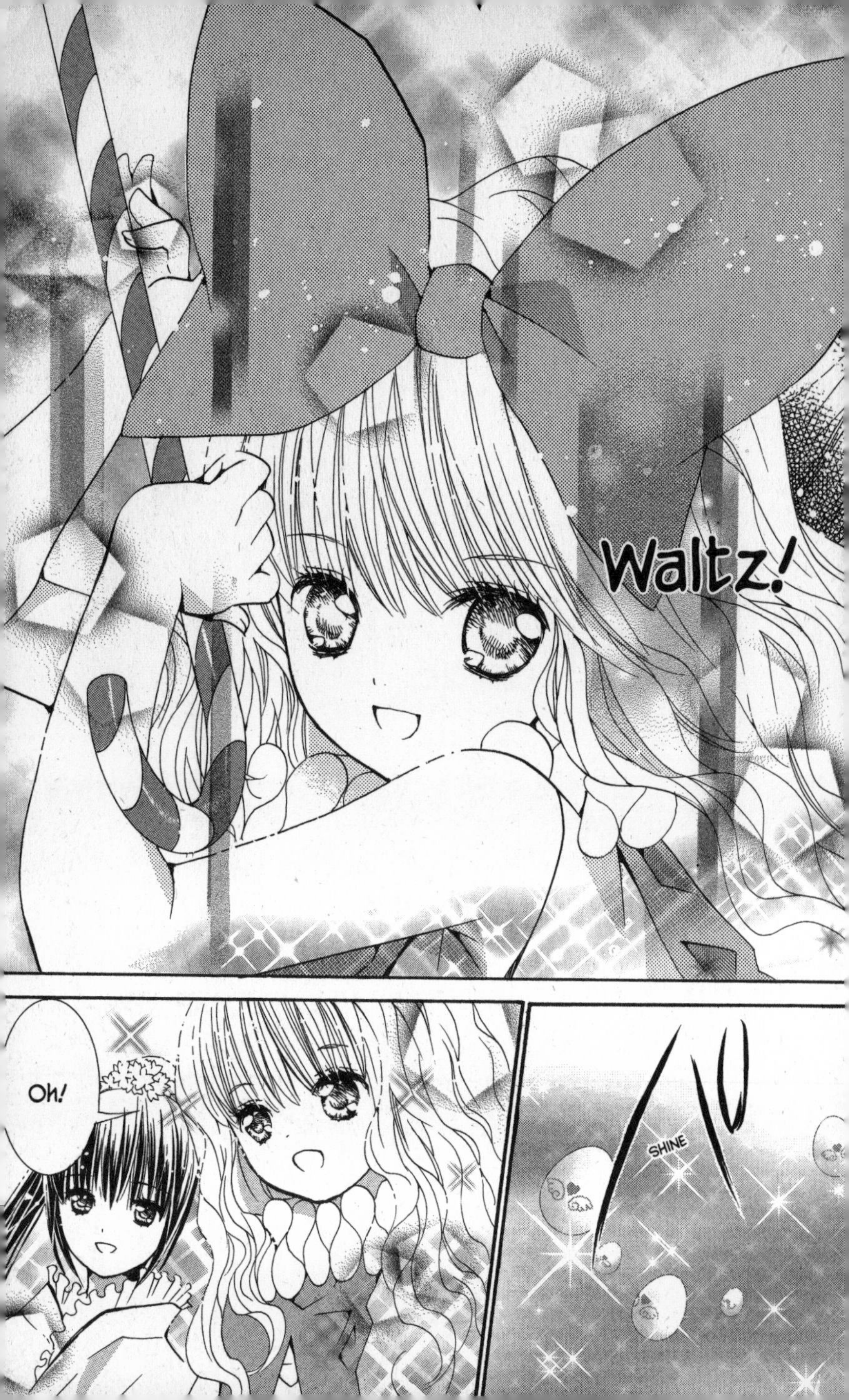
Waltz!
SHINE
Oh!

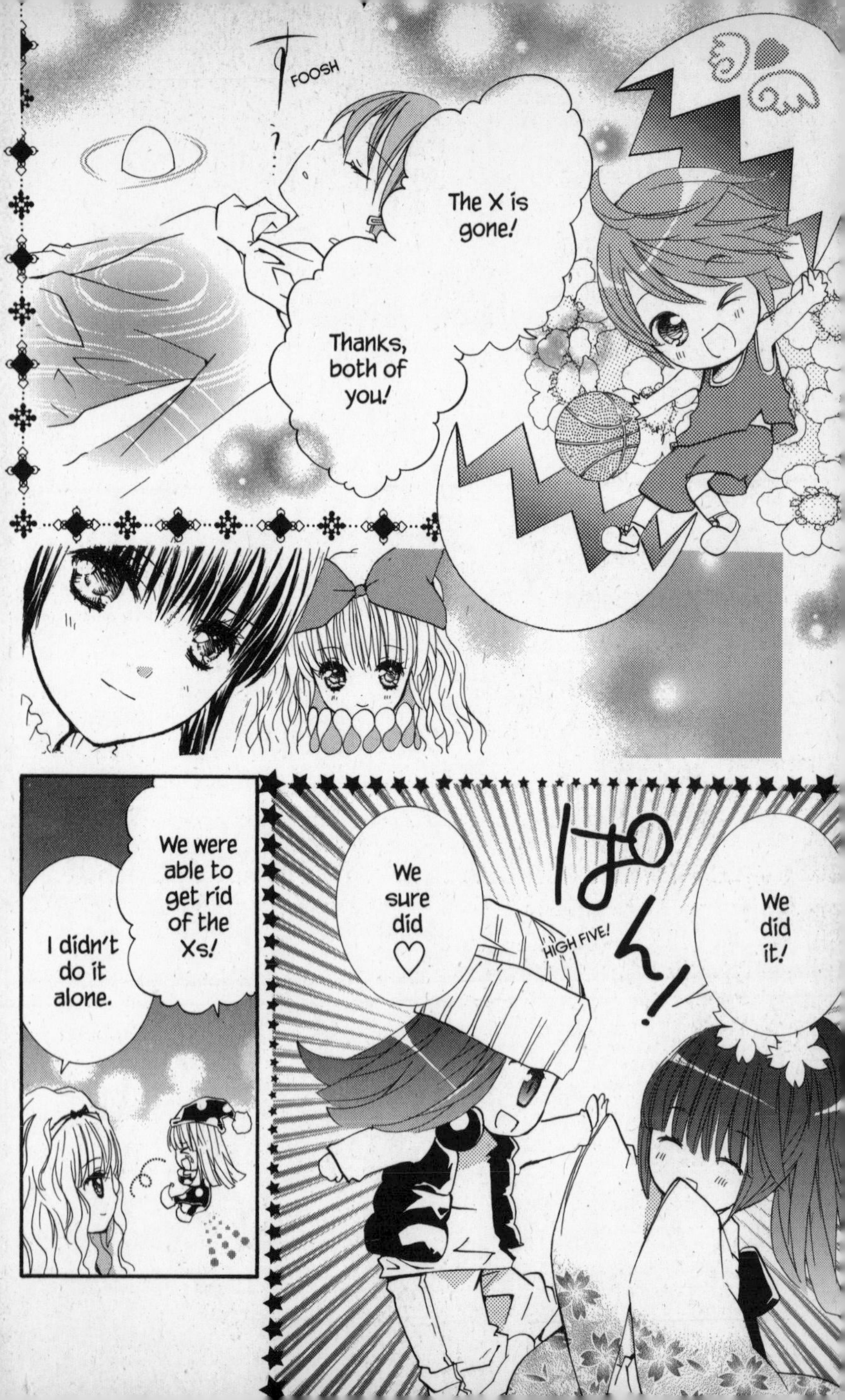
FOOSH
The X is gone!
Thanks, both of you!
We did it!
ぽん!
HIGH FIVE!
We sure did ♡
We were able to get rid of the Xs!
I didn't do it alone.

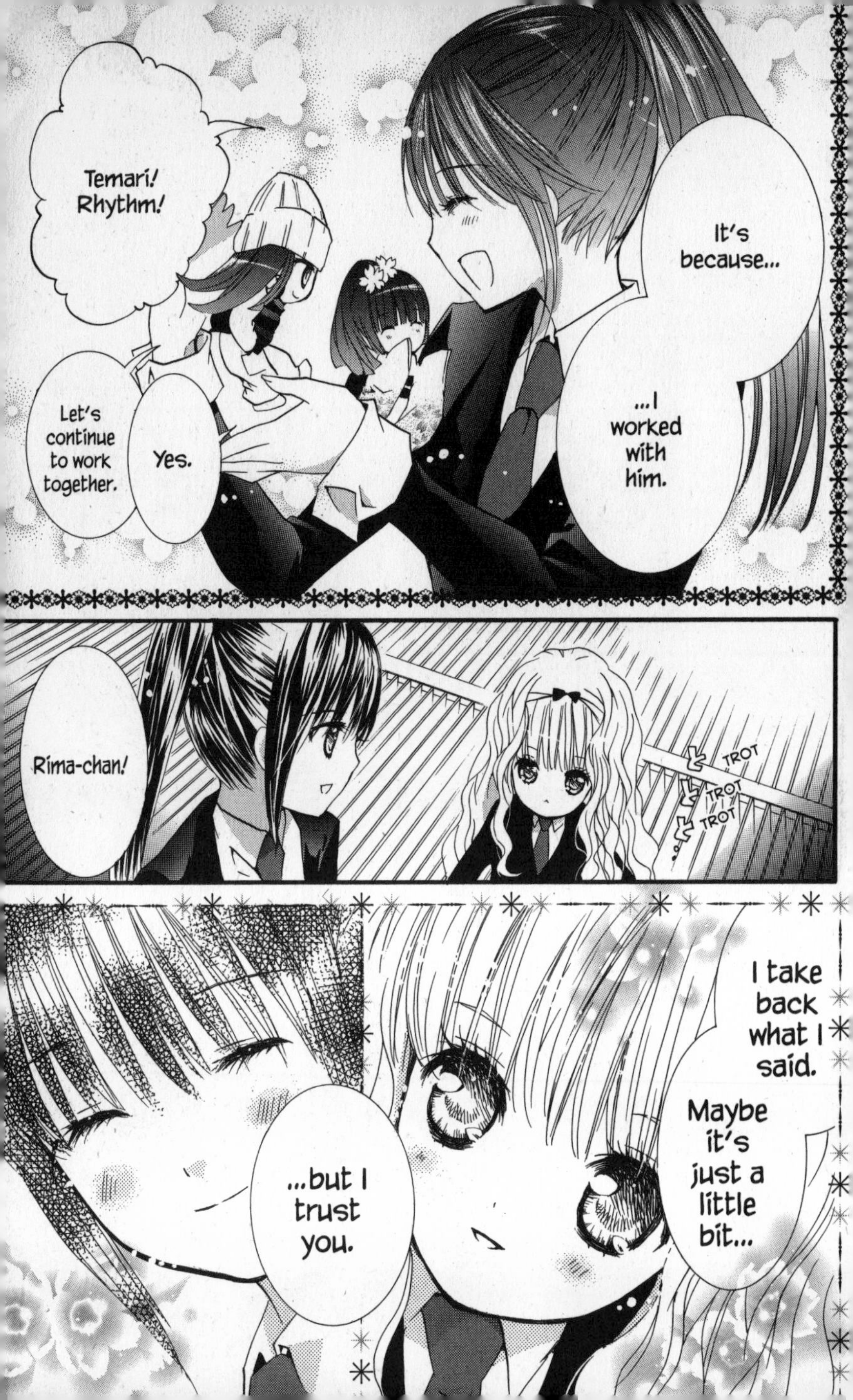
It's because...
...I worked with him.
Temari! Rhythm!
Yes.
Let's continue to work together.
TROT TROT TROT
Rima-chan!
I take back what I said.
Maybe it's just a little bit...
...but I trust you.

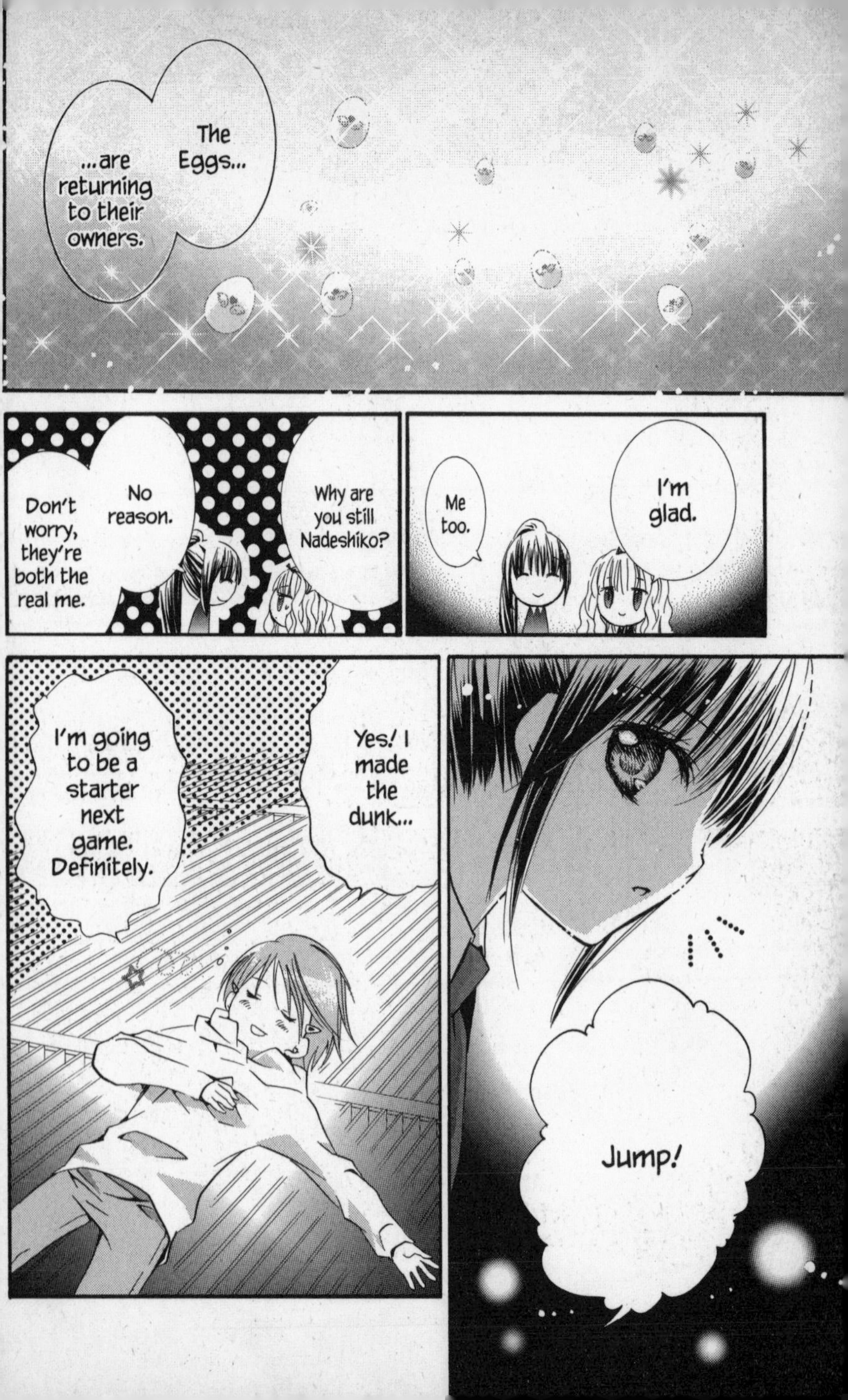
The Eggs... ...are returning to their owners.
I'm glad.
Me too.
Why are you still Nadeshiko?
No reason.
Don't worry, they're both the real me.
Jump!
Yes! I made the dunk...
I'm going to be a starter next game. Definitely.

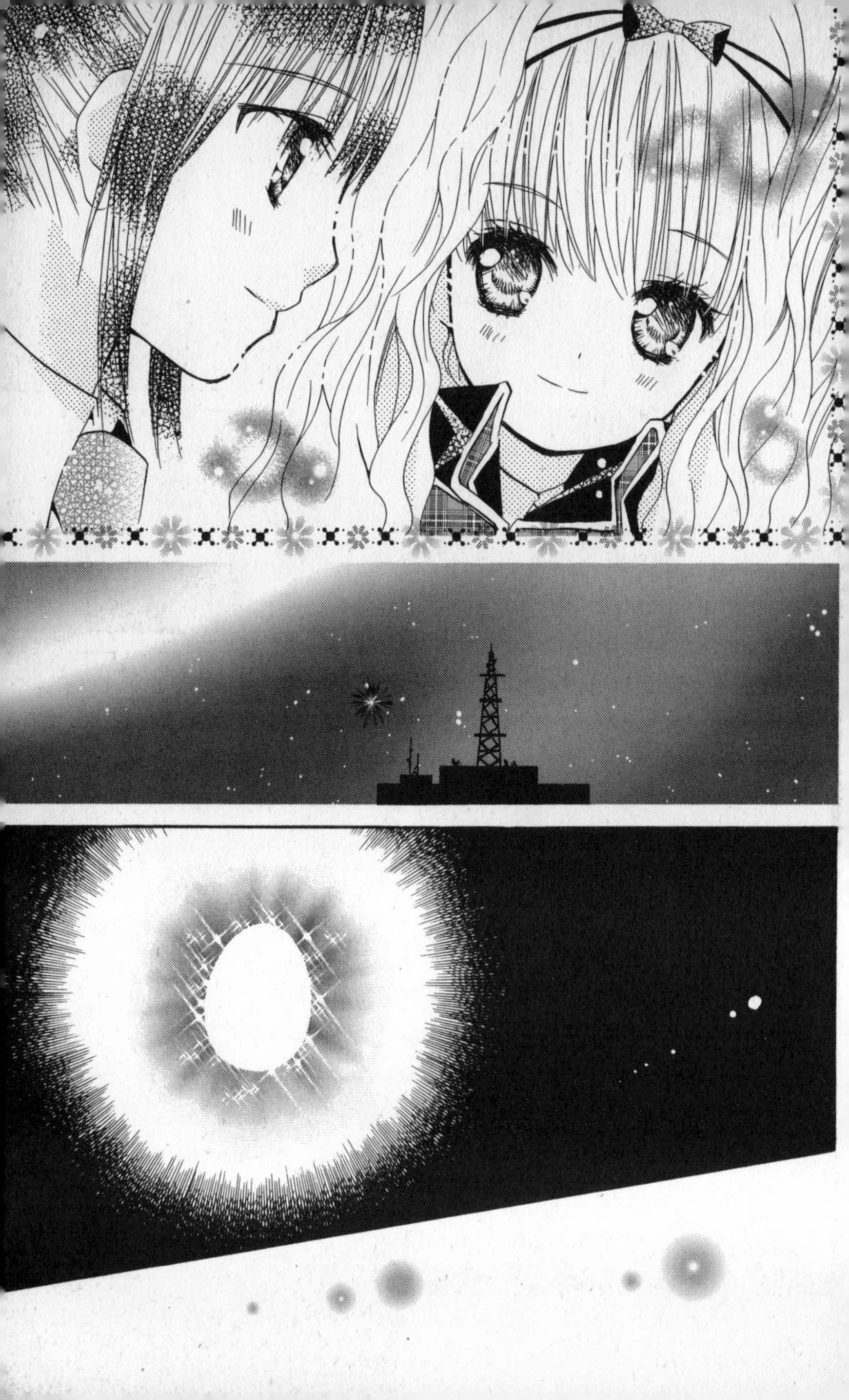

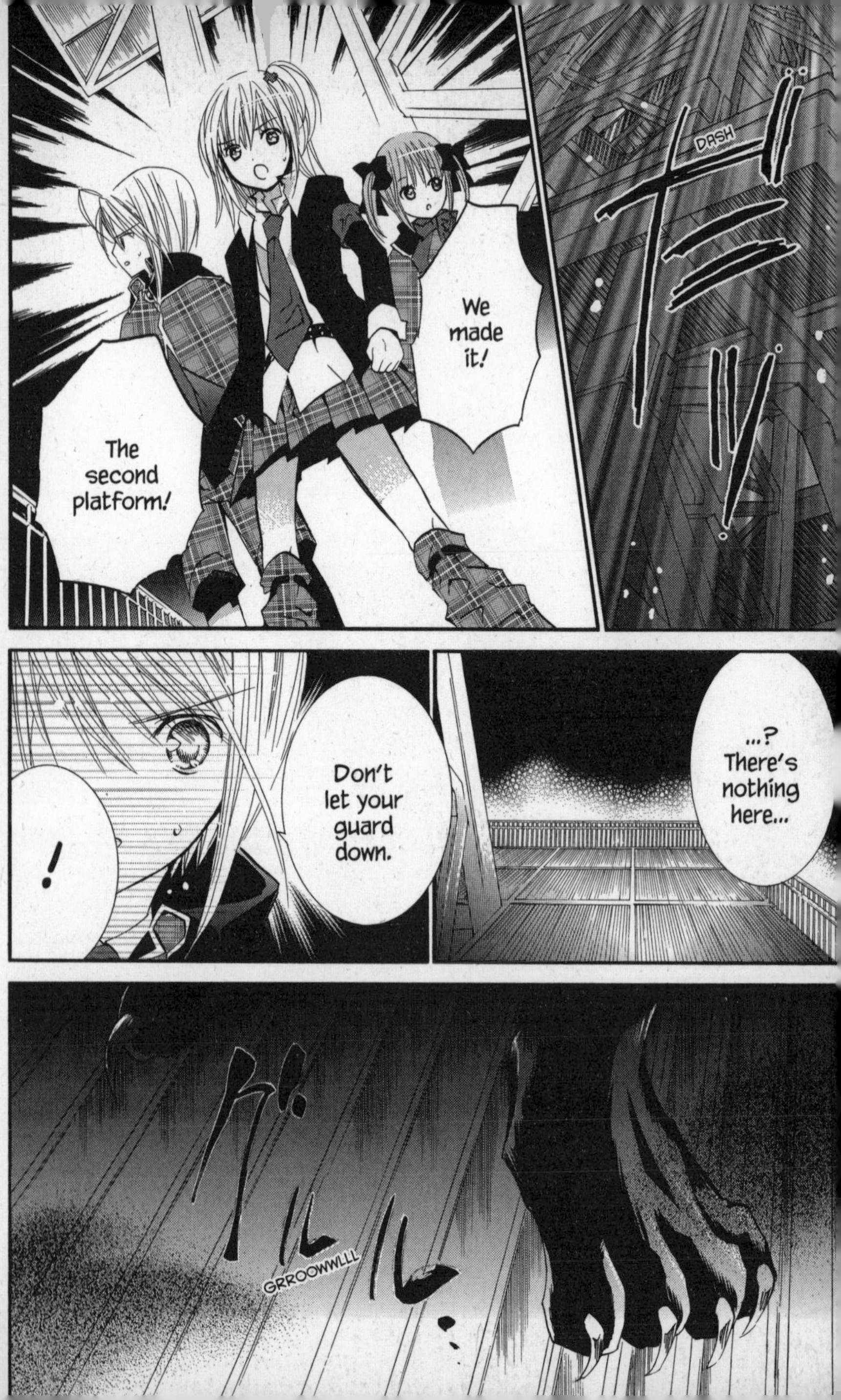
DASH
We made it!
The second platform!
...? There's nothing here...
Don't let your guard down.
!
GRROOWWLLL

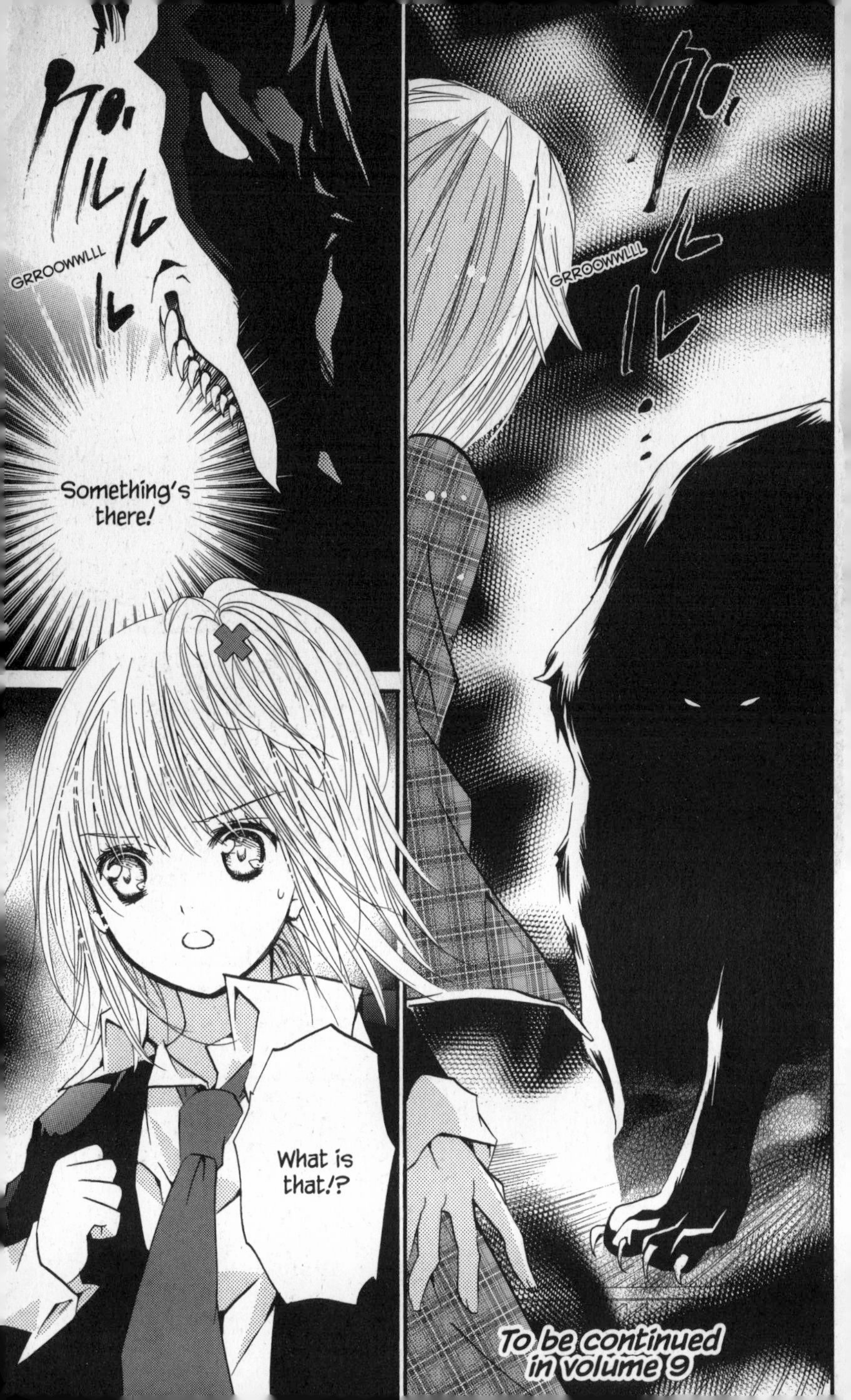
GRROOWWLLL
To be continued in volume 9
GRROOWWLLL
Something's there!
What is that!?

About the Creators

PEACH-PIT:
Banri Sendo was born on June 7. **Shibuko Ebara** was born on June 21. They are a pair of Gemini manga artists who work together. Sendo likes to eat sweets, and Ebara likes to eat spicy stuff.

"Whenever we draw manga, we try to decorate our room with flowers. We hope that the soothing power of the flower translates into the manga!" —PEACH-PIT

Translation Notes

Japanese is a tricky language for most Westerners, and translation is often more art than science. For your edification and reading pleasure, here are notes on some of the places where we could have gone in a different direction in our translation of the work, or where a Japanese cultural reference is used.

Taiyaki, page 11

A *taiyaki* is a Japanese snack made with batter and usually filled with red beans. It's shaped like a fish and can also be filled with various other things including cream, custard, or chocolate.

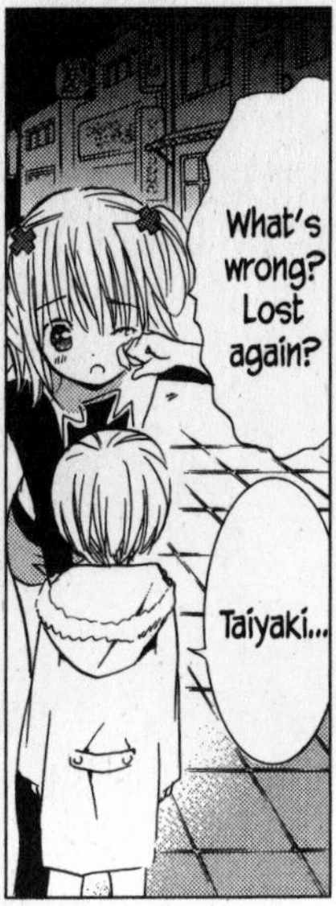
What's wrong? Lost again?
Taiyaki...

Good morning, page 115

In Japan, any business person who works long hours (or works at night, like at a bar or a television station) says "good morning" when they arrive at work no matter what time it is.

...Yamato Mai Hime!

Yamato Mai Hime, page 167

"Yamato" means Japan. It is a name that was used to refer to Japan until the 6th century. *Mai* is "to dance", and *hime* is "princess." So the Character Transformation move would be translated as "Japanese Dancing Princess."

Preview of *Shugo Chara!* volume 9

We're pleased to present you a preview from volume 9. Please check our website (www.delreymanga.com) to see when this volume will be available in English. For now you'll have to make do with Japanese!

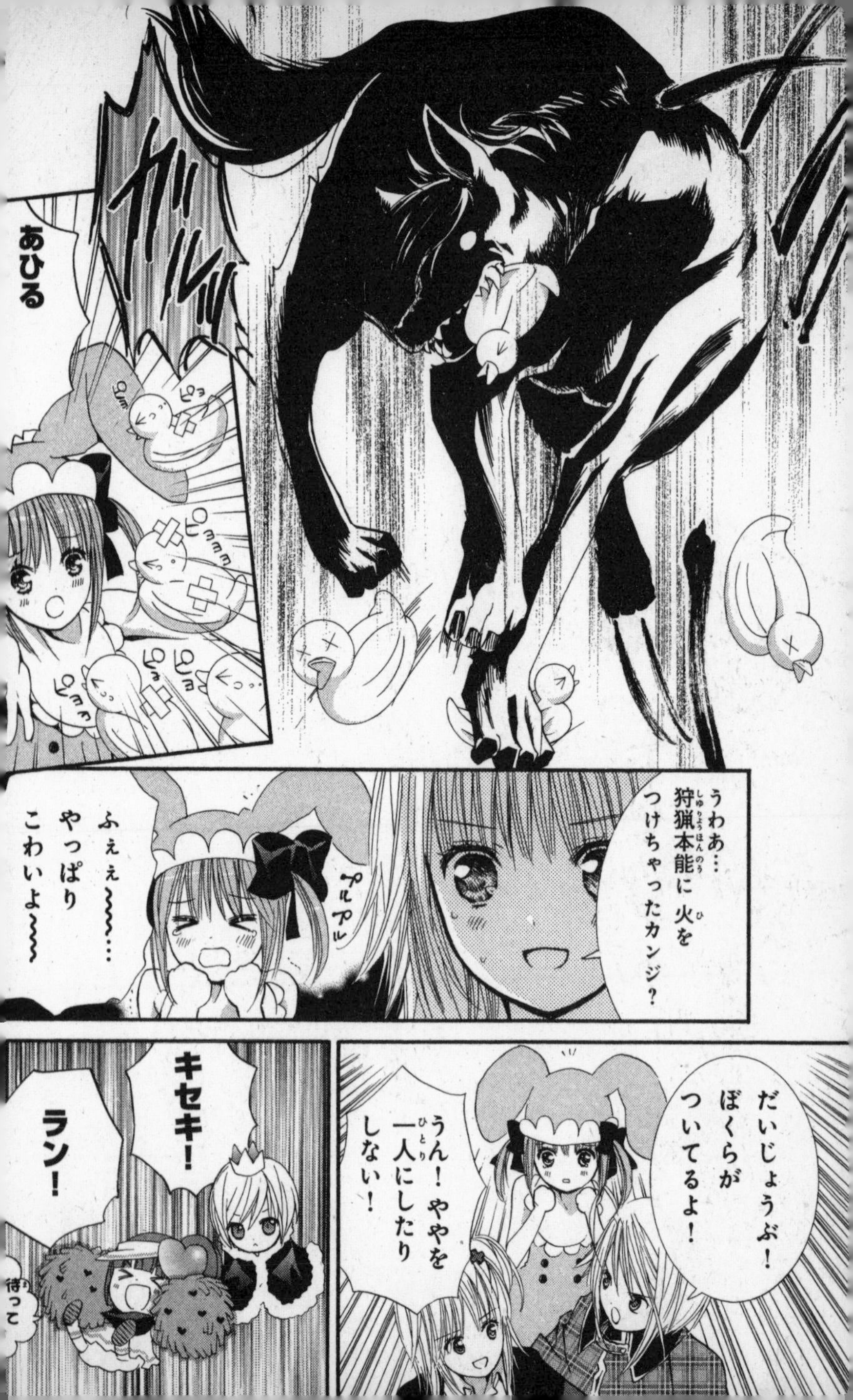
ガルルッ
あひる
うわあ…狩猟本能に火をつけちゃったカンジ?
プルプル
ふぇぇ〜〜〜…やっぱりこわいよ〜〜
だいじょうぶ!ぼくらがついてるよ!
うん!ややを一人にしたりしない!
キセキ!
ラン!
待って

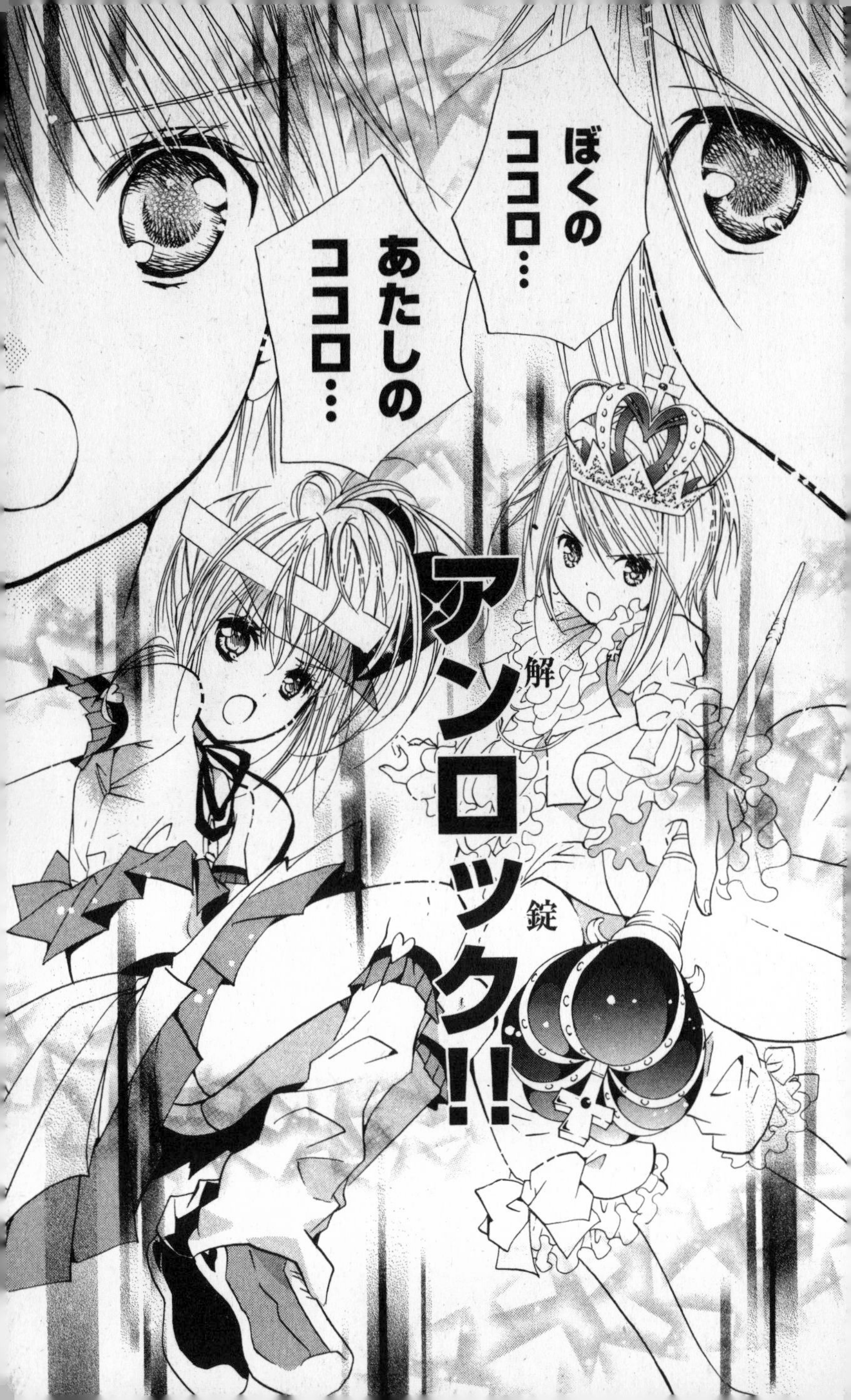
ぼくのココロ…
あたしのココロ…
解錠
アンロック!!

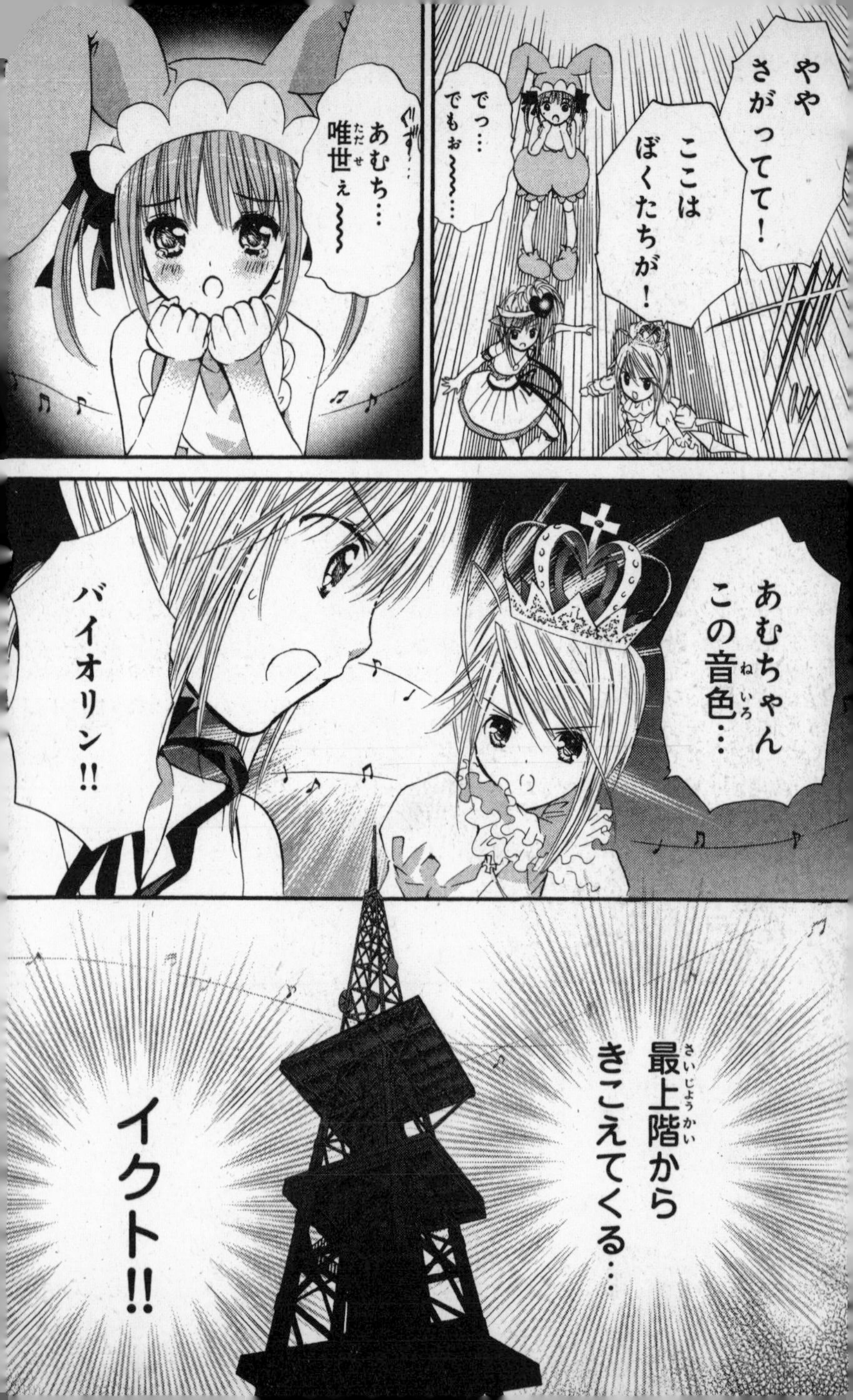
ややさがってて！
ここはぼくたちが！
でっ…でもぉ〜〜〜…
ぐずっ…
あむち…唯世ぇ〜〜〜
あむちゃんこの音色…
バイオリン!!
最上階からきこえてくる…
イクト!!

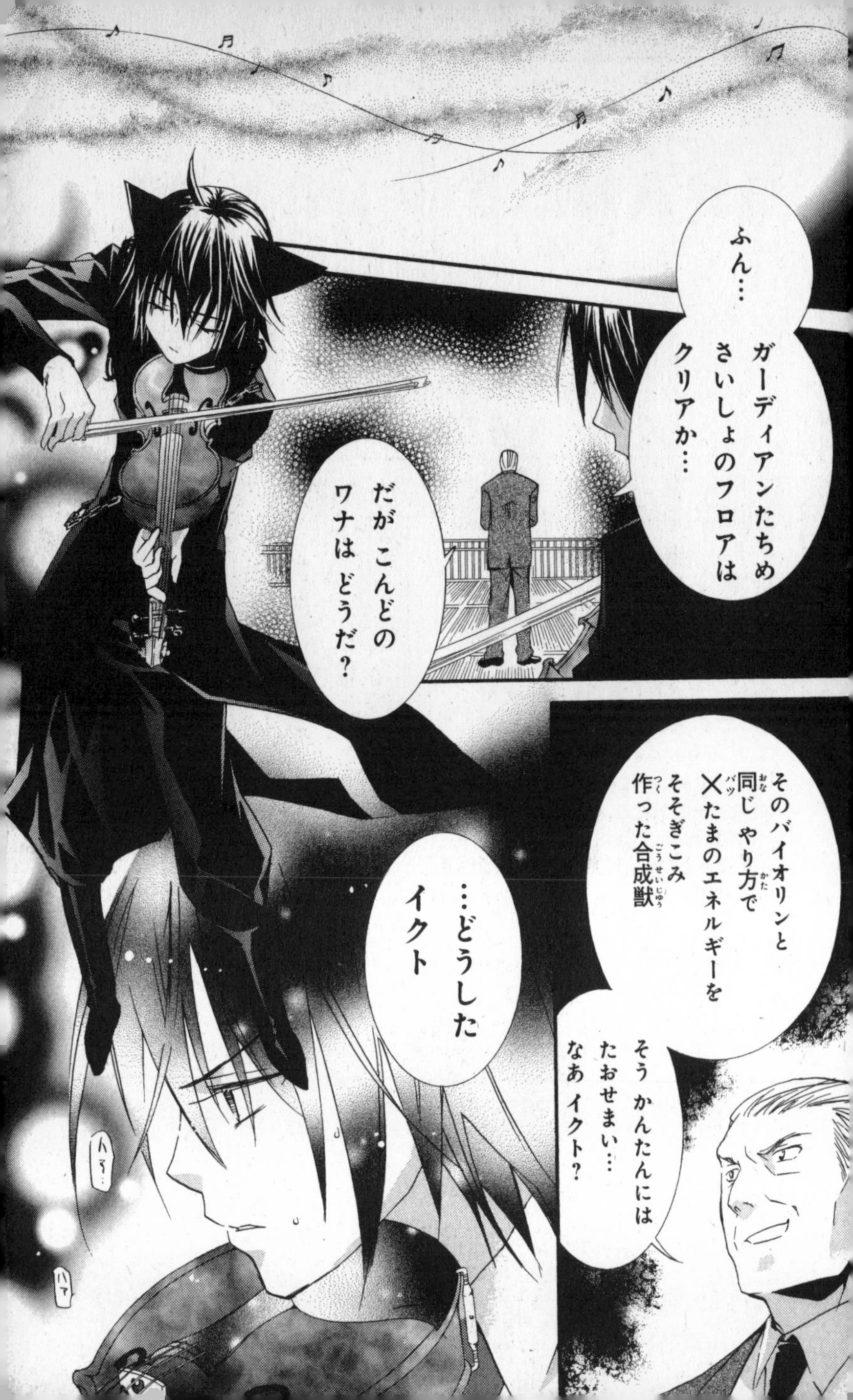
ふん…
ガーディアンたちめ さいしょのフロアは クリアか…
だが こんどの ワナは どうだ?
そのバイオリンと 同じやり方で ×たまのエネルギーを そそぎこみ 作った合成獣
そう かんたんには たおせまい… なあ イクト?
…どうした イクト
ハァ…
ハァ

ORANGE PLANET

BY HARUKA FUKUSHIMA

A ROMANTIC COMEDY IN THE TRADITION OF *KITCHEN PRINCESS*

It's hard enough being in love when you're thirteen. It's even harder when you're part of a secret love triangle! Rui's in love for the first time ever—with her dreamy classmate, Kaoru. But Rui's the target of someone else's major secret crush—her own best friend's, the adorable boy next door. Then to make matters worse, her hot teaching assistant moves in with her! Which lucky boy will Rui choose?

Available anywhere books or comics are sold!

TOMARE!

[STOP!]

You're going the wrong way!

Manga is a completely
different type of reading
experience.

To start at the *beginning,*
go to the *end*!

That's right! Authentic manga is read the traditional Japanese way—from right to left. Exactly the *opposite* of how American books are read. It's easy to follow: Just go to the other end of the book, and read each page—and each panel—from right side to left side, starting at the top right. Now you're experiencing manga as it was meant to be!